Jewish Christianity

THE ANCHOR YALE BIBLE REFERENCE LIBRARY is a project of international and interfaith scope in which Protestant, Catholic, and Jewish scholars from many countries contribute individual volumes. The project is not sponsored by any ecclesiastical organization and is not intended to reflect any particular theological doctrine.

The series is committed to producing volumes in the tradition established half a century ago by the founders of the Anchor Bible, William Foxwell Albright and David Noel Freedman. It aims to present the best contemporary scholarship in a way that is accessible not only to scholars but also to the educated nonspecialist. It is committed to work of sound philological and historical scholarship, supplemented by insight from modern methods, such as sociological and literary criticism.

John J. Collins
General Editor

THE ANCHOR YALE BIBLE REFERENCE LIBRARY

Jewish Christianity

The Making of the Christianity-Judaism Divide

MATT JACKSON-McCABE

Yale

NEW HAVEN

UNIVERSITY AND

PRESS LONDON

Yale University Press books may be purchased in quantity for educational, business, or promotional use. For information, please e-mail sales.press@yale.edu (U.S. office) or sales@yaleup.co.uk (U.K. office).

Set in Adobe Caslon type by Newgen North America, Austin, Texas.
Printed in the United States of America.

Library of Congress Control Number: 2019952803
ISBN 978-0-300-18013-8 (hardcover : alk. paper)

A catalogue record for this book is available from the British Library.

This paper meets the requirements of ANSI/NISO Z39.48-1992 (Permanence of Paper).

10 9 8 7 6 5 4 3 2 1

*For friends and teachers from my Chicago days
and, as always, for my family.*

For the distinction between Christians and other men is neither in country nor language nor customs . . . This teaching of theirs has not been discovered by the intellect or thought of busy men, nor are they advocates of any human doctrine as some men are.
—Epistle to Diognetus 5.1–3

Is there a Platonic Idea of Christianity hovering somewhere in the ontosphere?
—Daniel Boyarin, "Rethinking Jewish Christianity"

The Christian faith did not exist in the beginning. In the beginning there existed merely the "heretical" Jew, Jesus of Nazareth.
—Hans Dieter Betz, "Orthodoxy and Heresy in Primitive Christianity"

Contents

Acknowledgments

This is a project I have been sneaking up on in some sense ever since I was a graduate student at the University of Chicago in the 1990s. What eventually became a dissertation, "Logos and Law in the Letter of James," was initially supposed to have been only one section of one chapter of a study arguing that the Letter of James was better interpreted as an expression of early Judaism—albeit one with great interest in a messiah, Jesus—than as a "Jewish Christianity." My intention was to use James as a sort of case study in the problem of the category Jewish Christianity. Disentangling the complex exegetical issues surrounding James, however, became a job in itself. I continued thinking about the larger problem, though, and eventually came back around to it some years later in an edited volume called *Jewish Christianity Reconsidered*. I was shocked—though also intrigued—to find my work there interpreted in some quarters as a defense of the category. I continued to dig more deeply into where this notion of "Jewish Christianity" came from, how it became so embedded in the scholarly imagination, and how our understanding of Jewish and Christian antiquity might look different without it.

Some of the published results of those efforts have been incorporated in one way or another into the present study. An essay published under the title "The Invention of Jewish Christianity in John's Toland's *Nazarenus*" in *The Rediscovery of Jewish Christianity: From Toland to Baur* (ed. F. Stanley Jones; Society of Biblical Literature, 2012) has been revised and integrated into Chapter 1. The treatment of Thomas Morgan in Chapter 2 represents a condensed and more substantially reworked version of another study published in that same volume as "'Jewish Christianity' and 'Christian Deism' in Thomas Morgan's *The Moral Philosopher*."The analyses of the Ebionites and of the so-called Nazoraean exegesis of Isaiah in Chapter 6 draw freely on an essay titled "Ebionites and Nazoraeans: Christians or Jews?" that I wrote at the invitation of Hershel Shanks for a volume called *Partings: How Judaism and Christianity Became Two* (Biblical Archaeology Society, 2013). I am grateful to the publishers of these works for their permission to use this material here.

When John Collins asked whether I would be interested in producing a volume on Jewish Christianity for the Anchor Yale Bible Reference Library, I jumped at the chance to work through the issues more systematically. I am exceedingly grateful to him for the invitation—and for not balking when I came back with a proposal that was more critical history of a modern interpretive construct than analysis of an ancient phenomenon. I also owe him tremendous thanks for his patience as I wrote it, and for shepherding the whole project from start to finish. The anonymous reviewers of the initial proposal were invaluable in pushing me both conceptually and at the level of detail as I was first thinking through the project. The anonymous reviewers of the full manuscript likewise gave immensely important feedback that resulted, I hope, in a clearer, stronger argument. I am deeply grateful to them and to the book's editor, John Kloppenborg, for their exacting and insightful readings of the manuscript. It goes without saying that all remaining errors and problems are my responsibility alone.

Everyone at Yale University Press has been a pleasure to work with, including Jennifer Banks, Piyali Bhattacharya, Eric Brandt, Whitney Schumacher, and Ann-Marie Imbornoni. Susan Laity provided a number of helpful suggestions that led to an improved manuscript. I am especially indebted to Jessie Dolch for her expert copyediting, and to Katherine Ulrich for her careful indexing. Above all, I cannot thank Heather Gold enough for giving me the time and space I needed to follow the project where it led me, and for reliably wise counsel at many critical junctures along the way.

It goes without saying that I owe a great debt to many scholars, past and present, named and unnamed, who have explored the same or related problems before me. By its nature, this study engages extensively in a critical analysis (of some, at least) of their work. I have undertaken this with no small trepidation. Doing my best to understand other people's writings, ancient and modern alike, I have found evidence time and again of intellects far more capacious than mine; of philological abilities and sheer breadths of knowledge surpassing anything I will ever hope to accomplish. I have spent considerable time, for example, with the writings of F. C. Baur. The more I read him, and read about him, the more I marvel. The same goes for any number of the other authors treated in these pages, including not least those contemporary scholars with whom I engage extensively in later parts of the book. A special word of thanks goes to Annette Yoshiko Reed for generously sharing with me the page proofs of her outstanding collection *Jewish-Christianity and the History of Judaism*, which made it possible for me to account for it in Chapter 5. I have learned a great deal from her, as well as from F. Stanley Jones, Petri Luomanen, Daniel Boyarin, Edwin Broadhead, and the many other contributors to the Society of Biblical Literature's Jewish Christianity/Christian Judaism section. A number of the ideas published here were first presented to this group, and I have benefited greatly from the constructive criticism I received there. I hope I have done justice to these and other writers in my attempt to engage critically, in turn, with their work.

Different kinds of thanks are owed to a number of others. I have long suspected that if scholarly reconstructions are too complicated or convoluted to convey to intelligent and interested people who do not also happen to be specialists, then something is probably wrong. I am grateful to my students at Cleveland State University for feedback on ideas I have tried out in the classroom. I also benefited from the illuminating interactions that resulted from invitations to speak to the truly remarkable people of both Beth El–The Heights Synagogue in Cleveland Heights, Ohio, and the Community of St. Peter's in Cleveland during the writing of this book. I must also thank my colleagues in CSU's Department of Philosophy and Comparative Religion for their ongoing interest and support, especially those on the comparative religion side of the house—Sucharita Adluri, Stephen Cory, and Steve Taysom—and our former chair (and now dean), Allyson Robichaud.

This book is dedicated in part to those who were there when I first started thinking about the problem of Jewish Christianity in earnest, and who have shaped my thinking about it in innumerable ways both direct and indirect. This goes first of all for my teachers and mentors at the University of Chicago: Hans Dieter Betz, Adela Yarbro Collins, John J. Collins, Arthur Droge, and the late Arthur W. H. Adkins. Equally important, however, are the other students whose time in Swift Hall overlapped with my own. There are too many to name here, but a few deserve special mention. Jim Hanges, Chris Mount, and Dale Walker remain my most regular conversation partners on matters of scholarship as well as dear friends. Chris in particular read the entire manuscript with his characteristically incisive and insightful eye at a crucial point in its development and provided extremely helpful feedback for which I am beyond grateful. Bert Harrill, Paul Holloway, and Clare Rothschild have likewise been trusted colleagues and supportive friends in many ways for many years.

Finally, the book is also dedicated to my family. The McCabes, Boysels, and Jacksons have provided constant support and encouragement—and much needed laughter and relief—for years, not least those spent writing this book. This goes most especially for A.J. and Jeremy, who have lived with this project as much as I have, and who have contributed immeasurably to it. Jeremy has been a source of more strength and pure joy than he can possibly know. The same is true of A.J., who could envision the completion of this book even (and especially) in moments when I could not, and who, much more importantly, changed my life forever and infinitely for the better when she decided to travel with me to Chicago those many years ago.

Jewish Christianity

Introduction

Since the Second World War, scholars have been engaged in a fundamental reconsideration of the relationship of Christians and Jews, and of Christianity to Judaism, in antiquity. The anti-Semitism that reached a tragic crescendo in Nazi Germany was abetted by a traditional Christian historiography that explained the origins of Christianity as the result of an intervention by the creator of the world to supplant a sanctimonious, hollow, and finally rejected Judaism with the one true religion. Concerned with the implications of this narrative for Christian treatment of Jews in their present, twentieth-century scholars began to replace its inherently adversarial, zero-sum nature with the more complex and ambivalent metaphors of family: Judaism as mother who gave birth to a Christianity that eventually grew up and went off on its own; or the story of a sibling rivalry that gradually issued in a mutual parting of Christianity and Judaism. Such reframing laid the groundwork not only for a more tolerant and even potentially affectionate coexistence of Judaism and Christianity in the present, but for a much more nuanced reconstruction of their relationship in the historical past. New energy was poured into investigating the complex historical processes involved in the emergence of Christianity as a religion distinct from Judaism. Attention was focused increasingly on the local level, with the separation now recognized as something that happened in fits and starts over decades, perhaps as much as a century or more in the making. In recent decades, reconstructions have become even more complex as this "Parting of the Ways" model, as it came to be known, was itself subjected to serious criticism. Interest in the question of early Jewish-Christian relations and of the historical emergence of Christianity and Judaism as separate religions has only continued to intensify in the absence of any new, widely accepted historical paradigm.[1]

These developments have generated fresh interest in what scholars have traditionally called "Jewish Christianity." Developed alongside—and indeed, as we shall see, as an integral component of—critical New Testament scholarship, the idea of an early Jewish Christianity has long been imagined as the historical site where Christianity and Judaism, for good or ill, had once touched each other most profoundly. From the point of view of the Parting of the Ways model, it represented not only the transitional phase between a Jewish Jesus and the full flowering of Christianity as its own religion, but in some cases evidence for an ongoing relationship between Christianity and Judaism even after their split.[2] More recently, with the breakdown of the Parting of the Ways model, the notion of an early Jewish Christianity has taken on a new significance, precisely as a "way that never parted." It has become "the third term," as Daniel Boyarin has put it, "that unsettles the opposition between the 'two religions'"; a concept, in the words of Annette Yoshiko Reed, that "serves to disturb—literally by definition—any unquestioned assumptions that we might harbor about the essential incompatibility and inevitable 'parting' of Judaism and Christianity, while also reminding us that we have yet to settle some basic definitional issues about 'Judaism' and 'Christianity.'"[3]

At the same time, the breakdown of the Parting of the Ways model has quite exacerbated the definitional and taxonomic confusion that has always surrounded the concept of an early Jewish Christianity. Not only the historical significance of the supposed phenomenon, but the very identification of that phenomenon—what it is we are talking about when we say "Jewish" (or "Judaistic" or "Judaic" or "Judaeo-," etc.) Christianity—remain the subjects of endless and seemingly irresolvable debate.[4] The current scholarly climate has sparked both a new round of ruminations about this problem of definition and even more fundamental questions about whether the category has any enduring utility at all for the purposes of a critical reconstruction of Jewish and Christian antiquity. Implicit challenges to the concept have come in the form of an increasing number of specialized studies analyzing ancient texts or groups traditionally classed as "Jewish Christianity" as examples, instead, of Judaism—Christian or otherwise.[5] If even the apostle Paul—traditionally interpreted as both the quintessential Christian in general and the antithesis of Jewish Christianity in particular—was not himself a Christian, as some now argue, what can "Jewish Christianity" possibly signify?[6] Meanwhile, studies of Jewish Christianity continue to appear and to grapple with the ever more challenging problem of delineating what, exactly, its actual referent is.[7] Others have suggested alternative formulations meant either to nuance or to supplement "Jewish Christianity."[8] More recently, explicit calls for the outright abandonment of "Jewish Christianity" as an inherently flawed category have begun to materialize.[9]

Among other things, these developments have served to underscore the fact that "Jewish Christianity," like the Parting of the Ways model, is first and foremost a modern interpretive construct—not an ancient phenomenon, but one possible way to organize and thus make sense of ancient phenomena; a lens that lends particular shape, color, and meaning to the raw data of antiquity.[10] Taking this insight seriously necessitates critical consideration of the nature and interpretive impact of that lens. Who crafted it, and for what purpose? What historical or theoretical assumptions are built into it? What does it bring into focus, and how might it distort? How have modifications to it over time affected modern understandings of Christians and Jews, and of the history of their relationship to one another? Will this lens be a help or a hindrance to contemporary scholars seeking to move beyond the Parting of the Ways model in order to make new and better sense of the historical emergence of Christianity as a religion distinct from Judaism?

It is this line of questioning about the *concept* "Jewish Christianity" that is the guiding concern of the present book. To avoid the tedium of constant and repetitive punctuation, I will not normally place quotation marks around the term to remind readers of that fact. Readers should nonetheless understand that, with or without scare quotes, my use of the term is *never* intended with reference to an ancient phenomenon, but *always and only* to a modern interpretive construct. Indeed, as will soon become clear, I find the interpretive category "Jewish Christianity" to be thoroughly problematic for the purpose of reconstructing Jewish and Christian antiquity.

While the bulk of the book is devoted to tracing a history of the concept, in no way does it pretend to be exhaustive. Given the centrality of the idea of an early Jewish Christianity to the historical-critical study of the New Testament and early Christianity more generally, the very idea of such a comprehensive study is mind-boggling.[11] My much more limited aim is to elucidate major trends in the evolution of its scholarly application, from its initial formulations in the English Enlightenment through the present day. I selected the particular authors and publications that receive detailed treatment primarily for their usefulness in illustrating those trends. Specialists will no doubt feel the absence of others who could (and in some cases, perhaps even should) also have been analyzed along the way. To them I can only concede, up front, the limitations of the book and its author.

What remains to be done in this brief introduction is to frame out, in a bit more detail, the central problem of Jewish Christianity as I currently understand it, and how I seek to address it in the present book.

Christian Apologetics, Historical Scholarship, and Jewish Christianity

Christianity is profoundly concerned with history. Christian doctrine traditionally involves not only beliefs about the inner workings of a sacred, metaphysical realm, but concrete historical claims about particular people and events in Galilee, Judea, and elsewhere during the first century of the Common Era. The central such claim is that Jesus of Nazareth and the apostolic community that continued after his death were the locus of a uniquely transformative hierophany: the irruption of a transcendent, immutable reality into the otherwise mutable realm of human culture. The idea is expressed classically in the Trinitarian notions of Jesus as God incarnate and a Holy Spirit active in the apostolic church. By the second century, the claim that Jesus and the apostles represented something more than mere human culture was also being formulated in Greek philosophical terms. Not only did Christ and the Holy Spirit exist before the creation of the world, but the Christianity they revealed corresponded to a divine law immanent in that very world itself, particularly in the rational nature of humanity.[12] This latter formulation became particularly pronounced in the Enlightenment era as Christian intellectuals, increasingly uncomfortable with traditional supernatural claims, began to reconceptualize the presumed transcendence of Jesus and the apostles in more thoroughly humanistic terms as "natural religion" or a uniquely epiphanic "consciousness."[13] Armed with the new notion of "religion" as a discrete, cross-cultural phenomenon distinct from culture, such writers effectively reformulated the Christian incarnation myth.[14] If Jesus no longer represented the appearance of a preexistent god in literal human flesh, Christianity nonetheless represented the perfect disclosure of an immanent spiritual reality in the metaphorical flesh of human cultural discourse. The underlying assumption nevertheless remained: Christianity in the truest sense of the term was not simply one more artifact among many produced over the ongoing history of human creativity, but a stable reality in its own right, transcendent of that history even as it manifested itself within it. To borrow language crafted at Nicaea to safeguard the similarly immutable transcendence of Christ, Christianity was still not so much made in history as begotten into it.

The transcendent and historical claims of Christianity coalesce powerfully in the idea of an "original Christianity": a primal, uniquely authoritative instantiation of true Christianity in the apostolic community. Over Christianity's long history, this notion of an original Christianity has served as an important cipher for claims of essential continuity between the values of contemporary Christians and those of Jesus and the apostolic community despite otherwise apparent difference. From antiquity through the present day, Christian thinkers have legitimized any number of views not merely by demonstrating their logical or ethical superiority, or even by direct appeals to supernatural revelation, but through concrete historical claims that Jesus and the apostles had held them as well. A given Christian's own most cherished values are regularly said also to have been at the heart of the social movement that sprang up around Jesus of Nazareth in first-century Palestine, representing, in a word, what "original Christianity" was really all about.[15]

The inevitable problem of cultural change over time, combined with the multiplicity of actors seeking to authorize various and often conflicting viewpoints by means of this same historical appeal, gave rise to a long-standing tradition of competitive Christian historiography. Apologetic histories were built around the twin goals of (1) affirming the essential continuity of the writer's own position with "original Christianity" (despite otherwise apparent differences with Jesus and apostles), and (2) explaining the competing views of the writer's rivals as subsequent deviations from that original (despite otherwise apparent similarities with Jesus and the apostles). Early Catholic heresiologists, focusing particularly on the latter concern, constructed elaborate taxonomies of heresy, showing how rival claimants on the transcendent authority of Jesus and the apostles had "really" derived their teachings from other, merely human (or even demonic) sources. Centuries later the same basic strategy was deployed against the Roman Catholic Church itself, as Protestant reformers appealed to the New Testament as the sole arbiter of apostolic Christianity in order to reject key elements of Catholic doctrine as corrupting additions to what had now become a Protestant "original." In the Enlightenment era, freethinking

Christians began turning the same strategy against Protestant orthodoxy, arguing that even the New Testament contained later accretions that had to be stripped away in order to recover an original now correlated with an enlightened liberalism.[16]

In this crucible the modern critical study of the New Testament and its notion of an early Jewish Christianity were formed. Judging by the available evidence, it never occurred to anyone before the Enlightenment era to imagine such a thing as a "Jewish Christianity."[17] As far as the heresiologists were concerned, there was Christianity and there was heresy; and heresy, not Christianity, was subject to the vagaries of human diversity. To be sure, individual Christians came either from Jews (*ex Ioudaiōn*) or from Gentiles (*ex ethnōn*); but even if there might in this sense be Jewish *Christians*, there could be no Jewish *Christianity*. The latter concept arose, rather, among freethinkers of the Enlightenment era, specifically as the centerpiece of revisionist histories designed to subvert traditional Christian orthodoxy. Around the turn of the eighteenth century, John Toland sought to delegitimize what he considered the "priestcraft" and intolerance of orthodox Christianity by framing them as corrupting pagan impositions on the original Christianity of Jesus and the apostles. That original, Toland argued, represented a liberal, rational vision of a "unity without uniformity" in which diverse cultural institutions and practices, including not least those of the Jews, could serve equally well as the external vehicles of an internal and natural—and thus universal—religion. Indeed, the actual religion of Jesus and his disciples had represented nothing more than the instantiation of that transcendent religion in Jewish cultural forms—a *Jewish* Christianity. To be sure, Jesus and the apostles had envisioned from the beginning analogous and equally legitimate *Gentile* cultural incarnations existing alongside their Jewish one. The problem was that Gentiles, in practice, came to confuse their own cultural inventions and prejudices with the transcendent truths of Jesus's natural religion.[18]

Subsequent intellectuals, seeking a broadly similar end, flipped Toland's script. The most significant corruptor of Jesus's primal Christianity, they argued, was not Greek philosophical mumbo-jumbo, but the Judaism of Jesus's own setting. Reckoning more squarely with the fact that the New Testament does not obviously reflect Enlightenment values, these writers argued that the very apostles of Jesus themselves had already failed to fully distinguish the transcendent interiority of Jesus's revolutionary religion from the external, particularly Jewish forms in which he had couched it.

For the English Deist Thomas Morgan and, more consequentially, the later German theologian F. C. Baur, therefore, Jewish Christianity represented not so much, as Toland had it, the first cultural *incarnation* of transcendent Christianity as its earliest and most enduring (because canonized) *occlusion*. What was needed, they argued, was a thoroughly critical approach to the New Testament that would remove the Jewish barnacles from the "original Christianity" they imagined as lying beneath it all.[19]

Such liberal assaults on the twin pillars of Protestant authority—the New Testament and the apostolic community—became a defining anxiety in what would subsequently emerge as the field of critical New Testament studies. Lying squarely at the center of all of this was the new idea that the apostles represented a peculiarly Jewish Christianity. Concern to salvage the apostles and the canon for traditional orthodoxy led to further reformulations of the category. The incarnational model pioneered by Toland was combined with the occlusionistic one proffered by Baur in order to differentiate an apostolic and canonical Jewish Christianity from that of the Ebionites and the noncanonical literature in new and increasingly complex taxonomies of the category. The key problem now was specifying the particular Jewish features correlated with each type. What specific Jewish trait or traits demarcated heterodox varieties from the apostolic one? Which shared trait or traits, on the other hand, allowed these disparate types to be grouped together—and yet still distinguished from Paul and others—as a peculiarly *Jewish* Christianity? Unable to formulate any generally acceptable answers to these questions, scholars produced a bewildering variety of definitions and idiosyncratic technical distinctions (e.g., "Jewish" vs. "Judaic" vs. "Judaistic" Christianities, among others). Making sense of Jewish Christianity quickly became "one of the chief problems of the history of early Christianity."[20]

As critical scholarship on the New Testament and early Christianity continued over subsequent generations to disentangle itself from Christian theology, the theological and apologetic underpinnings of this discussion became increasingly muted. Nonetheless, the interpretive paradigms and resulting conundrums persisted, not least in the enduring problem of Jewish Christianity. The twentieth-century Parting of the Ways paradigm discussed above was itself a new iteration and combination of these incarnational and occlusionistic models. It too imagined an early Christianity that began, like a pupa within a chrysalis, "within Judaism" before its inner nature gradually but inexorably issued in its full emergence as a clearly distinct entity; and it too accounted for later, stunted forms of Jewish Christianity that either failed to fully hatch or even further occluded Christianity's inner nature with ongoing syncretistic additions. Scholars thus continued to wrestle with the problem of parsing the various types of Jewishness they imagined as "combined" with an assumed underlying Christianity.[21]

More recently, deepening awareness of the many and varied ways Christian apologetics have shaped the critical study of antiquity has led to a reconsideration not only of the historical origins and development of Christianity, but of the basic categories we use to tell the story and interpret the data. The criticisms leveled against the Parting of the Ways paradigm concern especially its interrelated assumptions of Christian essentialism and teleological inevitability—foundations that come from Christian apologetics, not from theoretical or methodological considerations derived from a more general history of culture. A fundamental problem facing critical historians today, then, is how to analyze Jewish and Christian antiquity apart from these specifically Christian constructs. How are we to explain the origins of Christianity if not as the sudden irruption of a new spiritual reality—a uniquely Christian essence—into the history of human culture? How are we to understand the separation of Christianity and Judaism if not by appeal to the inevitable outworking of that unique essence? To what extent can we talk about Christianity and Judaism as different religions in the context of the ancient world at all? Cut loose from their theological moorings, the most fundamental interpretive categories of the field are no longer the givens they once were, but the focal points of provocative debates: whether and in what sense even Paul, let alone other members of the early Jesus movement, should be considered "Christian"; whether the terms "Jew" and "Judaism" should be used in the context of the ancient world; and whether any of this in any case represents "religion."[22]

The problem of Jewish Christianity, lying precisely at the intersection of these issues, has become a flashpoint for some of the most fundamental questions driving scholarship on Jewish and Christian antiquity today. The central question of the present book, accordingly, is whether the concept can be of any use as we seek to move forward out of our present impasse. Can the category "Jewish Christianity" be useful for reconceptualizing the origins of Christianity and the Christianity-Judaism divide beyond the parameters of Christian apologetic historiography and the Parting of the Ways paradigm? My basic thesis, in a word, is no, it cannot. To be clear, I am not denying that the category might have other uses.[23] But the reason it cannot move us forward with respect to the question of Jewish and Christian antiquity is that the concept itself is only a pithy encapsulation of the apologetic paradigm scholars are currently seeking to move beyond. The very idea of an early Jewish Christianity posits a Christianity that existed in some sense from the beginning, albeit initially bound up with a Judaism from which it would eventually become separate. Jewish Christianity, in other words, does not explain the existence of Christianity and the Christianity-Judaism divide so much as it continues, even if only for analytical purposes, to assume them—and indeed from the very beginning. The evacuation of Christian theological assumptions from critical scholarship, in short, has left us with a problem that the concept "Jewish Christianity" is singularly ill-equipped to answer: how to explain the origins of Christianity and the Christianity-Judaism distinction themselves as cultural constructions. But if Christianity and the Christianity-Judaism divide must now be reconceptualized as something made in history rather than begotten into it, by whom, under what circumstances, and to what end were they made? The notion of an early Jewish Christianity not only does not help us answer these questions, it conceals them almost by design.

The Plan of the Book

Annette Yoshiko Reed has recently suggested that since the category "Jewish Christianity" "was invented at an important modern moment for the construction and naturalization of the very notion of 'religions,'" a consideration of "its genealogy may . . . prove especially promising as a means by which to revisit and reassess our present presumptions and practices."[24] While less overtly concerned with the question of "religion" per se, the present book was born out of an analogous conviction.[25] The bulk of the book traces the developments outlined above in detail in order to show how Christian apologetic assumptions and concerns, coupled with the rise of critical, history-of-religions scholarship, led to the making of a modern category. In Chapter 1 I explain why John Toland, in eighteenth-century London, began to reclassify groups long categorized as heresy as "Jewish Christianity." More specifically, I argue that Toland invented what I call an incarnational model of Jewish Christianity as the centerpiece of a freethinking reappropriation of Christian apologetic historiography. In Chapter 2 I explore the subsequent development of what I call an occlusionistic model of Jewish Christianity, and its relationship to the rise of a newly critical analysis of the New Testament, in the work of the English Deist Thomas Morgan and especially the German theologian F. C. Baur. In Chapter 3 I show how Baur's more traditionally minded critics, in an effort to turn back his assault on apostolic and canonical authority, combined the disparate models of Toland and Baur into new and more complex taxonomies of Jewish Christianity, and how this in turn resulted in the notorious problems of definition and terminology that have plagued the category ever since.

I turn in Chapter 4 to central developments in the study of Jewish Christianity in the post-Holocaust era, not least in relation to the Parting of the Ways paradigm. I examine the ways that Christian apologetic assumptions, and the interpretive problems they generate, continued to shape discussion of Jewish Christianity and treatments of Jewish and Christian antiquity more generally even as Christian theology became increasingly marginalized in critical scholarship. I also show how this evacuation of Christian theology from historical analysis created a new problem that the concept "Jewish Christianity" is ill-equipped to address—namely, how to theorize Christianity and its historical origins in the absence of appeals to hierophanic disclosures. In Chapter 5 I consider the contemporary debate about the enduring utility of the category "Jewish Christianity" in light of this new historical problem, with special focus on recent and promising attempts to resolve it by approaching Christianity and Judaism as socially constructed terms of identity. Finally, I show in Chapter 6 how we can get around the problems created by "Jewish Christianity" by approaching the question of the origins of Christianity and the Christianity-Judaism division as a study in the production and dissemination of ancient social taxonomies.

A word, finally, about terminology. As noted above, there is considerable debate at present about whether the ancient Greek term *Ioudaios* should be translated as "Jew," which tends to conjure up a particular cultural complex or even a religion, or as the more transparently geographical-genealogical "Judean." The issues that have led to this debate are exceedingly important, but the distinction itself should not be overblown. While *Ioudaioi* in the ancient literature clearly refers to a people linked to a particular ancestral territory, that people was also commonly correlated with what might today be called a distinct ethnic culture—much as Greeks, Persians, and Egyptians were. That culture, which included a cultic dimension, was occasionally, if apparently rarely, described as *Ioudaïsmos* as in 2 Maccabees, where it is paired precisely with *Hellēnismos* (2:21, 8:1, 14:38; cf. 4:13). That being said, *Ioudaioi* and *Ioudaïsmos* were not used with reference to a "religion" any more than *Hellēnes* and *Hellēnismos* were. The same goes, once they were invented, with the terms *Christianoi* and *Christianismos*. It seems to me that we both miss and even misunderstand a great deal about the ancients in general, and about early *Christianoi* and *Ioudaioi* in particular, if we lose sight of that fact. In what follows, then, I typically render *Ioudaios* "Judean" as a useful defamiliarization and reminder.[26] I do not, however, religiously (as it were) avoid the terms "Jew" and "Jewish," which after all have a similar ambiguity themselves. Conversely, when referring to the ancient concept *Christianismos*, I regularly render it "Christianism" in the service of an analogous defamiliarization—in this case to remind us that it functions alongside terms like *Ioudaïsmos* and *Hellēnismos* rather than within an assumed taxonomy of "religions" like the modern idea of Christianity.

1 The Invention of Jewish Christianity: From Early Christian Heresiology to John Toland's *Nazarenus*

Jewish Christianity, as has frequently been observed, is a modern category. While it is not unusual for early Christian writers to characterize some who allied themselves with Jesus as being Jewish in one sense or another, no one seems to have considered such people as representatives of a distinctly Jewish form of Christianity. They are classed as Christians "from the Judeans" (*ex Ioudaiōn*) and sometimes identified by group names like Ebionites or Nazoraeans; but abstractions equivalent to "Jewish Christianity" are not found in the ancient literature.[1] The move to the latter category was first made in the Enlightenment era, in close connection with the rise of critical New Testament scholarship. The earliest known formulation was by an Irish freethinker named John Toland who, in the early eighteenth century—initially in French as *Christianisme Judaique* and subsequently in English as "Jewish Christianity"—made the concept the centerpiece of a revisionist account of Christian origins.[2] By the end of the nineteenth century, above all because of the influential work of the German scholar Ferdinand Christian Baur, the concept had become a given within the emerging field of historical-critical scholarship on early Christianity.

The extent to which Toland and Baur were successful in redefining the scholarly imagination of Christian origins is underscored by the title of a recent volume framing their contribution as *The Rediscovery of Jewish Christianity*.[3] The implication is that Jewish Christianity had always been "out there"; that what was new with Toland and Baur was simply a methodology that led them to recover an ancient phenomenon that had been lost to view. This understanding of the matter would no doubt have delighted Toland. The claim was crucial to his thesis, and he himself had anticipated significant pushback precisely along these lines of "new" versus "old." "I foresee," he wrote, "that many of 'em . . . will say, that I advance a new Christianity, tho I think it undoubtedly to be the old one."[4] We should be very careful, however, to distinguish "Jewish Christianity" as the interpretive category Toland fashioned to bring new meaning to the ancient data from the ancient data itself. Whatever Toland may have rediscovered, it was not the *concept* "Jewish Christianity."

This distinction is important. Among other things, it allows us to highlight two separate lines of questions regarding Toland's accomplishment. First, how did he arrive at the category that would become not only the keystone of his new account of early Christianity, but a bedrock concept for subsequent generations of critical New Testament scholarship? Why did Toland reframe groups long known as Ebionites and Nazoraeans as "Jewish Christianity"? Second, what new claims about the past does this category signal? What particular historical points did Toland seek to assert over against previous accounts of early Christianity and to encapsulate within this new notion of a Jewish Christianity? The present chapter answers these questions by situating Toland between the earlier heresiological treatment of these groups on one hand and the rise of critical biblical scholarship on the other. Toland's critical sensibilities led him to both a new appreciation of the Jewish character of the early Jesus movement and a new thesis regarding the relationship of the Ebionites to the apostolic community. The resulting interpretive construct "Jewish Christianity," however, if thus fashioned with the tools of critical scholarship, rested nonetheless upon the same apologetic foundations laid long before by the Christian heresiologists themselves. In that sense, Toland did not discover "Jewish Christianity" so much as invent it as part of his Enlightenment-era retelling of the Christian incarnation myth.

On the Absence of "Jewish Christianity" in Antiquity

Distinctions along Jewish-Gentile lines were made within early Jesus groups presumably from the moment Gentiles became a factor in the movement. Paul, for example, presented himself as the apostle God had sent to the *ethnē* in particular, both to evangelize them and to secure their obedience (Gal 1:16; Rom 1:5, 15:15–18). He told his recruits in Galatia that an agreement had been struck among the movement's leaders back in Jerusalem to divide their missionary efforts along these very lines (Gal 2:7–10). Nor was this distinction merely a neutral observation of ethnic difference. It is quite clear from Paul's ongoing efforts to address issues that arose in relationship to it that Jewishness carried a special cachet within the movement. Singular prestige could be accorded to a Judean pedigree (2 Cor 11:21–22, Phil 3: 4–5), while a Gentile background was associated with particular sinfulness (e.g., Gal 2:15, 1 Thess 4:5; cf. Rom 1:18–32). More consequentially still, many within the group placed special value on the enactment of mores associated especially with Judeans (e.g., Gal 4:21), or what was sometimes called simply "living like a Judean" (*ioudaïzein*).[5] This latter was a source of significant tension within the movement, not least between Paul and those he referred to as the "acknowledged leaders" of the group (Gal 2:1–14). The open conflict between Paul and Peter over this matter in Antioch, apparently at the instigation of James the brother of Jesus, would reverberate for centuries.[6]

As noted above, however, there is no evidence that anyone involved conceptualized these distinctions abstractly in terms of different forms of Christianity. In the earliest generations, of course, there was not yet a concept of Christianity at all, let alone of distinct subclasses of it. But even once the abstraction "Christianism" (*Christianismos*) came to be used with reference to a self-defining culture, it was not delineated into Jewish and Gentile varieties. The operative distinctions where Jewishness was concerned remained simply Judean pedigree on one hand and "living like a Judean" on the other—the latter being used increasingly, as already by Paul, with a critical, polemical edge.[7] Indeed, far from developing a concept of Jewish Christianity along these lines, Ignatius of Antioch—the first known writer to invoke "Christianism" as a substantive—uses the term precisely in the context of a categorical distinction between "living in accord with Christianism" (*kata Christianismon zēn*) and "living like a Judean" (*ioudaïzein*).[8]

The category is similarly absent from the writings of the later Catholic heresiologists, who made it their business to build more or less systematic taxonomies of rival claimants on the authority of Jesus. When Irenaeus, toward the end of the second century, came in *Against Heresies* to that group that was distinguished by its particularly "Jewish way of life" (*iudaico charactere vitae*), he simply called them Ebionites (1.26). This was more or less standard practice, at least until Epiphanius and Jerome, some two centuries later, introduced the additional name "Nazoraeans."[9] Even then, while both writers associated the Nazoraeans closely with the Ebionites, neither conceptualized that association in terms of membership in a broader, generic class of Jewish Christianity.[10]

The lack of such a concept in the ancient literature is not accidental, nor is its explanation far to seek. Simply put, the early heresiologists did not consider Ebionites and Nazoraeans to be representatives of Christianism at all. Jerome's explicit denial of this, grounded in a categorical distinction between Christianism and Jewish observance reminiscent of Ignatius, is well known: "What shall I say of the Ebionites who claim to be Christians [while observing Jewish law]? . . . Until now a heresy is to be found in all parts of the East where Jews have their synagogues . . . Usually they are named Nazoraeans. They believe in Christ . . . in whom we also believe, but since they want to be both Jews and Christians, they are neither Jews nor Christians."[11] Epiphanius makes the same point in more generic terms. "Even today," he writes, "people call all the *haireseis*, I mean Manichaeans, Marcionites, Gnostics and others, by the common name of 'Christians,' though they are not Christians [*Christianous tous mē ontas Christianous kalousi*]. However, although each *hairesis* has another name, it still allows this one with pleasure, since the name is an ornament to it."[12] As is clear from these passages, the term "Christian" is not used by heresiologists as a generic descriptor of Jesus groups within some neutral taxonomy of religions. It is, rather, a highly charged term of identity, an honorific signifying a claim on transcendent truth within a context of cultural competition. As such it is reserved exclusively for those deemed as "truly" embodying the values associated with it, which is to say the writer's own group.[13] The fact of diversity among Jesus groups, therefore, is not conceptualized in terms of a taxonomy of Christianism. The operative distinction, rather, is between a singular Christianism on one hand and subcategories of *hairesis*—sects or "heresies"—on the other.

Ancient Heresiological Taxonomies

The term *hairesis*, particularly as used by early Jesus groups, poses certain challenges to the translator. The English equivalent "heresy," insofar as it conjures up doctrines concerning Jesus at odds with what was ultimately established as "orthodoxy," is potentially misleading. The term cannot be adequately understood apart from the Hellenistic literature, where it is used in a more neutral sense, especially of philosophical groups and their defining schools of thought.[14] Comparison of Judean intellectual life with Greek philosophy led to analogous usage with respect to Judean groups like Pharisees and Sadducees.[15] This wider understanding of *haireseis* played interestingly—and quite distinctly—into the efforts Jesus groups made to differentiate themselves from others in their social environment. Claims regarding the qualitative uniqueness of their own doctrines vis-à-vis any and all others were articulated in terms of a categorical distinction between "the Church" and its defining doctrines on one hand and the *haireseis* and theirs on the other. As a divine disclosure from God himself, the Christian-ism that defined the Church was no mere "school of thought" established by some human.[16] Hippolytus makes the point plainly in the opening of *Refutation of All Heresies*, portraying his own group as the successors of apostolic mediators of a Holy Spirit and rival "heresies" as appropriators of ideas "devised by those denominated philosophers among the Greeks."[17] An analogous exemption of the apostles from the consequences of human intellectual creativity is made by Tertullian in the beginning of *Prescription against Heretics*. Reflecting on the derivation of the word *hairesis* from the Greek *haireō*, "choose," he explains that the heretic can be described as "self-condemned because he has himself chosen that for which he is condemned. We, however, are not permitted to cherish any object after our own will, nor yet to make choice of that which another has introduced of his own private fancy . . . [The apostles] did not of themselves choose to introduce anything, but faithfully delivered to the nations . . . the doctrine which they had received from Christ" (*Praescr.* 6.3–4; cf. 37.2). The implication is spelled out still more clearly in a formula repeated elsewhere in the work: "the churches received [their doctrine] from the apostles, the apostles from Christ, Christ from God" (21.4; cf. 37.1). If Christian doctrine, therefore, is more than merely human in nature and origin, it is once again Greek phi-losophy, tellingly, as "the material of the world's wisdom," that represents the chief source of heresy.[18] Indeed, while Christian heresiologists were especially keen to differentiate themselves from rival Jesus groups in par-ticular, the category *hairesis* could still include earlier Hellenistic and Jew-ish groups as well. Epiphanius's *Panarion*, in fact, opens by treating twenty "heresies" that arose prior to Christ's incarnation before turning to the sixty that followed it.[19]

For the early Christian heresiologists, therefore, the *hairesis*/orthodoxy distinction was not conceived as a subdivision within Christianism. On the contrary, the first and most basic division in heresiological taxonomies was that between Christianism on one hand and *hairesis* on the other.[20] The ultimate basis for this dichotomy was an assertion regarding their fun-damentally different derivations. *Haireseis* were understood as innovations arising from within human history, from the thought processes of human founders, if perhaps at demonic instigation. They were contingent novelties of human opinion at best, and diabolical false prophecies at worst.[21] Christianism, on the other hand, was declared to be something altogether different. It was not a belief invented *within* history, but an eternal truth established by a god—indeed, the one true God—and revealed *into* history in the person of the incarnate Christ and through his Holy Spirit.[22] In the heresiological literature, then, Christianism is correlated not with diversity and division, but with a stable, singular unity said to underlie the "Church universal" (*ekklēsia katholikē*)—and this in stark contrast to the multiplicity of localized human opinion that was the hallmark of *hairesis*.[23]

Epiphanius's attempt to provide a comprehensive account of *hairesis* is especially instructive in this respect. Based in part on the work of earlier heresiologists—including "Irenaeus, Hippolytus, and many more" (*Pan.* 28.33.3)—his *Panarion* presents a creative synthesis and elaboration of key themes glimpsed throughout the earlier heresiological literature.[24] Epiphanius is especially concerned "to reveal the roots and beliefs of the *haireseis*" (*Pan.* Proem II, 3.2), and his project as a whole has a decidedly historical bent.[25] In book one, he outlines a history of *hairesis* beginning with Adam and the rise of "Barbarism," through the era of "Scythianism," to the emergence of more formal *haireseis* during the era of "Hellenism."[26] In the beginning, he says, there were no *haireseis* at all. Epiphanius imagines instead a primordial, pristine human piety that he equates with natural law (*Pan.* 1.1–2).[27] Adam, at least at first, "was unspoiled and innocent of evil and had no other name, for he had no additional name of an opinion, a belief, or a distinctive way of life. He was simply called 'Adam,' which means 'man'" (*Pan.* 1.1.1). The first deviations from this primordial state came in the form of Adam's own disobedience (*Pan.* 1.1.3), which is to say as the sort of "natural error" that is "not learned from teaching or writings" but arises simply from "each individual's will" (*Pan.* 2.2.3). The era of "Barbarism" arose as such human choices eventually gave rise to sorcery, witchcraft, and improper ethical behavior (*Pan.* 1.1.3). By the time of the flood, "everyone served as a law to himself and conformed to his own opinion" (*Pan.* 1.1.9). New manifestations of the same problem gave rise to still more human diversity in subsequent historical eras. The division of human languages from one to seventy-two as punishment for the tower of Babel defined the era of "Scythianism" (*Pan.* 2). The problems came to a head in the era of Hellenism, when a new emphasis on reason and learning produced all sorts of new evils, including idolatry: "The human reason invented evil for itself and with its freedom, reason and intellect, invented transgression instead of goodness," first with "paintings and portraits" and eventually with "carved images" and "reliefs in stone, wood . . . or any other material" (*Pan.* 3.3.4).[28] It was during this era, Epiphanius tells us, that *hairesis* in the more proper sense of the term—which is to say, the organized schools of Greek philosophy—finally appeared.[29]

The upshot of all this is that *hairesis* in the sense of a particular school of thought is said to be nothing more than a more formal, systematic, and learned manifestation of the same basic proclivity to be a law unto oneself (cf. *Pan.* 1.1.9) that first led humanity from the natural piety of primordial times to the wild diversity of human opinions and cultures that currently defines the world. "These [celebrated sects of the Greek philosophers] agree among themselves in error and produce a concordant science of idolatry, impiety and godlessness, but within the same error they clash with each other" (*Pan.* 4.2.8). The *haireseis* that arose after God became incarnate on earth as Jesus, in turn, represent nothing more than a continuation of this same phenomenon, often under the direct influence of the earlier *haireseis*.[30]

Christianism, in contrast, is neither the fruit of human thought nor the product of any social-cultural process, but something ultimately transcendent of human history. "The Church," Epiphanius says, "has always been but was revealed in the course of time, through Christ's incarnation" (*Pan.* Proem I, 1.3). For Epiphanius, then, Christianism refers to an ontological reality that exists beyond the realm of historical time and is only inflected hierophanically in the empirical, human world. Though used to categorize people and groups, then, Christianism in Epiphanius's usage is less a term of social-historical description than a construct of apologetic myth. Thus Epiphanius can speak meaningfully about the historical reality of Christianism in some sense even before the rise of "the Church": "in a sense there was [even before Judaism, Hellenism, or any sect at all] the faith which is now native to God's present day holy catholic church, a faith which was in existence from the beginning and was revealed again later. Anyone who is willing <to make an> impartial <investigation can> see . . . <that> the holy catholic church is the beginning of everything" (*Pan.* 2.2.3–4). Though fully "revealed" only with the incarnation of Christ, this transcendent Christianism is nonetheless correlated historically, at least incipiently, with the "natural," primordial piety of the first human. From this point of view, various heroes associated with the time before "the Church" can be redescribed in terms of—and thus appropriated for—Epiphanius's own Christianism.

"Without circumcision [Adam] was no Jew and since he did not worship carved images or anything else, he was no idolater. For Adam <was> a prophet . . . What was he, then, since he was neither circumcised nor an idolater—except that he exhibited the character of Christianity? And we must take this to be the case of Abel, Seth, Enosh, Enoch, Methuselah, Noah and Eber, down to Abraham" (*Pan.* 2.2.5–6).[31]

Given early Catholic claims on the God and scriptures of the Judeans, Judaism represents a singular and singularly ambivalent category within these heresiological taxonomies. On one hand, the orthodox fathers understand it, like Christianism, to have a divine origin: unlike *hairesis*, Judaism was no mere human invention. On the other hand, it is imagined as having historical limitations in a way that transcendent Christianism does not. In the eyes of the orthodox fathers, in short, Judaism was intended by God to serve a limited purpose within a particular historical circumstance. And once that circumstance had passed, continued practice of Judaism became little more than a *hairesis* of its own.[32]

Epiphanius's treatment is once again particularly illuminating. Within his historical taxonomy, Judaism functions above all in tandem with Hellenism. Historically, it is said to have begun soon after the latter, so that "everything was [then] divided into Hellenism and Judaism" (*Pan.* 8.2.2). Hellenism, as pointed out above, represented the full flowering of *hairesis*. Judaism, on the other hand, arose not as the result of any human design, but from a direct command of God to Abraham (*Pan.* 4.1.3). Indeed, Abraham himself, Epiphanius tells us, had until then been an exemplar of that primordial, adamic piety he imagines as an incipient Christianism (cf. *Pan.* 2.5–7): "characteristically of the holy catholic church," Abraham "was perfection itself in godliness, a prophet in knowledge, and in life, conformed to the Gospel" (*Pan.* 4.1.1).

Epiphanius is nonetheless quite clear that Judaism is not to be identified with that primordial piety itself. Adam, he insists, "was no Jew" (*Pan.* 2.2.5). "The character of Judaism" (*ho charactēr tou Ioudaïsmou*), rather, is correlated with the circumcision that God demanded of the ninety-nine-year-old Abraham (*Pan.* 4.1.3). What is more, that command was not issued for the sake of Abraham himself, in whom the faith of "the holy Catholic Church" was manifest (*Pan.* 4.1.1; cf. 2.3–5), but only for that of his future descendants, who would eventually find themselves surrounded by Hellenism and its *haireseis*—and thus in need of some tangible reminder of the original piety of Abraham. "It was so that his descendants would not repudiate the name of God on becoming strangers in a foreign land, but would bear a mark on their bodies instead to remind and convict them, and keep them true to their father's religion" (*Pan.* 8.4.1).[33] Similar divine commands were subsequently issued in the law given to Moses, with a similar object of giving "bodily" reminders of the primordial, "spiritual" piety of their ancestors: "The legislation God gave them taught them like a pedagogue—indeed the Law was like a pedagogue in giving its precepts physically, but with a spiritual hope [*somatikōs men diastellomenos, pneumatikēn de echōn tēn prosdokian*]" (*Pan.* 8.5.4; cf. Gal 3:24–25). At the same time, both circumcision and the law also served to point Abraham's descendants toward Christ by providing fleshly "types" of the spiritual "truths" that were to come with his incarnation—a function further supported by prophetic oracles pointing more explicitly to the coming Christ (*Pan.* 8.4.2; cf. 8.5 and 8.6.5–8.7.1). For Epiphanius, then, Judaism represented neither Hellenism nor the incipient Christianity of Adam and Abraham. In the period until Christ, at least, it was rather a *tertium quid*: a symbolic, fleshly hedge around the spiritual reality of incipient Christianity; a temporary protection against the *haireseis* of Hellenism until Christianity was fully revealed in the person of the incarnate Christ.

In fact, far from being identified with incipient Christianity, Judaism is ultimately classed by Epiphanius among the *haireseis* (e.g., *Pan.* Proem I, 3). The rationale for this remarkable move would seem to be twofold, and relative to Epiphanius's historiographical scheme. According to his account, the Judeans, despite God's best efforts, were ultimately infected by Hellenism. The sojourn among the Egyptians narrated in Genesis and Exodus seems to be especially important here, perhaps as the proximate cause of the additional legislation beyond circumcision given at the time of Moses.[34] Eventually, after Israel's experience of exile, full-blown *haireseis* are said to have arisen both from Judaism (Samaritanism) and within it (Sadducees, Pharisees, etc.).[35] If this clarifies Epiphanius's notion of Jewish *haireseis*, however, it does not yet explain his classification of Judaism itself as *hairesis*—a move that is remarkable considering his assumption of its divine origin. Here one can only surmise that Judaism is imagined as having *become* a *hairesis* in the postincarnation era, when it was deprived of its divine purpose and sanction. After the full revelation of the spiritual reality of Christianity in the historical Church, that is, continued insistence on the "fleshy" symbols of Judaism is no less an act of willful rejection of the primordial human piety than those *haireseis* against which it had previously been intended to guard.[36]

In any event, the idea that there could be subtypes of Christianity—let alone a distinctly Jewish Christianity in particular—is entirely nonsensical from the point of view of the early Christian heresiologists. Though at one time divinely commanded, Judaism as such is no more "spiritual" than *hairesis*; and neither, in the era after Christ, does it have any purpose or value. To opt for fleshly Jewish things after Christ is no less a rejection of the transcendent, spiritual reality of Christianism and the "Church universal" than were *haireseis* in the era before him. Groups like Ebionites or Nazoraeans who, as Jerome put it, "want to be both Jews and Christians . . . are neither Jews nor Christians," but simply *hairesis* (*Ep.* 112.13). There is no in between.

To be sure, Judeans could become "believers" just as surely as Gentiles could. Skarsaune's search for ancient analogues for the term "Jewish Christian," not surprisingly, yields a variety of ways of conveying this idea. Equally unsurprising, however, is the lack of any analogue for the substantive "Jewish Christianity."[37] If there can of course be Christians "from the Jews," or even "Jewish believers" in Christ, there can be no distinctly Jewish *Christianity*. The strikingly similar results produced by Matti Myllykoski's search for analogues in the English literature in the centuries before Toland only underscores the novelty of Jewish Christianity as a modern category.[38] Seen from this point of view, the interesting question is not why earlier writers failed to formulate the concept, but why Toland and others in the Enlightenment era suddenly did.

The Making of a Modern Category: John Toland

F. C. Baur is widely and rightly credited with making a dichotomy between Jewish Christianity and Gentile Christianity paradigmatic within the critical study of early Christianity. If, however, it was largely through Baur's immense influence that this division made its way into the standard vocabulary of the field, the distinction itself was not his own coinage. More than a century before Baur began publishing his seminal works, the Irish-born John Toland had already placed the same dichotomy at the center of his own provocative reconstruction of early Christianity, published under the title *Nazarenus* in 1718.[39]

The ostensible occasion for Toland's study was his chance discovery of the Islamic Gospel of Barnabas—a text, he says, that "*naturally*" led him to "*resume some former considerations I had about the* NAZARENS; *as being the Primitive Christians most properly so call'd.*"[40] It was in the context of this study that the term "Jewish Christianity," along with its inevitable mate "Gentile Christianity," is first known to appear. What led Toland to these categories? How can we understand his decision to redescribe a group long known simply as Nazoraeans in terms of Jewish Christianity?[41]

For his part, Toland wished to present *Nazarenus* as being the work of someone who was "only a historian"—albeit one who might comment from time to time on the wider implications of his study.[42] His readers, however, have long recognized that there was something much more at stake here than simply accurate description of the past. In fact, Toland composed *Nazarenus* not merely as an account of *early* Christianity, but as an account of *true* Christianity.[43] Whether he did so sincerely, with a genuine interest in reforming the religion, or satirically, to subvert the whole project of ecclesiastical historiography itself, is a matter of debate.[44] What is plain at any rate is that the category "Jewish Christianity," if supported by historical argumentation, was a by-product of Toland's attempt to divert the authorizing power of Jesus and the apostles from traditional orthodoxy to his own enlightened humanism.[45]

Toland's Taxonomic Project

Toland's formulation of a new taxonomy of Christianity was emphasized boldly in the very title of his work: "*NAZARENUS:* or, *Jewish, Gentile,* and *Mahometan* CHRISTIANITY." If it is the first of these categories that is our chief interest here, the one that sounded the most exotic to Toland's ears—and that his study would be particularly concerned to establish—was actually the third: "and tho the very title of *Mahometan Christianity* may be apt to startle you (for Jewish or *Gentile Christianity* shou'd not sound quite so strange) yet I flatter my self, that, by perusing the following *Dissertation,* you'll be fully convinc'd there is a sense, wherin the Mahometans may not improperly be reckon'd and call'd a sort or sect of Christians."[46] In fact, when Toland first began to conceive of the project that would eventually be published as *Nazarenus,* the main title he gave it was simply "Mahometan Christianity."[47] The title evolved as the project did. By the time he produced a French version of the work in 1710, its title had been reformulated to highlight two categories: *Christianisme Judaique et Mahometan.*[48] When the published version finally appeared eight years later, the title was reworked again to emphasize three distinct categories— "Jewish, Gentile, and Mahometan Christianity"—but with all this as an alternate title to a monograph now called simply *Nazarenus.*[49]

It is plain both from Toland's sensitivity to the extent to which his categories might "startle" and from his repeated reworking of the title that the formulation of a new taxonomy of Christianity was a very conscious and deliberate dimension of the project that would eventually be published as *Nazarenus*.[50] If we wish to understand how Toland came to formulate the category "Jewish Christianity," then, we will do well to begin by contextualizing this move within his larger taxonomic project.

The few extant portions of the initial draft of the work's introduction, apparently from the time when the project was still being called "Mahometan Christianity," are very helpful in this respect.[51] In a passage that would eventually evolve into the one quoted above, Toland can already be seen anticipating that his reader "might look on the title of the present dissertation [i.e., "Mahometan Christianity"] to be somewhat singular," and thus hoping to demonstrate precisely the point that "Mahometans may not improperly be call'd and reckon'd a sort of Christians."[52] It is quite plain, then, that Toland had conceived this project from the very start as an attempt to establish and defend a new classification of Islam as "Mahometan Christianity." What led him to make this provocative taxonomic move?

In the same passage, though in a portion that would eventually be edited out of the published *Nazarenus*, Toland elaborates further on the context in which he is doing this. However "singular" his notion of "Mahometan Christianity" might seem, he was not, he says, "the first, who put *Christian* and *Mahometan* together." He refers specifically in this connection to a certain "Doctor of Divinity"—namely, one Robert South—who had put the terms together precisely for the purpose of dismissing Toland as a "Mahometan Christian" on the basis of the seemingly Unitarian vision of Christianity Toland had promulgated in *Christianity not Mysterious* in 1696.[53] Notably, the question of Islam's relation to Christianity—and, more to the point, of Unitarian doctrine's relationship to Islam—had become a regular topic in the Unitarian-Trinitarian debate flourishing in Toland's England.[54] Toland's "startling" formulation of the category "Mahometan Christianity," then, represented an ironic appropriation and reification of a term of slander directed against himself in the context of an ecclesiastical debate about true Christian teaching.

Toland's response to this charge is a study in ambiguity.[55] He characterized the intended slander ironically as an "odd complement" but feigned not to understand its rationale. Compliment or not, he did not hesitate to hurl the characterization right back at his critic, and for reasons less than flattering either to South or to Islam.[56] He was in any case clearly perturbed by the charge—enough, indeed, to conceive of a full-blown treatise on "Mahometan Christianity" and to develop it over more than a decade into *Nazarenus*. And though he was quick to insist that this sort of Christianity was none of his own, the aim of this treatise would be to show precisely that there was an ironic truth to South's intended slur: that Islam itself should be considered a form of Christianity—"and not the worst sort neither, tho farr from being the best."[57] Indeed, he would press still further, arguing that this conclusion had immediate sociopolitical implications for Christian Europe; "that consequently . . . [Muslims] might with as much reason and safety be tolerated at London and Amsterdam, as the Christians of every kind are so at Constantinople and thro-out all Turkey."[58] Toland's strategy for establishing these points was to develop a second, more historically oriented thesis regarding the relationship of Islam to the Ebionites and Nazoraeans, and indeed to "the original plan of Christianity" itself.

Toland's Historical Argument

If Toland began ruminating about this project soon after the publication of *Christianity not Mysterious*, his chance discovery in 1709 of the Muslim Gospel of Barnabas, previously unknown to Christian Europe, provided an ideal occasion for him to make his historical case.[59] Though he remained rather coy regarding the authenticity of this gospel, he argued that its discovery showed that the Islamic understanding of Jesus did not come—as some, he says, have "rashly charg'd"—from forged or "Apocryphal books," but from this work, which was in all likelihood the very same Gospel of Barnabas known to Christian antiquity, even if "not in its original purity."[60] In any event, by examining the views of this gospel in light of the early Christian literature itself, he argued, "it manifestly appears from what source the Mahometans . . . had their peculiar Christianity, if I be allow'd so to call it" (*N.*, 61). Indeed, Toland's treatise would show that "some of the fundamental doctrines of Mahometanism . . . have their rise . . . from the earliest monuments of the Christian religion."[61]

By way of substantiating this claim, Toland showed that several distinctive aspects of the understanding of Jesus and Paul in the Gospel of Barnabas were also to be found in early Christian reports about Nazoraeans and Ebionites.[62] Their unitarianism represents a major case in point: "as to the making of JESUS a mere man," he says, the Gospel of Barnabas presents nothing other than "the ancient Ebionite or Nazaren System."[63] He notes further that even the gospel's report that someone else had been crucified in the place of Jesus was reported to have been taught already during the apostolic era by Cerinthus (*N.*, 17–19)—the Cerinthians, in Toland's view, being themselves "a branch of the Ebionites" (*N.*, 34). And if the Gospel of Barnabas singles out the apostle Paul as one who was later deceived into spreading false teachings about Jesus, this too only reflects an ancient Ebionite position: "this notion of PAUL's having wholly metamorphos'd and perverted the true Christianity (as some of the Heretics have exprest it) and his being blam'd for so doing by the other Apostles, especially by JAMES and PETER, is neither an original invention of the Mahometans, nor any sign of the novelty of their *Gospel*: but rather a strong presumtion of its antiquity, at least as to some parts of it; since this was the constant language and profession of the most ancient Sects [i.e., the Ebionites and Nazoraeans]" (*N.*, 24).

It is this last point that receives the fullest elaboration. Toland seeks first to establish "beyond any room for doubt" (*N.*, 24) that Nazoraeans and Ebionites considered Paul "an intruder on the genuin Christianity" who "substitut[ed] his own pretended Revelations to the doctrines of those with whom CHRIST had [actually] convers'd" (*N.*, 29). Having done this to his satisfaction (chap. 9), Toland proceeds to a consideration of Paul's relationship to the Jerusalem apostles as understood by the Ebionites and as told by Paul himself (chap. 10). Paul, Toland observes, not only did not deny the Ebionite charge that he did not get his gospel from the Jerusalem apostles, but he positively insists on it when recounting the history of his interaction with them in Galatians 1–2 (*N.*, 30).

At this point Toland's argument takes a critical turn. The focus shifts from simply proving that Islamic teaching about Jesus reflects ancient Nazoraean teaching to establishing a more comprehensive theory regarding the origins of Christianity itself. "But we ought not," Toland says, "slightly to run over this passage, since from the history of the Nazarens we shall take occasion (and a very natural occasion it is) to set THE ORIGINAL PLAN OF CHRISTIANITY in its proper light" (*N.*, 32–33).[64] The heart of Toland's theory is that Jesus and the apostles had from the beginning envisioned a religion that Toland would sum up as a "*Union without Uniformity*" (*N.*, v), in which Christianity as practiced by Jews would necessarily and for all time be different from Christianity as practiced by Gentiles. Interestingly, however, Toland develops this point not in relation to christological doctrine, but in relation to practice, specifically of Jewish law.[65] At this point the argument becomes essentially exegetical, based primarily on an interpretation of Galatians 1–2 in light of Acts 15 and 21.

In discussing Galatians 1–2 Toland highlights the fact that the Ebionites accused Paul of lying when he claimed that James, Peter, and John granted the legitimacy of his mission; for if James had actually acknowledged the validity of Paul's gospel, he could scarcely himself have been—as Paul implies—the source of the subsequent conflict in Antioch.[66] Toland does not, however, side with this Ebionite position. His key point, rather, is this: "There's but one way in the world," he says, of "reconciling these things" (*N.*, 32): "Paul can never be otherwise defended against the Ebionites" unless it was the case that his law-free gospel was understood by all the apostles to have been relevant for Gentiles only, not for Jews (*N.*, 38; cf. 36–37).

Toland found ample support for this position in the canonical Acts— a work, he notes, that the Ebionites rejected as spurious (*N.*, 34–35). Given Acts 21 and 25, Toland considered it an "incontestable matter of fact" that "all the Jews which became Christians were still Zealous for the Levitical Law" (*N.*, 38). Insofar as this law was, however, particularly "expressive of the history of their peculiar nation," being in this sense "no less national and political, than religious and sacred," none but "a few private persons" among them considered Gentiles to be in any way bound by it.[67] This, Toland says, was not only the position of the apostles, but of Jesus as well.[68] What is more, he argued, Acts 21:26 shows "irrefragably" that Paul himself agreed.[69] To argue otherwise would be to accuse not only Paul, but the other apostles as well, of "dissembling": "for if the matter was not so, how cou'd it be truly said [by James], *that those things were nothing*, with which he [i.e., Paul] was charg'd? namely, that he taught the Jews to forsake MOSES, and that they ought not to circumcise their children, neither to walk after the customs" (*N.*, 36–37; cf. Acts 21:20–24). In a remarkable anticipation of the so-called new reading of Paul advanced in recent decades by Lloyd Gaston, John Gager, and others, Toland thus argued that every negative word about the law in Paul's letters concerned only its relation to Gentiles, not Jews.[70] The Apostolic Decree, for its part, was instituted not out of any principled concern for Gentile diet, but simply for the pragmatic purpose of making social interaction possible between Jews and Gentiles in Judea.[71]

In short, Toland argued that "the original plan of Christianity" envisioned not one, but in fact multiple ways that the religion was to be practiced, depending upon the ethnicity and geographical location of its practitioners. Jewish followers of Jesus were forever bound to practice their own ancestral laws. The Gentiles who lived among them in Judea were not to observe that law, but only the minimal dietary restrictions required to permit fellowship with Jews. Those Gentiles who lived outside of Judea, on the other hand, didn't need to bother with dietary restrictions at all. According to Toland, then, the difference between Jews and Gentiles in early Christianity was not just a matter of ethnic backgrounds, but of distinct practices and even separate social institutions.[72] The distinction, in other words, was not simply between Jewish and Gentile *Christians,* but between Jewish and Gentile *Christianities.*[73]

Toland remains strangely vague as to how exactly Islam figures into this scheme.[74] But its general significance for his thesis, at least, he takes to be quite obvious: "Now, from all these things . . . it manifestly appears from what source the Mahometans (who always most religiously abstain from things strangl'd and from blood) had their peculiar Christianity, if I be allow'd so to call it; and that their *Gospel,* for ought I yet know, may in the main be the ancient *Gospel of* BARNABAS" (*N.,* 61). The Islamic understanding of Jesus and the apostles, in short, was not the creation of Muhammad but was in fact "as old as the time of the Apostles" (*N.,* 84–85). If different from the Gentile Christianity practiced in Europe, that is only because its roots lie in what was always meant to have been a distinctive form of the religion—what was indeed the original form of the religion practiced by Jesus and the apostolic community: *Jewish* Christianity.

"Jewish Christianity" as Apologetic Construct

Thus far Toland's argument for the redescription of Islam as "Mahometan Christianity" is basically historical, and his taxonomy apparently genealogical: insofar as Islam is rooted in the practices of early Christianity, it is itself properly classified as a type of Christianity. Toland's novel taxonomy, however, cannot be adequately explained as the product of his critical historiography. When stating at the outset his thesis regarding Islam, Toland draws an analogy between its historical origins and those of Christianity: "by perusing the following *Dissertation,* you'll be fully convinc'd there is a sense, wherin the Mahometans may not improperly be reckon'd and call'd a sort or sect of Christians, as Christianity was at first esteem'd a branch of Judaism" (*N.,* 4–5). If the analogy sums up Toland's historical argument for reclassifying Islam as "Mahometan Christianity," it also exposes an element of tension between that argument and his other novel category, "Jewish Christianity." If the issue is simply one of historical roots, how can we explain the fact that he came ultimately to formulate the category "Jewish Christianity" rather than—as his own analogy would seem to suggest—"Christian Judaism"? Why was the end result of Toland's historical argument a new taxonomy of Christianity rather than a new taxonomy of Judaism, now accounting for Christian and "Mahometan" varieties?

The answer to this question lies less in Toland's historical analysis than in the rhetorical and cultural contexts in which it was produced—namely, a competition among Christian intellectuals of the English Enlightenment to authorize rival mythic and ethical values as "true Christianity." There are two specific issues that must be reckoned with. The first is the authorizing power in Toland's Europe of the word "Christianity" itself—and most especially "original Christianity." The second is Toland's own mythic conception of Christianity, particularly as it relates to Judaism.

It should be remembered at the outset how Toland came to the terms of his taxonomy in the first place. The category with which he began, "Mahometan Christianity," was formulated as an ironic and quite pointed appropriation of a term of ecclesiastical polemics. If Trinitarian intellectuals were characterizing Unitarians as "Mahometan Christians" in order to suggest that their views were something less than "actual" or "true" Christianity, Toland aimed to show that such "Mahometan Christians," on the contrary, had more right to the name Christianity than their Trinitarian critics.[75] Indeed, Toland would press further: not only Unitarianism, but Islam more generally should be understood to count as Christianity—and thus, moreover, granted the same social and political rights in Christian Europe as any other form of the religion. Laying claim to the term "Christianity," in other words, was precisely the point. It was this word, not "Judaism," that carried rhetorical power in Toland's Europe.

The same dynamic is at work in Toland's move from a category apparently familiar to his contemporaries—Jewish *Christians*—to one much less common, if indeed yet known at all: Jewish *Christianity*. If this latter concept, along with its inevitable companion "Gentile Christianity," were somewhat less "apt to startle" than "Mahometan Christianity" (*N.*, 4), it was not, evidently, because it was widely used. Toland, to be sure, takes for granted the long-standing tradition of distinguishing types of Christians with reference to their ethnic derivations, specifically "*those from among the Jews, and those from among the Gentiles*" (*N.*, iv). But he was not merely restating a distinction, he says, "*which no body denies.*" On the contrary, his move from Jewish and Gentile Christians as distinct types of *people* to Jewish and Gentile Christianity as discrete categories of *religion* gets to a point, he says, that "*every body denies,*" and that is in fact a central thesis of *Nazarenus*: not only that such a distinction existed in antiquity, but "*that of right it ought to have been so*"; "*that it was so design'd in THE ORIGINAL PLAN OF CHRISTIANITY*" that there should for all times be different and yet equally legitimate forms of Christianity itself, one for Jews and one for Gentiles (*N.*, iv).

In fact, Toland's criticism of traditional accounts of Ebionites and Nazoraeans had less to do with any details of historical description than with their normative evaluation. "*Their history,*" he says, "*I have here set in a truer light than other writers, who are generally full of confusion and misrepresentation concerning them; making them the first, if not the worst, of all* Heretics" (*N.*, iii). His reconstruction of the Ebionites and Nazoraeans largely echoes the reports of the Catholic heresiologists, with one primary and very crucial difference: they were not, as portrayed there, a heretical deviation from apostolic Christianity, but rather a reflection of "the TRUE ORIGINAL PLAN OF CHRISTIANITY" as envisioned and practiced by both Jesus and the apostles (*N.*, 52). The whole point of redescribing the Nazoraeans as "Jewish Christianity," then, was simply to dignify and authorize their religion precisely *as* Christianity—indeed, as the primal Christianity of Jesus and the apostles themselves—rather than as some heresy. The Nazoraeans, he concludes with a scathing irony, were disavowed as heretics "not only [on account] of their Judaism, but I may say of their Christianity too" (*N.*, 56).

It is important to note in this connection how seamlessly the rhetoric of *Nazarenus* moves between the descriptive and the normative, the historical and the apologetic. The hinge on which the discourse swings in this respect is precisely the notion of "original Christianity"—a concept that recurs throughout *Nazarenus*, beginning with its subtitle and ending with its closing thought: "If in the history of this *Gospel* [*of Barnabas*] I have satisfy'd your curiosity, I shall think my time well spent; but infinitely better, if you agree, that, on this occasion, I have set THE ORIGINAL PLAN OF CHRISTIANITY in its due light, as farr as I propos'd to do."[76] In Christian rhetoric, the notion of original Christianity is not merely or even primarily a term of history but one of myth and, inevitably, politics. To characterize something as "original Christianity" is less to draw a temporal distinction than to lay claim to the mythic authority of a transcendent reality.[77] Indeed, Toland's argument for the normative legitimacy of "Jewish"—and thus by extension "Mahometan"—Christianity ultimately boils down to a single point: it was authorized by, and indeed practiced by, Jesus and the apostles.

For all its significant historical innovations, then, Toland's *Nazarenus* represents another, albeit subversive version of the historiographical paradigm long employed by his orthodox adversaries.[78] The most basic of their shared assumptions is that there is in fact such a thing as a "true Christianity" that can—and indeed must—be distinguished from the social and cultural realities of Christianity as actually practiced by varying self-described Christians over the course of history. This assumption is apparent throughout the text of *Nazarenus*, but perhaps never more so than when Toland, taking a page from the book of his adversaries, denies *their* claims on the title "Christianity," accusing them indeed of "downright ANTICHRISTIANISM."[79]

Two additional shared moves served to transpose this normative and fundamentally ahistorical assumption onto the stage of human history. Both Toland and his adversaries agreed, first, that this true Christianity was embodied in the historical teachings of Jesus and the apostles. Transcendent Christianity is in this way anchored definitively in time and space, with the temporal category "original" becoming essentially synonymous with the ecclesiastical category "authoritative."[80] Where they disagreed was on the particular values that had been authoritatively embodied in these first-century people. Second, all parties similarly assumed that this "original Christianity" quickly became subject to human corruption as it moved beyond the apostolic sphere—and that the nature of that corruption is such that even heretical innovators are wont to falsely identify their own teaching as the apostolic original. Toland quite agreed with his adversaries, for example, that this was how "papism" was to be explained.[81] The disagreement on this matter was simply the extent to which the same was true of their own beliefs and values. Toland saw something analogous to "papism" at work in his adversaries even as he anticipated that they, in turn, would interpret his own reconstruction along similar lines. "I forsee that many of 'em . . . will say, that I advance a new Christianity," he says, "tho I think it undoubtedly to be the old one."[82]

The historical-critical posture adopted in Toland's work, in short, represents the refraction of the apologetic historiographical paradigm of his heresiological predecessors through an Enlightenment-era sensibility. The twin ideas that Jesus and the apostles manifested a pure and authoritative Christianity and that their true religion was subject to subsequent corruption by syncretizing followers remain the driving assumptions. The natural next step in the age of reason was to turn critical inquiry to the task of separating the later accretions from the unadulterated original. If Toland conceived this simply as a matter of doing good history, it was because his unquestioned conceptual framework remained Christianity's own myth of pristine origins and its rhetoric of transcendent authority. His innovative reconstruction, in other words, was in this sense Christian apologetic historiography in a newly critical mode: another means of claiming the power inherent in the concept of an "original Christianity" in order to authorize whatever it is one might value in the present.

From this perspective, the root difference between Toland's historiography and that of the early heresiologists he criticized was less a matter of historical method than of the particular values each correlated with that most powerful of ciphers, "original Christianity." Where the latter identified it with Catholic orthodoxy, the values that *Nazarenus* sought to authorize were those of an Enlightenment humanism.[83] The traditional theorization of Christianity's transcendence was modified accordingly. Long-standing appeals to Jesus as the incarnation of a preexistent deity and to special revelations of a Holy Spirit were set aside in favor of a different sort of transcendence—one no less present in the early heresiological literature but traditionally used in tandem with the former: the identification of Christianity with a primordial "Law of Nature."[84] Toland, in the argot of his era, correlated this idea with the notion of a generic, "natural religion" imagined as underlying all the particular forms of piety found over the history of human culture.[85] For Toland, this natural religion comprised a "Moral Law of Nature" that, closely correlated with rationality, represented "the fundamental bond of all society."[86] As such, it was not the special possession of any one people, but a human universal immanent in the very nature of humanity itself. Indeed, while the various "civil and national rites" that one might designate as the world's religions are necessary means toward realizing the ends of the Law of Nature in human societies, they are themselves, in Toland's understanding, less religion in a proper sense than politics.[87] In fact, in the wrong hands—specifically, in the hands of priests—such social-cultural institutions can be twisted into something entirely opposed to religion in Toland's strict and normative sense of the term. Ironically, then, so-called religious leaders are themselves among the principal causes of irreligion: *"for the little effect of Religion procedes in most places from the too great influence of the CLERGY, who make that to pass for Religion which is none, or quite the reverse, as they make Piety often inconsistent with Probity; and this they do to serve their own private ends, which in such places are ever opposite to the public good of the people* . . . [I]n order to secure [wealth, and thus power] . . . they train up their hearers in Ignorance, and consequently in Superstition and Bigotry." It is not actually religion that such people preach, Toland says, but *"metaphysical riddles, or mythological tales, or mystical dreams"*—in short, precisely the sort of "mystery" he had exposed as the cynical invention of power-hungry priests in *Christianity not Mysterious.*[88]

What was actually promulgated by Jesus and the apostles, Toland argues, was no such "mystery." Nor was it even a new set of doctrines, practices, and social institutions intended to displace existing ones. "And tis evident to all, but such as will not see," he writes, "that one main design of Christianity was to improve and perfect the knowledge of the Law of nature" (*N.*, 67). And if the second design was "to facilitate and inforce the observation of the same," it was less by creating a new institution than by breathing new life into those, like Judaism, that already existed. Indeed, if there could be said to be any "mystery" in "original Christianity," it was precisely the idea that humans could be unified in religion even as the differences in their cultures were otherwise affirmed and perpetuated. The *"Mystery that* PAUL *rightly says was hid from all other ages, till the manifestation of it by* JESUS," according to Toland, is just that *"Union without Uniformity"* that became manifest in the simultaneous existence of Christianity, as pure natural religion, in distinct and separate Jewish and Gentile forms (*N.*, iv). The actualization of natural law in historical societies does not mean replacing the multiplicity of human cultures with a singular new one, but rather disclosing the transcendent "true religion" that all, at least latently, already have in common by virtue of their underlying humanity.

For Toland, then, Christianity represents something qualitatively different from all those systems of discourse, practice, and social identity—in a word, those cultures—that one might otherwise be inclined to call religion. Christianity alone, precisely as *"true religion,"* is not culture at all, but rather the end for which culture, and most especially other so-called religions, should serve as means. The gospel, he says, *"consists not in words but in virtue; tis inward and spiritual, abstracted from all formal and outward performances: for the most exact observation of externals, may be without one grain of religion . . . wheras true religion is inward life and spirit"* (*N.*, v). Christianity properly so-called, in other words, is not social and empirical but individual and spiritual. It does not consist in any particular discourse or practice but is an internal disposition that one brings *to* cultural practice and that is thus characterizable only in generic terms like "Faith," "Piety," and "Virtue." As such, it can become manifest within virtually any social-cultural institution, thereby producing the "Union without Uniformity" envisioned, according to Toland, by Jesus and his apostles in the "original plan of Christianity."

If Christianity thus stands for a spiritual disposition transcendent of all culture, Judaism, for Toland, is a prime example of the sort of external culture that Christianity simultaneously affirms and overcomes. This emerges with particular clarity as he discusses Jesus and the apostles in relation to their Jewish context:

> Without this Faith and Regeneration (as a change from vice to virtue was properly call'd even by the Heathens) the ever so punctual performance of Ceremonies cou'd not justify a Jew, or render him a good man, agreeable and well-pleasing to God: but JESUS and his Apostles made it manifest that the Gentile, who believ'd one God and the necessity of Regeneration, might, contrary to the notions of the degenerate Jews (who then plac'd all religion in outward practices) be justify'd by such his Faith, without being oblig'd to exercise the ceremonies of the Law, being things no way regarding him, either as to national origin or civil government; while the Jew, on the other hand, must, to the outward observance of his country Law by eternal covenant, add this inward Regeneration and the Faith of the *Gospel*, or the Levitical Law wou'd avail him nothing tho ever so strictly observ'd. (*N.*, 64)

In short, Jews, as Jews, are bound by covenant to observe their own national laws forever and always. The fundamental mistake made by "degenerate Jews," he says, was simply the confusion of this "outward observance" with *religion*—a misidentification of means and end that issued, among other things, in an utterly misguided ethnocentrism in their estimation of Gentiles.[89] By demonstrating that Gentiles could themselves have true religion simply by an internal disposition of "Faith" rather than by adopting Jewish cultural institutions, Toland argued, Jesus and the apostles laid bare the distinction between Judaism and religion—and thus too, effectively, the need by Jews as much as Gentiles for "Regeneration" by such "Faith" in order to become truly "religious." As he put it the preface to *Nazarenus*, "*something else besides the Legal Ordinances, most of 'em political, was necessary to render a Jew religious: even that Faith, which is an internal participation of the divine nature, irradiating the soul*" (*N.*, v). Christianity, in Toland's understanding, is precisely that transcendent "something else," realized historically in the person of Jesus and in the community of his apostles.[90]

As a purely internal disposition with no concrete doctrines and practices of its own, however, this "natural religion" can only become a social reality through the medium of particular cultures. Historically speaking, there cannot be any generic Christianity, only the "Jewish" or "Gentile"— or "Mahometan"—*Christianities* that result when human cultures are "regenerated" by the infusion of religion in Toland's sense of the term. The Christianity of Jesus and the apostles, then, was more specifically a *Jewish* Christianity—the embodiment of natural religion in Jewish cultural forms—albeit one that necessarily envisioned, from the beginning, an equally viable if socially and culturally distinct *Gentile* Christianity that would exist alongside it, and indeed for all time.

In Toland's telling, however, it was this Gentile Christianity that would prove in practice to be the source of historical Christianity's subsequent degradation into the perversion that passed, in his own day, for Christian orthodoxy. "*These* [converts from the Gentiles] *did almost wholly subvert the TRUE CHRISTIANITY, which in the following Treatise [Nazarenus] I vindicate; drawing it out from under the rubbish of their endless divisions, and clearing it from the almost impenetrable mists of their sophistry*" (*N.*, vi). What is more, these Gentile miscreants combined their sophistic priestcraft with a corrosive bigotry, specifically in the form of an "inveterate . . . hatred of the Jews" (*N.*, vi). In the ultimate irony, they came to condemn Jesus's own religion itself—namely, Jewish Christianity—by replicating, in inverted form, the very error of the "degenerate Jews" that Jesus himself had corrected: "confounding political with religious performances." If "*the Jews generally mistook the means for the end*," these Gentiles who now "*better understood the end, wou'd not onely absurdly take away the means; but even those other civil and national rites which were to continue always in the Jewish Republic*" (*N.*, v–vi). In the end, then, heresiologists like Epiphanius and Jerome denied the title "Christian" to those they called Ebionites and Nazoraeans for nothing more than practicing the very Christianity of Jesus "Nazarenus" himself.[91]

Incarnation Reconceived

The idea that there was such a thing as an early Jewish Christianity was an innovation of the English Enlightenment. Though a product of the same humanistic spirit that would eventually produce the fields of critical biblical studies and the history of religions more generally, it was built upon a foundation laid long ago by the inventors of Christianism and subsequently assumed by its many apologists and heresiologists. Christianity, it is insisted, is qualitatively different from anything else ever produced over the history of human culture. This is precisely because, in the truest sense, it is not itself culture at all, but an ontological reality that came to be embodied historically and authoritatively in Jesus and his apostles. The key departure that led from the ancient heresiological assumption of a singular Christianism to a wider taxonomy of Christianity in Jewish and Christian (and even "Mahometan") varieties was not a newly critical, more empirical methodology, but a new theorization of Christianity's transcendent nature: one that set aside traditional notions of an incarnate deity and special revelations in favor of a more humanistic notion of "natural religion."

While aided by ancient reports of tension and division among Jesus's followers around matters of Jewish law, Toland's formulation of a new taxonomy of Christianity—not, tellingly, of Judaism—was all but inevitable quite apart from any new findings his historical analysis of these already long-known sources might have generated. The generative assumption of his work is that Judaism and Christianity represent fundamentally different kinds of things. Judaism is the quintessential expression of the historical, the ethnic, the external, and the political. Christianity, in contrast, is the timeless, the universally human, the internal, and the religious. Judaism represents the very problem of cultural and civic difference that *Nazarenus* seeks to overcome, while Christianity, as a universal, transcendent law of nature, represents the solution. Indeed, Judaism cannot properly be called "religion" at all until it becomes "Jewish Christianity."[92] Christianity, on the other hand, insofar as it represents an internal spiritual disposition, cannot manifest itself historically unless embodied in particular social-cultural institutions like Judaism.

Seen in this light, Toland's concept of Jewish Christianity can be understood as a humanistic retelling of Christianity's traditional myth of origins. What had formerly been told as the story of the historical embodiment of a preexistent god in a particular Jewish man has now become, in Toland's hands, the story of the historical embodiment of an immanent spiritual reality—a "natural religion"—in a particularly Jewish culture. The divinity is less anthropomorphic, and the locus of its hierophany is moved from a specific individual to, at least potentially, all humanity; but the incarnation—

a divine spirit's ultimate transcendence of the "body" it must nevertheless assume in order to manifest itself historically—remains. In either telling, Christianity was not created by human history so much as disclosed within it. Toland's new concept "Jewish Christianity," in sum, was not the result of historical discovery. It was invented as a humanistic reclamation of Christianity's incarnation myth.

2 Jewish Christianity, Pauline Christianity, and the Critical Study of the New Testament: Thomas Morgan and F. C. Baur

While apparently the invention of an Irish freethinker, the idea of an early Jewish Christianity became a staple of New Testament scholarship mainly because of a German theologian. How exactly this interpretive construct made its way from Toland's *Nazarenus* to the influential work of F. C. Baur is not entirely clear. While the influence of the English Enlightenment on nineteenth-century German theology is plain enough, a specific chain of influence linking Baur to Toland's *Nazarenus* is difficult to identify.[1] The question is even more intriguing given the combination of similarities and differences in the two men's use of the concept. Baur, like Toland, presented his notion of Jewish Christianity as being first and foremost the result of historical scholarship; and he too correlated Jesus's original apostles closely with the Ebionites within the new category. In stark contrast to Toland, however, Baur made this taxonomic move not to authorize the Ebionites as genuinely apostolic but—quite the contrary—to deauthorize the apostles as representatives of a tainted Christianity. In Baur's hands, in short, "Jewish Christianity" was no longer the honorific it had been for Toland. It was a term of denigration meant to drive a wedge between Jesus and Paul on one hand and Jesus's first apostles on the other.

Any satisfactory explanation of this development must account in some way for the English Deist Thomas Morgan, whose key work, *The Moral Philosopher*, stands chronologically between *Nazarenus* and Baur's many publications. To be sure, there is no evidence to my knowledge that Baur was aware of Morgan at all, let alone *The Moral Philosopher* in particular. It is all the more remarkable, then, that Morgan's controversial reconstruction of early Christianity, once again centering on a concept of Jewish Christianity, anticipates Baur and his characteristic divergences from Toland to an astonishing degree.[2] Intellectual genealogies aside, comparison of the work of Morgan and Baur both with each other and with Toland greatly illuminates the role played by the idea of an early Jewish Christianity within the emerging discipline of critical New Testament scholarship. Most important for our purposes, it highlights the fact that Baur's concept of Jewish Christianity was not a straightforward result of the historical-critical method that, along with the problem of Jewish Christianity, would become his chief academic legacy. While elaborated by means of historical criticism, Baur's Jewish Christianity, no less than Toland's, was first and foremost a product of Christian apologetics.

Both Morgan and Baur, like Toland, were fundamentally concerned to advance the cause of Enlightenment humanism over against the traditional Christian theology that dominated their social environments. Both, to this end, adopted the same two-pronged strategy pursued by Toland. Most fundamentally, each claimed the mantle of "true Christianity" for his respective theological values. More consequential for our present purposes, however, was their second move. Given the compulsory correlation of "true" with "original" in traditional Christian rhetoric, both also translated their normative judgments into specific historical claims, namely, that their own humanistic values had also comprised the essence of the movement started by Jesus of Nazareth in first-century Palestine. As a corollary to this claim, both men—again like Toland—explained the divergent views of their more traditionalist rivals as the result of a historical degeneracy from the presumed original.

Where Morgan and Baur differed crucially from Toland was in their surrender of two central pillars of traditional Christian authority: the apostolic community and the New Testament. Conceding that the New Testament does not plainly express the liberal humanism they identified as primal Christianity, Morgan and Baur each argued that the adulteration of the pure original had begun already among Jesus's apostles themselves. Inevitably limited by their ingrained Jewish sensibilities, the original apostles had failed to clearly distinguish the transcendent Christianity at the heart of their master's teaching from the Jewish concepts in which he had couched it. It was Paul alone who truly grasped the import of Jesus's religion. For both Morgan and Baur, then, Jewish Christianity signaled something distinct not merely from Gentile Christianity, but more significantly from Pauline Christianity.

This move would prove to be momentous for the rise of critical New Testament scholarship. Concomitant with Morgan and Baur's historical thesis was a methodological insistence on a thoroughly critical study of the New Testament, precisely to extricate a pure Christianity from the Judaism of the apostles and the New Testament. Here again the driving assumption, both of the project in general and of its key concept of Jewish Christianity in particular, is that there actually is some primal Christianity to be so distilled. Morgan and Baur, in other words, did not abandon Toland's humanistic retelling of Christian myth so much as simply reconfigure the role of Jewish Christianity within it. The apostles no longer stood alongside Jesus as examples of an authoritative incarnation of transcendent Christianity in Jewish cultural forms. Now they represented the first *occlusion* of transcendent Christianity *by* those Jewish forms. The normative authority traditionally ascribed to the apostles and their purported writings, accordingly, was effectively reduced to the singular apostle Paul and his letters. The commingling of the latter with the former in the New Testament was explained in terms of a pervasive and multifaceted miscoloration of transcendent Christianity by its first, Jewish receptacle during the apostolic and postapostolic eras. Thus Morgan and, more consequentially, Baur both sounded a clarion call for a systematic and thoroughly critical study of the New Testament itself, precisely to distill from all its Jewish trappings the true, transcendent Christianity they assumed it concealed.

Jewish Christianity Reinvented: Thomas Morgan

Within twenty years of the publication of John Toland's *Nazarenus*, a second book proposing a revisionist history of early Christianity centering on the notion of an early Jewish Christianity was published in the same city by yet another freethinker, Thomas Morgan. Morgan was an ordained Presbyterian minister who, having apparently later become a physician, had been publishing works on both medicine and theology since 1725. It was, however, the 1737 appearance of *The Moral Philosopher, in Dialogue between Philalethes a Christian Deist, and Theophanes a Christian Jew* that generated the most attention, touching off a heated debate that would be carried out in a series of back-and-forth publications in London until Morgan's death in 1743. By the end of the century, Morgan was considered among the most notorious English freethinkers of the era.[3]

Like Toland, Morgan was concerned not only to defend Enlightenment humanism in itself, but to legitimize it specifically in historical terms by identifying it as the original Christianity of Jesus and the apostolic era. While it cannot be established with certainty that Morgan knew his predecessor's work—the latter receives no mention in *The Moral Philosopher*—Toland's notoriety in this effort, the fact that both published out of London, and the central place of Toland's recent coinage "Jewish Christianity" in Morgan's own revisionist history makes his familiarity with *Nazarenus* more probable than not.[4] It is all the more remarkable, then, that Morgan deploys the category with a force quite opposite that given it by Toland. Rather than signifying the true original, Jewish Christianity in Morgan's hands represents Christianity's primal perversion and the ultimate source of a later, misguided orthodoxy. Underlying this new iteration of the category was a more general strategic departure from traditional Christian apologetics. The paradigmatic authority traditionally ascribed historically to the apostolic community and canonically to the New Testament was limited by Morgan to Paul and his writings alone. The result was a comprehensive retelling of Christian history and a critical orientation to the New Testament that was less a continuation of Toland's project than an anticipation of Baur's.[5]

Morgan's Project

The Moral Philosopher is written in the form of a dialogue on "the Grounds and Principles of Religion in general, and particularly of Christianity as a Revelation distinct from the Religion of Nature."[6] Presented as the distillation of a long-running conversation among a "Club of Gentlemen," the dialogue comes in the form of a debate between two symbolically named and provocatively categorized men: "*Philalethes* a Christian *Deist*, and *Theophanes* a Christian *Jew*."[7] While the subtitle promises to present "the Arguments of both sides impartially," Morgan was scarcely a detached observer in the debate. Philalethes, the Deist "Lover of Truth," is quite plainly the protagonist here, with Theophanes—the defender of orthodox, revelation-based Christianity—cast in the role of interlocutor and foil.

The work opens with a troubled Theophanes coming to visit Philalethes. The source of his anxiety is twofold. First and most generally, he is troubled about "the present growth of *Deism*," not only among "Men of little Sense and less Virtue," but most especially among those who would otherwise seem to be models of "Sobriety, Benevolence, and all the social Virtues." More to the point, he is concerned because a mutual friend has suggested that Philalethes himself "might be a little, or perhaps not a little tainted with Deism." Though Philalethes will explicitly and proudly confirm that suspicion over the course of the dialogue, he does not immediately address the question of his own religious and philosophical leanings. What he seizes on, rather, is Theophanes's characterization of Deists, virtuous or not, as being "no great Friends if not real Enemies to Christianity." This, Philalethes suggests, depends entirely on how one defines Christianity: "This modern Controversy which has given you such Apprehensions may . . . be very much about Words of an indeterminate or no Signification; in my Opinion, we are not well agreed about the Meaning of the Words, *Deism, Christianity, Revelation, Inspiration,* &c. . . . I should be glad to know what you mean by *Christianity,* or *reveal'd Religion,* as oppos'd to, or contradistinguish'd from the *Religion of Nature.*" Thus begins the extended dialogue of *The Moral Philosopher,* the driving concern of which will be to clarify the relationship of Deism and Christianity.[8]

Morgan, of course, does not pursue this question simply out of academic interest in generating a usefully descriptive taxonomy of English Enlightenment religion. The debate is engaged, rather, with a normative and in fact quite competitive edge. The shared assumption around which the whole dispute is built—as Theophanes will later put it when summarizing Philalethes's position—is that "the Christian religion, when rightly understood, is the true Religion" (358). Christianity is no neutral designation for a particular species of religion here, but a legitimizing honorific for which the two men will compete by means of their debate. To suggest, as Theophanes does, that Deists—regardless of what they might say about themselves—are not "really" Christians is in itself to discredit them. Conversely, to characterize Deism as Christianity is to authorize it as "true religion." If, then, as Theophanes will ultimately articulate it, "the great and main Question" at issue is "wherein Christianity consists," the central object is to determine "how a Man may know whether he be *truly and really* a Christian or not" (391, emphasis mine).

Morgan's strategy in *The Moral Philosopher,* accordingly, is not merely to demonstrate the philosophical and ethical superiority of Deism to Christian orthodoxy. To be sure, Philalethes is made to argue throughout the work that it is neither intellectually defensible nor morally responsible to determine proper belief and practice by appealing to supernatural revelation or authorizing miracles, as orthodox Christianity does; and that the only "certain and infallible Mark or Criterion of divine Truth . . . is the moral Truth, Reason or Fitness of the Thing itself" as determined by rational reflection.[9] But Morgan is satisfied neither with such philosophical arguments nor with labeling his position Deism. His ultimate goal is to legitimize his Deism precisely as true Christianity. As Philalethes candidly puts it, "I am a profess'd Christian Deist. And, therefore, I must take Christianity, as to the Substance and doctrinal Parts of it, to be a Revival of the Religion of Nature" (392). The core thesis of the work, then, is that Christianity in the *true* sense of the word has nothing to do with revelation and mystery, with the "speculative Opinions, doubtful Disputations, external Rituals, arbitrary Laws, and mere positive Institutions" of so-called orthodox doctrine, nor with the hierarchy of clergymen who trade in such things.[10] Much as for Toland, true Christianity is, rather, "purely an internal Thing, and consists ultimately in moral Truth and Righteousness, considered as an inward Character, Temper, Disposition, or Habit in the Mind."[11]

Given the logic of Christian apologetic rhetoric, however, this claim on *true* Christianity inevitably requires an additional, historical claim regarding *original* Christianity. The whole debate of *The Moral Philosopher*, in fact, is predicated on the assumption by both parties that how one should conceive of the world and act within it in the present ultimately depends on the way certain, specially authoritative individuals had answered such questions in the distant past. Philalethes's identification of Deism as true Christianity, in short, all but obliges him to make the historical argument that Deism was also the heart of the Jesus movement. "I take . . . Christianity to be that Scheme or System of Deism, natural Religion, or moral Truth and Righteousness, which was at first preached and propagated in the World, by Jesus Christ and his Apostles, and has since been convey'd down to us by probable, human Testimony, or historical Evidence, strengthened and confirm'd by the necessary, natural Truth, and intrinsick Goodness of the Doctrines themselves."[12] In the end, then, it is the establishment of this historical thesis that will form the principle object of *The Moral Philosopher*.[13]

The principle challenge Morgan faced in this regard was the fact that Christianity, as it actually exists in history and tradition, consists of precisely the sort of things that he, as a Deist, rejected. Fortunately for him, the basic strategy for overcoming this challenge was near at hand in the rhetorical paradigm that had long defined inter-Christian polemics, and never more so since the Protestant Reformation: an apologetic historiography correlating one's own values with Jesus and the apostolic era and identifying those of one's rivals as corrupting deviations from it.[14] The more formidable obstacle in this case was the fact that the acknowledged literary authority of Protestant Christianity, the apostolic writings of the New Testament, clearly contained much of the same. This problem required a more radical solution: not only a comprehensive retelling of early Christian history, but the adoption of a more critical posture toward the Christian canon itself.

Apostolic Authority Redefined

In line with traditional ecclesiastical rhetoric, it is not only the religion of Jesus that Morgan claims for his Christianity, but that of the apostolic era as well. Assertions that Deism was the religion of Jesus are routinely rounded off with the stock phrase "and his [or simply 'the'] Apostles," as in the statement quoted above: "I take . . . Christianity to be that Scheme or System of Deism, natural Religion, or moral Truth and Righteousness, which was at first preached and propagated in the World, by Jesus Christ *and his Apostles.*"[15] The stock nature of this claim is underscored by the fact that it will turn out to be significantly qualified, if not outright contradicted, by the actual historical argument developed in *The Moral Philosopher*. Indeed, narrowing the traditional sphere of apostolic authority from the community and writings of the apostles, *plural*, to the singular apostle Paul was crucial to Morgan's rhetorical strategy.

It was not lost on Morgan that much of the New Testament, traditionally regarded as the authoritative, apostolic guide to true Christianity, stood in marked tension with the Deism he claimed Jesus to have taught. The book of Revelation, which Morgan accepted as an authentic work of the apostle John, is singled out for special comment in this respect: contrary to Jesus's Deism, its doctrines are "very agreeable to the Nature and Genius of the *Jewish* Religion"—indeed, the very Jewish religion that Jesus, according to Morgan, was rejecting.[16] Nor is this an isolated case. The New Testament canon in general, he says, "leans strongly towards *Judaism*." Indeed, "if a man reads the *New Testament* as a plain, historical, and uncorrupted Account of Things . . . he might be tempted to imagine, that *Judaism* and *Christianity* are both one and the same Religion, or at least have a necessary Dependence on, and Connexion with each other" (441). For reasons we shall see shortly, this was from Morgan's point of view an entirely unacceptable conclusion. His solution was a radical modification of what was, next to Jesus Christ, the most fundamental authority construct in Christian rhetoric. Others before him, of course, had faced analogous incongruences between their views of true Christianity and the New Testament. But where they had responded by rejecting the genuinely apostolic status of the offending texts, Morgan effectively deauthorized the apostolic community itself. If Deism was the true Christianity of Jesus, and if the apostolic writings do not teach Deism, then the apostles are no authoritative guide to true Christianity.[17]

There is, to be sure, some tension between this marked departure from traditional Christian rhetoric and Morgan's repeated claim, noted above, that Deism is what was actually taught by "Jesus and his Apostles." The tension is somewhat mitigated, however, by the fact that Morgan's strategy is not so much a wholesale abandonment of the construct "apostolic authority" itself as a constriction of it to one apostle alone. It is Paul, in fact, who is put forward by Philalethes as the definitive arbiter on the question of true Christianity: "For what relates to St. *Paul,* I can assure you, Sir, that I have as good an Opinion of him as you can have, and shall willingly abide by the Judgment and sense of that great Apostle in the present Debate between us . . . [I]f I cannot make it appear that *St. Paul* (when he comes to be rightly understood) is plainly on my Side, I will give up the Argument."[18] As with the more traditional notion of apostolic authority, Paul's authority has both historical and literary dimensions. The paradigmatic function traditionally ascribed to the apostolic era in general is now restricted specifically to Paul and his "*Gentile* Churches" in particular—who are now recast, remarkably and quite tellingly, given their later arrival on the scene, as "the first [!] and purest Part" of "the Apostolick Age" (395). Likewise, access to the religion of this time of primal purity can be found only in the Pauline literature rather than the New Testament as a whole. In short, Paul and the writings associated with him have replaced the apostles and the New Testament as the authoritative embodiment of true, original Christianity. Much of the dialogue, then, will be spent negotiating Philalethes's crucial parenthetical caveat: what exactly it means to render Paul's letters "rightly understood," especially as this concerns revelation and the miraculous in general and the apostle's understanding of Jewish scripture, law, and the death of Christ in particular.[19] While the details of Morgan's account of Paul lie outside the bounds of the current book, his core claim is well captured by the striking characterization of him as "the great Free-thinker of his Age, the bold and brave Defender of Reason against Authority" (71).

Judaism and Christian Origins

Of course it was not merely Paul, in Morgan's view, who had championed Deism, but Jesus as well. The Deist Christianity of Jesus is a recurring, though largely undeveloped, theme of the dialogue. "The Religion of Jesus," Philalethes says, "consists in the inward, spiritual Worship of one true God, by a strict Regard to all the Duties and Obligations of moral Truth and Righteousness" (393–94). As the "complete System of moral Truth and Righteousness, Justice and Charity," it is in short "the best Transcript of the Religion of Nature" (439). Jesus "was sent from God to restore, revive, and republish this Religion, after it had been lost in the general Superstition, Idolatry, and gross Ignorance of Mankind, both *Jew* and *Gentile*" (394).[20] This latter characterization effectively and categorically separates the true, natural religion of Jesus from all the cultures of his environment, Jewish or otherwise. Indeed, as for Toland, Jesus's religion did not represent culture at all, but a transcendent reality: "the eternal, immutable Rule of moral Rectitude, or the Religion of God and Nature" (439).

It is, however, above all Judaism, in Morgan's view, that epitomizes what Jesus was rejecting. According to Philalethes, "no two Religions in the World can be more inconsistent and irreconcileable, than *Judaism* and *Christianity*."[21] In Judaism, the immutable, internal, moral law established by God became indistinguishable from the variable, external rites established through claims of magic and revelation by a self-serving hierarchy of kings, priests, and corrupt prophets.[22] As Morgan saw it, Judaism had twisted Abraham's original vision of a future in which all nations might be unified in this universal, natural religion into a nationalistic expectation that God, by miraculous means and according to a predetermined historical plan, would send a king from Israel's royal dynasty—a messiah—to establish Israel's political sovereignty over all other peoples of the world.[23] In an act of divine irony, then, the same providential God who sent Jesus as "the last great Prophet" of natural religion to the Jewish nation (327) eventually made that same Jewish nation "an Example to the World in all future Ages, of the natural Effects and Consequences of Ignorance, Superstition, Presumption, and Immorality . . . [God] gave them up as an everlasting Name of Reproach, an eternal Scandal to the Profession of Religion,

without moral Goodness, or any rational Dependence on God and Providence."[24] Judaism, in short, stands quite literally for everything Jesus's transcendent Christianity opposed.

As noted above, Morgan concluded from the preponderance of Jewish ideas in the New Testament that the earliest apostles had already
fundamentally misunderstood the teachings of their master. Indeed, the
corruption of original Christianity with Judaism had begun virtually simultaneously with its preaching by Jesus himself. Morgan explains this by appealing to the inevitable limitations of the apostles' Jewish culture. "No *Jew*,
at that Time, would ever have embraced the Religion of Jesus" apart from
the assumption that it had to do with traditional messianic hopes of national restoration and world domination (441). "The Prejudices even of his
own Apostles and Disciples, and of the whole Circumcision," he says, "were
invincible" (375–76). Their embrace of Christianity, therefore, amounted effectively to a profession of "Faith in Jesus, as their national Messiah." It did
nothing to change "their old Religion": "Christianity, or the Faith of Christ,
as receiv'd and profess'd by them, was nothing but a political faction among
themselves, and a new State Division added to three or four more which
they had before." In short, it was not so much *true* Christianity as merely "a
Jewish Christianity, or Christian *Judaism*, exactly agreeable to . . . the gross
Notions they always had of Religion" (374).

Seen in this light, the whole point of contrasting Jesus and Paul with
Jewish Christianity is to signal that they *did* transcend Judaism. Interestingly, the mechanism by which Jesus became a special exception to the
otherwise "invincible" force of Jewish culture—that is to say, how exactly
we are to understand the actual origins of Christianity—is never clearly
explained. The closest we come to an account of what can only have been
the sudden, exceptional advent of "the eternal, immutable Rule of moral
Rectitude, or the Religion of God and Nature" (439) in the historical figure
of Jesus, strikingly, is an apparent appeal to superhuman forces: Jesus, Morgan repeatedly tells us, was a prophet, sent by God.[25] In the case of Paul,
Morgan is more explicit still. Having begun in "the true Spirit of *Judaism*"
as a member "of the *establish'd Church* . . . this great Apostle was convinced
by a Miracle. For this, I think, is plain, that nothing less than Miracle could
have convinced this great Rabbin, that he had mistaken the Glory of God,
and the Good of Mankind" (120). Even for the Deist Morgan, the origins
of Christianity could be explained only with reference to the intervention
of superhuman forces.[26]

Jewish Christianity and the Critical Study
of the New Testament

For all its significant departures from traditional Christian historiography, Morgan's theory of an early Jewish Christianity is in the end only another iteration of the same underlying paradigm that had long defined Christian apologetics. The lynchpin of that paradigm is a theory of Christian origins. A given writer's own values are said ultimately to have originated in the sudden irruption in human cultural history of a transcendent, immutable reality in the person of Jesus. This primal Christianity was then carried forward by an apostolic community, who captured it definitively in writings that could serve ever forward as authoritative guides to its truths. The competing views of one's rivals, on the other hand, are mere human creations. Morgan's principle departure from this traditional Christian narrative—and, too, from the similarly liberalizing version of it already formulated by his freethinking predecessor, Toland—was his admission of his rivals' claims that they represented an apostolic Christianity suffused within the New Testament. His bold, new strategy was to argue that this, while apostolic and canonical, was nonetheless not the true, primal Christianity of Jesus and the apostle Paul's Gentile communities, but a perversion of it created by Jesus's still-Jewish apostles.[27]

Toland, of course, had already recast the apostolic era in terms of a dichotomy between Jewish and Gentile Christianities in the service of an argument for a primal Christian humanism. As we have seen, however, his own strategy was strikingly different.[28] In the first place, this dichotomy illustrated Toland's claim that the religion of Jesus and the apostles was envisioned from the start as a "Union without Uniformity" grounded in a humanistic universalism. Second, it allowed him to explain present-day orthodoxy as the result of undue pagan influence on a later, Gentile Christianity. Morgan, working with the same taxonomic distinction toward the same broad end, took a very different tack. An authentic, primal rationalism was now assigned to only one of these Christianities, namely, the Gentile one championed by Paul. The corruptions of orthodoxy, accordingly, were not due to subsequent *pagan* influence but began virtually simultaneously with Jesus's teaching itself because of the inevitable religious limitations of his original *Jewish* followers. Thus did a new understanding of Jewish Christianity come to form the centerpiece of yet another Enlightenment-era retelling of early Christian history.

The key to Morgan's rhetorical strategy was the historical thesis of a fundamental and enduring difference between the Christianity of Paul and the Jewish Christianity of Jesus's earlier apostles. He found evidence for this difference above all in Galatians 2 and Acts 15. The "standing Controversy" between Paul and Jewish Christianity was not whether the law should be observed—Morgan conceded that Paul himself sometimes observed it—but on what principle and under what circumstances this was to happen. The conflict reported in Galatians 2 is interpreted in terms of a distinction between religious and political intention familiar from Toland. Paul, he argued, "submitted to this Law only in a civil or political Capacity, as the Law of his country" rather than as "the Law of God" and a matter of "Conscience in Point of Religion." The other apostles, in contrast, "obey'd the Law as a Law of Righteousness, or as a necessary Part of Religion and means of Justification with God" (54; cf. 71).[29] While there from the beginning, Morgan argued, this essential difference remained masked for as long as the movement stayed in a Jewish context. It began to surface only as Christianity spread beyond the Jewish homeland to Gentile proselytes, coming fully to a head "as a Schism never to be healed" after Paul and Barnabas started preaching "to the idolatrous *Gentiles* also" in Asia Minor (74–75). At this point Paul's position became fully clear: no one, Jew or Gentile, was bound by Jewish law "without the Boundaries of *Judea*" (57). The Apostolic Council, Morgan says, was convened to settle the "great concerning Debate," which came down to two questions: "First, Whether the *Jewish* Converts were still obliged, in Point of Religion and Conscience, to obey the whole Law? And secondly, Whether the *Gentile* converts, as Matter of Religion and Conscience, were bound to comply with the Mosaick Law of Proselytism, as the necessary Condition upon which the Christian *Jews* were to hold Communion with them?" As Morgan sees it, when the apostles' affirmative answer to both questions was codified in the Apostolic Decree, what had always been an essential breach in principle between Paul and the earlier apostles became translated into the unmistakable social reality of a difference between Jewish and Gentile Christianities. Paul now "saw plainly" that this decree amounted to a "joining of two contrary and inconsistent Religions" and henceforward began "to advance a new Doctrine of his own," namely, that the law was no longer binding even on Jews "out of the confines of Judea" (57).

Far from Jesus's intention from the beginning, then, the emergence of a distinction between Jewish and Gentile Christianity represented the signal failure of the original apostles to grasp the true force of Jesus's teaching. The full realization of the natural religion of Jesus in Paul's Gentile mission brought to the surface an essential conflict between the Christianity of Jesus and Paul on one hand and the lingering Judaism of the original apostles on the other. Effectively isolated by the Jewish church leadership, Paul became the champion of a distinctly Gentile Christianity. "The rest of the Apostles, not excepting *Peter, Barnabas*, and *John Mark*, not being able to come into St. *Paul's* Scheme, thought themselves obliged to separate from him, and leave him to preach his *own Gospel*, as he call'd it, among the *Gentiles*, in his *own Way*" (79). Peter in particular became "the Head and Ring-Leader of the *Judaizers*, who would still keep up the Separation between *Jews* and *Gentiles* in the Christian Churches" (364). The end result were two separate and essentially incompatible forms of Christianity, "*Jewish* and *Gentile* Christianity, or *Peter's* Religion and *Paul's* . . . as opposite and inconsistent as Light and Darkness, Truth and Falshood" (377). The overall conclusion, for Morgan, "is so very plain, that one would think, Men must willfully shut their Eyes not to see it":

> The Truth is, that St. *Paul* was the great Free-thinker of his Age, the bold and brave Defender of Reason against Authority, in Opposition to those who had set up a wretched Scheme of Superstition, Blindness, and Salvery [*sic*], contrary to all Reason and common Sense; and this under the specious, popular Pretence of a divine Institution and Revelation from God. But our truly Christian Apostle continually laboured under this Disadvantage, of being opposed in all his Ministry by the whole *Jewish* nation, and having a Decree of Council standing out against him, pass'd at *Jerusalem* by a large Assembly of Apostolical Christian *Jews*; yet he still stood to his Point.[30]

In the end, in other words, Morgan found the lot of the "truly Christian Apostle" Paul to be much the same as his own: a freethinker and lone defender of true Christianity, bravely resisting the "Apostolical Christian Jews" who outnumbered him.

The only thing that remained to be explained was how these mutually contradictory religions came "so soon afterwards, to unite into one Catholick, Christian Church" (377–78)—a Church that placed Peter and Paul side by side, and not least within its New Testament canon. Morgan found his solution in the postapostolic era. Once Paul was dead, he argued, Jewish Christianity quickly prevailed (396). When Nero's persecution provided a common enemy for Gentile and Jewish Christians, the former forged an unholy alliance with the latter, "to the great Advantage of *Judaism* in the Christian Church" (378). Considering it was this "Judaizing" Church that "at first collect'd, revis'd, and published" the New Testament, he observed, "it is no Wonder it leans strongly toward *Judaism.*"[31] The formation of such an authoritative canon, Morgan argued, was but one of a variety of strategies devised by the Church to quash dissent, not least from the remnants of their freethinking critics.[32] The pinnacle of this development was the establishment of the Pope as "*a living, infallible Judge,* with temporal Power enough in his Hands to controul and prevent all Difference of Opinion" (399).

Morgan finally comes to his ultimate target as he correlates this Jewish Christianity-cum-Catholicism with the orthodoxy of his own Protestant rivals. Insofar as they continue to insist that the New Testament is an authoritative statement of true Christianity, their rejection of the papacy represents little more than a changing of the Catholic guard: "they set up the Scriptures in gross in its Prophecies, Histories, and Morals without Exception, as a *dead, infallible Rule,* in Opposition to a *living, infallible Judge*" (403). As a result, they are less true Christians than "modern disciples" of Peter's Jewish Christianity (265), which is to say—as Theophanes is himself styled in the title of the work—simply "Christian Jews." Separation of the wheat of the true Christianity of Jesus and Paul from the Jewish chaff of the earlier apostles, therefore, required nothing short of a new, historical-critical approach to the Christian canon. "The Books of the *New Testament* ... ought to be read critically, with an Allowance for Persons, Circumstances, and the Situation of Things at that Time; and not taken in gross, as if every Thing contain'd in them had been at first infallibly inspired from God, and no Corruptions could have ever since happen'd to them" (442). It would be nearly a century before Morgan's call for a critical study of the New Testament along these lines was taken up systematically in the disciplined scholarship of F. C. Baur and his Tübingen School.

Jewish Christianity in the Work of F. C. Baur

Over the course of the eighteenth and nineteenth centuries, the new interpretive construct "Jewish Christianity" made its way from the controversial publications of London freethinkers to the central institutions of German theological learning. By the early twentieth century, clarification of the historical significance of Jewish Christianity was considered "one of the chief problems in the history of *Urchristentum.*"[33] No single writer was more instrumental in mainstreaming the twin concerns of Jewish Christianity and the critical study of the New Testament than the Tübingen scholar Ferdinand Christian Baur.[34] To be clear, there is nothing in the evidence to suggest that Baur was directly familiar with Morgan's work or, for that matter, with Toland's *Nazarenus*.[35] There can be little doubt, however, that the new German scholarship Baur represented owed much to its English forebears, by whatever particular route the latter may have been mediated to him. What is plain at any rate is that Baur's influential model of early Christian history cannot be adequately explained—and thus facilely dismissed—as a consequence of his Hegelianism, as his critics have sometimes found it convenient to do.[36] Baur's lifework, rather, was a much more philosophically sophisticated and historically rigorous iteration of an apologetic strategy devised nearly a century earlier by Thomas Morgan.

Though Baur's name is virtually synonymous with historical-critical New Testament scholarship, the foundational presupposition of his work, no less than Morgan's, was an apologetic assumption that Christianity, as true religion, is an ontological reality transcendent of mere human culture. Much like his freethinking predecessors, moreover, Baur was concerned to divert the legitimizing power attached to this understanding of Christianity from the supernatural doctrine of traditional orthodoxy to a manner of thinking more at home in the age of liberal Enlightenment. As always within the framework of Christian apologetics, such a claim on *true* Christianity required a simultaneous claim on *original* Christianity, and thus a negotiation of the central historical and literary authorities traditionally correlated with the latter: Jesus, the apostolic community, and the New Testament. Conceding, like Morgan, that the New Testament as such did not reflect his humanistic vision, Baur adopted a remarkably similar strategy. He identified his own theological values with Jesus, then divided what was traditionally imagined as a unified apostolic sphere into two distinct types of Christianity: a Pauline one correlated with the true, transcendent religion of Jesus; and a Jewish one that failed, precisely as a result of its Jewishness, to really grasp that true religion. The central strategy, in other words, was once again to confine the authority traditionally invested in the apostolic community and the New Testament in general to Paul and his writings in particular. As for Morgan, the New Testament was no longer an authoritative literary statement of true Christianity but a misguided synthesis of Christianity with Jewish culture produced by a later Catholic orthodoxy. The authoritative original, therefore, could not be found by reading the New Testament in a straightforward manner, but only by subjecting it to a rigorously critical analysis. Here again the concept of Jewish Christianity and critical New Testament scholarship were bound up tightly together.

Baur's Apologetic Project

The precise nature and development of Baur's theology is a complex and contested matter that neither can be nor, fortunately, need be resolved here.[37] Regardless of how exactly the boundaries of his Hegelian period are to be defined, how thoroughly his Hegelianism eclipsed his interest in Friedrich Schleiermacher, or the extent to which it is accurate to character-ize him in his various phases as orthodox, rationalist, or atheist, two basic elements of Baur's understanding of Christianity are abundantly clear. First and most fundamentally, the term "Christianity" functions in Baur's writ-ings not merely or even primarily as a historical descriptor of *a* religion but—just as for Toland, Morgan, and during the centuries of Christian apologetics preceding them—as a normative indicator of *true* religion: an ontological reality independent of the social groups and cultural expressions that manifest it in only better and worse forms in history. Second, Baur—again like Toland and Morgan—was concerned to reconceive Christianity's supposed transcendence in terms more at home, and more defensible, in an era of Enlightenment humanism than the more traditional appeals to supernatural powers were.[38]

Baur was fundamentally appreciative of freethinking rationalism. In-sofar as it was an expression of "the primacy of faith and free subjectiv-ity in the actualization of the Christian Gospel," it represented for him an authentically Protestant autonomy.[39] As Peter Hodgson has observed, however, Baur was also acutely aware of the mortal threat such freethinking posed to the objective, historical claims about Jesus made by that very same faith. "To dissolve an historically mediated faith into subjective rational truth is to vitiate not only the heritage of Protestantism but of the Chris-tian Church as a whole, throughout its entire history."[40] The fundamental apologetic challenge of the era, as Baur understood it, lay precisely in the resolution of this paradox. How could one embrace the free subjectivity of rationalism while simultaneously guaranteeing the objective, historical claims of Christianity? If the objective truth of the latter was to be affirmed in this new intellectual climate, it would not be by continued appeals to special supernatural forces, but only through free, scientific inquiry itself.

Christianity's truth claims were to be defended not against critical study, but precisely by means of it.[41]

Baur considered Schleiermacher to be a pivotal figure in this task.[42] The transformative originality of Schleiermacher's approach to Christianity was clear to Baur as early as 1823, when he summed it up succinctly in a letter to his brother:

> I know of no representation of Christianity in which the peculiar essence of Christianity is so acutely comprehended and made so thoroughly the middle point of the whole system, none which could be held as being more Christian and orthodox. And yet, in the last resort, everything is conceived entirely otherwise, from a completely different viewpoint as in the previous dogmatics. The distinction between this new viewpoint and the old customary one consists, to put it briefly, in the fact that while the old view accepts the external revelation or writings of the New Testament as the sole source of knowledge of Christianity, according to Schleiermacher, the primary source of Christianity lies in the religious self-consciousness, out of whose development the principle doctrines of Christianity are to be obtained.[43]

What Baur found new and compelling here was just that synthesis he sought: a liberating deauthorization of the New Testament as "external revelation" as in rationalism, yet without the latter's indifference to "everything positive and ecclesiastical."[44] This was accomplished by means of an identification of the "peculiar essence of Christianity" not with canonical doctrine per se, but with a "religious consciousness" imagined as lying beneath it, as its ultimate source. The ultimate arbiter of authentic Christianity, therefore, was neither a specially revealed New Testament nor orthodox dogma, but a religious consciousness internal to the human individual. This correlation of Christianity first and foremost with such a "consciousness" would be fundamental to the writings of Baur throughout his career.[45]

As Baur saw it, however, Schleiermacher had not yet been entirely successful in negotiating the logical gap between the subjective consciousness of the individual and the objective, historical truth claims of Christianity.[46] Schleiermacher's God remained too much of an abstraction—merely an implication of the subjective feeling of dependence—to satisfy Baur's concern for objective truth. It was precisely at this point that he found Hegel helpful. Unlike Schleiermacher's abstraction, Hegel's God was a more concrete "Absolute Spirit": an "infinite and eternal consciousness" that "dirempts" itself into the finite forms of the world in order to know itself, above all in the finite human consciousness with which it is, therefore, "implicitly identical." This correlation of human consciousness with an immanent divine consciousness provided just the bridge between subjectivity and objectivity Baur was seeking. Conceived along these lines, human consciousness comprised not merely feeling, but rational ideas. "Thinking Spirit . . . is a category that transcends human subjectivity; it is the concrete, fundamental, universal reality in which human existence is grounded," an objective, universal truth immanent in the historical particular.[47] From this starting point, Baur could reframe Christian consciousness not merely as the subjective feeling of God-dependence, but as objective, divinely revealed truth. As he put it in the introduction to *Lectures on the History of Dogma*:

> The movement of Christian dogma is . . . to be considered from the general point of view of the activity of Spirit manifesting itself in thinking. Christian dogma has as its presupposition Christian revelation. Revelation is an act of Spirit in which an objective reality confronts subjective consciousness as an immediate given, and becomes for the subject the object of a faith whose content is the Absolute Idea. Moved by the power of the Absolute Idea, the entire thinking activity of the subject feels the compulsion to become absorbed into this objective reality, given as an immediate divine power, in order to bring its content into consciousness—as it were, to lay it out in all its components for the representative consciousness.[48]

In effect, then, the appeal to supernatural revelation on which the claim of Christianity's qualitative difference from other forms of culture was traditionally based was rehabilitated in a humanistic, panentheistic mode.[49]

An important result of this move was a radical historicizing and relativizing of traditional orthodoxy in general and of the New Testament in particular. With the ultimate source of Christianity now identified as the revelation of an "Absolute Spirit" immanent in human consciousness, the real essence of Christianity could be boiled down to a single, elemental idea: the perfect realization of the immanent unity of the particular and the universal, of the infinite and the finite, in the person of Christ.[50] All forms of Christian dogma, consequently, were only second-order phenomena—so many historically located, culturally conditioned responses to the transcendent truth comprised by Christian consciousness. From this point of view, any absolute distinction between canonical and extracanonical literature—or even between orthodoxy and heresy—simply evaporated.[51] The whole history of dogma, including the New Testament, was simply the ongoing story of the expression of this Christian consciousness in concepts furnished by different cultural epochs. For Baur, then, the task of the theologian was not to preserve and defend past doctrinal formulations, but to translate the underlying Christian consciousness ever more effectively into the terms of one's own cultural era. To this end, all prior iterations of Christian dogma—including those found in the New Testament—were to be subjected to rigorous historical-critical analysis in order to differentiate the "absolute consciousness" of Christianity from the relative "consciousness of the age" in which it expresses itself, the transcendent from the merely cultural.[52]

For all its radical implications, Baur's theory of Christianity remained consistent with the centuries of Christian apologetic discourse that preceded him in several fundamental respects. Most basic is his starting assumption that Christianity is qualitatively different from everything else in the history of human culture by virtue of its unique transcendence. Here again Christianity is something not so much *of* culture as incarnate *within* it. In a manner reminiscent of the early heresiologists, for example, it is Christianity's revelatory character that distinguishes it from mere philosophy.[53] Its radical transcendence of historical particulars, moreover, renders Christianity wholly unique even among religions as the lone "absolute religion." This latter point is developed at length in Baur's *Church History*:

> But what is it in Christianity that gives it its absolute character [*worin besteht aber das Absolute seines Wesens*]? The first and obvious answer to this question is, that Christianity is elevated above the defects and limitations, the one-sidedness and finiteness, which constitute the particularism of other forms of religion . . . To speak broadly, it is a more spiritual form of the religious consciousness [*eine geistigere Form des religiösen Bewusstseins*] than these are, and stands above them . . . We find Christianity to be far more free than any other religion from everything merely external, sensuous, or material. It lays its foundations more deeply in the inmost essence of man's nature and in the principles of moral consciousness . . . When we inquire what constitutes the absolute character of Christianity, we must point to its spirituality . . . Looking away from all that is unessential, and asking what is the element in Christianity which makes it a religion in the absolute sense, we find that it rests on man's knowledge of himself as a moral subject.[54]

In other words, as Hodgson has well put it, "Christianity frees Spirit from everything particular and subjective, bringing it into unity with the Universal, the Absolute, which is the principle of Christianity."[55]

As Baur sees it, moreover, the spiritual reality underlying Christianity does not merely transcend culture; it actively guides it as a singularly constant and constantly determinative factor in the otherwise variable history of Christian dogma.[56] This assumption, obviously reminiscent of appeals to the Holy Spirit in more traditional Christian thinking, is fundamental to Baur's whole theory of Christian history. It surfaces with particular clarity in *Church History*, as he argues pointedly for the basic thesis that it is a certain "moral and religious consciousness"—not "faith in the person of Jesus" per se—that constitutes the true essence of Christianity. Baur begins with the by-now familiar correlation of the normative idea of a "true Christianity" with the temporal notion of an "original Christianity":

> When we look back at its earliest elements, Christianity appears as a purely moral religion; its highest and most peculiar distinction is that it bears an essentially moral character, and is rooted in the moral consciousness of man ... There are other elements which belong to the character and the contents of Christianity [including "faith in the person of Jesus"], and the relation which these bear to its original and simple beginnings may be variously determined; but there can be no question that the purely moral element which lies at its first source has ever been its unchangeable and substantial foundation ... The element which appears at the outset with all the significance of far-reaching principles, which has always remained the same though other parts of the religion changed, and which contains in itself the evidence that it is true,—this surely must be held to be the proper substance of the whole.[57]

Given this assumption of a generative Christian essence, the various groups and texts that have laid claim to the legacy of Jesus must be not only described historically, but evaluated normatively as better and worse approximations of the "Christian consciousness" that lies beneath them. "Christianity has never been removed from this foundation without denying its true and proper character."[58] What is more, the generative character of this "unchangeable" essence remains ever at work, actively propelling the history of Christian dogma ever forward toward its more perfect actualization. As true, original Christianity, this consciousness thus represents an inescapable "foundation" to which historical Christianity "has always been forced to return as often as it went astray in that exaggerated dogmatism, whose logical conclusions were found to undermine the very foundations of moral and religious life."[59]

As is also typical of Christian apologetics, then, Baur's theory of Christian history builds decisively around the key matter of origins.[60] Once again we find a crucial convergence of the normative and the historical in the notion of an especially authoritative "original Christianity"—not merely one more cultural artifact among countless others produced over the history of human societies, but a transcendent reality suddenly disclosed by revelation into the vehicle of culture. To be sure, in a radical departure from traditional apologetics, this original was no longer correlated straightforwardly with the New Testament and the apostolic community. With the source of revelation relocated from a supernatural realm external to humanity to a divine Spirit immanent in the inner workings of the individual human consciousness, the apostolic era became simply the first among many epochs in the wider history of Christian dogma. As much as any other, then, the apostles and the canonical writings attributed to them were thus subject not only to critical, historical analysis, but to normative evaluation vis-à-vis the moral universalism Baur identified as the true essence of Christian consciousness. This move, however, only underscored the more fundamental problem of historical origins. What account could be given, in historical terms, of the origin of that generative Christian consciousness? How, within a chain of historical cause and effect, was a decisive, quantum leap to "the absolute" to be imagined? And when and in whom, exactly, was that leap first made? Would historical-critical analysis support the idea that Jesus actually manifested such a consciousness, sharing the values Baur identified as true Christianity?

The Problem of Historical Origins

The question of the historical origins of this "absolute religion" was of the utmost importance to Baur. "In no field of historical study," he wrote in the opening line of *Church History*, "are the whole scope and character of the successive events of which the history is composed so largely determined by the starting-point from which the movement issues, as in the history of the Christian church: nowhere therefore does more depend on the conception which we form of that first point with which the whole historical development begins."[61] In traditional Christian rhetoric, of course, this assumption of determinative origins is part and parcel of a broader claim regarding Christianity's superhuman character. Christianity, it is said, began with the momentous arrival of otherworldly realities—an incarnate

God and a Holy Spirit—in the human realm, events that imbue it ever after with a supernatural aura and thus an extrahuman authority. Baur found this traditional formulation, which he called "the miracle of the absolute beginning," to be fundamentally problematic. Given the immanence of the Absolute Spirit in human consciousness, the historical appearance of Christianity was not to be understood as the result of an otherworldly disruption of the normal cause-and-effect workings of history, but as something that occurred entirely within them. Christianity was simply the end point of a wider historical-spiritual process, the ultimate step to which Greek philosophy and Judaism, particularly in its Alexandrian and "Essene" forms, had long been leading.[62]

In the end, however, it was more the appeal to supernatural forces than the notion of an "absolute beginning" per se that Baur seems to have rejected. His central premise that Christianity, as "absolute religion," is qualitatively different from every other phenomenon in the history of human culture virtually demands the postulation of some singular and singularly decisive moment when this leap to a radically new, transcendent type of consciousness was first made.[63] Though the end result of a historical progression, Christian dogma, as the direct reflection of a new and qualitatively different type of religious consciousness, was ultimately self-generated: "The point of view from which the first major period [in the history of dogma] is to be considered is that of dogma as it first emerges, developing out of itself and determining itself."[64] As we have seen, in fact, Christianity's origins are ultimately no less hierophanic for Baur than for traditional orthodoxy. It is still explained as revelation, albeit now reconceived and relocated: no longer the advent of a supernatural divinity within the natural world, but the perfect actualization of a divine reality immanent in human consciousness; an incarnation not of a God in literal human flesh, but of an "absolute consciousness" in the discursive flesh of human culture. Miracle or not, the origins of Christianity are still imagined in fundamentally mythic terms as a singular moment when the sacred and the human suddenly and decisively came together, forever changing the possibilities of human existence and setting in motion, more specifically, the history of Christianity.

Not surprisingly, it was precisely in this crucial matter of origins that Baur felt most acutely the logical gap between the subjective experience of the individual consciousness—the new seat of Christianity's generative revelation—and the objective, historical claims made about Jesus in traditional Christianity.[65] No doubt, he reasoned, some particular person had to have made the momentous leap to this new absolute consciousness, and no doubt this leap at some point became crystallized in the notion of Christ as the God-man. But could the claim that this had actually been true of Jesus himself be anything more than bare assertion? Baur recognized that Schleiermacher's Christ functioned both ideally as "the personification of this consciousness" and historically as "the point at which the God-consciousness, in its power of sensible consciousness, has entered into the history of humanity via a specific individual in an epoch making way." As Baur saw it, however, Schleiermacher's signal failure was his inability to provide a clear basis for the second of these claims. "Schleiermacher's Christ," he wrote, "is actually only an abstraction of Christian consciousness, a postulate whose reality is not so much empirically demonstrated as simply presupposed."[66] And on this matter, at least, Hegel was of no help.[67] For Hegel, the crucial moment in the spiritual history of humanity—the actual "reconciliation" of the divine and the human—was not the historical appearance of Jesus per se, but the "faith" that recognized in him the perfect unity of the finite and the infinite, the human and the divine. But here again Baur found no clear explanation as to why this subjective experience of "faith" requires Jesus himself really to have been any such thing in objective history. "The Hegelian philosophy of religion," he wrote, "views Christ as the God-man only in his relation to faith, without expressing more precisely what objective point of contact in the actual appearance of Christ faith has for its presupposition."[68]

To be sure, Baur was himself inclined to believe that Jesus actually was in objective, historical fact what subjective Christian faith had made him out to be. "But how could faith in him as the God-man have arisen," he wondered, "without his having also been in some fashion objectively what faith claimed for him?"[69] Nonetheless, the historical problem remained. "Whether or not," Baur wrote, "the person of Jesus really possesses the attributes ascribed to him by Schleiermacher in the concept of the Redeemer . . . is in fact a purely historical question which can be answered only through a historical investigation of the literary documents of the Gospel history, documents which in the introduction to [Schleiermacher's] *Christian Faith* are certainly nowhere brought forward as actual sources of knowledge for Christianity."[70] In short, while the origins of Christianity had to be correlated with the transcendent consciousness of some particular individual, the only way to determine whether that individual was Jesus or someone else was a consideration of the actual evidence. In the end, then, the only way to close the gap between subjective faith and objective, historical truth was historical-critical analysis of the New Testament.[71]

Given the crucial nature of this question for Baur, it is remarkable that he did not publish a statement of his own view on the historical Jesus until the first edition of *Church History* in 1853. How exactly we are to explain this is not entirely clear, though there can be little doubt that the publication of the *Life of Jesus, Critically Examined* by Baur's one-time student, longtime friend, and fellow Hegelian David Friedrich Strauss was a major factor. Picking up on the same basic problem Baur had identified, Strauss argued forcefully that critical analysis of the gospels rendered Schleiermacher's idealized portrait of the historical Jesus fundamentally problematic.[72] Consequently, when another of Baur's students, Albert Schwegler, sought to flesh out Baur's historical paradigm more comprehensively in his massive *Das nachapostolische Zeitalter in den Hauptmomenten seiner Entwicklung* (The Postapostolic Age in the Principal Moments of Its Development), the whole question of the historical Jesus was reduced quite literally to a footnote in the study of early Christianity.[73] Baur himself, while fundamentally appreciative of the critical spirit of Strauss's work, was nonetheless dissatisfied with both its methodology and its largely "negative" results. More generally, he continued to find it difficult to understand the rise of Christian faith—particularly after Jesus's death—apart from an assumption that Jesus was in objective fact what faith subjectively saw in him. "If Jesus in his whole appearance was not more than results from [Strauss's] investigation," he wrote, "then it remains all the more puzzling how the conviction of the disciples, that he *must* have risen from the dead, could have developed."[74]

It is perhaps less than surprising, then, that once Baur finally did take up the subject, he found precisely what he had long surmised. Identifying Matthew's sayings material, especially the Sermon on the Mount and the Kingdom parables, as the most direct reflection of the historical Jesus in all the gospels, Baur argued that beneath it all was nothing other than that universalizing religious consciousness he had identified as the core "principle of Christianity." His interpretation is worth quoting at length:

> All that the most developed dogmatic consciousness can comprise is already here [in Matthew's Beatitudes] . . . All the beatitudes, variously as they sound, are but different expressions of the same original idea and mood which lie at the root of the Christian consciousness . . . the simple feeling of the need of redemption, which contains in itself implicitly, though as

yet undeveloped, the antithesis of sin and grace . . . The original and radical element of Christianity appears further in the form of the absolute moral command in the controversial part of the discourse which is directed against the Pharisees, and in other parts of it . . . The inner is opposed to the outer, the disposition to the act, the spirit to the letter . . . And this is what Jesus means when [summarizing the law and prophets with the love command in Matt 7:12] . . . He who loves his neighbor as himself must renounce everything egotistical, subjective, or peculiar to himself; above the plurality of separate subjects, each of whom now is the same as we are, there comes to stand the objective universal, where everything particular and subjective is done away with . . . Here then we meet again the characteristic feature of the Christian principle. It looks beyond the outward, the accidental, the particular, and rises to the universal, the unconditioned, the essential. It places a man's moral value only in that region of his life where he is in the presence of absolute considerations, and his acts possess absolute value . . . [T]he earliest and most essential element of the teaching of Jesus . . . appears to be purely and entirely moral in its tendency, and what it aims at is simply to throw men back on their own moral and religious consciousness.[75]

If this move to Matthew's sayings material represented a key step toward bridging the gap between the subjective experience of "religious consciousness" and the objective claims of Christianity regarding the singular significance of Jesus of Nazareth, it did not yet address the larger problem of the "absolute beginning" itself. How exactly did Jesus manage to make this leap to transcendence when others had not? Was he born this way, or did he experience a sudden, radical shift in consciousness at some point during his life? Baur remains curiously silent on these problems. Much as for Morgan, the decisive moment when the transcendent became the historical—when immutable Christianity suddenly irrupted into the otherwise mutable history of culture—is passed over without explanation.

From Christian Consciousness to the Christian Religion: Paul the Apostle

Though personally tending to the view that Jesus himself must have represented the historical origins of Christianity's "absolute consciousness," Baur conceded that critical study of the gospels, particularly as this "concerns the life of the Founder of Christianity," would "long remain the most important object of the critical labors of our time." Be that as it may, "the ultimate, most important point of the primitive history of Christianity," as Baur saw it, was actually less the historical Jesus than the more general question of "how Christianity . . . asserted itself as a separate, independent principle . . . and took its stand as a new enfranchised form of religious thought and life, essentially different from all the national peculiarities of Judaism," which is to say the social-cultural context in which it first appeared. And if there was a "single life" that forms "the peculiar object of the historical and critical enquiry" on this matter, it is in any case not Jesus, but Paul.[76] "That Christianity, in its universal historical acceptation, was the work of the Apostle Paul," he wrote, "is undeniably an historical matter of fact." It was Paul who was "the first to lay down expressly and distinctly the principle of Christian universalism as a thing essentially opposed to Jewish particularism"—an "antagonism of principle," Baur said, that Jesus himself had left merely implicit in his teaching.[77] Moreover, if "the conscious idea of Christianity and its principles [were] originated by [Jesus], and by him carried out through the devotion of his whole being," it was in any event Paul who was ultimately responsible for the "practical realization" of that idea in history, particularly in the form of Gentile Christianity.[78] In short, while Baur correlates Christianity in the sense of "absolute consciousness" with Jesus himself, Paul, as the "true herald, and logical founder and expositor" of Gentile Christianity, represents a "new beginning" in his own right. He "did of himself what no one had done before,—introduced Christianity to its true destination as a religion for the world, and enunciated, with a full sense of its vast significance, the principle of Christian universalism."[79] Much as for Morgan, then, Paul and his writings were in Baur's view all but synonymous with "original Christianity."

In Paul, moreover, Baur found precisely the sort of singular historical moment his notion of Christianity as "absolute religion" demanded: a decisive conversion experience. Here, according to Baur, was revelatory Christian consciousness par excellence.

> In order to apprehend the principle of Christian consciousness in all its depth and peculiarity, as it existed in the view of the apostle, it is necessary for us to refer as far as possible to what was characteristic in the fact of his conversion . . . not less decisive than rapid and immediate, not merely from Judaism to Christianity, and from one form of religious consciousness to another, but also from one direction of life into the very opposite direction . . . Of all those who have been converted to faith in Christ, there is no one in whose case the Christian principle broke so absolutely and so immediately through everything opposed to it, and asserted so triumphantly its own

absolute authority, as in that of the apostle Paul . . . The spiritual process he passed through in the act of his conversion is simply the key to the Christian principle as unfolded in his person.[80]

For Baur, of course, the supernatural event narrated in Acts "can only be regarded as the outward reflection of an inner spiritual process," and where there is process there must be some transitional step. Here, however, historical analysis fails. "No analysis, either psychological or dialectical," he wrote, "can detect the inner secret of the act in which God revealed his Son in him." To be sure, Baur speculated that this moment can only have arisen out of the profoundest contemplation of Jesus's death—which is to say the paradox of a crucified messiah. Nonetheless, so abrupt, so improbable, and so absolute was Paul's leap to a new, transcendent form of consciousness that even Baur—strikingly, like Morgan before him—can only mystify the precise transformational moment in terms of miracle: "We cannot call his conversion, his sudden transformation from the most vehement opponent of Christianity into its boldest preacher, anything but a miracle [*nur ein Wunder*]; and the miracle appears all the greater when we remember that in this revulsion of his consciousness he broke through the barriers of Judaism and rose out of the particularism of Judaism into the universal idea of Christianity."[81]

For this reason it is above all the writings of Paul—or simply "the Apostle," as Baur routinely calls him—where Baur found most clearly and authoritatively that "consciousness" he identified as the generative essence of Christianity. It was precisely this notion of consciousness, in fact, that provided the starting point and touchstone of Baur's lengthy and systematic treatment of Pauline theology in the third part of his extensive *Paul the Apostle of Jesus Christ*—a move Baur himself considered among the most distinctive features of his treatment.[82] The result is a tour de force in the modern demythologizing—or better, remythologizing—of Pauline thought. The section opens with a chapter titled "The Principle of the Christian Consciousness" (*Das Princip des christlichen Bewusstseins*) in which this absolute consciousness of Paul's conversion experience is shown to underlie the core concepts of his doctrine, particularly the identification of Jesus as Son of God, the distinction between spirit and flesh, and the notion of freedom:

This is what [Paul] asserts when he says of his conversion . . . that it pleased God . . . to reveal his Son in him, that is, to disclose the person of Jesus . . .

in his consciousness, through an inward act of consciousness, as that which he really was, the Son of God . . . The apostle therefore saw in the death of Christ the purification of the Messianic idea from all the sensuous elements which cleaved to it in Judaism, and its elevation to the truly spiritual consciousness where Christ comes to be recognized as (that which he was to the apostle) the absolute principle of the spiritual life . . . A further definition of the absoluteness of the principle of the Christian consciousness . . . is this: that in this principle the apostle is conscious of the essential difference of the spirit from the flesh, of freedom from everything by which man is only outwardly affected . . . It is the same absolute character of the Christian consciousness which finds its expression in all these relations. The term "spirit" is used by the apostle to denote the Christian consciousness . . . [T]his identity of the spirit as it appears in us with the spirit as it is in God, is thus the highest expression for the absolute truth of that which the Christian consciousness asserts as its own immediate contents . . . Being in this sense spiritual, the Christian consciousness is also absolutely free, absolved from all limits of finality, and unfolded to the full clearness of the absolute self-consciousness . . . In all this we have the explanation which the apostle himself has given us of the principle of his Christian consciousness.[83]

Baur proceeds in Chapters 2 and 3 to demonstrate at length that Paul's doctrine of justification in particular "was entirely within the sphere of the individual consciousness."[84] In the remaining chapters he explains, among other things, the relationship of this consciousness to the social reality of the Church and its rituals (Chapter 4);[85] how it underlies the basic differences in (and constitutes the spiritual hierarchy of) "Heathenism," Judaism, and Christianity (Chapter 5);[86] how it provides the wider meaning of Paul's contrast between Adam and the resurrected Christ (Chapter 6);[87] and how it underlies too, finally, Paul's emphasis on faith, hope, and love (Chapter 7; cf. 1 Cor 13:13).[88]

Christianity, Judaism, and Jewish Christianity

As we have seen, Baur draws a basic distinction between the "absolute consciousness" of Christianity and the relative "consciousness of the age" in whose concepts it seeks to express itself within any given historical epoch. If there is always a certain ambivalence in the relationship of the transcendent to its historical forms, this was never more so than in the formative first epoch of Christianity when this new revelatory consciousness found itself in something of a double bind. With the dogmas articulating it as a distinct religion not yet formulated, the only conceptual forms to which it had recourse were those furnished by the very "consciousness of the age" from which it sought fundamentally to differentiate itself, namely, Judaism and paganism.[89] As the immediate context of both Jesus and Paul, it was Judaism above all that was the primary factor in earliest Christianity, and in two ways: as a key source of conceptual forms on one hand, and as "the chief obstacle to its universal historical realization" on the other.[90] If Baur thus considered it "entirely natural that in the first stage of its own development [Christianity] still bore within it the character of Judaism," he also felt there could be "no doubt" that "the thought in which the apostle [Paul] first discerned the truth of Christianity" was at the same time nonetheless precisely its transcendence of "the particularism of Judaism."[91] The process by which Christian consciousness gradually disentangled itself from Judaism, actualizing its essential difference from it in both dogma and social reality, is thus for Baur "the ultimate, most important point of the primitive history of Christianity."[92]

As noted above, Baur identified Paul as the pivotal figure in this process. Nonetheless, he argued, it took collective Christendom decades to come to terms with what Paul had grasped so immediately and absolutely in his extraordinary revelatory moment. It is precisely this theory of a gradual historical actualization of Christianity's essential non-Jewish nature that allowed Baur to account for the fact that so much of the New Testament seemed inconsistent with the enlightened values he identified as primal Christianity.[93]

More specifically, Baur's reconstruction allowed for two possible interpretations of the prevalence of characteristically Jewish elements in what he imagined as a new and fundamentally non-Jewish religion. The first amounts to the same sort of humanistic adaptation of Christianity's incarnation myth that we have already seen in Toland: the transcendent, spiritual reality of Christian consciousness "borrowed" existing Jewish forms in order to manifest itself in the realm of historical human discourse. In practice, however, Baur used this incarnational paradigm primarily to interpret the Jewishness of Jesus and Paul. Indeed in his view, the bulk of the New Testament could not be sufficiently explained along these lines. Baur, in fact, found Jewish ideas positively at odds with his own vision of true Christianity throughout the Christian canon, and even explicit opposition to Paul among the first apostles themselves. Such evidence demanded a second interpretive paradigm, less of incarnation than of obscurantism. Despite their intuitive response to Christ, Baur argued, most early Christians struggled to fully transcend the limited consciousness of their epoch and continued to confuse the Jewish medium with the new message. Not yet realizing the profound implications Jesus's Christian principle had for Judaism, they continued to value Jewish forms in themselves rather than recognizing them for what they really were: convenient but ultimately disposable receptacles of a radically new and fundamentally not-Jewish truth. In most cases, then, Baur found the Jewishness of early Christianity to be less the cultural flesh in which absolute consciousness first became incarnate than the primary cultural barrier it had to overcome in order to fully actualize itself as an independent dogmatic and social reality. It was this malformed, positively obscurant Christianity—not the more purely incarnational one of Jesus and Paul—that Baur designated "Jewish Christianity."

THE INCARNATIONAL MODEL: JESUS AND PAUL

It is of course above all Jesus and Paul who represented for Baur the appropriate and effective use of Jewish discourse in the service of the new Christian consciousness. Jesus's fundamental aim, according to Baur, was "simply to throw men back on their own moral and religious consciousness." His was thus a "purely moral religion" in which particular religious forms were so fundamentally unimportant that even "faith in the person of Jesus" was unnecessary.[94] In order for that consciousness to actually have an impact on history, however, some concrete "form was needed"—a "firm centre . . . around which the circle of its disciples might rally, so as to grow into a fellowship which should be able to win dominion over the world." Jesus, Baur said, found just such a conceptual "fulcrum supplied by the circumstances of the place and time" in Jewish eschatology and its concept of a messiah. "It was in the Messianic idea that the spiritual contents of Christianity were clothed . . . with the concrete form in which it could enter on the path of historical development."[95] Jesus's use of this most nationalistic of Jewish "forms," moreover, was said to be wholly ironic and subversive. Following the synoptic account, Baur suggests that Jesus began identifying himself as messiah only as his death in Jerusalem became imminent—and that he did so in this context precisely to force a decision on the Jewish people: "the whole nation must be called on to declare whether it would persist in that traditional Messianic belief which bore the stamp of selfish Jewish particularism, or if it would accept such a Messiah as he was, and had shown himself in his whole life and influence to be."The answer, in the form of his crucifixion, "made a complete and irreparable breach between him and Judaism. A death like his made it impossible for the Jew, as long as he remained a Jew, to believe in him as his Messiah."[96] If old wineskins were used by Jesus, one might say, it was precisely so that he might burst them with new wine.

Baur nonetheless conceded that this "principled opposition" to Judaism was only implicit in Jesus's teaching.[97] It was in the writings of Paul, as we have seen, that Baur found Christianity's essential antagonism to Judaism first expressed in explicit and decisive terms. Even here, however, Jewish "forms" remained fundamental. Paul's revelatory experience, according to Baur, was precipitated precisely by reflection on the death of the messiah, and his own subsequent doctrine remained couched in eschatological terms. In fact, Baur found even what he took to be Paul's most incisive articulation of Christianity's opposition to Judaism—the idea that "man is justified, not by works of the law, but by faith," which Baur considered the "chief proposition of Pauline doctrine"—to have been articulated in fully Jewish terms. The whole notion of *dikaiosynē*, Baur said, "has its roots in the soil of the Jewish religion, to which that conception belongs; but in the peculiar Christian conception of faith, it departs from that religion, and takes up an attitude of decided opposition to it."[98] As in the case of the messianic idea itself, in other words, a concept was conscripted from Jewish discourse to serve as the vehicle of a spiritual reality fundamentally opposed to Judaism. Like Jesus then, Paul the convert did not think like a Jew so much as merely borrow Jewish concepts in order to think like a Christian.[99]

THE OCCLUSIONISTIC MODEL: JEWISH CHRISTIANITY

Not all early Christians, according to Baur, were as readily equipped as Paul to think like Christians rather than Jews. As he saw it, Paul's revelatory experience, while not the lone such experience in early Christianity, was singular nonetheless in its depth and impact. Accordingly, Baur found all too many instances in the New Testament of Jewish ideas that were less receptacles of primal Christian liberalism than obscurers of it. What is more, he found widespread evidence in a variety of sources—Paul's own letters, the canonical Acts of the Apostles, the Pseudo-Clementine literature, and patristic reports about the Ebionites—that Paul's efforts to translate the universalistic consciousness of Christianity into social reality met with strong and sustained opposition from within the Jesus movement itself. His analysis of the ancient literature led him to the conclusion that the ultimate source of this opposition was none other than Jesus's original apostles.[100]

Baur encapsulated this theory of a new, generative Christian consciousness choked by an ongoing, improper valuation of Judaism in a variety of more or less synonymous expressions over the course of his many publications. It can be described, among other things, as "clinging tenaciously to Judaism," having a "judaistic stamp," or simply "Judaizing," and its substantive result as an "anti-Pauline Judaizing Christianity" or, more straightforwardly, "Jewish Christianity" (*Judenchristenthum*).[101] As far as I have found, Baur nowhere offers a formal definition of this latter term. His basic understanding of the concept, however, is sufficiently clear both from his larger theory of the nature and origins of Christianity and from various comments about "Jewish Christians" and "Jewish Christianity" found throughout his writings. In the context of Baur's theory of Christian history, Jewish Christianity represents the obfuscation of the transcendent religious consciousness of Jesus and Paul by the particular values of Judaism.[102] From Baur's point of view, this supposed phenomenon, if far from surprising from a historical point of view, is especially egregious insofar as Judaism is said to represent particularism par excellence. "The very principle of Judaism," he said, was a notion of "true religion as a thing bound down to special ordinances and localities."[103] As such, Judaism is not only the polar opposite of Christianity in principle, it was literally what Jesus and Paul rejected in historical fact.

Baur understood this obscurantist phenomenon to have manifested itself in a variety of forms. Most fundamental was the soteriological "principle that . . . salvation could only be obtained in the form of Judaism": "To Judaism there must always belong an absolute right over the Gentiles. It was therefore simply impossible that a man should be saved by Christianity unless he acknowledged Judaism, and submitted to everything which Judaism prescribed as the necessary conditions of salvation."[104] In practice, this meant an emphasis on observance of Jewish law "in all its particulars." From this point of view, then, the "highest principle" of Jewish Christianity could also be articulated as a doctrine of justification, namely, *dikaiosynē ex ergōn nomou*, "righteousness out of works of the law."[105] It might also manifest itself still more specifically in an emphasis on circumcision insofar as the latter, according to Baur, "included all Judaism in itself."[106] Whether in these or other forms, the generative impulse of Jewish Christianity is to place "absolute importance" rather than merely "relative value" on Judaism alongside Christianity.[107] For such "Judaists," Baur said, "it is in vain to be a Christian without being a Jew also," while for Paul "it is in vain to be a Christian if, as a Christian, one chooses to be a Jew as well."[108]

If Baur's understanding of the Jewishness of Jewish Christianity is thus clear enough, what is perhaps less immediately obvious is the sense in which he understands this supposed phenomenon to represent Christianity at all.[109] As long as Jewish religious forms are valued in their own right, to what extent can one assume the presence of that "absolute consciousness" that Baur identifies as Christianity? At this point it is helpful to recall Baur's distinction between the actual historical dogmas of Christianity and the one implicit dogma said to lie beneath them.[110] The absolute consciousness of Jesus, particularly once given "concrete form" as an idea, set in motion the possibility of subsequent revelatory replications of it, transmitted by means of historical doctrine. The history of Christian dogma represents the continual and progressive actualization of that singular idea in the consciousness of the Church. Seen from this point of view, Christianity is not imagined merely as the actual historical experience of absolute consciousness like that of Jesus and Paul, but as a spiritual potentiality for such consciousness transmitted specifically within the historical forms of the Church. According to Baur, in other words, some forms of human discourse—namely, those of the Church—are qualitatively different from others insofar as they are vehicles of a transcendent, revelatory potentiality (albeit one that is realized only to varying degrees by its actual historical tradents). All such forms of discourse—orthodox or otherwise—can thus be called Christianity insofar as they are assumed to be carriers of an autonomous spiritual reality that they variously reveal or conceal. In short, the "Christianity" of Jewish Christianity represents nothing other than Baur's claim that his own theological and ethical values were concealed all along within the otherwise Jewish culture of Jesus's early followers.[111]

The general dynamic is well illustrated by Baur's treatment of what is for him the formative Christian notion of a crucified messiah. As noted above, Baur understood Jesus to have framed himself in messianic terms precisely with the dual intention of providing his religious consciousness a historically impactful form while simultaneously exploding Jewish nationalism. The essential (if only implicit) breach between his religion and Judaism, Baur said, was crystallized for all time by the historical fact of his crucifixion: "A death like his made it impossible for the Jew, as long as he remained a Jew, to believe in him as his Messiah."[112] Two major developments in Christian consciousness, both resulting in further doctrinal advances, are said to have resulted directly from this subversive messianism. In the immediate aftermath of Jesus's death, the cognitive dissonance inherent in the notion of a crucified messiah spurred an "inward spiritual process"—the same sort of "subjective psychological miracle" to which Baur appealed in the case of Paul—that moved Jesus's earliest disciples from unbelief to belief and resulted more specifically in the idea of the resurrection.[113] "Certain as [this] seemed to bring the minds of the disciples who believed in Jesus into direct conflict with Judaism," however, this idea was in itself "still too narrow to accomplish much" in terms of formulating that conflict clearly, let alone bringing it to social reality. Indeed, so limited was these disciples' grasp of the essentially anti-Jewish meaning of their own revelatory experience that their new faith was simply "a new and stronger form of the old Messianic expectations," different from that of other Jews only insofar as their messiah had already come. Baur's own emphatic declarations about the impossibility of the notion of a crucified messiah for the Jew qua Jew notwithstanding, then, they represented "a mere Jewish sect in whose keeping the whole future of Christianity would have been imperilled." A new "principle" had indeed "entered into the world in Christianity," but it had yet "to triumph over every influence which opposed it and threatened to hinder or obscure the all-commanding universalism of its spirit and aims."[114] The early disciples, in other words, became unwitting carriers of the revelatory potential of this new Christian consciousness, albeit in a form still constrained by "the cramping and narrowing influence of the Jewish national Messianic idea."[115] It was thus these Jewish Christian disciples themselves who—quite despite themselves—set the stage for a second and altogether more momentous dogmatic advance, when their notion of a crucified and resurrected messiah awakened a more profound revelatory experience in Paul. The result was not only doctrinal formulations that would finally make the decidedly not-Jewish essence of Christianity explicit, but a Gentile mission that would translate it into social reality.[116]

Jewish Christianity in History

Insofar as it was Paul's revelatory experience that inaugurated this crucial dogmatic advance, Baur apparently considered all forms of Christianity not directly indebted to Paul—whether because coming before him, actively opposed to him, or simply not exposed to his teaching—to be more or less occluded by Judaism. He thus conceived of the whole of early Christianity beyond the sphere of Pauline influence as Jewish Christianity, in contrast to Pauline or Gentile Christianity. If in this very broad sense a single "party," Jewish Christianity in Baur's reconstruction was nonetheless subject to a variety of historical manifestations and even internal divisions both before Paul and especially after him. Baur found evidence of this diversity already in the New Testament, which, as he saw it, placed ideas reflective of true Christian consciousness alongside ideas derived from Judaism in many and various combinations. Like Morgan, Baur explained this perceived juxtaposition by theorizing that the defining trend of the postapostolic era was reconciliation of these opposites, most especially in the emerging Catholic Church and its canon.[117]

That the supposed phenomenon he called Jewish Christianity should have occurred in the first place is anything but surprising from Baur's point of view given "the two elements" combined "in the person of Jesus": "the unconfined humanity . . . which gave his person its absolute significance" on one hand, and "the cramping and narrowing influence," on the other, "of the Jewish national Messianic idea."

> The latter was the form which the person of Jesus was obliged to assume if the former element was to have a point of vantage from which to go forth into the stream of history, and to find the way on which it could pass into the general consciousness of mankind. What, then, could be more natural than that one set of his followers should hold to the national side of his appearance, and attach themselves to it so firmly as never to surmount the particularism of Judaism at all, while the other of the two elements . . . found in another quarter a much more distinct and energetic expression than the first set of his followers ever could have given it?[118]

As Baur understood it, the initial social-historical manifestation of Christianity after the death of Jesus was precisely this "first set of followers," still firmly wedded to the Jewish messianic "form" itself rather than the spiritual Christian essence ensconced within it. He found the first glimmers of that more insightful "other quarter" in the "Hellenists" of Acts (6:1–8:1, 9:29), who, as Baur's historical bridge between the Jewish Christianity of the first apostles and the full-blown Gentile Christianity of Paul, are given a somewhat ambiguous position between them. Stephen in particular is said to have somehow "attained a clearer consciousness" of Christianity's inherent antagonism to Judaism than had the first apostles and was in this sense less a Jewish Christian than a "forerunner of Paul."[119] It was the public preaching of Christianity in Stephen's form in particular, Baur said, that aroused the violent hostility of Jews, and with very consequential results. An already implicit divide between Stephen's liberal "Hellenists" and the more conservative "Hebraists" now played out socially and geographically as the former—but not the latter—were driven from Jerusalem in the wake of Stephen's martyrdom. Purged of these Hellenists, Jerusalem now became the seat of a "strictly Judaizing" Christianity led by the original apostles. Antioch, on the other hand, would emerge as the center of a "liberal Hellenistic Christianity" (*das freiere hellenistische Christenthum*) that, becoming ever more independent "of the cramping connection with the Mother Church at Jerusalem" and its "cramping forms of Judaism," eventually took the step of proclaiming its gospel to Gentiles rather than "exclusively to the Jews." Meanwhile, a "strenuous opposition" to this liberal development arose in the Jerusalem Church, which sought to bring these increasingly far-flung communities more securely within its own sphere of influence "in order to further its Jewish interests" while hindering "the free development of Hellenistic principles."[120]

Baur situates the revelation of Paul and his subsequent tensions with the Jerusalem apostles within this already existing division. To be sure, Baur was careful to safeguard Paul's originality and independent authority, even with respect to these Hellenists; Paul's gospel, Baur insisted, did not ultimately derive from any group or person, but from a revelation grounded in his own absolute consciousness. Baur posited nonetheless that Paul got his first glimmers of this "Christian consciousness" precisely from Stephen.[121] After his revelation, Baur said, the newly converted Paul "avoided intentionally and on principle all contact" with the Judaizing apostles in Jerusalem, working instead from Antioch alongside the Hellenists he had formerly persecuted. If a brief meeting with Peter several years after Paul's conversion left Peter with "nothing to allege against Paul's apostolic call" in theory, it also did not result in any formal authorization of him by the original apostles—an authorization Paul did not in any case seek.[122]

After some fourteen years of Paul's successful Gentile mission, however, the apostles could no longer put off what had by then become a pressing, practical issue, namely, "whether such a Gentile Christianity as the Pauline Christianity had now become, ought to be recognized and tolerated from a Jewish standpoint."[123] Direct interference by their representatives in Antioch, Baur said, prompted Paul to visit Jerusalem in order to bring the matter to some resolution. What transpired, according to Baur, was thus no mere dustup between Paul and a few Pharisaic-minded individuals as Acts reports, but a clash of core principles in a historic first confrontation of Jewish Christianity with Pauline, Gentile Christianity.[124] The divisive question was "whether the Gentiles could become Christians directly as Gentiles, or only through the mediation of Judaism by first becoming Jews," and it played out particularly around the symbolic matter of circumcision in a contest between Peter and Paul: "man against man, teacher against teacher, one Gospel against another, one apostolic office against another."[125] Though the fact of Paul's success among the Gentiles forced the apostles to concede that it had come with God's blessing, they were unprepared to adopt the principles of his gospel. While unable to produce rational objections to Paul's argument, "still they could not free themselves from the limited standpoint of Judaism on which they had hitherto stood."[126] The matter was resolved, therefore, only by means of a truce: the two would go their separate ways, with an understanding that the Jerusalem apostles would no longer interfere in Gentile Christianity.

This superficial resolution, Baur said, soon proved untenable. If their inability to mount a successful counterargument against Paul forced the Jerusalem community to adopt a stance of a passive tolerance toward Gentile Christianity, that concession was ultimately out of step with their own driving religious principles. The result, according to Baur, was a division within Jewish Christianity itself in Jerusalem. Insofar as they did not insist on enacting their own Jewish principles where Pauline Christianity was concerned, the apostles represented a (relatively!) "liberal" Jewish Christian party. Others, however, finding this disharmony of principle and practice intolerable, "could not be indifferent to the Pauline Christianity" and became "declared opponents of the Apostle Paul." Apparently under the leadership of James, this more "strict" Jewish Christian party began to jostle for influence in Jerusalem while ever more actively intervening in Paul's Gentile communities.[127] The tensions quickly came to a head in the so-called Antioch incident, which exposed the shakiness of the earlier truce. When push was brought to shove by certain "people from James" (Gal 2:12), Peter ultimately sided with his Jewish Christian principles, effectively denying the equality of Gentile and Jewish Christians. Paul's harsh critique of Peter created a lasting breach between the two apostles, effectively ending their fragile truce. Newly energized, the Jewish Christians spread their anti-Paulinism throughout his Gentile Christian communities; even the apostle John would make his way to Ephesus in an effort to turn back Paulinism from Asia Minor.[128] Paul, on the other hand, would spend the remainder of his life—the period during which his authentic letters were written—defending Christianity and its Gentile communities against the encroachments of Jewish Christians. The fateful clash between Peter and Paul would echo for decades beyond their deaths in both Jewish and Pauline Christianity.[129]

If the apostolic age was thus defined by conflict between Jewish Christianity and Pauline Christianity, it was evident to Baur from the shape of early Catholicism and its New Testament that the central tendency of the postapostolic era must have been their reconciliation.[130] To be sure, it was clear to him from the ongoing reports of Ebionites as well as the Pseudo-Clementine literature that some continued to nurture the old opposition for centuries. But such hardliners became increasingly marginalized as Jewish Christianity itself splintered along these lines. The Ebionites were eventually reduced to an isolated "sect" as a more tolerant, Nazoraean faction traded outright hostility to Paul and Gentile Christianity for mere indifference.[131] Others on both sides of the Jewish Christianity–Gentile Christianity divide, meanwhile, increasingly funneled their creative energies into new strategies of reconciliation. This impetus toward unity, however, was according to Baur more pragmatic than doctrinal. All but the most stubborn Jewish Christians finally bowed to the reality of a Gentile Christianity without circumcision; but they made peace with it less by acceptance of Pauline doctrine than through the formal substitution of baptism—a ritual already accepted within Gentile Christianity—for circumcision.[132] Pauline Christianity, for its part, tended to seek common ground simply by emphasizing the moral consequences of faith—the "works" that would attend it—over its doctrinal significance in relation to justification.[133] Equally important on both sides was the erasure from historical memory of the antagonism that had originally obtained between the apostolic heads of each party.[134] New historical narratives—most notably the Acts of the Apostles—were generated to portray Peter and Paul as fully harmonious both in life and in death. Baur located the impulse for this development particularly in Rome, where a certain preeminence for Peter was also maintained. Its accomplishment marked "the point in which the final completion of the [Catholic] Church was arrived at."[135]

The character of the resultant Catholic Church, in Baur's view, is especially telling of its original dual nature. If "it was Paulinism that conquered

the soil for Catholic Christianity" by supplying members from every nation, "it was Jewish Christianity which supplied the forms of organisation
and erected the hierarchical edifice upon this basis," first in the form of the
episcopate and ultimately in the papacy.[136] Among the chief products of this
Catholic Church, and indeed its "essential basis," was the New Testament
canon.[137] Writings of Paul were placed alongside those ostensibly written
by Peter, James, and John—the very "Pillars" from whom Paul distances
himself in Galatians 2. Thus "what the Acts desired people to believe did
actually come to be believed, and the belief never afterwards wavered."[138]
In reality, however, almost all of these writings actually represented some
manner of conciliatory hybrid of what originally, according to Baur, had
been two essentially opposing principles, whether as Paulinizing forms of
Jewish Christianity or a Paulinism working in some way to accommodate
Jewish Christianity.[139]

Much as for Morgan, this theory allowed Baur to explain why the New
Testament as a whole, and indeed all but a handful of its individual works,
was in one way or another out of step with the enlightened consciousness
he identified as primal Christianity.[140] In order to recover the true original,
then, the Protestant had to do more than merely liberate the New Testament from the Catholic hierarchy and its traditions. More fundamentally,
the liberal consciousness Baur posited as the primal, generative essence
of Christianity had to be disentangled from the Jewish conceptual forms
that variously conveyed and obscured it already within the New Testament
canon itself. Proper distillation of this singularly authoritative Christianity thus required critical, historical analysis in general and an awareness
of the distinction between Jewish Christianity and Pauline Christianity in
particular.[141]

Like John Toland before them, Thomas Morgan and F. C. Baur claimed
the authorizing power attached to the idea of an "original Christianity" for
their own respective brands of Enlightenment humanism. Here again the
central strategy in both cases was to produce a new account of Christian
history to explain how traditional orthodoxy rather than their own theological values came to be associated with Christianity, specifically by postulating the existence of an early "Jewish Christianity." At this point, however,
the approach taken by Morgan and Baur diverged significantly from that
adopted by Toland. Conceding that the New Testament was largely out of
step with their own vision of true Christianity, they surrendered the two

long-standing pillars of Christian authority—the New Testament and the apostolic authority behind it—to traditional orthodoxy. More specifically, the traditional construct "apostolic authority" was channeled principally into Paul and his letters as the only fully authentic expression of the true Christianity of Jesus. Elements of the early record deemed irreconcilable with their Enlightenment values, on the other hand, were attributed to a virtually insurmountable influence Judaism had on Jesus's first followers—an influence that Jesus and Paul, nonetheless, had themselves somehow transcended. If apostolic Christianity was once again recast as a *Jewish* Christianity, the point was not, as for Toland, to denigrate orthodoxy as a later Gentile corruption; the point now was to explain orthodox Christianity and its New Testament as the legacy of a *Jewish* corruption against which Paul himself had already struggled tirelessly. The implied contrast was no longer simply *Gentile* Christianity, but more specifically *Pauline* Christianity. The result was not only a momentous reconceptualization of the interpretive construct Jewish Christianity, but a new urgency surrounding the critical study of the New Testament as the only way to recover original Christianity from the Judaism in whose terms the apostles had variously revealed and concealed it.

3 Apostolic vs. Judaizing Jewish Christianity: The Reclamation of Apostolic Authority in Post-Baur Scholarship

Baur's provocative account of early Christianity had a profound impact on subsequent scholarship. Though revisionist accounts of Christian origins and the New Testament had already been built around concepts of Jewish Christianity in eighteenth-century London, the rigorously critical and methodical discipline Baur brought to the matter made his publications—not Toland's or Morgan's—the center of a furious debate regarding Jewish Christianity not only in Germany, but back in England as well. Baur's elegant twofold thesis—that the apostolic era was defined by a fundamental conflict between Pauline and Jewish Christianities, and the postapostolic era by their gradual synthesis in Catholic Christianity and its New Testament—was variously developed by his students, who came to be known collectively as the Tübingen School.[1] Ironically, however, it was less his students than his ardent opponents who would ultimately ensure Baur's enduring legacy in the critical study of early Christianity. While some summarily dismissed Baur as a Hegelian, others found it impossible to overlook the impressive results of his critical approach to the New Testament. Rather than ignoring his theory of an early Jewish Christianity, such scholars sought instead to defuse it by engaging Baur on his own critical terms. This effort was led above all by Albrecht Ritschl, a former student of Baur who, in the second edition of his own study of the emergence of early Catholicism, sought to refute systematically the views of his teacher.[2] In England, meanwhile, it was especially Joseph Lightfoot who came to be celebrated as the slayer of the Tübingen dragon.[3]

Thanks to the efforts of these and other scholars, obituaries for Baur's Tübingen School were being written already by the second half of the nineteenth century.[4] Reports of its death, however, were greatly exaggerated. School aside, important elements of Baur's approach quickly became commonplace in the analysis of early Christianity, and not least in the work of his critics themselves. Most important for our purposes, neither Ritschl nor Lightfoot was interested in disputing Baur's bifurcation of early Christianity into Jewish and Pauline varieties, nor even his premise that its first generation was defined largely by a principled conflict between them. Lightfoot was every bit as insistent as Baur that the apostolic era was not the irenic idyll the Christian imagination had traditionally made it out to be. "The systematic hatred of St Paul," he wrote, "is an important fact, which we are too apt to overlook, but without which the whole history of the Apostolic ages will be misread and misunderstood." Any commentary on Galatians could now be considered "incomplete" without "the attempt to decipher the relations between Jewish and Gentile Christianity in the first ages of the Church."[5] The existence of a fundamental conflict in principle, and of outright hostility in practice, between Jewish Christianity and Pauline Christianity also remained central to the work of Ritschl.[6]

What these and other critics sought to turn back, rather, was mainly two of Baur's more specific theses. First, they wanted to refute the idea that the apostles themselves were on the wrong side of the conflict—that they were any less clear than Paul that Christianity was essentially other than Judaism. As Adolf Hilgenfeld observed in 1886, "What the reigning theology sought to ward off at any price was only a dualism of the *apostolic* Christianity . . . the view that the *Urapostel* as a whole in no way progressed beyond Judaism in their manner of thinking."[7] Second, Baur's critics similarly rejected not his critical approach to the New Testament per se, but only the idea that the canon was in any way tainted with a problematic, anti-Pauline Jewishness. The basic aim of Baur's critics, in short, was not to repudiate the whole of Baur's historical model, much less his critical methodology. They simply sought, within this new framework, to restore the early apostles and the canonical writings associated with them to their traditional role as authoritative expressions of an authentic, primal Christianity.[8]

The central challenge on this front, as Hilgenfeld put it, was that "even Baur's opponents were unable to deny that Jewish Christianity had been the *urapostolic* form of Christianity."[9] In the wake of Baur's analysis, the relationship and apparent similarities between the early apostles and Paul's opponents had become too obvious to ignore. The only option, then, was to rehabilitate the apostles *precisely as* Jewish Christianity. The heart of their strategy, accordingly, was to subdivide Jewish Christianity itself into two different classes. The anti-Pauline party highlighted by Baur, it was argued, was neither the only nor even the most significant kind of Jewish Christianity in antiquity. The apostles represented a different kind: one that was actually in essential agreement with Paul regarding Christianity's absolute transcendence of Judaism. While superficially similar to the anti-Pauline "Judaizers" with respect to Torah observance, their apparent Jewishness was only civic or cultural, not a function of essential religious principle. In their case, in other words, primal Christianity was ensconced not only within forms of Jewish discourse (as for Paul), but within forms of Jewish practice as well. In effect, the incarnational model of Jewish Christianity pioneered by Toland was placed alongside Baur's occlusionistic model within a new taxonomy of the category.

With this move, the conflict Baur highlighted between Paul and Jewish Christianity was safely expunged from the apostolic sphere proper, relegated instead to a marginal faction of outlying "radicals" who sought to impose on apostolic Christianity Jewish principles essentially at odds with it.[10] Variations on this broad counternarrative served to defend the integrity of apostolic authority at both key flashpoints assaulted by Baur: the early apostles themselves, especially as portrayed in Galatians 2, and the apostolic legacy of the early Catholic Church and its New Testament canon in particular. The price of this apologetic strategy, however, was a new and seemingly intractable confusion surrounding the terminology and definitions attending this new taxonomy of Jewish Christianity.

The Reclamation of the Apostolic Community

The basic premise of the counternarrative generated by Ritschl, Lightfoot, and other critics of Baur was that the early apostles were in essential agreement with Paul regarding Christianity's difference from Judaism in principle. Ritschl found it "unbelievable," given the clear statements of Jesus in Mark and Matthew, as well as Old Testament prophecy more generally, that it was only as a result of Paul's missionary efforts that the first apostles came to realize that the Kingdom of God was also to include Gentiles.[11] Lightfoot similarly emphasized, primarily on the basis of Acts, that "the first stage in the emancipation of the Church" from Judaism had already taken place in the pre-Pauline era: "The principle was broadly asserted that the Gospel received all comers, asking no questions, allowing no impediments, insisting on no preliminary conditions."[12] The subsequent conflict surrounding Paul's Gentile mission, Ritschl and Lightfoot agree, arose only because some Pharisaic converts to Christianity, as Lightfoot put it, "had imported into the Church of Christ the rigid and exclusive spirit of Pharisaism" and sought "to impose circumcision on the Gentiles, not only as a condition of equality, but as necessary to salvation" (cf. Acts 15:1).[13] The so-called Jerusalem council of Acts 15 and Galatians 2, accordingly, is interpreted as a formal acknowledgment of an essential Christian "principle" that, if first articulated explicitly and emphatically by Paul, had been implicit in the religion of the apostles—much as for Baur's Jesus—from the start.[14] When, therefore, these Pharisaic Jewish Christians continued to claim in Galatia and elsewhere that they represented the original apostolic position, they did so disingenuously.[15] The crucial point, stated plainly by Ritschl at the conclusion of his discussion of Jewish Christianity in the apostolic era, is this: "actual *Judenchristenthum*"—that is, the species of Jewish Christianity (*Jüdische Christenthum*) defined by its failure to differentiate Christianity from Judaism and emphasized by Baur—"is devoid of apostolic authority and does not form the basis of an enduring opposition between the Apostle of the Gentiles and the immediate disciples of Jesus."[16] Lightfoot's conclusion is similar: the historical separation of Christianity from Judaism unfolded as divisively as it did only because "the Church" was not a "religious machine" under the "absolute control" of the apostles. Human nature being what it is, a "bigoted minority" in Jerusalem "was little likely to make an absolute surrender of its most stubborn prejudices to any external influence," even that of the "leading Apostles."[17]

Ritschl and Lightfoot realized, however, that establishing apostolic unity on this supposed essential Christian principle was not quite so simple as all that, given the nature of the evidence highlighted by Baur. Both acknowledged that the early apostles continued to observe Jewish law much like the "extremist" Jewish Christians did.[18] Ritschl recognized other problems as well. If the first apostles had really known from the beginning that the Kingdom was meant for Gentiles as much as for Jews, why had they not actively pursued a Gentile mission themselves? And if their acceptance of righteousness and salvation by grace rather than by the law resulted in a "principled indifference" to the Torah, why did they apparently do nothing to moderate the Jerusalem community's zeal for the law (cf. Acts 21)? Moreover, did not the Apostolic Decree itself, by imposing restrictions on Gentiles in accord with Jewish law, actually signal an affirmation, even if only instinctively or indirectly, of the guiding principle of Paul's oppo-nents?[19] Lightfoot was similarly troubled by this decree. Given his thesis that the apostles had already transcended Judaism, he conceded, "it is not so easy to understand the bearing of the restrictions imposed on the Gentile converts."[20] While differing in the details, Ritschl and Lightfoot offered the same underlying solution to these various problems: the assertion of a distinction between internal (Christian) principle and outward (Jewish) practice where the apostles were concerned.

Ritschl was emphatic that the early apostles' continued adherence to Jewish customs was rooted in a fundamentally different religious principle (*Grundsatz*) than the one driving the otherwise similar practice of the "strict Jewish Christians." The latter, conceiving of Christianity basically as a Jew-ish national alliance, considered Torah observance in general and circumci-sion in particular to be absolute requirements for admission. The apostles on the other hand, for whom Christianity was a new covenant defined solely by "faith in Christ," maintained a principled indifference to Jewish law.[21] Neither the continued importance of the law within the apostolic commu-nity nor the apostles' seemingly ambivalent relationship to Paul's Gentile mission, he argued, reflected any interest in the law for its own sake. Such things are to be explained, rather, simply by the apostles' belief, based on "Old Testament prophecy," that "Israel as a whole nation must be accepted into the Christian community before the Gentiles."[22] While fully recogniz-ing Christianity's essential difference from Judaism in principle, in other words, the apostles had assumed that the full realization of that difference in actual social practice was to occur in distinct historical phases: first the collective conversion of Israel to Christianity, then the incorporation of the Gentiles. Radically relativized by faith in Christ, Israel's privilege was now reduced merely to the temporal honor of being first to come to Chris-tianity.[23] Understanding themselves to be in the midst of the first of these phases, the apostles continued their outward observance of Jewish customs, and even tolerated the misguided zeal for the law by less enlightened Jew-ish Christians, in the service of their mission to Israel. All this, Ritschl emphasizes, "was compatible with the pure perception of the Christian idea demonstrated by the apostles, because even Christ had allowed the same."[24]

The upending of their assumed timetable by Paul's successful Gen-tile mission, according to Ritschl, caught the apostles entirely off guard, and they were forced to work through both their resulting cognitive disso-nance and its practical implications on the fly. It was only in the negotiation of these secondary details—not in the essential principle of Christianity itself—that tensions with Paul arose. The first attempt to accommodate the sooner-than-expected Gentile mission was the Apostolic Decree, which, Ritschl argued, affirmed the core Christian principle and accepted Paul's mission while also making certain practical concessions to the strict Jewish Christians in the interest of the continuing mission to Israel. The Gentiles, they decided, were to observe a limited number of laws—namely, those associated with "proselytes of the gate"—not out of any religious scruples, but purely as a social accommodation to Jewish Christians.[25] While this policy was fully compatible with Pauline principles, Ritschl argued, differences over its practical implementation eventually resulted in the tensions that later surfaced in Antioch.[26] Paul understood the division of the mission field into Jewish and Gentile spheres geographically; James, however, considering the eschatological mission to Israel to include the diaspora, understood it as an ethnic division.[27] When Jewish Christians in Antioch, along the lines of Paul's understanding, began setting aside dietary restrictions in communal meals with Gentiles, James intervened and the unresolved differences were exposed. Paul, as apostle to the Gentiles, resisted even the notion of a temporal priority for Israel within Christianity, and this led him to an "open refutation" of the idea that even Jews were beholden to the law.[28] Peter—in line with what Ritschl calls his "well-known character"—waffled. Having initially laid aside Jewish customs in Antioch (not least because of his own earlier experience with Cornelius as narrated in Acts 10), he then overcorrected, requiring even more concessions from Gentiles than the Apostolic Decree had outlined.[29] Ritschl goes so far as to grant that it is ultimately unclear whether James and Peter ever did give up on their notion of the temporal privilege of the Jewish nation and its consequences for the law. The apostle John, at least, is to have been brought around in any event by the fall of the temple, which he, unlike the others, had actually lived to see.[30]

Lightfoot similarly framed the problem of "the relations between Jewish and Gentile Christianity in the first ages of the Church"—and more specifically the "progressive history" of "The Emancipation of the Jewish Churches" from Judaism—in terms of a distinction between an essential Christian principle and outward Jewish practice.[31] Jesus, he argued, "enunciated the great principle" that the gospel fulfilled and thus discredited the law and also commanded that this gospel be preached to Gentiles as well as Jews. He left, however, "no express instructions" about how exactly "a national Church must expand into a universal Church." Much as Baur before him, then, Lightfoot took this "emancipation" of Christianity from Judaism to be the "great problem" of the apostolic era, framing it specifically as a matter of the "long interval" "between asserting a principle and carrying it out to its legitimate results."[32] However, like Ritschl, Lightfoot is quite clear that the key events narrated in Galatians 2 show that the first apostles were actually as unified with Paul as they were "distinctly separated from the policy and principles of the Judaizers."[33] The Apostolic Decree, which addressed precisely this "question of principle," plainly articulated an "*emancipating* clause" asserting "the supremacy of the Gospel" over the "old dispensation."[34]

As noted above, Lightfoot thus found what he called the "*restrictive* clauses" of the decree—that is, those concerned less with this supposed Christian principle than with actual Jewish practice—somewhat perplexing. Much as Ritschl, he interprets these restrictions not with reference to any religious principle of the apostles, but rather as concessions made— quite despite the apostles' own principles—to the Jewish sensibilities of the "Pharisaic party" and other Jews.[35] While Lightfoot thus similarly insisted that these restrictions were "relative rather than absolute,"[36] he was not interested in Ritschl's appeal to eschatological beliefs about Israel's temporal priority to explain either the decree or the apostles' continued adherence to Jewish law more generally. He offered instead his own threefold explanation for why the law might be thus observed for reasons other than simple piety. In the first place, he argues, as a civic institution "the law had claims on a Hebrew of Palestine wholly independent of his religious obligations … To be a good Christian he was not required to be a bad citizen. On these grounds the more enlightened members of the mother church would justify their continued adhesion to the law." Second, condescension by "the more enlightened" to the scruples of the less enlightened for the larger good of the mission was in any case the standard practice even of Paul himself: "The Apostles of the Circumcision … [were] conscious themselves that the law was fulfilled in the Gospel … [but] strove nevertheless by strict conformity to conciliate the zealots both within and without the Church, … acting upon St Paul's own maxim, who 'became to the Jews a Jew that he might gain the Jews' [cf. 1 Cor 9:20]." Finally, he suggested, the expectation of an imminent "catastrophe" made it unnecessary for the apostles to force the issue of the law in any case, since they could simply "leave all perplexing questions to the solution of time."[37]

Lightfoot's thesis that apostolic interest in the Torah was an accommodation to external circumstance rather than an expression of the apostles' own pious convictions is well illustrated by his interpretation of each of the "Pillars" identified by Paul in Galatians 2. James was a "scrupulous observer of the law" who differed from the Judaizers "less in the external forms of worship than in the vital principles of religion." Unlike the Judaizers, Lightfoot suggests, James's "rigid observance of the Mosaic ritual" was simply a function of his role as a "purely local" official within "the Church of the Circumcision" at Jerusalem as opposed to the wider responsibilities of an apostle. His limitation to a Jewish civic sphere, in other words, meant that "he was required only to be 'a Jew to the Jews.'" It is thus ultimately his presence at the meeting of Paul and the Pillars that explains the "restrictive clauses" in the decree—not as an imposition of rules for "proselytes of the gate," but simply in deference to the less enlightened Pharisaic voices in the community he represented.[38] Peter and John, on the other hand, as apostles like Paul, "were required to become 'all things to all men'"—a complex responsibility that sometimes led to "conflicting duties, such as entangled St Peter at Antioch."[39] Peter came to his "liberal principles" through the vision narrated in Acts 10, and his "normal practice" since that time was "to live as a Gentile" when among Gentiles. His conflict with Paul at Antioch thus represented simply a temporary lapse: "sanctioning the Jewish feeling which regarded eating with the Gentiles as an unclean thing" was an "exceptional departure" from Peter's "normal principles" and represented a "hypocritical compliance with the Jews." As with Ritschl, this waffling is explained with reference to an assumed weakness in Peter's general character. His moral lapse was in any case fleeting. "The weighty spiritual maxims thrown out during the dispute at Antioch" by Paul—Peter's "superior in intellectual culture, in breadth of sympathy, and in knowledge of men"—Lightfoot speculates, could only "sink deep into [Peter's] heart."[40] John similarly varied his practice depending on the surrounding circumstances: during the first part of his apostolic career he "lived as a Jew among Jews" in Palestine, but after moving to Asia Minor he became "as a Gentile among Gentiles."[41]

The Reclamation of the New Testament

Baur's critics were concerned to restore authority not only to the apostolic community, but to the New Testament as its literary legacy. Baur's subversion of the authority of the canon, like Morgan's before him, was based in part on the historical theory that the early Catholic Church—and thus, by extension, its New Testament—was a synthesis of the authentic Christianity of Paul with the obscurant Jewish Christianity of his opponents. Baur's critics, therefore, were also fundamentally interested in the rise of early Catholicism.[42] Here again the basic strategy was not to reject Baur's concept of Jewish Christianity per se, but simply to move it safely to the fringes of history and beyond the boundaries of the canon. While again varying in any number of details, the crux of the historical argument was that Jewish Christianity—in both its apostolic and nonapostolic varieties—became increasingly irrelevant over the course of the first and early second centuries, not least as a result of the Jewish wars with Rome. Catholic Christianity was by default, therefore, an essentially Gentile Christian phenomenon. This historical reconstruction was paired with exegetical arguments attempting to demonstrate that the New Testament in general, and the writings associated with the Jerusalem "Pillars" in particular, were no more problematically Jewish than Jesus and Paul had been. Here again, Ritschl and Lightfoot can serve to illustrate both the underlying shape of the argument and the various ways it could be elaborated.

Among the most basic moves made by both men was the correlation of Epiphanius's (and less obviously, Jerome's) fourth-century distinction between Ebionites and Nazoraeans with their own new distinction between apostolic and nonapostolic Jewish Christianity. The Nazoraeans—said to be pro-Pauline and essentially orthodox in all but their insistence that Jews (and Jews alone) should continue practicing Jewish law—are interpreted as direct descendants of apostolic Jewish Christianity.[43] The anti-Pauline Ebionites, on the other hand, are considered "the direct spiritual descendants of those false brethren, the Judaizers of the apostolic age."[44] Ebionite attempts to claim an apostolic legacy for themselves were thus no more legitimate than those of the early Pharisaic Christians whose legacy they preserved. The appearance of such claims in the Pseudo-Clementine literature is rendered doubly problematic in this respect insofar as these texts are said to have been the products, more specifically, of an "Essene Ebionism" that arose only as the result of an influx of Essene refugees into Ebionism after the fall of Jerusalem. As Lightfoot put it, "if Pharisaic Ebionism was a disease inherent in the Church of the Circumcision from the first, Essene Ebionism seems to have been a later infection caught by external contact."[45]

According to Ritschl and Lightfoot, moreover, neither the Ebionites nor even the Nazoraeans had any meaningful impact on the development of early Catholicism in the postapostolic era. Both groups, it is said, became increasingly marginalized and irrelevant as a result of the Jewish wars with Rome. According to Ritschl, the Nazoraeans had been almost entirely out of contact with "the rest of the Church" since the destruction of the temple.[46] Whatever special consideration the Gentile Christians may have continued to give them due to their historical connection to the original apostolic community was in any event all but lost as a result of the Bar Kochba rebellion, when leadership of the Jerusalem community passed into Gentile hands after the banishment of Jews from Aelia Capitolina. The Nazoraeans' interactions with Gentile Christians were always limited because of their ongoing observance of Jewish law, and by the time of Justin, their acceptance in the Church at all had become a matter of controversy. Mutual hostilities between the Ebionites and Gentile Christianity meant that there was even less interaction between the two of them. The Ebionites in any event were utterly rejected as a heretical sect by Justin's day. Over time, Ritschl argued, it became increasingly difficult for Gentile Christians to tell these two superficially similar groups apart, so that even the Nazoraeans were eventually declared a heresy—primarily as a result of guilt by association.[47] All things considered, he concludes, it is "impossible" that Jewish Christianity could have been a major force in the second-century Church.[48] "Catholic Christianity," in short, "did not issue from a reconciliation of Jewish Christians and Gentile Christians . . . it is a phase of Gentile Christianity alone."[49]

The same basic point is made even more strongly by Lightfoot, who approaches the matter from a somewhat different angle. Here again the Jewish wars with Rome are identified as the crucial turning point in the history of Jewish Christianity, but now only as the final steps in a progressive "emancipation" of the "Jewish Churches" themselves from Judaism. Here, finally, was the very "catastrophe" the apostles, according to Lightfoot, had been waiting for: "all those who had hitherto maintained their allegiance to the law purely as a national institution were by the overthrow of the nation set free henceforth from any such obligation." For the less enlightened, the destruction of the Jewish temple amounted to a "stern teaching of facts" about the transitory nature of Jewish sacrifice (as opposed to that of "the one Paschal Lamb"!), and thus about the efficacy of the law more generally.[50] In Lightfoot's view, in fact, the "star of Jewish Christendom was already on the wane" well before the first revolt and even by the time Paul and Barnabas had embarked on their first Gentile mission. Citing Acts 11:27–30, Lightfoot postulates that a severe and apparently ongoing famine in Palestine had left the Judean churches generally beholden to the Gentile churches and thus "deposed from the level of proud isolation which many of them would gladly have maintained." More importantly, the Jerusalem Church had been devoid of apostolic leadership—and thus "half her prestige and more than half her influence"—since Herod's execution of James son of Zebedee (cf. Acts 12:1–19).[51] The Bar Kochba rebellion and establishment of Aelia Capitolina, therefore, simply brought what had long been a steady, inexorable decline to its decisive conclusion. "By this second catastrophe the Church and the law were finally divorced." "The Church of Jerusalem ceased to be the Church of the Circumcision"—and not, moreover, merely because of an absence of ethnic Jews. "Of the Christians of the Circumcision not a few doubtless accepted [Hadrian's] terms, content to live henceforth as Gentiles"—which is to say, just as the "Apostles of the Circumcision" themselves had already modeled decades earlier, under considerably less extreme circumstances. Others, however, neglecting the divine lessons of history, "clung to the law of their forefathers with a stubborn grasp which no force of circumstances could loosen." It was these "malcontents," now as "declared separatists," who formed the Nazoraean and Ebionite sects.[52] Regardless of the details, then, Lightfoot is in fundamental agreement with Ritschl on the big picture: neither the Ebionites nor the Nazoraeans had any significant impact on the emerging Catholic Church.

More directly to the point, Ritschl and Lightfoot also agree that the New Testament, including not least the texts bearing the names of the Jerusalem "Pillars," is in no way tainted by failures to properly differentiate Christianity from Judaism, let alone a synthesis of such views with Pauline Christianity. Ritschl argues systematically that James, 1 Peter, and Revelation are as little "Jewish Christian" in Baur's occlusionistic sense as they are Pauline. Far from a later reconciliation of opposing Jewish and Christian principles, such texts represent expressions of authentic Christianity in forms provided by the apostles' Jewish environment—just like the Jesus and Paul of Baur.[53] Lightfoot, arguing similarly for the authenticity of these texts, interprets them in light of his own analysis of the individual Pillars as explained above. The Letter of James, coming from a man who "mix[ed] only with those to whom the Mosaic ordinances were the rule of life," lays great stress on the *idea* of law—but only as a virtual synonym for "the Gospel": "he nowhere implies that the Mosaic ritual is identical with or even a necessary part of Christianity." Indeed, the letter's notorious comments on faith and works, Lightfoot proposes, were not directed at Paul or even any perversion of Pauline doctrine at all, but rather at "the self-complacent orthodoxy of the Pharisaic Christian."[54] First Peter, for its part, "occupies a place midway between the writings of St James and St Paul": on one hand it "speaks of the truths of the Gospel . . . through the forms of the older dispensation"; but on the other "the law [is] never once named," nor is there even any "allusion to formal ordinances of any kind."[55] As with Peter, the apostle John's "larger sphere of action and wider obligations" translated "necessarily" into "a neutral position with regard to the law" and thus a virtual absence of the concept from his writings. What's more, the notorious differences between the Apocalypse and the other canonical texts ascribed to John are simply the result of the apostle's chameleon-like reflection of differing cultural circumstances: the former was written while he still "lived as a Jew among Jews" and the latter after he had begun living "as a Gentile among Gentiles."[56]

The Thematization of Jewish Christianity in Critical Scholarship

Ritschl and Lightfoot represent prominent and especially influential examples of what became a widespread strategy of response to Baur and his Tübingen School: the construction of alternative historical-critical accounts of Jewish Christianity, in which the apostles and the New Testament, though thoroughly Jewish, nonetheless retained their traditional roles as authoritative expressions of an authentic, primal Christianity. As fundamental now to Baur's chief critics as to the Tübingen School itself, the idea of an early Jewish Christianity (by whatever particular name) became all but bedrock in the emerging discipline of critical New Testament scholarship. Treatments were increasingly included in historical surveys of early Christianity, and attempts to delineate its nature and history became the central focus of specialized studies.[57] By the beginning of the twentieth century, the nature and history of Jewish Christianity could be considered "one of the chief problems in the history of *Urchristentum*."[58] With the Tübingen theory widely considered discredited, historical reconstructions were increasingly built around the basic interpretive moves exemplified by Ritschl and Lightfoot. Thus did the idea of an early Jewish Christianity, and even the broad outlines of a historical narrative about it, become central building blocks in the critical study of the New Testament and early Christian history.

Among the most elemental premises of the new, post-Baur narrative about Jewish Christianity was the fundamental unity of Paul and the early apostles on essential gospel principles. Paul's activity, it was now generally agreed, did indeed expose a basic conflict of principle between his Christianity and a problematically Jewish Christianity at work in the Jerusalem community. But it was widely concluded, with Ritschl and Lightfoot, that the apostles actually agreed with Paul where the essential matter of Christianity's transcendence of Judaism was concerned. To be sure, they continued to observe Jewish law much as the anti-Pauline "Judaizers" did. But unlike the latter, the apostles' observance was only a pragmatic and ultimately conditional accommodation to transient social-historical circumstances—not a matter of their own, active religious scruples. The apparent similarity between them and Paul's opponents, then, was indeed only apparent. If Jewish Christians, the apostles were no "Judaizers." Indeed, while superficially resembling the latter in day-to-day practice, the apostles ultimately showed themselves to be as different from them in essential religious principle as Paul himself was. Detailed explanations of the tensions otherwise evident between Paul and the Jerusalem "Pillars" continued to vary, but the general conclusion was that they concerned merely the secondary matters of translating their shared Christian principle into practice—whether, as for Ritschl, all but inevitable bumps in the road as the early apostles adapted to changing circumstances; or, as for Lightfoot, a function of differing opinions about the importance of appeasing the less enlightened who still valued Judaism in itself. In any event, such tensions did not signal a substantial rift, let alone an enduring one, on essential matters of gospel principle within the apostolic sphere proper.[59] In short, Baur's model of an obscurant Jewish Christianity remained quite intact in the growing discussion of early Jewish Christianity. The central difference was that the apostles in particular were exonerated, their Jewishness interpreted instead on an incarnational model after the fashion of Baur's Jesus. As Harnack put it, the "primitive Christianity" of the apostles, if originally "within the framework of Judaism," already "pointed far beyond Judaism" thanks to the unique "consciousness" at its generative essence—"the new experience of a direct union with God" that "makes the old worship with its priests and mediations unnecessary."[60]

Variations on the view that Jewish Christianity had at any rate become basically irrelevant by the Jewish wars with Rome at the latest, and thus of little or no significance for the rise of early Catholicism, similarly took root.[61] This thesis found particularly powerful expression in the work of Adolf von Harnack. As Harnack saw it, Jewish Christianity—and indeed Judaism more generally—was a virtual nonfactor in the development of Catholic Christianity precisely because its "national element" precluded it from exerting any meaningful influence on what from the start had been a new and avowedly universalistic religion.[62] "As a consequence of the complete break with the Jewish Church"—a break that "was essentially accomplished in the first two generations of believers"—"there followed . . . the strict necessity of quarrying the stones for the building of the Church from the Graeco-Roman world . . . The separation from Judaism having taken place, it was necessary that the spirit of another people should be admitted."[63] Elsewhere Harnack puts the matter in more strikingly mythical terms reminiscent of Genesis 1:

> Even had this youthful religion not severed the tie which bound it to Judaism, it would have been inevitably affected by the spirit and civilisation of [the] Graeco-Roman world . . . But to what a much greater extent was it exposed to the influence of this spirit after being sharply severed from the Jewish religion and the Jewish nation. *It hovered bodiless over the earth like a being of the air; bodiless and seeking a body . . . by assimilating what is around it.* The influx of Hellenism . . . and the union of the Gospel with it, form the greatest fact in the history of the Church in the second century.[64]

The defining dogma of early Catholicism, in short, "in its conception and development is a work of the Greek spirit on the soil of the Gospel." In a manner interestingly reminiscent of Toland, then, it was Hellenism—not Judaism—that was the key factor in primitive Christianity's transformation into Catholicism.[65]

The not incidental upshot of all this was an increasing insulation of the Christian canon from any especially problematic Jewishness and thus a restoration of its traditional status as the expression of an authentic, primal Christianity.[66] If the New Testament was increasingly recognized as being thoroughly Jewish, its Jewishness was not interpreted in the obscurant sense postulated by Morgan and Baur, but once again along more incarnational lines. In these early writings the new Christian religion was still being couched in the Jewish forms in which it was first disclosed. The exemption of the apostles from the Judaizing Jewish Christianity of Paul's opponents, in other words, found a literary correlation in the Christian canon just as in the work of Ritschl and Lightfoot.

The new subdivision of Jewish Christians and their texts into apostolic and Judaizing varieties was elaborated and reinforced by additional correlations. As for Ritschl and Lightfoot, the distinction drawn by Epiphanius in the fourth century between Ebionites and Nazoraeans was interpreted as the difference between Judaizing and more legitimately apostolic Jewish Christians. Hegesippus's general portrayal of the time after the death of James as an era of *hairesis* (Eusebius, *Hist. eccl.* 4.22), together with Epiphanius's claim that Ebion had begun as a Nazoraean before starting his own *hairesis* (*Pan.* 1.30.1.1), however trustworthy in detail, seemed to some to reinforce the marginal status of "Judaizers" relative to apostolic Jewish Christianity. Such passages, along with Justin's distinction between observant Jews in the movement who insisted on Gentile observance and those who did not (*Dial.* 47)—and especially his own endorsement of fellowship with the latter but not the former—facilitated the translation of the normative distinction between legitimate and illegitimate Jewish Christians into the more sociological terms of "mainstream" or "Great Church" ones as opposed to marginal, schismatic, sectarian ones.[67] Taken together, these various interpretive moves appear as so many tips of an apologetic iceberg, elements in a historical narrative designed to neutralize Baur's assault on the traditional pillars of Christian authority: the apostolic community and its legacy in the New Testament. Actual Jewish observance aside, any failure to differentiate Christianity from Judaism in principle is removed to the fringes of both history and canon: so many multifarious misapprehensions of the transcendent Christianity authentically disclosed by Jesus and specially manifest in the apostolic church and its New Testament.

The Problems of Terminology and Definition

The identification of the apostolic sphere as a distinct subclass of Jewish Christianity placed problems of terminology and definition front and center in the scholarly discussion. While Baur didn't offer a formal definition of the category, its meaning in his work had been clear enough: Jewish Christianity was a fraction of early Christianity whose insistence on the importance of elements of Judaism for their own sake obscured the underlying "absolute consciousness" that constituted Christianity's unique status as "absolute religion."[68] Where both anti-Paulinists of the apostolic era and the postapostolic Ebionites and Nazoraeans were concerned, Baur's critics basically agreed. Each, in one way or another, was still viewed as having clouded an essential and distinctly Christian principle with unwarranted

Jewishness. The exemption of the apostles and the New Testament from this characterization, however, necessitated some methodological decisions. Either the apostolic sphere was not to be distinguished from Paul as Jewish Christianity at all, or the latter category had to be newly defined so as to include acceptable as well as unacceptable forms of Jewishness. While there were a few notable exceptions, it was the second alternative that became the most widely adopted. Scholars were thus forced to clarify this new taxonomy of Jewish Christianity, providing more specific terms and definitions in order to distinguish the licit Jewishness of the apostolic sphere from both the problematic Jewishness of the "Judaizers" on one hand and the analogously licit Jewish traits exhibited by Paul on the other. What was it that made Jewish Christianity, apostolic or otherwise, especially Jewish in a way that Paul was not? The problem of defining the category, centering on this question of parsing its Jewishness, quickly became notorious, and it has remained so ever since.

The production of more exacting terminology and definitions to replace Baur's more singular concept of Jewish Christianity is evident as early as 1844, in Adolph Schliemann's study of the Pseudo-Clementine literature. Like the later, more influential proponents of the post-Baur counternarrative, Schliemann was especially concerned to show that Ebionism, which he correlated with the Pseudo-Clementines, was neither a significant presence in the New Testament nor a central basis of early Catholicism.[69] Most fundamentally, he rejected the thesis—which he attributes, interestingly, to both Baur and Toland—that "the original Jewish Christianity, and thus the original form of Christianity" had been Ebionite.[70] In order to counter these claims, Schliemann argued that the Christianity of the original apostles, while distinctly "conditioned" by Judaism, was not, however, obscured by it, as was the Ebionite "error."[71] Accordingly, he criticized Baur's simple identification of Jewish Christianity with Ebionism and proposed in its place a more complex taxonomy of the category.

Like Baur, Schliemann assumes a correlation of primal Christianity with a certain "consciousness" or "faith" essentially distinct from a Judaism whose "external forms" were nonetheless initially maintained, and whose "manner of thought" (*Denkweise*), therefore, had at first "conditioned" it in an admittedly limiting way.[72] He also conceded that proto-Ebionite heretics (*Irrlehrer*) were to be found in the apostolic era and that even the apostles, at first, had clung to Jesus's "sensual appearance."[73] Unlike Baur, however, Schliemann posited an early and decisive turning point for Jesus's apostles as a result of "the outpouring of the Holy Spirit" on them at Pentecost. Their reception of this "spirit" represented "the beginning point of [the apostles'] deeper understanding of the essence of the Christian religion"—and later, as Schliemann saw it, ensured their underlying unity with Paul, regardless of any practical differences or even occasional tensions that may have risen between them.[74] In effect, then, what Baur had said of Jesus and Paul's relationship to Judaism, Schliemann extended to the Jewish Christianity of the early apostles as well: their Christianity was not so much obscured by Judaism as incarnate within it, even if in an inherently limiting way.[75] For Schliemann, the New Testament, containing writings by both Paul and the "Jewish Christian apostles," is indeed theologically diverse; but that diversity consists only in the multiplicity of forms in which the same underlying "Christian truth" was able to "reveal itself." Jewish Christian heresy, on the other hand—like other heresies—arose when such forms, "present in full purity in the New Testament writings," were subsequently developed in increasingly "one-sided, obscuring, and polluted" ways into more rigid types of thinking.[76] Identifying Baur's straightforward correlation of Jewish Christianity with Ebionism as a fatal step in the direction of a wrong-headed interpretation of the apostles, Schliemann thus drew a terminological distinction. The term "Jewish Christian" (*Judenchristen, judenchristlich*), he proposed, was to be used only with respect to Jewish ethnic derivation (*Abstammung*) and a particular conception (*Auffassung*) of Christianity that went along with it—one that was "conditioned" or even "constrained" by Judaism, but "not at all in a way that essentially clouds Christianity over." "Judaizing" or "Judaistic" (*judaisierende, judaistisch, judenzende*) Christianity, on the other hand, refers to a "line of thought" (*Richtung*) that "carries over into Christianity in an inappropriate way" one or more "clouding elements from Judaism."[77]

Ritschl agreed that the historical reconstruction of Jewish Christianity was hindered by terminological problems. In particular, he echoed Schliemann's criticism regarding the simple correlation of Jewish Christianity with Ebionism and, more to the point, the identification of the latter as "original Jewish Christianity."[78] He found Schliemann's proposed distinction, however, to be an inadequate parsing of the Jewishness of early Christianity, and on two counts. First, he argued, Schliemann's new categories were too broadly conceived to be analytically useful: even Paul and Barnabas would count as *Judenchristen* by Schliemann's definition, while early Catholicism, insofar as it fell back on Old Testament legalism, would count as "Judaistic" or "Judaizing" Christianity. Second, he said, Schliemann's normative distinction was insufficiently clear regarding what constitutes proper as opposed to improper Jewish influence on Christianity. Ritschl thus sought to improve on Schliemann's proposal by offering additional terminological distinctions with still more exacting definitions. In particular, he aimed to better clarify the difference between legitimate and illegitimate Jewishness in early Christianity by elucidating more specifically the basic "principle" (*Grundsatz*) underlying the disagreement between Paul—the implicit standard for legitimate Jewishness!—and his opponents.[79]

The result was a replacement of Schliemann's two categories with a fourfold distinction—and one, moreover, that basically reversed the meanings Schliemann had assigned to the terms *Judenchristenthum* and *judaistisch*. According to Ritschl, the core issue separating Paul from his opponents was essentially the latter's failure to recognize that Christianity was not Judaism. The basic principle of the anti-Pauline "line of thought" (*Richtung*), in a word, was the idea that "the law, which God has given through Moses, is also the essence of Christianity." Contrary to Schliemann, then, Ritschl assigned the compound term *Judenchristenthum* to this "line of thought" because "that name best expresses the identity of Judaism and Christianity."[80] As we have seen, Ritschl argued that the apostles, in contrast, continued to observe Jewish law for merely pragmatic reasons, quite despite their rejection of this principle. *Judenchristenthum* thus represented only one "species" of a larger category for which he used the uncompounded term *jüdisches Christenthum*. This larger category was not defined with reference to attachment to Judaism itself, but simply by observance of its law: a Christianity, once again, that was only "conditioned" by Judaism, if now more specifically "by a consideration for Jewish nationality and customs." This latter category, moreover, was to be further distinguished from the other, more general kinds of Jewish influence on Christianity, found in both Paul and early Catholicism, that Schliemann had called *Judenchristenthum* and that Ritschl thus now renamed *judaistisches Christenthum*.[81] This "Judaistic Christianity," finally, was to be kept analytically distinct from other forms of Christianity that were said to be simply *alttestamentlich*—that is, which merely exhibited forms of "Old Testament religion" (*alttestamentlichen Religion*) as opposed to apocalypticism and other features characteristic of postclassical Judaism.[82]

Matters of terminology and definition were no clearer or more uniform among Baur's British critics. Lightfoot likewise deployed an array of terms to the same end in his analysis of "St Paul and the Three," albeit without such overt concern for sharp or even explicit definition. "Jewish Christianity" seems to be the most comprehensive term, as when Lightfoot frames his general interest as "the relations between Jewish and Gentile Christianity in the first ages of the Church."[83] Problematically Jewish groups within that overarching category are differentiated as either "Judaizing" or "Judaic" and their religion as a "Judaic Christianity."[84] The term "Hebrew Christianity," in contrast, is apparently used to denote distinctly Jewish "thoughts and feelings" insofar as they are expressed within the pale of early Catholic orthodoxy.[85] F. J. A. Hort, in his posthumously published lectures on "the various stages in the emancipation of the church from the trammels of Judaism," was more explicit about the need for terminological distinctions to differentiate appropriate from inappropriate Jewishness in early Christianity.[86] Groups or texts deemed problematically Jewish—what Ritschl called *Judenchristenthum* and Lightfoot "Judaic Christianity"—are here distinguished as "Judaistic Christianity." Hort's definition of the term, moreover, placed special emphasis on the historicizing dimension of the counternarrative: "The only Christianity which can properly be called Judaistic is that which falls back to the Jewish point of view, belonging naturally to the time before Christ came ... It ascribes perpetuity to the Jewish Law, with more or less modification; thus confounding the conditions Providentially imposed for a time on the people of God when it was only a single nation ... confounding these Providential conditions with God's government of His people after its national limits were broken down and it had become universal." For this reason, he continued, "Judaistic Christianity, in this true sense of the term, might with at least equal propriety be called Christian Judaism." In contrast, the more general and generally acceptable types of Jewish influence on Christianity that Ritschl had called *jüdisches Christenthum* and Lightfoot "Hebrew Christianity" Hort somewhat hesitantly designated "Judaic" Christianity—thus assigning to this latter term the exact opposite meaning it had for Lightfoot. To make matters more confusing, the term "Jewish Christianity," though oddly unaddressed in Hort's otherwise exacting opening remarks on definition, is also used, apparently as a wider category encompassing all the others.[87]

By the early twentieth century, complaints about the elasticity and opacity of the category "Jewish Christianity" and the practical problems it posed for historical analysis had become all but standard in treatments of the subject, which nonetheless continued in a steady, ever-widening stream. None of the technical terminological distinctions proffered by the first generation of Baur's critics found any real traction, and the discussion returned largely to the singular term "Jewish Christianity" (*Judenchristentum*). Analyses routinely opened with programmatic statements of what should—and just as importantly, what should not—be included in the category. But the ongoing production of varying definitions only multiplied the confusion. Scholars continued to build analyses around differentiations of problematic from unproblematic Jewishness in early Christianity, and to correlate those differences with the traditional apologetic divisions restored by Baur's critics: original and apostolic versus subsequent and deviant; "mainstream" or "Great Church" versus partisan or sectarian; orthodox versus heretical; and New Testament versus noncanonical. Where they continued to differ, however, was in the translation of the underlying normative distinction into formal terms and definitions that could be used for purposes of historical analysis.

A few scholars responded to the resulting confusion by limiting the category once again to groups who were Jewish only in a problematic sense. Seeberg's definition of *Judenchristentum* as "the religious and moral mindset of Jewish national Christendom," while on the face of it reminiscent of Schliemann's broad use of the term, clarifies the relevant "mindset" as one that actually obscures the "essential content" of "original Christianity" by insisting on the necessity of Jewish religious forms.[88] Harnack was more adamant still. Assuming the same contrast between "original Christianity" (*das ursprüngliche Christenthum*) and Jewish Christianity (*Judenchristenthum*), Harnack insisted that the latter term "should be applied exclusively to those Christians who really maintained in their whole extent, or in some measure, even if it were to a minimum degree, the national and political forms of Judaism and the observance of the Mosaic law in its literal sense, as essential to Christianity, at least to the Christianity of born Jews, or who, though rejecting these forms, nevertheless assumed a prerogative of the Jewish people even in Christianity."[89] Harnack was particularly explicit in rejecting as entirely arbitrary the designation of general Jewish influence on Christianity as Jewish Christianity. "Christianity," he wrote, "took possession of the whole of Judaism as religion, and it is therefore a most arbitrary view of history which looks upon the Christian appropriation of the Old Testament religion, after any point, as no longer Christian, but only 'Jewish-Christian' ['*judenchristlich*,' with his scare quotes]. Wherever the universalism of Christianity is not violated in favour of the Jewish nation, we have to recognise every appropriation of the Old Testament [simply] as Christian."[90] For Harnack, then, the contrasting value invoked by the term "Jewish Christianity" is not "Gentile Christianity, but the Christian religion itself, in so far as it is conceived as universalistic and anti-national in the strict sense of the term . . . that is, the main body of Christendom in so far as it has freed itself from Judaism as a nation."[91]

Most, however, pursued the path forged by Baur's earlier critics, replicating the distinction Baur had drawn between incarnational (Jesus and Paul) and occlusionistic (Jewish-Christian) models of Christian Jewishness within the category of Jewish Christianity itself. Groups deemed problematically Jewish, in other words, were interpreted merely as marginal, deviant subsets of a more broadly conceived Jewish Christianity—a category now reformulated so as to ensure that inclusion of the apostles and the New Testament within it implied in no way that they were anything less than authentically Christian, which is to say anything more than accidentally Jewish. Gustav Hoennicke's *Das Judenchristentum* (1908), for example, was quite explicit in differentiating Christians of Jewish ancestry, even those with a certain "national feeling" for the Jewish people, from two types of Jewishness he found more troubling: an affirmation of "the bond between religion and nationality" that was so strong as to insist that salvation could be mediated only by Judaism, resulting in what he considered a "clouded formation of Christianity" (*getrübte Gestaltung des Christentums*); and more generally the presence of "Old Testament–Jewish elements within Christianity that were not in accord with the essence of the Gospel [*welche dem Wesen des Evangeliums nicht entsprechen*]." All three were nonetheless included within *Judenchristentum*, with the first of the problematic varieties specially marked out as a subclass by forms of the term *Judaismus* (*der jüdaistische Richtung, die Judaisten*, etc.).[92]

In the 1930s, Hugh Schonfield produced a significant variation on this approach, formulating the category broadly enough to encompass authoritative apostles, yet without the usual concern to differentiate them from a deviant "Judaizing" subset.[93] The diffuse (and ultimately undefined) category at the center of his ambitiously comprehensive *History of Jewish Christianity from the First to the Twentieth Century* was not, however, the result of an attempt to dislodge the concept of Jewish Christianity from Christian apologetics, but rather to repurpose it for a Christian apologetics of a new kind. At base, Schonfield's Jewish Christianity is construed as a category of ethnic descent, comprising not only the first followers of

Jesus and those later branded heretical by early Catholicism, but also all Jews throughout history who had ever been converted, willingly or unwillingly, to Christianity.[94] Implicit in this ostensibly ethnic category of Jewish *Christians*, however, is an assumption that a particular form of religion— a Jewish *Christianity*—was somehow transmitted in its collective members. For Schonfield, who was himself a Messianic Jew, grouping together all Jews, throughout history, who had ever been Christian in one sense or another under the singular heading of Jewish Christianity created a sense of unbroken continuity between an idealized apostolic past, romanticized as a "simpler faith in Christology," and his own present. He perceived that present, moreover, to be on the brink of an eschatological transformation: Jewish Christianity would be restored to its "original position of authority," resulting in a final healing of "old wounds" that had become more painfully evident than ever in Hitler's Germany.[95] Jewish Christianity, in Schonfield's hands, had come full circle, becoming once again what Toland created it to be in the first place: a rhetorical recasting of the dominant orthodoxy of his own day as an errant Gentile development, with his own position now in the role of primal, authoritative Christianity.[96]

The enduring legacy of Baur's concept of Jewish Christianity within the critical study of early Christianity was ensured less by his students than by his critics. Baur's central distinction between a Pauline Christianity that enlisted concepts from its Jewish environment to express a new and radically transcendent reality, and a Jewish Christianity that obscured that new reality by confusing an incidental Jewish medium with an essential Christian message, was accepted by Baur's chief critics as much as by his Tübingen School. Ritschl, Lightfoot, and other like-minded scholars did not reject Baur's theory of Jewish Christianity; they simply produced alternative histories of it. Underlying the varying details of these new accounts was a common counternarrative that restored the integrity and authority traditionally accorded to the apostolic and canonical spheres by revising Baur's theory at two critical junctures. First, the apostles, while superficially similar to Paul's "Judaizing" opponents in outward practice, were said to have been aligned with Paul, not with those opponents, in essential religious principle. Second, the "Judaizers" were said to have quickly become a nonfactor in the development of the early Catholic Church and thus to have had virtually no meaningful influence on the New Testament.

A few scholars concluded that the term "Jewish Christianity" therefore should not be used with reference to the apostles and the canon. Most, however, increasingly cognizant of both the apostles' generally Jewish character and their evident tensions with Paul, responded instead by drawing a categorical distinction within Jewish Christianity itself. The incarnational and occlusionistic models deployed by Baur to differentiate the Jewishness of Jesus and Paul from that of Jewish Christianity now became the basis for a distinction between apostolic and "Judaizing" varieties of Jewish Christianity itself. In effect, the conception of an early Jewish Christianity articulated by Morgan and Baur was placed alongside the one pioneered by Toland in what was now a twofold taxonomy of a Jewish Christianity in obscurant and incarnational varieties. The problem now was translating what was effectively a normative distinction into terms and definitions useful for a descriptive, historical analysis. Scholars scrambled to parse the various senses in which groups considered not-Jewish in essential principle might nonetheless be characterized as decidedly and distinctively Jewish for purposes of historical interpretation. The definition of Jewish Christianity quickly became a notorious problem. It has remained one ever since.

4 The Legacy of Christian Apologetics in Post-Holocaust Scholarship: Jean Daniélou, Marcel Simon, and the Problem of Definition

Jewish Christianity remained a central concept in twentieth-century accounts of the origins and development of Christianity and its relationship to Judaism. The meanings attached to the idea, however, continued to evolve. The rise and fall of Nazi Germany and the creation of the modern state of Israel lent new urgency to the critical reassessment of the historical relationship between Christians and Jews and, more abstractly, of Christianity to Judaism. Imagined as a site where the two religions had touched one another most profoundly, Jewish Christianity became a renewed focus of interest for Jewish and Christian scholars alike. The idea that "original Christianity"—that most charged of apologetic Christian concepts—had actually been a *Jewish* Christianity took on fresh resonances and rhetorical possibilities in this new climate.[1] Meanwhile, the critical approach to early Christianity pioneered by Baur continued to extricate itself from Christian theology. The assumption, common to both Baur and his critics, that Christianity was a uniquely valuable religion—and not least in comparison with Judaism—became increasingly muted in historical reconstructions. So too did appeals to the spiritual forces and authentic revelatory events that had long provided the basis for that assumption. In short, as critical reconstruction became less overtly Christian in orientation, the scholarly discourse around Jewish Christianity changed. The incarnational and occlusionistic models of Christianity's relationship to Judaism conveyed by the category in generations past were pushed increasingly below the surface. What had initially been formulated as a term of Christian apologetics was gradually transformed, over the course of the twentieth century, into an ostensibly neutral term of social history.

The result was a new phase in the debate about the definition of Jewish Christianity. Overt notions of Jewish taint on Christian purity—which now had a new and quite sinister resonance of their own—receded significantly into the background. Largely disappearing with such notions was the limitation of the category to groups and texts deemed Jewish in an occlusionistic sense, as in the work of Morgan, Baur, and Harnack. Debates about definition narrowed instead to the alternatives outlined by Ritschl. The tone was set when the French scholars Marcel Simon and Jean Daniélou, each in critical response to the work of Harnack, produced their own fresh analyses of Jewish Christianity—each, however, based on fundamentally different definitions. Simon, in a manner reminiscent of Ritschl's uncompounded *jüdisches Christenthum*, defined it strictly with reference to Torah observance.[2] Daniélou's iteration, on the other hand, was formulated along the lines of what Ritschl had called *judaistisches Christenthum*: *"the expression of Christianity in the thought-forms of Later Judaism."*[3] Over the next half-century, analyses of Jewish Christianity coalesced largely around one or the other of these two approaches. The already notorious confusion about what did and did not belong in the category was compounded as attempts to resolve problems inherent in both of these definitions yielded ever new and more exacting variations on each one. Reflecting much of the same underlying apologetic anxieties that had driven earlier generations, moreover, these efforts continued to correlate different types of Jewishness in the early Jesus movement with the same pregnant distinctions around which Baur's critics had built their response to the Tübingen School: primal and apostolic as opposed to deviant and Judaizing; moderate as opposed to radical and extremist; mainstream as opposed to partisan; Great Church as opposed to sectarian; orthodox as opposed to heretical; New Testament as opposed to extracanonical. The discussion came complete with a new round of proposals that different synonyms for "Jewish" be used to differentiate the various senses in which early Christianity might be said to have been such. The effective result was a replay—if in terms generally less overtly disdainful of Jews and Judaism—of nineteenth-century attempts to isolate the Jewishness of the early Jesus movement as an incidental attribute, ancillary to a more elemental Christianity assumed to lie beneath it.

What went largely unnoticed, however, was how fundamentally problematic this latter assumption had become. Up to now, its theoretical basis had been provided by apologetic Christian theology. Christianity, in the Christian imagination, was begotten into history by revelatory means, not made in it like any other instance of culture. The eclipse of Christian theology in critical reconstructions of early Jewish and Christian history, then, created a new problem. How was the existence of Christianity and its distinction from Judaism to be accounted for if not hierophanically? If the Jewishness of Jesus and the movement he inspired had become increasingly obvious, to whom was the making of Christianity to be attributed? Absent theology, what theory regarding the nature and origins of Christianity is at work in the redescription of the early Jesus movement as a Jewish *Christianity*? Through most of the twentieth century, such questions went largely unasked. That Christianity existed in some sense "from the beginning" of the movement—not during the life of the Jewish Jesus, to be sure, but somehow immediately in the wake of it—remained more routine assumption than critically contemplated thesis, neatly encapsulated within, and held firmly in place by, the very concept of Jewish Christianity itself. The problem that continued both to preoccupy and to stump scholars, therefore, was how to isolate and define this presumed Christianity's Jewishness. By the end of the twentieth century, the intractable nature of that problem was leading some to question whether Jewish Christianity was a useful category at all.

Jewish Christianity and Its Theology: Hans Joachim Schoeps and Jean Daniélou

The last major work to define Jewish Christianity strictly with reference to the Ebionites was Hans Joachim Schoeps's *Theologie und Geschichte des Judenchristentums* (*Theology and History of Jewish Christianity*).[4] A German Jew writing during a period of "involuntary leisure" as an emigrant to Sweden during Hitler's regime, Schoeps did not limit the category in this way out of any apparent concern to distinguish good from bad Jewishness in early Christianity. His intention was simply to avoid the confusion that resulted from categorizing all Christians of Jewish descent in terms of Jewish Christianity.[5] What had been for all intents and purposes a heresiological understanding of Jewish Christianity in the work of Baur, Seeberg, and Harnack was thus drained of its overtly normative and theological force and translated into the seemingly neutral terms of social history.

In Schoeps's hands, describing the Ebionites as "Jewish Christianity" did not signal a Jewish occlusion of some authentic Christianity, as for Harnack; nor, for that matter, the incarnation of such a Christianity in Jewish forms, as for Toland. Schoeps took over this concept, rather, simply to differentiate what he considered a sectarian form of early Christianity from the one comprised by the "Great Church."[6] So important was this sociological perspective, in fact, that Schoeps considered Jewish Christianity to be a postapostolic phenomenon insofar as the "radical" faction of anti-Paulinists of which it consisted did not actually separate themselves from the wider Christian community until after the Jewish revolt.[7] Indeed, even the so-called moderate group of "Christians of Jewish derivation" reported by Justin in the second century—that is, those who observed the law themselves but did not require the same of Gentiles—were now excluded from the category insofar as they remained, at least to some extent, in communion with the "Great Church." While now explained entirely on sociological grounds, the resulting category was nonetheless strikingly similar to Harnack's in several respects. Jewish Christianity represented a "radical" and "intransigent" form of Christianity, distinct by definition both from the apostolic community and from early Catholicism.[8] Explicitly normative or not, key structural elements of the apologetic Christian narratives about Jewish Christianity remained firmly in place.

Schoeps's primary impact on subsequent discussion of Jewish Christianity was in any case only indirect. While his limitation of the category to the Ebionites found little traction in post-Holocaust scholarship, his study did inspire in the Roman Catholic cardinal Jean Daniélou an "ambition to do for orthodox what Schoeps has already done for heterodox Jewish Christianity," namely, analyze its theology.[9] The result was a correlation of Jewish Christianity particularly with a certain type of theology: a Christianity expressed in Jewish forms of discourse. Definitions of the category along these lines would dominate the specialized literature on Jewish Christianity for most of the remainder of the twentieth century.[10]

If Schoeps's concept of Jewish Christianity as a radical, separatist form of Christianity was shaped by an apologetic historiography whose theological concerns were not his own, Christian theology and apologetics remained the clear and explicit foundation of Daniélou's analysis. Daniélou was particularly concerned to combat Harnack's view that Christian theology was a phenomenon "born from the union of the Gospel message and Greek philosophy"—a conclusion, from Daniélou's point of view, that had the "damaging consequence" of forcing a choice between what to him were two equally unappealing alternatives: "either the full Catholic faith did not develop until the fourth or fifth century or else . . . it must be assumed *a priori* to have been present in the earliest period in default of documentary evidence."[11] Daniélou escaped this dilemma in two basic moves. First, he defined theology as a response to genuinely revelatory events: "By Theology is here meant the attempt to construct a systematic world-view on the basis of the data provided by the divine events of the Incarnation and Resurrection of the Word . . . the product of reflection on the Revelation." Second, he identified the first historical phase of that "reflection"—that is, the phase "between the Incarnation and the emergence of Hellenistic theology"—as one that processed revelation not in Greek philosophical terms, but in "*the thought-forms of Later Judaism*": not a Hellenistic, but a Jewish Christianity.[12] From there, Daniélou was able to provide just the "documentary evidence" he needed to disprove the notion that "the complexities of orthodox doctrine, the teaching of the Great Church," was merely "a superstructure added to some simple basic Gospel by later centuries"; to demonstrate, conversely, that "in all major features the Christian faith in its most archaic expression was even then what it always has been."[13]

The result was an incarnational theory of Christian history structurally reminiscent of the one worked out a century earlier by Baur and intimated already in the early eighteenth century by Toland. Beneath historical Christianity and its developing theology lies a stable ontological reality radically transcendent of the various human cultures that have served over time and space as its vehicle. In Daniélou's work as much as in Baur's, this assumption provided the basis for the all-important assertion of an essential continuity between contemporary Christians and the ancient individuals claimed as their authoritative forebears. Seen from this perspective, the chief differences between Daniélou's general theory of Christian history and Baur's are two: first, Daniélou restored the traditional appeal to supernatural revelation that Baur had displaced in favor of a more humanistic revelatory consciousness; and second, it was now Roman Catholic orthodoxy, not Baur's liberal Protestantism, that was correlated with its timeless essence.

Inevitably, this model of Jewish Christianity had normative and even teleological implications. In Daniélou's view, "archaic" Jewish Christian theology, while entirely orthodox, nonetheless "suffered from serious limitations in its terminology and in some of its conclusions." It was, in short, "an incomplete expression of Christian truth" that was later superseded "by a more adequate instrument"—which is to say, the "more comprehensive understanding" afforded by the discourses of other cultural complexes, culminating ultimately in Daniélou's own Roman Catholicism.[14] If this theorized process—though not, of course, its historical conclusion!—is reminiscent of Baur's *History of Dogma*, Daniélou's reinstatement of supernatural revelation as the foundation of Christianity's transcendent essence resulted in a clearer boundary between orthodoxy and heresy than Baur's humanistic formulation allowed. According to Daniélou, it was precisely the inherent "defects" of Jewish Christianity's conceptual apparatus that "exposed it to heresies and misinterpretations which vitiated its usefulness as a vehicle of salvation." In Daniélou's reckoning, moreover, such heresies—which is to say, the very sectarian groups that in Schoeps's view represented Jewish Christianity in the strict sense—were only marginal to the category at best. These "heretical Jewish Christian sects," he said, "sprang up in abundance" only later, around "the tradition of the Great Church" that had itself been there "from the beginning." If this much is reminiscent of Schoeps, Daniélou seems only grudgingly to consider such groups as "Jewish Christianity" at all. Less a development of "archaic Christian theology" than a "continuation of heterodoxies in Judaism," such heresies, he said, are of interest to the history of theology—that is, theology in Daniélou's technical sense of a "product of reflection on Revelation"—only "in so far as they preserve certain elements which they *had in common with Jewish Christianity*."[15]

The Impact of Daniélou: Problems and Attempted Refinements

Daniélou's theory of an original Christianity expressed in Jewish "thought forms" struck a major chord in the second half of the twentieth century. A concept of Jewish Christianity in which Christianity and Judaism, if fundamentally different, were nonetheless originally compatible furnished a much more irenic paradigm of Jewish-Christian relations for a post-Holocaust era than Schoeps's sectarian model, let alone the theory of Jewish taint on Christian purity postulated by Baur and Harnack.[16] Its overtly theological basis, however, drew remarkably little notice. In fact, while some of Daniélou's followers continued his explicit appeal to superhuman forces, most simply appropriated his formulation of the category as a matter of course. Supernatural revelation or not, the idea that Jewish discourse, where Jesus groups were concerned, was merely the temporary vehicle of a deeper and more fundamental Christianity subsequently passed on to later Christians for translation into new cultural forms was more routine assumption than conscious, critically contemplated thesis. Indeed, the incarnational character of Daniélou's notion of a transcendent Christianity in

Jewish "thought forms" seems hardly to have registered at all, even among his critics, who focused more on problems in the practical application of Daniélou's broad definition than on its theoretical viability for anything other than an apologetic Christian historiography.[17] Here again it was the Jewishness of Jewish Christianity that was understood to demand further clarification, not its Christianity.

The practical problems, at any rate, were quickly recognized. As one follower of Daniélou observed, it now became "impossible to define the term 'Jewish-Christian' because it proved to be a name that can readily be replaced by 'Christian'"—at least where the first generations of the movement were concerned.[18] The analytical uselessness of what had become in effect a category of the whole, recognized as much by those who embraced Daniélou's formulation as by those who did not, soon became the chief complaint against it. Undaunted, Daniélou's followers sought to rectify the problem by introducing analytical subdivisions within the more general category. The end result, predictably, was a proliferation of idiosyncratic taxonomies and definitions and a "terminological chaos" that only added to the already notorious confusion surrounding the category.[19]

Such subdivisions, moreover, largely fell back on the same apologetically loaded distinctions introduced already in the nineteenth century by Baur's critics. Most common were the basic genealogical, theological, and sociological divisions assumed by Daniélou himself: an apostolic and orthodox "main stream" versus nonapostolic and heterodox sects.[20] These were elaborated, however, in new and various ways. Johannes Munck, "attempt[ing] to reach a clearer usage of the term Jewish Christianity," in his presidential address to the *Societas Novi Testamenti Studiorum* in 1959, further correlated these distinctions with ethnic and temporal ones in a way that bolstered the thesis of a special continuity between the apostolic sphere and later orthodoxy. What Daniélou treated simply as "orthodox Jewish Christianity," Munck argued, actually should be separated into two distinct subcategories: a "Primitive Jewish Christianity" that "perished with the destruction of Jerusalem in A.D. 70," and a "post-apostolic Gentile Church" that was only *"Jewish-Christian in the sense that its founders were Jewish-Christian apostles such as Paul, and . . . therefore possessed a tradition that contained Jewish elements."*[21] Heretical Jewish Christianity, on the other hand, represented a deviant offshoot not of "Primitive Jewish Christianity," but of "the post-apostolic Gentile Church." These heretical "so-called Jewish Christians," Munck argued, were a "new type" of Jewish Christianity that had "no connexion" to the original, apostolic one at all. In effect, then, Munck linked Gentile orthodoxy directly to the apostolic sphere while severing a heretical Jewish Christianity decisively from it.[22] An analogous (if somewhat less absolute) distinction between early and later Jewish Christianities was similarly foundational to Longenecker's analysis in *The Christology of Early Jewish Christianity*, which further complicated the picture by formally excluding Pauline Christianity from early Jewish Christianity in a way that Munck did not.[23]

Not surprisingly, such divisions were further correlated, again as in the nineteenth century, with the distinction between canonical and non-canonical Christian texts. This too, however, only exacerbated the confusion about what exactly Jewish Christianity was. In marked contrast to Daniélou's study, scholars like Longenecker and Munck came to consider the New Testament itself, as Robert Murray put it, as "the supreme monument of Jewish Christianity," at least in its "early" and "orthodox" form.[24] Klijn, meanwhile, drew from the same series of divisions precisely the opposite conclusion. The proper subject matter of "Jewish Christianity," he argued, is not the New Testament at all, but "the presence, the origin, the development and the disappearance" of a "Jewish influence" on Christianity precisely "*apart from the many ideas already adopted in the New Testament and taken over by ecclesiastic writers of a later date.*" The term "Jewish Christianity," in other words, should be reserved for groups and texts that are Jewish in ways beyond which "the Apostolic Church and later orthodoxy were able to accept."[25]

A number of scholars attempted to rein in the ever-growing chaos surrounding the category by suggesting—as Baur's critics had done a century before—that different synonyms for "Jewish" be assigned to different heads of the hydra. Stanley Riegel proposed that the term "Jewish Christianity" be reserved for the "canonical" and "apostolic" expression of Christianity "in Semitic-Jewish thought-forms." The mainly postapostolic, "heterodox" groups "who, in contrast to Jewish Christianity, over-emphasized the Judaistic character of Christianity almost to the exclusion of the Christian aspect," on the other hand, were differentiated as a "Judaistic" or "Judaic Christianity." The overarching category that included all this, finally, was to be called "Judaeo-Christianity."[26] Robert Murray published two separate proposals of his own that differed not only from Riegel's, but seemingly from one another. In an initial article he argued first that Daniélou's category should be rendered "Judaeo-Christianity" in order to differentiate it from "Jewish Christianity" as "the sociological phenomenon of Jews who were Christians."[27] Some years later, he proposed a more complex, fourfold distinction between the "Jewish" and "Hebrew" Christianities purportedly reflected in the apostolic period and canonical texts, and the "Judaistic" and "Hebraistic" Christianities of "the Sub-Apostolic Church."[28] Bruce Malina, meanwhile, pointedly observing that "Jewish Christianity" had become a "rubber bag term, applied to a host of phenomena yet saying nothing with any clarity about the phenomena that would warrant this specific label," proposed a "hypothetical" distinction of his own. Like Riegel, he used the term "Jewish Christianity" to describe the "historically perceived orthodox Christianity that undergirds the ideology of the Great Church." This, he argued, was to be distinguished from a "Christian Judaism" that represented a *"tertium quid* between the Judaism of the post 70 A.D. world and the Christianity of the Great Church."[29] Even among those who embraced Daniélou's definition of Jewish Christianity as a Christianity incarnate in Jewish "thought forms," the meaning and historical referents of the category were as variable as ever.

Jewish Christianity and the Parting of the Ways: Marcel Simon

Marcel Simon was among those who responded to the confusion by suggesting that different technical terms be used for various types of Jewish phenomena found among early Jesus groups. A decade before Daniélou, Simon had produced his own account of Jewish Christianity. Here, however, the category was defined with reference to Torah observance, not theology. Simon's interest in Jewish Christianity, as part of a larger study of ancient Jewish and Christian relations, was first and foremost social-historical. Like Schoeps, he took over what was by then a generally assumed category with little or no regard for the apologetic theology that had produced it. On the other hand, Simon did not account for the existence of Christianity in the absence of that theology; the distinction between Christianity and Judaism, for his purposes, was simply assumed as a given. Consequently, when subsequently faced with Daniélou's alternative definition, Simon did not reject it in theory so much as question its analytical utility in practice. Such a definition, he pointed out, was "paradoxical and productive of confusion" insofar as it had the logical consequence of including "even the Marcionites" as Jewish Christianity. In the end, he simply renamed a refined version of Daniélou's concept "Semitic Christianity" in order to distinguish it from his own preferred understanding of Jewish Christianity as a class defined strictly with reference to observance of Jewish law.[30] When, by the 1990s, the majority of specialized studies had come to agree that Daniélou's definition was too broad to be useful, it was Simon's law-oriented approach that became the chief alternative.[31]

Simon's analysis of Jewish Christianity was part of a broader reconsideration of early Jewish-Christian relations produced in response to the rise of anti-Semitism in the early twentieth century.[32] Christian anti-Judaism was abetted by a narrative of Christian origins—reflected as much in the critical scholarship of Baur as in that of his critics—in which a stagnant and sanctimonious Judaism was replaced on the world stage by a spiritually vibrant and morally superior Christianity. Horrified particularly by policies enacted against Jews in Nazi Germany, academics responded by recasting the early history of Jewish-Christian relations in less starkly adversarial terms. The notion of a zero-sum replacement of a bankrupt religion by the perfect one gave way to the more potentially ecumenical metaphor of a sibling rivalry: competing "brothers" that grew up together before gradually—and mutually—"parting ways."[33] Published immediately in the wake of the Holocaust, Simon's groundbreaking analysis of Jewish-Christian relations in the era between the Bar Kochba rebellion and the demise of the Jewish Patriarchate in 425 CE gave powerful voice to this new historical model—and placed a concept of "Jewish Christianity" squarely at its center.

Simon was particularly concerned with the widespread and "unacknowledged assumption," exemplified especially in Harnack's work, that Christianity and Judaism, "developing on radically divergent lines, very quickly ceased to take any interest in each other . . . so that there was not the least occasion for contact between the two."[34] His central aim was to demonstrate that meaningful social interaction continued to occur between Christians and Jews for centuries, even after Christianity and Judaism had become separate religions. The historical disappearance of a "Hellenistic and universalistic" Judaism, he argued, did not result from the failed wars with Rome but was a Jewish strategy of self-preservation adopted only in response to Christianity's eventual rise to imperial power in the fourth century. Up until then, Judaism had remained "a real, active, and often successful competitor with Christianity" in a relationship defined not merely by a "conflict of orthodoxies" but by "contact and assimilation" beyond and quite despite them.[35] For Simon, the ongoing existence of Jewish Christianity in late antiquity was prime evidence that "contacts resulting in syncretism" between the two continued well into the Christian imperial era.[36]

As these outlines suggest, Simon's interest in Jewish Christianity was more social-historical than theological. His primary objective was to re-describe the social realities of Jewish-Christian relations in late antiquity. Quite unlike Daniélou, then, he neither cultivated the dogmatic notion of a transcendent, ontological Christianity nor showed any overt concern to en-sure historical continuity between modern Christians and their claimed ap-ostolic authorities.[37] Jewish Christianity is conceived first and foremost in sociological terms, as "a body midway between Church and Synagogue."[38] The historical emergence of Christianity as a religion distinct from Juda-ism, while more presupposition than concern of the study, is framed in similarly social terms. Rather than emphasizing new, divine revelations or even theological generalizations about Jewish particularism and Christian universalism, Simon focused above all on the "split" as it occurred on the ground. The separation of Christianity from Judaism, he noted, "came into being gradually, and at different rates in different places," with a final, deci-sive separation coming only as a result of institutional developments in the wake of the Bar Kochba rebellion—specifically, in the form of an "eccle-siastical organization . . . being laid down and made uniform" in Catholic Christianity on one hand and the Roman recognition of the Jewish Patri-archate on the other.[39]

Nonetheless, Simon's account of Jewish Christianity, like Schoeps's before him, did not so much displace the theological apologetics of his predecessors as simply push them below the surface. This is nowhere more evident than when Simon conceptualizes even the era preceding the insti-tutional separation of Christianity from Judaism as "Jewish Christianity" and is thus forced to wrestle with the definitional problem that results. "In the first Palestinian community," he writes, "Jewish Christianity and nor-mative Christianity were hardly to be distinguished, for until the preach-ing of St. Stephen and St. Paul, Jewish Christianity was the only kind of Christianity in existence." Given that this was an era, by Simon's own ac-count, in which "the Church" did not yet exist as a reality distinct from "the Synagogue," there is obviously something more at work in his idea of "Jewish Christianity" than simply a sociological identification of a group "midway between Church and Synagogue." Rejecting any "ethnic" criteria for the category, Simon argues that the term should have the "strictly re-ligious" sense of "Christians who continued to mix their religion with elements drawn from Judaism, and in particular, who went out of their way to observe all or part of the ritual law." The problem, as he himself perceptively observed, centered precisely around this notion of a "mixing" of distinct religions. "If we say simply that Jewish Christianity is a combination of elements drawn from Judaism with those derived from Christianity," he notes, "we shall find different interpreters, applying different criteria, affixing the label to very different articles. How are we to decide, in the context of early Christianity, what is originally and specifically Christian and what is drawn secondarily from Judaism?" Simon recognizes, in fact, that this whole exercise is the function of an ongoing Christian heresiology. "For the scholars of the Catholic Church, from the second century onward, Jewish Christianity was no more than a heretical body outside the pale of orthodoxy. By contrast, in Marcion's view the whole Catholic Church was Jewish Christian . . . Some of our present-day racist ideologies, venturing into the field of theology or religious history, similarly repudiate all existing forms of Christianity, Catholic and Protestant, as tainted with Judaism." Despite these provocative observations, Simon offers no alternative. His solution is simply to dismiss the Marcionite view as a historical curiosity and to adopt as established practice a definition of "Jewish Christianity with reference to the Catholic Church and with deference to the Catholic point of view." Though stripped of its normative theological basis in principle, the traditional heresiological framework remains firmly in place in practice.[40]

The question that remains unasked is why, in the absence of the dogmatic presuppositions of Christian apologetics, we should still be assuming that the early Jesus movement represented any such combination of disparate religions in the first place. Distinguishing "what is originally and specifically Christian" from "what is drawn secondarily from Judaism" is only a problem on the assumption that there *was* in fact something fundamentally not Jewish at the generative heart of the Jesus movement from the start: a Christianity that rendered its otherwise obvious Jewishness secondary. This, as we have seen, is an apologetic claim as old as the idea of Christianism itself, and the central assumption on which the whole notion of an early Jewish Christianity rests.[41] In early critical historiography, as in the subsequent analysis of Daniélou, its theoretical justification was supplied by the claim that a reality transcendent of culture—whether conceived in traditional terms of supernatural revelation or in the more humanistic idioms of radically transcendent religious consciousness or natural law—was at work among the early Jewish groups who laid claim to the authority of Jesus of Nazareth. Simon, focusing primarily on the social realities of human relationships, makes no such appeal. But without it, the rationale for the continued assumption that there was something fundamentally not Jewish about the early Jesus movement from the beginning entirely evaporates.

Comparison with Munck's subsequent characterization of "primitive Jewish Christianity" as an analogous "blend" of distinct religions is instructive. Munck's treatment, like Simon's, is devoid of any explicit theology. Unlike Simon, however, Munck is quite transparently eager to preserve the apologetic notion of an authoritative primal Christianity. Criticizing the idea that "circumcision and observance of the Mosaic Law" were "the distinguishing marks" of "primitive Jewish Christianity," Munck objects that if that were the case we would "have a religion that does not take its rise in Jesus but . . . becomes Christianity only by a *metabasis eis allo genos*." Far from having been subject to any such change of species, Munck insists, Jesus groups were essentially different from Judaism "from the start": "But if Christianity had a character of its own from the beginning, we get a historically probable blend of Jewish and Christian elements, in which the decisive factor is Jesus Christ, *and which is therefore from the start a new religion, Christianity*."[42]

Much is left unsaid in this highly compressed argument. It is far from obvious from a sociological perspective why a Jewish charismatic leader like Jesus might not be equally well—or even better!—understood as having inspired a Jewish movement. Clearly Munck's driving concern is to ensure that Jesus was a sufficiently "decisive factor" for those who followed him. But why we should expect Jesus to have been somehow more "decisive" for his followers than any of the various other charismatic leaders of ancient Palestine were for theirs is not explained.[43] Nor is it apparent why such "decisiveness," whatever that might mean, should in any event lead us logically ("therefore") to the conclusion that the resulting movement represented a "species" other than Judaism. The Dead Sea sect, for example, clearly differentiated themselves from other Judeans by all manner of peculiar beliefs, practices, and social institutions as a result of their faith in a revelatory "Teacher of Righteousness." And yet no interpreter, as far as I know, assumes that this faith represented something inherently not-Jewish, let alone the essence of a new religion ultimately transcendent of (even if still "within") Judaism.

Munck's argument calls to mind yet another similar formulation made a decade later by Longenecker: "In relation to Judaism, it was the allegiance of the earliest believers to Jesus, and the implications arising from their early commitment to him as Messiah and Lord, which set Jewish Christians apart as something more than just sectarians of or schismatics from the established faith [of Judaism]." If this statement of the matter is in itself no more probative than Munck's, Longenecker's claim is rendered more comprehensible by the explicit appeal elsewhere in his study to the genuinely revelatory character of the "Christ-event" as the decisive factor in Christian origins.[44] It is difficult to avoid the conclusion that analogous spiritual forces—or at the very least, romantic notions of the special uniqueness of Jesus or the "faith" he inspired in his followers—continue to haunt historical interpretations of Christian origins in these works, even as overt theology has been removed to the margins.[45] The result in any event is a perpetuation of the basic narrative of Christian apologetic historiography and a mystifying gloss of the nature and origins of Christianity as something other than Judaism.

Much as for Munck and Longenecker, the implication of Simon's concept of Jewish Christianity is that the essential—and essentially not-Jewish—core of the Jesus movement was precisely its "faith in Jesus."[46] The Pauline ring of this formulation is hardly accidental. According to Simon's later clarification, it was in fact Paul who marked the first moment at which "Jewish Christianity and Christianity ceased to be coextensive."[47] It is Paul, therefore, who serves as Simon's chief exemplum when he argues against the inclusion of an ethnic criterion in the definition of Jewish Christianity; for unlike other Jews in the Jesus movement "whose religion remained mixed with Jewish elements," he says, "Jews such as St. Paul . . . on being converted to Christianity broke all ties with their ancestral religion."[48] The implication is that Paul represents in pure, unalloyed form a Christianity that before him had been "mixed" with Judaism;[49] that Paul's piety, therefore, is to be characterized less in terms of cultural invention than simply a more penetrating insight into what had already been the essential nature of the Jesus movement from the start—whether anyone else in the group had known it or not![50] This was precisely the central thesis of Morgan and Baur, and the point of departure for their own notions of an early Jewish Christianity. As we have seen, the same premise was also accepted by Baur's critics, who rejected only the idea that the apostolic "mix" represented an actively obscurant religious syncretism as opposed to a purely pragmatic response to ephemeral civic and cultural circumstance.[51] By the time we get to Simon, what had begun as an attempt by freethinkers to claim the mantle of "original Christianity" for their Enlightenment values had become the subterranean foundation of a critical study of ancient social history. Though its dogmatic underpinnings are muted, the basic apologetic framework remains firmly in place, neatly encapsulated in the notion of an early Jewish Christianity.

This interpretive framework guides not only Simon's narrative of the apostolic era, but of postapostolic history as well. This is most clearly evident in his handling of the key matter of change over time, which is construed differently in the case of Catholic orthodoxy than that of heretical groups. Where Catholic Christianity is concerned, new developments—and not least those that distinguished early Catholicism from what Simon calls Jewish Christianity—are interpreted along the same lines as Paul. Such developments are less a matter of cultural invention than merely refinements of something implicit in the apostolic community from the start: a more complete "consciousness," as Simon puts it, of Christianity's "originality" and "universal mission."[52] New developments in groups classed as Jewish Christianity, on the other hand, are interpreted in markedly different terms. As "other manifestations of Christian life and thought that did not stem so directly from the original apostolic form of Christianity," they were not the result of any analogous insights, but rather of ongoing "syncretisms" beyond even the "mixing" already imagined in the apostolic era.[53] Conversely, to the extent that postapostolic "Jewish Christianity" was more similar to the apostolic community than to early Catholicism, its apparent continuity is interpreted as a failure to properly mature. The Ebionites shared some "elements of orthodox dogma" but "in an incomplete and, as it were, stunted form"—a "backward stage of doctrinal development" that rendered them "heretics, so to speak, by omission."[54] Even if Simon's "deference to the Catholic point of view" was purely methodological rather than principled, the result is the same. The early history of the Jesus movement continues to be narrated in a heresiological Christian mode.

Simon's Definition Problem

Simon's continued analysis of the early Jesus movement, even if only for analytical purposes, through lenses fashioned by Christian apologetics served among other things to perpetuate the problem of defining Jewish Christianity. As already observed, it is only on the assumption that there was something fundamentally not Jewish at the heart of the early Jesus movement that renders its otherwise apparent Jewishness in need of special dissection and definition. If critical analysis of Jewish groups contemporary with it, like the Dead Sea sect or the Pharisees, for example, has not been bogged down by an analogous preoccupation, it is only because no analogous assumption is at work in their interpretation. What, on the contrary, is *not* Jewish about them? The different presumption where Jesus and the apostles are concerned is a function of one of the oldest and most fundamental of all Christian apologetic claims: that the values uniquely definitive of Christianity, however exactly or inexactly specified, are essentially identical to, and thus authorized by, the first-century values of Jesus and the apostles. Much as for the early apologists who found "Christians" among the venerable heroes of ancient Israel and Athens, the terms "Christian" and "Christianity" are themselves key ciphers for such claims of authorizing continuity. And insofar as Christianity represents something that is not Judaism, claiming the apostles for Christianity virtually demands that any Jewish traits exhibited by them but not by later Christians be specially accounted for, not least in light of competing claims on their authority by rival groups like the Ebionites. The theory of an early Jewish Christianity represented a new, Enlightenment-era strategy for the negotiation of this old problem: the interpretation of the Jewishness of Jesus and the apostles as ancillary cultural flesh that variously revealed and concealed a more fundamental and radically transcendent Christianity. Whether supported by overt theological dogma or not, the concept of Jewish Christianity guides the interpreter to analyze early Jesus groups through Christian eyes, separating out "Jewish" traits as secondary to "Christian" ones—either as borrowed "forms" in which the latter were initially couched, or as holdovers with which they had been "mixed," in some cases as obscuring syncretisms. The problem of defining Jewish Christianity, as Simon himself seems to have intuited, is nothing other than the problem of drawing these imaginary lines.

The alternative—namely, to treat the whole idea of a distinct Christianity as the partisan invention of certain localized Jesus groups—apparently did not occur to Simon. He thus continued to ruminate on the problem of defining Jewish Christianity for decades, not least in conversation with Daniélou's influential formulation.[55] Considering the identification of the Christian component of the perceived "synthesis" to be relatively straightforward, Simon struggled particularly "to define the dose of Judaism necessary in order for a Christian to be labeled a 'Jewish Christian.'"[56] As noted above, he did not so much reject Daniélou's theological definition as simply accept it (with some refinements) as a rather less helpful alternative: a "broad sense" of Jewish Christianity he half-heartedly suggested renaming "Semitic Christianity" in order to distinguish it from his own "more precise" formulation.[57] He remained firm at any rate in his insistence that "the safest criterion, if not absolutely the only one" for defining Jewish Christianity was observance of Jewish law. For it was this, he argued, that not only created divisions between Paul and others in the apostolic era, but was actually denounced as "Judaizing" by subsequent Catholic writers like Chrysostom. Indeed, explicitly disallowing additional considerations of ethnicity or theology as inherently problematic, Simon continued to argue that observance of the law should in fact be the *sole* criterion of Jewish Christianity in what he considered the proper sense of the term.[58]

This did not, however, resolve his "dosage" problem. Defining Jewish Christianity strictly with reference to Torah observance rendered it effectively synonymous with the ancient notion of "Judaizing," albeit now reified as a syncretizing subclass of Christianity.[59] As used by early Christians, however, "Judaizing" was less a descriptive term than a normative, polemical one. It was invoked particularly in situations of inner-group conflict, by people with ambivalent attitudes toward what they called "Judaism," to marginalize competing values as being incompatible with those that should "truly" define the group.[60] Apart from arbitrarily picking a side in ancient squabbles, then, it is far from obvious where—let alone why—historians should draw the magic line between behaviors that are "Judaizing" and those that are "properly Christian." Faced with this problem, Simon simply deferred once again to "the official position of the Church on the question of Jewish observance"—specifically in the form of the so-called Apostolic Decree—as "the line of demarcation between the normal [!] type of Christian and the Jewish Christian."[61] His definition, in other words, normalized the partisan lenses of one early group as the methodological starting point for the analysis of others, and indeed for the whole history of the Jesus movement more generally.

While narrower than Daniélou's category on the face of it, Simon's approach nonetheless resulted in a similarly diffuse category, encompassing no less than three quite distinct phenomena. First was what Simon considered the "classical form" of Jewish Christianity: "the successor in Palestine of the primitive Christian community" whose Torah observance, correlated with an "incomplete and, as it were, stunted form" of Catholic orthodoxy, marginalized them as Ebionites. More important to Simon's own project,

on the other hand, was "a second form of Jewish Christianity, more difficult by nature to pin down and define": those within the Catholic Church
who did "not form themselves into independent bodies" but, whether Jews
or Gentiles, simply "took it upon themselves to keep some of the Mosaic rules." There were also, finally, the "motley assembly" of "syncretizing
sects" whose assimilationist tendencies resulted in doctrines as far removed
from Catholic orthodoxy as from "the doctrinal poverty of the Ebionites."[62]
What is more, the specification of the Apostolic Decree as the boundary
marker between Jewish and "normal" Christianity eventually led Simon to
introduce the supplementary idea of a "mixed Jewish Christianity" (*judéo-
christianisme mitigé*) in order to account for the *Didascalia*, which rejected
some elements of Jewish law as *deuterōsis* while continuing to endorse others beyond the requirements of Acts 15.[63]

The situation became still more complex as Simon's definition eventually came to displace Daniélou's "thought forms" model as the dominant
approach in the specialized literature on Jewish Christianity. Attempts to
resolve its own inherent problems resulted in yet another round of competing definitions, this time as so many variations on the law-oriented approach. While some scholars took over Simon's definition more or less as
it stood, others began introducing their own more and less idiosyncratic
modifications.[64] Gerd Luedemann, while giving unqualified endorsement
to Simon's definition in principle, considered anti-Paulinism to be a sufficient criterion for inclusion in the category in practice in the apostolic era
and an indication of at least a "Jewish-Christian past" for groups and texts
of subsequent generations.[65] Others continued to wrestle with the "dosage" problem, offering different suggestions regarding the specific types
of Jewish observance required for inclusion in the category.[66] More consequential departures resulted as still others, observing problems arising
from a singular focus on Jewish practice, began introducing additional criteria—including those that Simon had explicitly rejected. Some, blending
the approaches of Simon and Daniélou, defined the Jewishness of Jewish
Christianity with reference to Torah observance in combination either with
a distinctly "Jewish structure of theology"[67] or with more general "traditions . . . maintaining the 'symbolic world' of Jewish thought."[68] Others,
in order to distinguish ethnically Jewish Christians from Gentile "Judaizers," reintroduced Jewish descent as a key criterion,[69] effectively excluding
from the category precisely the phenomenon Simon had considered "the
most important manifestation [of Jewish Christianity] of all."[70] F. Stanley

Jones, meanwhile, drawing a temporal distinction between "Earliest Jewish Christianity" and "Early Jewish Christianity," introduced yet another criterion of "genetic relationship" that pared the category down even further to what Simon had considered only its "classical form." "Earliest Jewish Christianity" represented "the body of Jews who soon confessed Jesus as the Messiah," while "Early Jewish Christianity," as "*one* development out of" it, combined "confession of Christ" with "Jewish observance" in "some sort of direct genetic relationship to earliest Jewish Christianity."[71] James Carleton Paget, rejecting all these aforementioned criteria, removed "Judaizers" from the category by means of a sociological criterion reminiscent of Schoeps: in contrast to the "more haphazard and unstructured" character of Judaizers, "Jewish Christians formed coherent groups."[72]

Generally unnoticed was the fact that this law-based definition of Jewish Christianity did not in any event escape the chief criticism its proponents (somewhat ironically) leveled at Daniélou's definition, which is to say the analytical uselessness of a category that is functionally coextensive with early Christianity in general. As its advocates effectively concede, the problem is no less inherent in the law-based definition than the theological one. The only real difference is the duration of the period in which the tautology remains in effect. "In the first Palestinian community," Simon wrote, "Jewish Christianity and normative Christianity were hardly to be distinguished, for until the preaching of St. Stephen and St. Paul, Jewish Christianity was the only kind of Christianity in existence."[73] Subsequent reformulations have been equally explicit. According to Jones, "*Early* Jewish Christianity," to be sure, is only "one development out of earliest Christianity." That being said, "earliest Jewish Christianity is equivalent to the body of Jews who soon confessed Jesus as the Messiah and thus to all of earliest Christianity."[74] David Horrell, rejecting ethnic and theological definitions as being "too broad to be useful," acknowledges nonetheless that "at the time of its origins, all of what we now call Christianity was Jewish Christianity." "In the beginning," Carleton Paget writes, "all Christianity was Jewish Christianity." "With respect to origin," Stemberger similarly avers, "the whole Church is Jewish-Christian."[75]

As Annette Yoshiko Reed has observed, however, "it seems almost superfluous to speak of 'Jewish Christianity' in the first century CE, and it seems strange to limit 'Jewishness' to only one group or stream of the Jesus Movement."[76] This problem led some advocates of Simon's general approach to complicate matters further by introducing chronological caveats limiting particular definitions of Jewish Christianity, if not the category itself, to the postapostolic era. As noted above, Carleton Paget introduced a sociological criterion in order to distinguish separate, identifiably "Jewish Christian" groups from the more haphazard phenomenon of so-called Judaizing. Recognizing, however, that "it is by no means clear that Jewish Christians, as defined [by Torah observance], were always 'extra ecclesiam,' or indeed, for that matter, 'outside Judaism'" in the earliest era of the movement, Carleton Paget conceded, in a manner reminiscent of Schoeps, that this sociological criterion was "only valid from perhaps the second part of the second century onwards."[77] Simon Claude Mimouni similarly qualified his definition by saying that the Jewish Christianity it accounted for "was not exactly that of the first century"—or, as he put it in the initial version of the relevant essay, "that of the New Testament." Defining Jewish Christianity in the case of these latter, he said, was unnecessary insofar as Christianity in general, in their case, was still "within Judaism."[78]

Such caveats, however, only served to underscore the larger and still unresolved problems surrounding the category itself. If the idea of a Jewish Christianity is anachronistic in the context of the earliest era of the Jesus movement, in what terms *can* we analyze that period? Does the anachronism reside in interpreting such groups as Jewish, or—as historians had long come to conclude with respect to Jesus—interpreting them as Christianity? How is the historical emergence of Christianity and its distinction from Judaism to be modeled in the void left by the evacuation of Christian apologetics from critical historiography? Even in the context of the second century, does categorizing particular groups as "Jewish Christianity" do anything other than affirm and normalize the heresiological perspective of their early Catholic rivals?

Jewish Christianity or Torah-Observant Christians?

Given these ongoing problems, it is hardly surprising that by the end of the twentieth century a few voices had begun to raise questions about the viability of the category "Jewish Christianity" at all. A first step in this direction was taken already in the 1980s in a brief but widely cited article by Raymond Brown called "Not Jewish Christianity and Gentile Christianity but Types of Jewish/Gentile Christianity."[79] Brown's essential point was that the typical scholarly slippage from an ethnic distinction between Jewish and Gentile *Christians* to an assumption of "two types of *Christianity*"—

namely, Jewish and Gentile ones—results in an analytical distinction that is "imprecise and poorly designated," at least where "most of the first century" is concerned.[80] Brown proposed that these traditional scholarly categories be replaced by a more exacting morphological analysis of varying approaches to the law. What is more, insofar as ancient approaches to law cut across the Jewish-Gentile distinction, "one should not speak of Jewish Christianity and Gentile Christianity but of varying types of Jewish/Gentile Christianity."[81] Nonetheless, Brown still allowed that the more traditional distinction might at least "be justifiable in the second century."[82]

While Brown's study paved the way for the temporal caveats of Carleton Paget and Mimouni discussed above, it also opened the door to more global criticism of the category "Jewish Christianity" itself. In a subsequent treatment of the problem published in 2007, Carleton Paget himself took Brown's argument a step further, albeit hypothetically. Citing the analogy of Michael Williams's rejection of the category "Gnosticism," Carleton Paget imagined that some scholars might ultimately conclude that continued use of the category "Jewish Christianity" in antiquity more generally is "counter-productive"—that "the term is simply too slippery and has too complex a history to be worth preserving" at all. Envisioning how "the argument might go," Carleton Paget enumerates three specific objections. First, the term was not used by anyone as a self-designation in antiquity. Second, "typological definitions" of the category sometimes lead to "misreading of material" grouped within it.[83] Third, attempts to address the latter problem by appealing to diverse "Jewish Christianities" still fail to adequately explain "the 'Jewish' aspect of the name," resolving neither "the amount of Jewishness that makes a text Jewish Christian" nor its tautologous nature given the "dependence of early Christian culture on Judaism" more generally. As a possible (albeit "not unproblematic") alternative, Carleton Paget envisions "a new start" in which the category is jettisoned altogether and replaced with the sort of explicitly morphological analysis suggested by Brown. Rather than continuing to muddy the waters with the vague and problematically allusive notions of Jewish Christianity, he asks, "why not simply settle on" a more transparently analytical category "like 'Torah observant' and then introduce subcategories like Ebionite, Elchasaite, etc.? This would . . . do away with the problem of the Jewishness of 'Jewish Christian' . . . and transcend such complex issues as the role of ethnicity in the definition as well as the place of a term like 'Judaizer.'"[84]

While the analytical approach envisioned by Brown and Carleton Paget does indeed eliminate the long-standing problem of defining the "Jewishness" of the early Jesus movement, it does not, however, address the more fundamental problem raised by critical, post-Christian historiography: its assumed "Christianness." Nonetheless, Carleton Paget's incisive criticism represents a significant turning point in the history of the discussion. Within two years, the argument he began to sketch against continued use of the category "Jewish Christianity" would be developed extensively in Daniel Boyarin's full-throated rejection of it as a concept that does more to obscure than to elucidate the relationship of Christians and Jews in antiquity.[85] On the other hand, Carleton Paget's anticipation that some might consider the concept's abandonment "unrealistic" given how entrenched it had become in scholarly discourse has also proved prescient. Despite the arguments of Carleton Paget and Boyarin, studies of Jewish Christianity, as we shall see in the next chapter, continue unabated in the twenty-first century.

Over the course of the twentieth century, the apologetic Christian concerns that had led early generations of scholars to theorize the existence of an early Jewish Christianity, and to disagree about the implications of that act of interpretation, receded increasingly into the background in critical study. The idea of Jewish Christianity itself, however, remained firmly entrenched. That there was something essentially not Jewish about the early Jesus movement from the start—that it had always represented, in other words, a "Christianity," even if a "Jewish" one—remained the routine assumption, with or without continued appeal to the dogmatic theologies that provided its theoretical grounding. While overtly occlusionistic models of Jewish Christianity largely disappeared in the wake of the Holocaust, the incarnational model perdured, either explicitly in Daniélou's notion of a Christianity in Jewish "thought forms," or implicitly in the new historical model of a primal Christianity that initially appeared "within Judaism" before gradually "parting ways" with it. The intractable problem of isolating precisely what it was that made that "Jewish Christianity" Jewish persisted with it. By the turn of the twenty-first century, some scholars had begun to wonder whether it might be time to retire the concept as a modern interpretive construct that had outlived its usefulness.

5 Problems and Prospects: Jewish Christianity and Identity in Contemporary Discussion

The problem of Jewish Christianity has become only more complicated in recent decades as a result of broader developments in the study of Jewish and Christian antiquity. By the end of the twentieth century, the Parting of the Ways model pioneered by Simon and others had come in for major criticism as a theological construct.[1] This critique has pushed to the foreground, as a problem in its own right, what Simon had already intuited as the underlying problem of defining Jewish Christianity: "How are we to decide, in the context of early Christianity, what is originally and specifically Christian and what is drawn secondarily from Judaism?"[2] As already observed, this is a problem only on the assumption that there was in fact something "originally and specifically Christian" about the Jesus movement, and indeed from the very beginning, that rendered its otherwise apparent Jewishness "secondary." This assumption was as foundational to Toland's concept of Jewish Christianity as to Morgan's, to Baur's as to Ritschl's, and to Harnack's as to Daniélou's. For each of these writers, and in the discussion of Jewish Christianity more generally through most of the concept's history, its theoretical basis was supplied by Christian apologetics and theology. Christians who consider the defining values of their Christianity to be other than Jewish all but inevitably imagine Jesus and the apostles, as the primal authorities for those values, to have been similarly other than Jewish—or at any rate far more than merely Jewish—at their essential, spiritual core.

Questions resulting from the eclipse of Christian apologetics in critical reconstructions of antiquity have been raised with increasing insistence in the opening decades of the twenty-first century. How are historians to conceive of Christianity if not as a distinct ontological reality transcendent of the history that is their object of study? How is the story of Christianity's origins and separation from Judaism to be told if not by appeal to the revelatory disclosure of such a reality into history and its inexorable impact on human culture and society? When, where, among whom, and in what sense can we begin to talk about Christianity as an ancient phenomenon at all, let alone one distinct from Judaism? In the theoretical void left by the evacuation of Christian theology from critical historiography, scholars are seeking to reconceptualize the nature of Christianity, and the problem of its origins and development in relation to Judaism, in light of the more general human propensity to construct and maintain social and cultural identities. This paradigm shift has led to fundamental changes in the scholarly debates about Jewish Christianity. The question at issue today is no longer merely how to define the category. Among those who continue to use it, the question is whether it should be defined at all given the inevitable fluidity of cultural identity. Even more fundamental is the question of the continued utility of the very notion of Jewish Christianity. Can this category, bound up so long and so intimately in the critical study of early Christianity, have any place within this new theoretical orientation? Will the idea of an early Jewish Christianity be more help or hindrance in the attempt to rethink Jewish and Christian antiquity in light of the human production of social identities?

Shifting Paradigms

At some point in antiquity, some early Jesus group, in an effort to valorize its salient habits of practice and discourse over against those of Judeans and others, began to declare those habits the marks of an uncreated, noncontingent "Christianism" (*Christianismos*).[3] Jesus and the apostles were cited both as the locus of the hierophanic disclosure of this Christianism and as its primal authorities. With this general theory of the nature and origins of Christianism in place, any potentially troubling differences apparent either among Jesus and his apostles or between them and later Christians—and likewise, any potentially troubling similarities between Jesus, the apostles, and Judeans—could be safely marginalized as matters of transitory context as opposed to essential content: the all but inevitable by-products of Christianity's initial revelation within a Jewish society that ultimately would prove unable to contain it.[4] With or without its traditional theological underpinnings, this remained the dominant paradigm of early Christian history through the rise and development of critical scholarship in the post-Enlightenment era. From the eighteenth century on it found new expression in the idea of an early Jewish Christianity in either incarnational or occlusionistic senses. In the twentieth century it took the form of a broad historical reconstruction that came to be known as the Parting of the Ways.

Recognition of the decidedly Christian and apologetic character of this account of early Christian history has sent scholars searching for new paradigms with which to make sense of Christianity and its relationship to Judaism in antiquity.[5] Among the most important of these has been a reconsideration of Christianity and Judaism from the point of view of the social construction of identity.[6] Scholars today routinely treat Christianity and Judaism as socially and thus variably constructed terms of identity rather than as ontological realities, with the distinction between them therefore equally fabricated and contingent.[7] In place of earlier accounts of a teleological process in which Christianity and Judaism inevitably parted ways, one now finds analyses of "an imposed *partitioning*" of them—of "groups gradually congealing into Christianity and Judaism" by means of a deliberate "choice of specific indicia of identity and the diffusion and clustering of such indicia."[8] Assumptions of a monolithic Christianity or a similarly monolithic and normative Judaism have given way to discussions of plural Christianities and Judaisms. The narrative now, in short, concerns not so much a "parting of the ways" as a *"forming of the ways,"* including indeed some "ways that never parted."[9] According to some recent scholars, in fact, the definitive separation of Christianity and Judaism was not a first- or even second-century phenomenon, but a product of Christianity's rise to imperial power in the fourth century. Most notably, Daniel Boyarin, picking up on an idea advanced decades earlier by Rosemary Radford Ruether, has argued that "for at least the first three centuries of their common lives, Judaism in all of its forms and Christianity in all of its forms were part of one complex religious family, twins in a womb . . . It was the birth of the hegemonic Catholic Church . . . that seems finally to have precipitated the consolidation of rabbinic Judaism as Jewish orthodoxy, with all its rivals, including the so-called Jewish Christianities, apparently largely vanquished. It was then that Judaism and Christianity finally emerged from the womb as genuinely independent children of Rebecca."[10]

This development has caused significant upheaval in the basic taxonomies long used by scholars for the organization and analysis of the data of antiquity, not least where the terms "Christian" and "Christianity" are concerned. The displacement of the hierophanic "big bang" theory of Christian origins by this focus on the human production of social identities considerably complicates the question of when, where, of whom, and in what sense it becomes useful to begin to speak of Christians and Christianity in antiquity at all. So, for example, Judith Lieu, whose statement of the problem is worth quoting at length:

> When and of whom may we use the label "Christian"? The New Testament, notoriously, is far more sparing with the term than most of those who teach or write about it . . . [W]e can no longer confidently plot the growth of "Christian" ministry, doctrine or practice, as if in so doing we were telling the story of the origins of Christianity—a term yet even more rare in our earliest sources. Both "Judaism" and "Christianity" have come to elude our conceptual grasp; we feel sure that they are there, and can quote those "others," outsiders, who were no less sure . . . Yet when we try to describe, when we seek to draw the boundaries which will define our subject for us, we lack the tools, both conceptual and material. It seems to me equally justifiable to "construct" "Christianity" in opposition to "Judaism" at the moment when Jesus "cleansed the Temple," at least in the literary representation of that event, and to think of that separation only in the fourth century, stimulated by dramatic changes in access to power—and I could call to my defence advocates of both positions, no doubt determined by their own starting points and definitional frameworks.[11]

An increasing number of studies, in fact, now treat particular segments of the Jesus movement, or even the movement more generally up through a certain era, as forms of Judaism, with or without the qualifying descriptor "Christian." To be sure, similar moves had long been made by writers ranging from Epiphanius to Thomas Morgan to F. J. A. Hort. In contrast to these Christian polemicists, however, the current intention is not to relegate the relevant phenomena to the ranks of the less than "truly" Christian, but simply to avoid misleading anachronism—to describe more accurately the social-historical realities such phenomena represented in their own time rather than projecting our own modern assumptions about Christianity onto them.[12] Indeed, the same move is increasingly made with respect to Paul—the very apostle held up by previous generations of scholars as the quintessential expression of pure, unadulterated Christianity. According to a growing line of interpretation even *Paul*, as the title of one recent book has provocatively put it, *Was Not a Christian*.[13] Meanwhile, use of the terms

"Jews" and "Judaism," respectively, to translate the Greek *Ioudaioi* ("Judeans") and to refer to that people's characteristic culture has itself become a matter of contention, as scholars have grown analogously circumspect about projecting our modern notion of "religion" onto ancients who had no such concept.[14]

These taxonomic shifts have created fresh interest in and a new urgency surrounding the problem of Jewish Christianity. Emphasis on ancient social constructions of identity has made scholars much more acutely aware that it is a modern interpretive construct. On the other hand, redescription of data in our own terms in order to make our own analytical points about that data is a routine—and indeed quite necessary—element of critical, comparative analysis.[15] Contemporary debate about Jewish Christianity swirls largely around the tension between the interpretive constructs found in the ancient data and those constructs modern scholars fabricate to analyze that data for their own purposes. Some argue that the category "Jewish Christianity" is no longer analytically useful. Karen King, calling it "a particularly exasperating case of classificatory imprecision," suggests that "a more adequate analysis would replace the division of Christianity into static and inaccurate types [like Jewish Christianity], which do little more than reproduce ... the boundary-setting enterprise of ancient discourses of orthodoxy and heresy, with an analysis of the full range of Christian practices of mapping difference and identity."[16] Others, in a manner somewhat reminiscent of Simon, are repurposing "Jewish Christianity" yet again in order to subvert long-standing claims regarding an early and decisive separation of Christianity from Judaism. Seizing on the traditional conception of it as the historical site where Judaism and Christianity had touched one another most profoundly, these scholars point to category-busting hybrids throughout antiquity in order to underscore the fluidity and artificiality of the boundaries interposed between Christianity and Judaism. Among these scholars, the old debate about Simon's definition versus Daniélou's has been set aside in favor of attempts to account for ever-fluctuating identities, in some cases eschewing the very idea of definition in principle. At the beginning of the twenty-first century, in short, scholarly discussion of Jewish Christianity has become more complicated than ever. The debate is no longer merely how to define the concept, but whether it should be defined—or even still considered analytically useful—at all.

Daniel Boyarin: "Judaeo-Christianity" vs. "Jewish Christianity"

Daniel Boyarin is among the most active and provocative voices in the contemporary discussion.[17] Reflecting in 1999 on the current state of scholarship on the origins of Christianity in relation to Judaism, Boyarin argued that "what is required . . . is a deconstruction, in the full technical sense of the word, of the opposition between Judaism and Christianity, a deconstruction in which the name 'Jewish Christian' is pulled in from the marginal cold of 'those who owe something to both religions and set up camp in the territory between the two,' in Marcel Simon's words . . . [and] understood [instead] as the third term that unsettles the opposition between the 'two religions.'"[18] Rather than essentially distinct and clearly bounded entities with a hybrid Jewish Christianity between them, Boyarin reimagines "Judaism and Christianity in late antiquity as points on a continuum. On one end were the Marcionites . . . who believed that the Hebrew Bible had been written by an inferior God and had no standing for Christians and who completely denied the 'Jewishness' of Christianity. On the other were the many Jews for whom Jesus meant nothing. In the middle, however, were many gradations that provided social and cultural mobility from one end of this spectrum to the other." The underlying continuum is conceived as a broad cultural "circulatory system within which discursive elements could move from non-Christian Jews and back again."[19] Each of the various early Jewish and Christian groups, accordingly, represented some "choice of specific indicia of identity and the diffusion and clustering of such indicia" to create boundaries between themselves and others.[20] Given the inevitable artificiality of these boundaries, Boyarin observes, claims made by such groups regarding clear social and cultural separation of Jews and Christians should be treated with great suspicion. While not wishing to suggest "that there was no distinction at all between 'Judaism' and 'Christianity' by the second century," Boyarin strongly emphasizes that "the border between the two was so fuzzy that one could hardly say precisely at what point one stopped and the other began."[21] Rather than hard and fast boundaries between Judaism and Christianity, there were a range of overlapping groups, some "more Christian than others."[22]

Boyarin's treatment of Judaism and Christianity as thoroughgoing products of human social activity represents an important theoretical advance over the explicitly or implicitly theological models examined up to this point in the present book. As he acknowledges, however, his analysis produces "serious terminological problems." The central issue, as he well recognizes, is a certain paradox at work in his reconstruction: "at the same time that I wish to deny the early existence of separate Judaism and Christianity, I am also speaking of the relationship between two entities that are, in some senses, recognizably different."[23] Indeed, though "suggesting that Judaism and Christianity were not separate entities until very late in antiquity," Boyarin nonetheless is "not claiming that it is impossible to discern separate social groups that are in an important sense Christian/not Jewish or Jewish/not-Christian from fairly early on."[24] The difficulty lies in capturing in clear analytical terms a reconstruction in which Christianity and Judaism were not "separate" but nonetheless "recognizably different"—and indeed even included individual Jewish and Christian groups that *were* socially "separate." The resulting taxonomy is quite complex, bordering on confusing. Boyarin names his theorized "circulatory system" itself "Jud(a)eo-Christianity."[25] Though primarily a cultural category, it also takes on a clear temporal dimension in a manner interestingly reminiscent of the (otherwise quite different) *judéo-christianisme* of Daniélou and the Judaistic Christianity of Hort.[26] Correlated with the period before Christianity's rise to imperial power, Judaeo-Christianity is a comprehensive category that includes not only "the so-called Jewish Christianities" that were eventually suppressed by the emerging orthodoxies, but "Judaism in all of its forms and Christianity in all of its forms."[27] Accordingly, even those "separate social groups" that were already by the mid-second century "in an important sense Christian/not Jewish or Jewish/not Christian" are nonetheless themselves still included in Judaeo-Christianity. What is more, if early rabbinic Judaism is an iteration of Judaeo-Christianity, all of early Christianity, conversely, can also be categorized as "Christian Judaism"— a term, Boyarin clarifies, "which is not the same as Jewish Christianity, but rather an intentionally startling name for Christianity *simpliciter* as the 'brother' of rabbinic Judaism."[28] In this sense, then, "Judaeo-Christianity" and "Judaism" would seem to be virtual synonyms, with the latter now reconceptualized as a cultural complex broad enough to include all of late antique Christianity—including those varieties that were "in an important sense . . . not Jewish."[29]

Boyarin's terminological problem becomes more complicated still when, in a subsequent article, he develops his theory into a more specific and explicit argument against any continued use of the concept "Jewish

Christianity." Integrating Steve Mason's seminal study of the ancient meaning of *Ioudaios* and related terms into his own analysis, Boyarin emphasizes that ancient Judeans did not define themselves as a religion. *Ioudaïsmos*—a term rarely used in the pre-Christian era in any case—"doesn't mean Judaism the religion but the entire complex of loyalties and practices that mark off the people of Israel."[30] In a twist on Mason's thesis, Boyarin argues that Christians invented the religion of Judaism—and in the process the generic category "religion" itself—as a key by-product of their own self-definitional efforts. What is more, he argues, "the construction of ancient versions of 'Jewish Christianity'" was itself, in turn, "an important part of the production of that notion" of religion.[31] Citing a supposed "explosion of heresiological interest in the 'Jewish-Christian heresies' of the Nazarenes and the Ebionites" in the early fifth century, Boyarin observes a "new moment" in Christian heresiology as Epiphanius and Jerome suddenly find it "important . . . to assert a difference between Judaizing heretics and Jews."[32] This interest, he argues, reflects the new notion that Christianity and Judaism represent separate religions: "The ascription of existence to the 'hybrids' assumes (and thus assures) the existence of nonhybrid, 'pure' religions."[33] Correlating this move with the idea of "Jewish Christianity," Boyarin thus concludes that the latter term—"or rather its ancient equivalents, Nazoraean, Ebionite"—was "part and parcel" of the Christian invention of the notion of religion and "thus *eo ipso*, and not merely factitiously, a heresiological term of art." Consequently, "there should be as little justification for continued use of the term 'Jewish Christianity' as a scholarly designation as there is for the term 'heresy' itself."[34]

The central theoretical point that the postulation of hybrids is a necessary by-product of claims of purity is sound enough. The treatment of Jewish Christianity as a straightforward equivalent of the ancient terms Ebionite and Nazoraean, however, is problematic. It bears repeating that Epiphanius and Jerome, while the first to use "Nazoraean" alongside "Ebionite" as the names of heretical sects, knew nothing of any overarching category "Jewish Christianity."[35] The names they did use, moreover, had prior histories of their own, extending well beyond the Christian heresiological project. If "Ebionite," for example, signifies a monstrous hybrid for Epiphanius and Jerome, it seems also to have signified a pure kind for those who used it as a self-designation.[36] Thus even if one were convinced by the thesis that a late antique invention of "religion" was responsible for rendering such names "heresiological terms of art" for Epiphanius and Jerome in particular, it is unclear why that means other, different uses of them are thereby excluded in principle. What is more, the first self-conscious formulation of the actual category "Jewish Christianity"—while no doubt thoroughly heresiological and presuming the same fundamental distinction between Christianity and Judaism postulated by Jerome and Epiphanius—was actually meant to *subvert* the latter's polemical usage of "Ebionite" and "Nazoraean." As Toland's coinage, "Jewish Christianity" did not devalue Ebionites and Nazoraeans as hybrid nothings; on the contrary, it valorized groups that had formerly been dismissed as heresy as thoroughly legitimate and indeed primally authoritative cultural incarnations of Christianity. It was precisely this new theory of a "Jewish Christianity" that allowed Toland to reposition Ebionites and Nazoraeans as (at least potential) purities in contrast to the problematically hybrid *Gentile* Christianity he correlated with traditional orthodoxy.[37]

In any event, the provocative taxonomic conclusions Boyarin draws from this argument exacerbate his terminological problems. Since *Ioudaïsmos* is "not a religion," he argues, "it cannot be hyphenated in any meaningful way."[38] The implication of this dictum for his own foundational concept of "Judaeo-Christianity" is not explicitly addressed. The substantive point would seem to be that since hybrids and purities are codependent notions, there can be no hybrid (i.e., "hyphenated") Jewish-Christianity apart from the postulation of a pure and bounded Judaism, separate from Christianity. The point is clear and apposite, even if the special relevance of the category "religion" to it is not. (Can a *Ioudaïsmos* conceived as Judean culture along the lines of 2 Maccabees be either any more pure or any less hybrid than a Judaism conceived as religion?) In another sense, however, one might also say that where there are no purities, everything is effectively hybrid. In Boyarin's terms, then, if there can be no hyphenated "Jewish-Christianity," everything should be considered a hyphenated "Judaeo-Christianity." The underlying logic leading to both formulations (religion and literal hyphens aside) is clear enough. The result, however, is another terminological paradox.

Similar problems surround the declaration "There is no Judaism."[39] How, then, are we to understand Boyarin's earlier redescription of all Christians before the fourth century in terms of "Christian Judaism"? Here again the implication of the former for the latter is not developed. To be sure, underlying the apparently categorical rejection of any notion of ancient Judaism is a more nuanced and specific thesis, namely, that there is no *religion* of Judaism apart from Christianity's artificial "disembedding" of select

Judean practices and beliefs "from their landedness, their history," and from the wider range of "cultural practices and identifying markers" that 2 Maccabees, at least, called *Ioudaïsmos*.[40] Unless we are to conclude, then, that Boyarin means now to disallow his own "intentionally startling" classification of early "Christianity *simpliciter*" as a kind of Judaism, the implication would seem to be that Judaism in that formulation is to be understood not as a religion, but more generally as a culture.[41] Notably, however, insofar as this "Christian Judaism" includes groups who were in an important sense "not Jewish," this taxonomic move would seem to require a certain disembedding of its own—if not of a religion, of a discursive "circulatory system" that is in any event no less abstracted from the landedness and loyalties of ancient Judeans. In *Border Lines*, in fact, Boyarin uses the term "*Gentile Christianity* in a sort of subtechnical sense to refer to Christian converts from among non-Jews (and their descendants) who have neither a sense of genealogical attachment to the historical, physical people of Israel (Israel according to the flesh), nor an attachment (and frequently the exact opposite of one) to the fleshly practices of that historical community." Subtechnical or not, he imbues the category with tremendous historical significance: it is Boyarin's "strong intuition that it was this formation, Gentile Christianity, that first presented the structural irritant around which the notion of belonging by virtue of faith would arise."[42] From this postulation of a "Gentile Christianity," however, it would seem but a short step to its traditional mate, "Jewish Christianity," as the implied term of contrast—and indeed in something other than a heresiological sense: those Christians *from among Jews* who *do* have strong attachments to historical Israel and its practices. What, then, does the blanket rejection of Jewish Christianity do to his earlier concept of Gentile Christianity? What contrasting value does the latter imply, if not the former?

Boyarin's attempt to reimagine the invention and separation of Christianity and Judaism as thoroughgoing products of human efforts at self-differentiation represents a major theoretical advance. By his own admission, however, his analysis is beset with terminological problems that quickly devolve into a string of paradoxes. By the second century, Judaism and Christianity included "separate social groups" that were Christian-but-not-Jewish and Jewish-but-not-Christian; and yet Judaism and Christianity were not "separate entities" until the fourth century. Those early Christians who were "in an important sense . . . not Jewish" can nonetheless be thought of as representing "Christian Judaism," and perhaps even as

"Christian Jews."[43] There was no Judaism, except in the sense that all Jews and Christians before the fourth century represented Judaism. Since Judaism did not exist as a religion, it cannot be hyphenated—except in the sense that everything before the fourth century was Judaeo-Christianity. Gentile Christianity is a viable and indeed historically significant subset of "Judaeo-Christianity" (and of "Christian Judaism"); its traditional mate, Jewish Christianity, however, is not and can have no place in historical scholarship. Boyarin's analysis of the cultural overlaps underlying—and in some measure, at least, belying—the postulation of Christianity and Judaism as distinct things represents an important step forward in the disentanglement of critical scholarship from Christian apologetics. The production of clear analytical categories for the purpose of such analysis, however, remains a major desideratum.

The Deconstructive Repurposing of Jewish Christianity

Other scholars, meanwhile, have argued that the category "Jewish Christianity" still has an important role to play in this new era of scholarship—and for the very deconstructive ends sought by Boyarin. In a study published in a seminal essay collection titled *The Ways That Never Parted* in 2003, Annette Yoshiko Reed explained why she was "not quite ready to jettison" this "wholly modern invention." Citing its ongoing value "as a heuristic irritant," Reed argued that "the term [Jewish Christianity] serves to disturb—literally by definition—any unquestioned assumptions that we might harbor about the essential incompatibility and inevitable 'parting' of Judaism and Christianity, while also reminding us that we have yet to settle some basic definitional issues about 'Judaism' and 'Christianity' and that our scholarly categories (even the ones with ancient counterparts) are exactly that: categories shaped by our scholarly aims and modern experiences that we choose to impose, for better or worse, on our ancient evidence."[44] Petri Luomanen, agreeing with Boyarin's general point that "we can start speaking of [Judaism and Christianity as] two separate religions only after the Constantine turn," similarly concedes that the whole idea of Jewish Christianity is thoroughly modern: "it presumes two distinct religious bodies, Judaism and Christianity, which were less clearly separated from each other in antiquity than they are today." While thus "gladly admit[ting] that the concept of Jewish Christianity is anachronistic," he argues nonetheless that "it still provides the best starting point for historical analysis" precisely insofar as it "directs attention to the way our modern categories 'Judaism' and 'Christianity' overlapped in some ancient communities."[45] Edwin Broadhead's effort to exhaustively "gather the evidence for Jewish Christianity and to reconsider its impact" is likewise intended not only to "challenge presumptions of an early and decisive parting of the ways between Judaism and Christianity," but to "add further evidence that official Judaism and official Christianity are late, sometimes awkward constructs."[46] For these scholars, Jewish Christianity remains a significant concept precisely insofar as it represents those "ways that never parted"—"the third term," as Boyarin had put it, "that unsettles the opposition between the 'two religions.'"[47]

With this development has come a new phase in the discussion of the notorious problem of definition. Realization that Judaism and Christianity, as historical phenomena, are socially constructed and therefore entirely fluid forms of cultural identity has considerably complicated the matter of defining them at all, let alone as subcomponents of a hybrid Jewish-Christianity. Recent reformulations of the latter, accordingly, have sought to account in one way or another for the nature of Christianity and Judaism as mutable social identities variably constructed from the range of cultural materials available in the ancient Mediterranean world, much as in the analysis of Boyarin. Broadhead's attempt to provide a comprehensive study of early Jewish Christianity, for example, sets aside the late-twentieth-century debate between definitions that reduce its Jewishness to specific forms of either discourse (so Daniélou) or practice (so Simon) in favor of a more generalized—if, as he recognizes, rather more elusive—notion of "maintaining Jewishness." Jewish Christianity, by his definition, is "a scholarly label for persons and groups in antiquity whose historical profile suggests they both follow Jesus and maintain their Jewishness and that they do so as a continuation of God's covenant with Israel."[48]

Luomanen, on the other hand, considers the very attempt to define Jewish Christianity misguided.[49] The diversity of ancient Judaism and Christianity, he reasons, makes it "likely that there was not just one Jewish Christianity but several Jewish Christianities" as well—a likelihood that renders any "predetermined definition of Jewish Christianity," however "broad or narrow," problematic.[50] What is more, he argues, the formulation of categories "on the basis of sufficient and necessary traits . . . fails to capture social categorizations from the emic point of view," which tends to work with more fluid categories, "continuously revised . . . in changing social situations." To get around this problem, he advocates a polythetic approach to classification that, as in Boyarin's model, "allows degrees of 'Jewishness' and degrees of 'Christianness'" and that places special emphasis on factors "that are determinative in social relations—such as ideology, practice, identity, and group formation."[51] "The main idea of this approach is to list and analyze the 'Jewish' and 'Christian' components of a particular text or a community, paying special attention to . . . how its conceptions and practices create, maintain and cross boundaries between insiders and outsiders."[52] Luomanen identifies six such "indicators of Jewish Christianity." Three are indicators of "Jewishness" (Jewish practices, Jewish ideas, and Jewish pedigree) and two of "Christianness" (Christology and baptism). The final indicator considers the role played by the previous five particularly in the social construction of identity, thus allowing him to differentiate "simple Jewish-Christian inclinations" from "independent Jewish-Christian movements," or what he elsewhere calls "a Jewish Christianity on its own."[53]

Most recently, Reed has defended the deconstructive use of a (now literally hyphenated!) "Jewish-Christianity" against Boyarin's later objections in what is undoubtedly the most nuanced and theoretically sophisticated approach to the category yet formulated.[54] Reed fully acknowledges the heresiological dimension of the category highlighted by Boyarin. "Inasmuch as the term presumes a need to mark certain expressions of 'Christianity' as *too* 'Jewish' to be called *just* Christian," she agrees, "it functions to naturalize an understanding of 'Christianity' as essentially or inevitably distinct from 'Judaism' . . . To deploy the term in the context of the scholarly discussion of Christianity is therefore to make a normative judgment about what constitutes the Jewishness that goes beyond the bounds of what *should* be called 'Christian.'"[55] And yet this is not, she points out, the only function the category either has been or can be made to serve. In Reed's view, in fact, its enduring utility in the current scholarly moment lies precisely in its potential to lay bare—and thereby to subvert—the problematic assumptions underlying such normative Christian usage.[56] In short, Reed finds "the conceptual issues surrounding 'Jewish-Christianity' to be especially productive for the same reasons that Boyarin finds them especially problematic . . . [M]y argument for retaining the term is therefore both complimentary [*sic*] and inverse to Boyarin's argument to jettison it."[57] For this purpose, moreover, the concept's anachronism and vagueness are counted among its greatest virtues. "Perhaps precisely because 'Jewish-Christianity' is an anachronistic, clumsy, fraught, and contested category, I propose that it proves useful as a site for reassessing some of the interpretive habits that we take most for granted. Its definition has been much debated. Even the perceived need for such a hybrid term points powerfully to the limits of modern taxonomies of 'religions' for describing all of our premodern data."[58] In contrast to Broadhead's, then, Reed's interest in Jewish Christianity is purely analytical. The category is not a reflection of some ancient construction of identity but a strategic reappropriation of a taxonomic dichotomy she wishes to deconstruct. If more reminiscent of Luomanen in this respect, her approach to the matter of definition is much more straightforward. For Reed's purposes, "'Jewish-Christian' is used to denote those premodern figures, sects, and sources which can be meaningfully defined as both 'Jewish' and 'Christian' and which thus do not fit into a modern taxonomic system that treats 'Judaism' and 'Christianity' as mutually exclusive."[59]

Reed's continued interest in the category "Jewish-Christianity" itself is in this sense more deconstructive than reconstructive.[60] It is tied particularly closely to her concern with "lingering elements" of the Parting of the Ways model that perdure even in the work of that model's critics. Among the most basic of these is an ongoing preoccupation with locating some particular historical moment when Christianity and Judaism became decisively separate. Whether the key events are found in the first, second, or fourth century, she observes, scholars continue to frame "the issue of Jewish and Christian difference in temporal terms—as a question of *when*."[61] This insightful observation has profound historical implications. Such "narratives of dramatic change," Reed points out, are associated with broad historical models that bifurcate social histories into two contrasting eras: initial periods of "origins" characterized by "fluidity and dynamism" on one hand; and subsequent eras defined by the "static, substantial entities" that issued from them, "forever bounded and set," on the other.[62] Reed finds an analogous paradigm at work in late-twentieth-century scholarship on early Christian self-definition, at least to the extent that it is patterned after a psychological model in which selves form by means of gradual processes of individuation. "When applied to the 'origins' of 'religions,' this model of individuation ... naturalizes a narrative of inevitable development, from an early era characterized by fluid indifferentiation, to some pivotal crisis point catalyzing self-definition, to what is thereafter framed as the inevitable emergence of 'Christianity' as a bounded entity with a stable 'core' forever after."[63] Moving the catalytic hinge-moment forward or backward in time does nothing to change the overall effect. "Whatever date is deemed determinative ... the very question of *when* serves tidily to collapse any local . . . specificities into the service of a monolithic narrative about two 'religions' . . . The task of cultural history is thereby flattened into a simple narrative of before and after, and the past is construed as a reservoir of precedents for the presumed *telos* of our present (with whatever the presumed 'our' thereby naturalized as inevitable if not normative)."[64]

Reed's critique of this simplistic "before and after" model of history has significant implications for the use and interpretation of social taxonomies, ancient and modern. Many scholars, she observes, tend to correlate this sought-for watershed moment with the first known appearances of terms equivalent to the modern distinction between Christianity and Judaism. Ignatius of Antioch, for example, has often been "heralded as marking or confirming the 'Parting of the Ways.'" Not only do such correlations draw "globalizing conclusions about 'religions' *writ large*" from specific, local sources, they also represent a problematic leap from taxonomies to social realities that Reed rightly criticizes as a sort of "groupism": a facile conflation of discursive categories with actual social groups, as opposed to a critical inquiry into "the degree of groupness associated with a particular category."[65] The problem is exacerbated insofar as an ancient and decidedly Christian taxonomic scheme that divided Christianity from Judaism is elided with modern taxonomies of religion and made the ostensibly neutral terms of a critical analysis of antiquity. Such moves effectively privilege the contemporary Christian perspective as the "natural" one rather than historicizing it as one more among others. "Today," Reed observes, "'Judaism' and 'Christianity' are widely perceived as neutral, objective, and thus simply descriptive terms . . . But within late antique contexts . . . the very practice of sorting ideas and practices as 'Jewish' *or* 'Christian' is a *distinctively Christian practice*, unparalleled within Jewish sources. To the degree that scholars engage in this practice without self-consciousness of other perspectives and possibilities, we thus risk unidirectionally imposing (certain) Christian regimes of knowledge and power onto those thereby sorted and labeled into what became an increasingly totalizing imperial Christian system of classification."[66] Not only does this promote a conflation of the ancient distinction between *Christianismos* and *Ioudaïsmos* with modern understandings of religion, it also blinds us to the fact that the ancient distinction itself was, in its time, an experimental innovation—and thus too to any taxonomic alternatives with which it may have been competing.[67]

The key to escaping this problem, it would seem, is not so much to reject questions of *when* altogether as to temper them by insisting equally emphatically on questions of *where, by whom,* and *to what end.*[68] The location of any and all social taxonomies, ancient or modern, in particular historical settings not only serves to denaturalize the dominant and supposedly neutral ones operative today, but it allows us to reconsider history beyond the constraints of the narratives of origins that have been constructed to affirm and sustain them—in this case, the story of the decisive moment when Christianity went from being bound up in Judaism to being an independent reality all its own. It is precisely here, in Reed's view, that "Jewish-Christianity," as an avowedly modern, redescriptive category, has ongoing value. If frequently serving in the past to marginalize those sources "that cannot be readily sorted into this now-naturalized binary of 'Judaism'/'Christianity,'" those very same sources "also point to the problems in imposing a single classification scheme uniformly across our premodern sources; in late antique context, this binary is far from neutral, and it is also not the only organizing principle at play."[69] Recognition of this taxonomic relativity, in turn, provides an opportunity to rethink the history of Christianity and its relationship to Judaism. "The materials that modern scholars have labeled as 'Jewish-Christian' perhaps prove especially powerful for unsettling the very notion of a clear-cut *before/after* narrative of Christian identity formation. To take such materials seriously, in this sense, is to be pushed to craft more sophisticated diachronic narratives about Jews and Christians"[70]—narratives that account for fluidity not merely in some supposed era of "origins," but as an enduring condition of "Christian" and "Jew" as social and cultural categories. In Reed's view, in sum, "the puzzling case of 'Jewish-Christianity'" is "provocatively productive" precisely insofar as "it is exemplary of what must be ignored and elided" when the task of early Christian history is approached as "the search for precedents for the terms and taxonomies most familiar to us today."[71] And the more vaguely the category is formulated, she finds, the more productive it can be. "What might be effaced," she asks, "by the fixation on attempting to narrow the best definition for a term like 'Jewish-Christian' . . . or debating whether this-or-that sect or source fits therein? What might we learn by taking seriously, instead, just how different the religious landscape of Late Antiquity looks when viewed from the positions and perspectives articulated within 'Jewish-Christian' sources, and how they might challenge and enrich our understandings of 'Christianity,' 'Judaism,' and 'religion'?"[72]

Broadhead, Luomanen, and Reed are undoubtedly correct to emphasize the deconstructive utility, as Reed puts it, of "the materials that modern

scholars have labeled as 'Jewish-Christian.'"[73] Centuries of cultural labor
have been devoted to naturalizing the Christianity-Judaism distinction as
a simple given. Materials that resist easy compartmentalization within that
dichotomy carry a special potential to erode the ongoing power of those
efforts by highlighting not only its limitations, but its thoroughly historical (not natural) character as the product of a particular group's efforts at
apologetic self-definition. Historicizing the Christianity-Judaism dichotomy enriches our historical understanding by prompting us to investigate
not only the ancient alternatives that existed alongside it in antiquity, but
its own production and dissemination as an important exemplum in the
history of human efforts at social differentiation.

As these studies themselves emphatically underscore, however, there is
a significant difference between the categories one uses to group materials into sets for purposes of analysis and the actual materials themselves.
One can thus wholly concur regarding the special importance of (at least
some of) the data traditionally categorized as "Jewish Christianity" while
also questioning the value of the category itself.[74] To be sure, phenomena
interpreted as "Jewish Christian" by past scholars may provide a convenient place to begin the search for evidence of taxonomic alternatives to
the Christianism-Judaism dichotomy postulated by Ignatius and others
like him. What is far from clear, however, is the continued utility of the
actual category "Jewish Christianity" for any *constructive* analysis of that
material going forward. Indeed, insofar as our concern, with Reed, is to
historicize the Christianity-Judaism division as "part of a continuum of
experimentation with different modes of categorizing difference in Late
Antiquity," even a deconstructive deployment of "Jewish-Christianity" is
ultimately counterproductive.[75] To continue framing other segments of that
hypothesized continuum as so many hybrid combinations of Christianity
and Judaism is to carry on interpreting them decidedly through the eyes of
their Christian rivals, treating the very conceptual distinctions we are trying to historicize yet again as simple analytical givens. The category "Jewish
Christianity" (with or without a hyphen) does not explain the existence of
Christianity; it continues to assume it. Did the relevant groups view themselves as some such combination? Or did some make sense of their social
experience within a different taxonomic scheme altogether—perhaps even
one in which the "Christianism" postulated by their rivals was itself made
to play the role of hybrid vis-à-vis some differently imagined pure kinds?
What alternative ancient taxonomic scheme or schemes might we be con-

tinuing to overwrite by redescribing any and all such groups as a hybrid "Jewish-Christianity"?[76] How might our understanding of the origins and early history of Christianity and of the Christianity-Judaism divide change if we organized our analysis, instead, around those alternative ancient taxonomies themselves?

Problems and Prospects

The utility of a category is relative to the particular purpose for which it is enlisted. The interpretive construct "Jewish Christianity" has been used for a variety of purposes in the years since Toland first introduced it into the discussion of early Christianity. Over most of the history of its usage the ends it has served have been decidedly Christian and apologetic. Toland, Morgan, and Baur each deployed it as part of their respective attempts to transfer the authorizing power inherent in the notion of an "original Christianity" from traditional orthodoxy to their own Enlightenment values. Toland renamed what had until then been considered the Ebionite heresy "Jewish Christianity" in order to authorize it *precisely as Christianity*— indeed, the very Christianity of Jesus and the apostles, now reconceived as a natural, rational religion ensconced within the external forms of a newly vitalized Jewish culture. What eventually became Christian orthodoxy, on the other hand, was dismissed as a subsequent Gentile corruption of what should have been an analogously revitalized Gentile culture through the perverse imposition of Greek mysticism, priestcraft, and prejudice. Morgan and Baur, conversely, used the idea of an early Jewish Christianity to marginalize undesirable elements of the New Testament and orthodox theology as Jewish corruptions of an original Christian principle that found full flower only in the Gentile Christianity of Paul. Baur's critics, in turn, attempted to restore the apostolic and canonical authority Baur had undermined by dividing Jewish Christianity into two subspecies: an apostolic and canonical one that, analogous to Toland's Ebionites, represented the incarnation of a fully authentic Christianity in expendable Jewish forms; and heretical varieties, like those identified by Baur, that obscured true Christianity by insisting on the essential and enduring importance of those forms.[77]

These apologetic maneuvers contributed significantly to the development of a critical analysis of the New Testament and early Christianity that, among other things, drew more and more attention to the Jewish character of the early Jesus movement. The increasing disentanglement of this critical approach from Christian theology and apologetics over the subsequent history of scholarship has led to new reformulations of the category "Jewish Christianity" for new purposes. Simon redeployed it in order to subvert the widespread assumption that resulted from the counternarrative produced by Baur's critics, and evident not least in the influential work of Harnack: that of an early and decisive social separation of Christianity and Judaism. Jewish Christianity, for Simon, now became evidence for ongoing "contact and assimilation" between Judaism and Christianity well into the fourth century.[78] While this historical interest was no doubt motivated by disgust and horror at Christian treatment of Jews in his own day, Simon's actual concept of Jewish Christianity, like Schoeps's, was more a social-historical than an apologetic-theological construct: "a body midway between Church and Synagogue," or the phenomenon of Christians practicing Jewish law.[79] Even if no longer grounded explicitly in Christian theological claims, however, the continued assumption of an early Jewish Christianity itself left the underlying apologetic historiographical paradigm basically intact. Christianity was still imagined as a reality distinct from Judaism—even if "within it" or at least "mixed" with it—from the very beginning. Simon simply offered two main revisions to the traditional apologetic narrative. First, the (still-assumed) "original Christianity" was now identified with the ostensibly historical datum of "faith in Jesus" rather than some revelatory dogma or transcendent principle.[80] Second, the separation of Christianity from Judaism was depicted as a more gradual and mutual "parting of the ways," with the final severing of relations between them pushed back much farther in time than previously imagined—indeed, to Christianity's imperial era. Simon's simple correlation of Christianity with "faith in Jesus," however, does more to underscore than to resolve the new problem created by the evacuation of Christian theology from historical reconstruction. How did the concession of authority to a charismatic Jewish leader—let alone one interpreted in the typically nationalistic idiom of a "messiah"—ever come to be considered anything other than a Jewish trait? The continued assumption of a Christianity there "from the beginning" only perpetuated the long-standing Christian preoccupation with the seemingly irresolvable conundrum of isolating the particular ingredient that made a postulated early Jewish Christianity peculiarly Jewish.

Similar problems remain in practice, even if not in theory, in more recent redeployments of the category to subvert the Parting of the Ways paradigm itself. Informed now by critical theories of Christianity as an invented social identity, scholars today portray the separation of Christianity and Judaism not as the inevitable social outworking of an essential, underlying difference, but as the artificial construction and enforcement of social and cultural boundaries within an otherwise shared cultural milieu. This is, to be sure, a major theoretical advance—one that goes a long way toward addressing the problem of explaining the nature and history of Christianity and the Christianity-Judaism divide in the absence of apologetic Christian theology. But it is one that is more hindered than helped by continued appeal to categories like "Jewish-Christianity"—whether in the more restricted sense of Broadhead, Luomanen, and Reed or in Boyarin's more generalized theory of "Judaeo-Christianity." Even if no longer imagining Christianity as an essential principle either incarnate in or obscured by Judaism in theory, such formulations continue to portray the relevant ancient Jesus groups in practice as hybrids of Christianity and Judaism—and thus Christianity, once again, as something there "from the beginning," initially bound up in Judaism before gradually, at some point, becoming separate from it. While identifying Christianity as a term of identity in theory, in other words, such analyses continue to treat it as the functional equivalent of "faith in Jesus" in practice—or even, as when notions of "degrees of Christianness" are invoked, as a quality somehow *inherent in* rather than *ascribed to* belief in Jesus.[81]

At best, this dual usage of Christianity both as functional equivalent of (some manner of) belief in Jesus and as socially constructed term of identity is productive of analytical (and, in the case of Boyarin, terminological) confusion. At worst, it reintroduces into our historical reconstructions the very paradigm we are seeking to overcome: the idea of a Christianity that existed from the beginning, begotten not made. The effective result is the continued analysis of the whole history of the Jesus movement specifically through the eyes of one particular segment of it—the very ones who invented this notion of an "original Christianity" to begin with—and thus the continued interpretation of other segments of that movement as groups who exhibited lesser degrees of the former's claimed "Christianness." To persist in imagining some or all of the early Jesus movement as Jewish Christianity, in short, is to continue to assume a Christianity much like the one that Christians have always imagined: something that existed in the Jesus movement from the beginning and that was embodied more fully in some of Jesus's followers than others—whether any of them knew it or not. In a Jungian irony, the central building blocks of the Christian apologetic project persist in the very attempt to resist them with such deconstructive reappropriations of the traditional category "Jewish Christianity."

What, then, is the alternative? If our aim is to thoroughly historicize the Christianity-Judaism distinction as one taxonomic scheme among others, we would do well to stop treating it as an analytical given. More specifically, if our purpose is to rethink Christianity as a socially constructed term of identity in theory, we should stop treating it as the functional equivalent of belief in Jesus in practice. While Christians have of course long emphasized "faith in Christ" as a—and sometimes, if only for rhetorical purposes, even *the*—defining value of Christianity, the two are scarcely the same thing when seen from the point of view of this new theoretical perspective.[82] "Christian" and "Christianity" are terms of identity and belonging. "Christian" is something people claim (or are said) to *be*; "Christianity," in turn, is an idealized abstraction of the values whose enactment constitutes the experience of being such, of belonging to a group that identifies itself as Christian.[83] Belief in the authoritative power of Jesus, on the other hand, is a cultural meme. As such, it might be—and in historical fact, has been—construed in any number of ways and integrated into any number of social identities.[84] Isolated elements of culture, as Philippa Townsend has well observed, "cannot be classified as Jewish or Christian independently of the context of meaning within which they were being deployed; nor do they determine self-identification."[85] From this perspective, in short, belief in Jesus is neither inherently Christian nor inherently not-Jewish. Christianness and Jewishness, rather, are qualities that people *ascribe to* this cultural meme for their own rhetorical purposes, not qualities that are somehow *inherent in* the meme itself.

Accounting more clearly and explicitly in our redescriptive categories for this distinction between belief in the authoritative power of Jesus on one hand and Christianity on the other will allow us to turn our critical gaze more directly at the very ideas of Christianity and the Christianity-Judaism distinction themselves as cultural constructs to be explained rather than as analytical givens to be safely assumed. When various types of "faith in Jesus" are kept analytically distinct from the terms "Christian" and "Christianity," investigation of the history of Christianity and the Christianity-Judaism divide becomes first and foremost the question of the production and dissemination of a social taxonomy. Approaching the matter from this perspective allows us to move beyond both the loaded notion of an "original Christianity" and the closely related preoccupation, noted by Reed, with locating the moment of its final, decisive separation from Judaism. Such ideas themselves now appear as so many outworkings of a particular taxonomic scheme manufactured by a particular group of ancient people and continually reinvented by their successors for their own particular ends. Our attention turns instead to an investigation of the underlying taxonomy itself. Who produced it, and why? How widespread was it in antiquity? If the Christianity-Judaism distinction was in fact, as Reed suggests, only "part of the picture in Late Antiquity"—"part of a continuum of experimentation with different modes of categorizing difference"[86]—what alternative taxonomies contextualized and competed with it? While the idea of an early Jewish Christianity is counterproductive for such a historical reorientation, the materials Enlightenment-era Christians began reclassifying as such can indeed provide an illuminating point of departure.

6 Beyond Jewish Christianity: Ancient Social Taxonomies and the Christianity-Judaism Divide

Taking seriously Christianity's nature as a socially constructed identity means reconceiving the problem of its origins and relationship to Judaism first and foremost as a study in the production and dissemination of social taxonomies. The central question from this perspective is neither the similarities and differences in culture nor even the social interaction among ancient Christians and Jews, but how early Jesus groups imagined themselves and their characteristic cultures in relation to Judeans and theirs.[1] Similarities aside, at what point did some Jesus groups begin to assert that Judeans and their distinguishing culture were per se "other" and to reify that difference by postulating a distinction between Christianism and Judaism? Whatever its various social consequences, how widespread was this taxonomy before its imperial adoption in the centuries after Constantine?

There can of course be no question of anything like a comprehensive analysis here. My aim in what follows is only to demonstrate, through an examination of a few exemplary cases, that a significant distinction can be observed well into late antiquity between Jesus groups who made sense of their social experience with reference to such a notion of Christianism and those who did not; between those who came to differentiate a new "us" from the Judeans and the Nations alike, and those for whom Judeans and the Nations remained the primary division. This difference, and its implications for a historical understanding of the origins of Christianity and its relationship to Judaism, is as obscured by construing the latter group as "Jewish Christianity" as it is by construing the former as a "Christian Judaism."

The Making of Christianism and the Christianism-Judaism Divide

Like all cultural innovations, a taxonomic scheme separating Christians and their defining culture from Judeans and theirs undoubtedly began as a local invention. The question of when, where, and in whose hands Jesus and the apostles were first made to represent the embodiment of a cultural identity categorically other than Jewish is a complex one that, fortunately, need not be resolved for the purposes of the present study.[2] What is clear in any case is that by the second century Jesus and the apostles were being claimed for a Christianism that, according to its propagators, was different in kind from the cultures of all other peoples and from that of the Judeans in particular. The first extant uses of the substantive "Christianism" (*Christianismos*) are found in the letters of Ignatius, the self-described bishop of a Jesus group in Antioch.[3] These letters were apparently written over a matter of days, under somewhat extraordinary circumstances. Ignatius had been arrested for some activity connected to the group whose bishop he was, and was being extradited to Rome. Along the way he met with members of other local Jesus communities in Asia Minor and Macedonia. Written both to these communities and to one he anticipated seeing in Rome, Ignatius's letters reflect a social network of Jesus groups spanning the northern Mediterranean from Syria to Italy. The extent to which his appeals to Christianism were invoking a concept already widely assumed within that network or actively inculcating, through the medium of his letters, what was still at that point a more localized (Antiochan?) innovation is not immediately obvious.[4] In any event, by the end of the century a variety of authors connected to that network were propagating this same general taxonomy. Ignatius's letters, then, are a useful place to begin.

The social taxonomy espoused by Ignatius is complex but illuminating. A distinction between Judeans and "the (other) Nations" is taken for granted, as in the formulaic opening of his letter to Smyrna. Christ, he writes, was killed so that "through his resurrection he might eternally lift up the standard for his holy and faithful ones, whether among Jews or Gentiles [*eite en Ioudaiois eite en ethnesin*], in the one body of his church" (*Smyrn.* 1.2).[5] In Ignatius's usage, however, this Judeo-centric taxonomy has been subsumed under a differently self-referential division between "the holy and faithful ones [*pistous*]" or "the Church" on one hand, and those outside the Church—by implication, those who are *not* holy or faithful—

on the other. This primary division surfaces more explicitly elsewhere in the letters, as for example when Ignatius draws a contrast between "the believers [*hoi pistoi*]" who bear "the stamp of God the Father, in love, through Jesus Christ" and "the unbelievers [*hoi apistoi*]" who bear the stamp "of this world" (*Magn.* 5.2). Correlated more specifically with a translocal network of communities regulated by an assumed hierarchy of bishops, presbyters, and deacons, this Church is described more specifically as "the universal"— which is to say "catholic"—church (*Smyrn.* 8.2, *hē katholikē ekklēsia*) and its members as "Christians" (*Rom.* 3.2, *Eph.* 11.2).[6]

The description of the believers as those "among" either Judeans or the Nations (*Smyrn.* 1.2, *eite en Ioudaiois eite en ethnesin*) signals a certain ambiguity, if not an ambivalence, regarding the meaning of this distinction relative to Ignatius's primary division between Christians and nonbelievers. Judeans are not mentioned as such anywhere else in Ignatius's letters, let alone as a subcategory of Christians. The closest Ignatius comes to the latter idea is a passage that refers instead—and quite ambiguously—to "a man who is circumcised" (*andros peritomēn exontos*) and espouses Christianism (*Phld.* 6.1). The fact that Ignatius can refer explicitly to "Ephesian Christians" (*Eph.* 11.2, *Ephesiōn . . . tōn Christianōn*) might suggest that he considers Judean and Gentile as a subdivision that cuts across both "believers" and "unbelievers"; that everyone, Christian or not, is necessarily either a Judean or a Gentile simultaneously.[7] His only other use of the collective "Nations," however, refers clearly to a category of dangerous others: "Give no occasion to the Nations [*tois ethnesin*], lest on account of a few foolish persons the entire congregation of God be slandered."[8] This formulation of the matter suggests a quite different sense in which believers are "among" Gentiles and Judeans: one in which the latter distinction is not a division of believers at all, but of the unbelievers *among* whom Christians currently reside, and *from* whom believers can be recruited as in the more common ancient notion of believers "from" (*ex* or *apo*) the Judeans and the Nations.[9] In this case, "Ephesian Christians" would be a geographical designation functionally equivalent to Ignatius's address of his letter to "the Church . . . which is in Ephesus of Asia" (*tē ekklēsia . . . tē ousē en Ephesō tēs Asias*).[10]

Even if one were to postulate that Ignatius imagined that Christians must also simultaneously be Judeans or Gentiles, within the context of his wider taxonomic logic this could be so only insofar as these latter forms of identity were subordinated to and radically relativized by the former. More specifically, it would have implied a separation of the relevant people's salient habits and customs from the matters of familial descent and territorial derivation with which they are typically correlated in ancient (and modern) understandings of ethnicity.[11] In other words, one could be both a Christian and a Judean or a Gentile only insofar as the latter terms are reduced to what we might call ancestry or civic location—or what Ignatius, in a manner reminiscent of Paul, would likely have framed as one's identity "according to the flesh."[12] To be sure, it is not at all clear that Ignatius understood either "Judean" or "Gentile" in such a truncated way. Christians, in fact, are correlated with a kinship and a polity of their own: they can be addressed as "brothers" (e.g., *Rom.* 6.2) and owe primary allegiance to a "kingdom" quite other than any "of this age" (*Rom.* 6.1; cf. *Phld.* 3.3, *Eph.* 16.1). In any event, what marks someone as "Christian" for practical purposes is above all what we can call culture: certain learnable habits of discourse and practice that Ignatius portrays as being uniquely definitive of his own group's status as "faithful" and "holy." Thus can Ignatius distinguish between those merely *said* to be Christians and those who "really are" such (*Magn.* 4, *Rom* 3.2). It is these learnable habits that Ignatius reifies and essentializes as Christianism, as in his letter to Magnesia: "let us learn to live according to Christianism" (*Magn.* 10.1, *mathōmen kata Christianismon zēn*).[13]

In short, while the Judean/Gentile distinction is still a relevant subdivision of peoples for Ignatius, its significance is radically relativized by a new primary division: Christians and their Christianism on one hand, and everyone and everything else—Judeans, the Nations, and their respective cultures—on the other. "Let us learn to live according Christianism," Ignatius continues, "for whoever is called by a name other than this does not belong to God" (*Magn.* 10.1). As this stark opposition suggests, the assertion of difference between Christianism and the cultures of all other peoples is framed not merely as a matter of content, but as a difference in kind. Indeed, insofar as the term "culture" conjures up human creativity, Ignatius would likely have rejected such a characterization of Christianism entirely. Christianism, in his view, is decidedly *not* human or "fleshly"; it—and it alone—stamps a person with a character reflective of realities far beyond the ordinary human world, and indeed of God himself (*Magn.* 5.3). Such is the gulf between Christianism and "the world," in fact, that the greatness of the former can be measured in terms of the hatred directed to it by the latter (*Rom.* 3.3).

While Ignatius's language clearly implies a categorical and qualitative difference between Christianism and the habits of thought and practice of the world's other peoples, he is particularly explicit and emphatic where those of the Judeans are concerned. His exhortation to the Magnesian community to "live according to Christianity" (*kata Christianismon zēn*) comes specifically on the heels of a warning about "living according to Judaism": "Don't be deceived," he cautions, "by false opinions [*heterodoxiais*] or old fables [*mytheumasin*] that are of no use. For if we have lived according to Judaism [*kata Ioudaïsmon zōmen*] until now, we admit that we have not received God's gracious gift" (*Magn.* 8.1). The implication is clear: the salient culture of the Judeans is merely a matter of human opinions and tales—at best a "bad yeast, which has grown old and sour" (*Magn.* 10.2; cf. 9.1, "old ways"). As such, it is entirely incompatible with Christianism. "It is monstrous" [*atopos*]," he continues, "to speak of Jesus Christ and to live like a Judean [*ioudaïzein*]" (*Magn.* 10.3). The use of *atopos* here, if difficult to capture adequately in English, is quite telling. The incompatibility of living in accord with Christianism and living like a Judean—expressed equally well by the verbal form *ioudaïzein* or the substantive *Ioudaïsmos*—is such that attempting to do both leaves one utterly "without place" within Ignatius's social taxonomy.[14] He is equally emphatic in his letter to Philadelphia regarding the incompatibility of Christianity's divine transcendence with the mere humanness of Judaism: "if anyone should interpret Judaism to you, do not hear him. For it is better to hear Christianism from a man who is circumcised than Judaism from one who is uncircumcised. But if neither one speaks about Jesus Christ, they both appear to me as monuments and tombs of the dead, on which are written merely human names [*monon ono-mata anthrōpōn*]" (*Phld.* 6.1).

Even granting the possibility that Ignatius, beyond his extant letters, might sometimes have found reason to speak of "Judean Christians" in the same limited sense he spoke of "Ephesian" ones, his taxonomic logic makes the notion of a Jewish *Christianity* inconceivable. While we can of course point to any number of commonalities between Ignatius's cultural values and those generally characteristic of ancient Judeans—a shared deity, scriptures, and past heroes like Abraham, Isaac, Jacob, and "the prophets" among others (cf. *Phld.* 9.1)—Christianism and Judaism, from Ignatius's point of view, were entirely distinct and incompatible things. They had been such from the moment that God had manifested himself "humanly" (*anthrōpinōs*) in Christ—even a Christ who was descended from "the race of David according to the flesh" (*Eph.* 19.3; cf. 20.2)—if not already at the time of the "most divine prophets" who, even before the incarnation, had "lived according to Jesus Christ" (*Magn.* 8.2, *kata Christon Iēsoun ezēsan*). The apostles, by implication, are imagined not as practitioners of Judean culture, but as paradigmatic exemplars of the Christianism ideally embodied in Ignatius's own social network (e.g., *Eph.* 11.2; cf. *Phld.* 9.1, *Rom.* 13.3, etc.).

As noted above, the extent to which Ignatius's social taxonomy was already operative across that network at the time he was moving through it on his way to Rome is not immediately clear. What is plain in any case is that he was received by at least some members of these local communities as one of their own; that he was actively sought out by others who traveled as emissaries from their own communities to visit him along his journey (*Eph.* 1, 21.1; *Magn.* 2; 15.1; *Trall.* 1; cf. *Phld.* 11); and that some subsequently sought to acquire his collected letters as a source of ongoing edification (Pol. *Phil.* 13.2). Regardless of the extent to which his letters were the means or merely a reflection of its wider dissemination, then, it is not altogether surprising to find Ignatius's general taxonomic scheme at work in subsequent writings of others connected to this same network who, like him, self-identified as Christian.

The Martyrdom of Polycarp is an instructive example. The text was produced within the same Smyrnaean community that, decades earlier, had received both Ignatius and one of his letters. The subject of its narrative, the community's own bishop Polycarp, had been associated especially closely with Ignatius, serving as an important nexus of communication between him and the larger network of communities through which he traveled on his way to Rome (Ign. *Pol.* 8; Pol. *Phil.* 13). The account of Polycarp's martyrdom, like Ignatius's letters, identifies this network variously as "Christians," "the holy and universal [*katholikēs*, i.e., 'catholic'] Church," "the elect," and at least by implication "the believers."[15] It is understood as a class distinct from both the Judeans and "the whole multitude of the Nations" (Mart. Pol. 12.1–2). In what was becoming an increasingly common assertion, in fact, Christians are imagined as an entirely different kind or "race" (*genos*) of people.[16] On the face of it, this move would seem to render the notion that someone could be simultaneously Christian and either Judean or one of "the Nations" even more problematic than in the case of Ignatius's letters. In fact, the Christians in Smyrna and elsewhere are imagined not so much as being *of* the peoples who inhabit these regions as being resident aliens who live *among* them. The text is sent in the form of a letter from "the *ekklēsia* of God that temporarily resides in Smyrna [*hē paroikousa Smyrnan*] to the *ekklēsia* of God that temporarily resides in Philomelium [*tē paroikousē en Philomēliō*], and to all congregations of temporary residents everywhere, who belong to the holy and universal Church [*katholikēs ekklēsias paroikiais*]."

Be that as it may, what demarcates the Christian *genos* from both Judeans and "the (other) Nations" in practice is above all the presence or absence of certain cultural markers: a summarizable body of teaching reified here again as "Christianism." "If you wish to learn an account of Christianism [*ton tou Christianismou mathein logon*]," Polycarp says to the proconsul trying him, "appoint a day and listen" (Mart. Pol. 10.1). The identity declaration "I am Christian" (*Christianos eimi*) is said to be fundamentally incompatible, for example, with swearing by the *Tychē* of Caesar (Mart. Pol. 9.3–10.1). More generally, the Christians are identifiable as "atheists" relative to the Nations (Mart. Pol. 3.2, 9.2). The difference between Christianism and the defining practices of the Judeans, if less developed than in Ignatius's letters, is no less obvious. Indeed, Judeans are correlated with an *ethos* defined among other things by an especially violent strain of hostility to Christians. When it came time to actually burn Polycarp alive, "the Judeans" were "especially eager" to lend a hand, "as is their custom" (*hōs ethos autois*).[17] In practice, then, "Judean" and "Gentile" are less a subdivision of the Christian *genos* than of "unbelievers."[18] When the aborted martyr Quintus, therefore, is characterized emphatically as "a Phrygian, who had recently come from Phrygia," this long-standing term of ethnic identity is at best reduced to matters of geography and biological descent; at worst it signals an ambivalence regarding Quintus's status as a genuine representative of the Christian race at all.[19]

Irenaeus, a bishop of Lyons who eventually found his way to Rome, was part of the same social network to which Ignatius and Polycarp belonged and in which the Martyrdom of Polycarp was produced.[20] While Irenaeus undoubtedly knows the term "Christian," the substantive "Christianism," as far as I have noted, is not used in his extant writings. Likely because the "others" that most concern him in these particular texts are those found within his own "fractionated" group rather than outsiders, Irenaeus's more characteristic term of self-identification is orthodoxy.[21] The underlying taxonomic logic that produced the term "Christianism" and its distinction from Judaism is nonetheless clearly assumed. Irenaeus too considers human beings in three broad categories: the Judeans, the Nations, and the Faithful, with the former pair once again primarily a subdivision of the (by implication) unfaithful other.[22] In his hands, in fact, the notion of Christians as a distinct "race" is developed into a broad historical theory of human diversity. According to Irenaeus, humanity began as a singular "race of Adam" created in the likeness of a rational (*logikos*) God.[23] The "entire race of man," however, was quickly corrupted by the influence of apostate angels who, particularly after Adam and Eve's expulsion from paradise, introduced to their descendants a variety of new practices ranging from cosmetics, herbology, and metallurgy to magic and divination. Among the eventual consequences of these cultural innovations was the subsequent devolution of the singular human race into a multiplicity of races that Irenaeus considers positively "beastial" in nature.[24] In particular, Noah's sons are correlated with "three races of men" that, after Babel, were further subdivided into groups "according to their respective languages," resulting in the "diverse peoples" with varying customs that Irenaeus sees in his own day.[25] Christ, as *logos*, "became a man amongst men" precisely to restore these degenerate races to their primal humanity through a "regeneration" effected by baptism and, more specifically, a Holy Spirit "poured out in a new fashion upon the human race renewing man, throughout the world, to God" (*Epid.* 6–7). Christians, therefore, are not merely imagined as one more "race" alongside others, but as a qualitatively different one: the generic human race from which all others, Judean and Gentile, had devolved.[26]

If Christians are imagined as an altogether different type of race in theory, what distinguishes them from others in practice, for Irenaeus, is once again above all their adherence to a particular "way of life" (*Epid.* 98): a "rule of faith" (*Epid.* 3) that constitutes their special status as "the Faithful" over against both Judeans and the Nations. It is this way of life, which can also be called "the things of God," or simply "the truth," that Irenaeus seeks to outline systematically and authoritatively in *Demonstration of the Apostolic Preaching*. Like the Christian race itself, the way of life that defines it is understood to be different not only in fact but in kind from all others. Rather than the secondary cultural creations of demons or humans, it is simply an expression of the rational human nature itself in its ideal, divinely intended form: the natural law the Stoics had identified with "right reason."[27] It is less a culture at all, in other words, than simply the generically "right conduct" appropriate to a generically human race. Insofar as they are correlated with particular cultures, then, Judeans and the Nations represent a subdivision of the unfaithful other within Irenaeus's social taxonomy: the two categories of people *out of whom* generically human Christians can be made.

Judeans and their way of life represent a special and especially emphatic other with respect to the Christians and theirs within Irenaeus's theory of human diversity. Like other peoples, Judeans are associated with a particular territory, language, and patriarchal ancestry.[28] What sets them apart from "the (other) Nations," however, is a law divinely revealed to them through Moses. Originally intended to instruct them in the worship of God in an era when humanity had otherwise "forgotten, abandoned, and rebelled against" him (*Epid.* 8), this law has a somewhat ambiguous relationship to the natural law Irenaeus correlates with Christians. The Decalogue, at least, is understood to represent a verbal approximation of the law originally "implanted" in human nature and subsequently brought to fulfillment by Christ.[29] In any event, Jewish law was only ever intended as a temporary measure according to Irenaeus—one that now, in the wake of Christ's new covenant, is wholly past its expiration date: "We should no longer turn back . . . to the former legislation."[30] The Judeans, according to Irenaeus, never really lived up to that law in practice in any case, having forsaken God in favor of the same types of practices and allegiances that characterized the Nations.[31] Indeed, apparently because they—more than the Nations, who did not receive this extra divine guidance—should have known better, the Judeans, particularly after Christ, represent an actively "disbelieving people." According to Irenaeus, they were thus effectively disinherited in favor of a new people from "the foolish Gentiles, who were neither of the citizenship of God nor knew who God is" (*Epid.* 95). This new "chosen race," which can also be called "the Church," is thus correlated first and foremost with "the calling of the Gentiles" and placed in direct contrast to "the Synagogue."[32]

This taxonomy, in which Christians and their way of life are fundamentally other than the Judeans and theirs, is Irenaeus's framework not only for making sense of his own group in the present, but for imagining its origins in the historical past. Christianity, for Irenaeus, did not begin as yet one more cultural innovation. It was the result, rather, of a divine intervention to restore something that had been built into the very fabric of a divinely wrought human nature from the moment of its creation. Jesus and the apostles, as its primally authoritative embodiments, are thus portrayed in fundamentally ambivalent relationship to the Judeans among whom they lived. Christ himself, having descended from heaven, was born from a virgin who was herself, to be sure, "of the race of David and Abraham."[33] Ultimately, however, Christ's own *genos*, according to Irenaeus, "cannot be declared" insofar as his Father is not any man, but God himself (*Epid.* 70). If begotten "among the Judeans" then (*Epid.* 58), Christ is not himself to be considered a Judean in any but the most superficial sense. The apostles' relation to the Judeans is fraught with a similar ambivalence. As the title of *Demonstration of the Apostolic Preaching* already makes clear, Irenaeus assumes that the "rule of faith" said to demarcate his group from the Judeans and their way of life was embodied already by the apostles as a collective.[34] While they are no doubt to be included alongside the patriarchs and prophets among those exceptional few who would be saved from among the otherwise "disbelieving people" (cf. *Epid.* 47 and 56), the whole thrust of Irenaeus's racial theory implies that this is only so insofar as their distinctly Judean character had been effectively negated by their status as generically human Christians. To put it into the common terms of his day, they are less Judeans than believers *from* the Judeans. In fact, Irenaeus associates the apostles as a group—not just Paul—above all with the call of those from the Nations who, as Christians, would displace the Judeans as the "chosen race."[35]

It is within this taxonomic and historical framework that Irenaeus makes sense of other Jesus groups who exhibit features he associates with the Judean way of life rather than the Christian one. The primary impulse behind the writing of both *Against Heresies* and the *Demonstration of the Apostolic Preaching* was the existence of other ostensible "believers" whose teachings departed from his own in ways he found quite disturbing. To be sure, Irenaeus's primary concern was that "falsely so-called knowledge" which he associated principally with people directly connected to his own social network: Valentinus and Marcion.[36] Along the way, however, Irenaeus also produced the first extant treatment of the Ebionites, who, in stark contrast to these latter, "persevere in the customs which are according to the Law and practice a Jewish way of life."[37] Despite their allegiance to Christ, Irenaeus imagines the relationship of all such "heresies" to "orthodoxy" along the lines of the same qualitative difference separating the Christian race and its way of life from the Judeans and the Nations and theirs. Here again his own values represent the "single" way "illuminated by the heavenly light." Heresies, on the other hand, are only further instances of "the many, dark and divergent" ways "separating man from God" (*Epid.* 1). If his own "rule of faith" represents "the things of God," what others teach, by implication, are human things at best: "false opinions" generated by "schools"—that is, mere "schools of thought" (*haireseis*) as compared to the divine truths of orthodoxy. At worst they represent a continuation of the demonic innovations that had long characterized "the dominion of apostate angels."[38] Within Irenaeus's interpretive framework, then, even such apparent "believers," if not adhering in all salient respects to "the truth" as summarized in the *Demonstration*, should actually "be counted with the unbelievers" (*Epid.* 98–99). They are at most "sinful believers" who should expect judgment alongside the Judeans and the Nations (*Epid.* 8). Even if we might imagine Irenaeus conceiving of a category like "the Faithful from the Judeans" to account for the apostles and other like them, then, the Ebionites would scarcely qualify—at least, not without this quite literally damning caveat. Within Irenaeus's system of racial and cultural classification, the gap between the Christian way of life and the Judean one is the gap between faithfulness to God and rebellion against him; between a generic human nature created by God and the degenerate customs of demonically inspired "ethnic" people. The persistence of distinctly Judean values among the Ebionites does not represent a peculiarly Judean form of Christianism but a rejection of the Christian way of life tantamount to unbelief.

It is clear from these works that the formulation of a categorical distinction between Christians and their way of life and Judeans and theirs—that is to say, a taxonomic separation of Christianism and Judaism—was being increasingly disseminated through a second-century social network represented by Ignatius, Polycarp, and Irenaeus. Examples of the same broad taxonomic scheme could be multiplied, including works whose links to this particular network are not always equally clear.[39] Of course we must always reckon with the gap between prescriptive texts produced by intellectuals and institutional leaders of a group and the actual social realities attending its rank and file on the ground. Ongoing concerns among self-described orthodox writers into the third century and beyond about "Judaizing" on one hand and "Gnostics" on the other indicate quite clearly that there were varying views as to where, exactly, the boundary between Christianism and Judaism was to be drawn, both socially and culturally. But while figures like Irenaeus, Marcion, and Valentinus disagreed sharply about *where* the line between themselves and Judeans should be drawn, what was not apparently in dispute among them was the more fundamental taxonomic premise that such a line between Christianism and Judaism *was in any event to be drawn.* Undoubtedly these intellectuals sought, with whatever degree of success, to inculcate that same basic assumption within the communities to which they belonged.[40] Seen from this perspective, what changed in Christianity's imperial era was not some final separation of Christianity and Judaism; it was the sphere of influence—the power, the reach, and the numbers—of a group that had been actively propagating this taxonomic separation for centuries.

The Pseudo-Clementine Homilies

Reimagining the origins of Christianity and its separation from Judaism as the invention and dissemination of a new social taxonomy raises the question of alternative taxonomies, at work in other Jesus groups, that the propagators of the Christianism-Judaism division sought to displace. Once again there can be nothing approaching a comprehensive analysis here given the limits of space and the range and complexity of the data. The question of the first generation of the movement—both during Jesus's lifetime and after the conflict that led to his violent death—is a particularly thorny one. While it is clear by all accounts that there was no concept of Christianism per se in this period, how either Jesus or his first followers viewed themselves and their salient habits of practice and discourse in relation to those of other Judeans is not immediately self-evident given the nature of our sources, and it remains a contested issue.[41] In any event, it seems plain from the various conflicts reflected in the letters of Paul that some, at least, within the broader Jesus movement did not imagine their alignment with Jesus to be the mark of anything other than proper Judean practice. The problems involved in moving from Paul's rhetoric to conclusions regarding the group or groups to whom he's reacting, however, are sufficiently complex to warrant a separate study. Indeed, even how Paul viewed himself and the assemblies he founded in relation to what he called *Ioudaïsmos* (Gal 1:13, 14) is a live question whose answer would require much more space than is possible here.[42] Somewhat regretfully, then, I leave the matter of the first generation aside in what follows and focus instead on select examples from later generations. In particular, I examine some classic cases from Irenaeus's time and later in order to highlight the problem with using a term like "Jewish Christianity" even once the distinction between Christianism and Judaism was becoming increasingly disseminated.

The Pseudo-Clementine literature has long been considered a classic exemplum of Jewish Christianity.[43] Baur's theory of early Christian history and of the place of the Pseudo-Clementine literature within it spawned more than a century and a half (and counting) of source-critical theories seeking to distinguish which parts of this complex corpus represent Jewish Christianity and which do not.[44] Recent scholars, on the other hand, while of course acknowledging the source-critical issues, have turned increasing attention to analysis of the *Homilies* and *Recognitions* as compositions in their own right.[45] For my purposes I focus solely on the present form of the *Homilies*. Apparently written in mid-fourth-century Syria, this work postulates a network of communities between Caesarea Maritima and Antioch with institutional authorities consisting of bishops, presbyters, and deacons established by Peter himself.[46] Though composed out of various sources, the Pseudo-Clementine *Homilies* present a coherent understanding of the relationship of disciples of Jesus to Judeans on one hand and to the Nations on the other. The Homilist develops a comprehensive theory of human diversity, in fact, that is similar in many respects to the one articulated by Irenaeus. The social taxonomy that theory is meant to support, however, is significantly different. In the *Homilies* the primary division of peoples is simply the Judeans and the Nations; and its central cultural division, accordingly, is what it calls "the things of the Judeans" as opposed to those of the Nations, above all "the things of the Greeks." There are, in other words, neither Christians nor Christianity in the *Homilies*; there are only Judeans, the Nations, and those called "from the Nations" to become proselytes of the Judeans and even Judeans themselves.

The Judeans, the Nations, and the Human Race

Much like Irenaeus, the Homilist assumes that a singular human race underlies human social and cultural diversity (e.g., 5.24.5, *to pan genos*).[47] Here again that race is both analyzed in Greek philosophical terms as a particular "nature" (*anthrōpou physis*, e.g., 3.31.4) and historicized in Judean scriptural terms as a primal human ancestor created in the image and likeness of a divine creator to be "ruler and lord" of the world (10.3.3). Human nature consists of body and soul, each in turn divisible into three parts: the body into the three passions of desire, anger, and grief; and the soul into reason (*logismos*), knowledge, and fear (20.2, 4; cf. 19.21). This nature was created with a divine purpose, and it is the creator's will that humans live in accord with their nature and its reasoning faculty in particular. In this sense the Homilist imagines a "perpetual law" (*nomon aiōnion*) equally available to and relevant for the whole human race, obedience to which yields "freedom from grief and fear."[48] Human nature is nonetheless subject to perversion by "formed habits" or "customs" that can become almost as powerful as nature itself, even to the point of constituting a "second nature" (5.25.1, *deutera physis hē synētheia*; cf. 4.11.2 and 8.16). Such perverse behaviors are correlated with lack of restraint in the passions that effectively render people "irrational animals," with souls so degraded as to lose their likeness to God in the present and to be subject to eternal punishment when they depart the body at death.[49]

The rise of such unnatural and irrational customs is explained, much as by Irenaeus, with reference to demonic innovation, and more specifically with reference to the biblical story of the Giants and the flood (see especially *Hom.* 8.9–23). Some lower-order angels, it is said, took advantage of the malleability of their "god-like substance" to metamorphose into various earthly forms—mineral, animal, and human—in order to entice people away from God; but upon adopting human nature (*tēn anthrōpōn physis*) they fell prey to desire and became stuck in the human realm (8.13.1). Wishing to please the human women they desired, these fallen angels introduced all sorts of innovative corruptions, from magic and astronomy, to the valuation of precious stones and metals, to the dying of garments and other forms of adornment (8.14). Their sexual relations with women produced Giants: unholy angelic-human hybrids who developed an unnatural (*para physin*) taste for meat (8.15–16). These Giants ultimately gave rise to a "new race" (*kainon genos*): a "bastard race" (*nothoi tō genei*) of demons whose specially powerful souls survived the flood God had sent in the meantime to purify the world (8.17–18). This demonic race, which has remained in the world ever since, satisfies its ongoing cravings for meat and sex by inhabiting human bodies and hijacking their reasoning faculties in order to lead them into illicit behaviors (9.10). God thus instituted a second (this time angelically mediated) law to govern this new demonic race: specifically, a decree that they would have no power over anyone who followed God's original, eternal law, but only over those who actively subjected themselves to demons by "pouring libations and partaking of [their] table" and otherwise engaging in their unclean (*akathartou*) diet.[50] It is through diet above all, in fact, that humans become subject to demons. The *Homilies* assume a fascinating physiological psychology in which demons infect the soul through the medium of food, replacing right reason (cf. 10.18.4, *orthos logismos*) with a demonic reasoning correlated with irrational desire (11.11.5, *alogos epithymia*), hostility to God, and phantasms of false gods—in a word, fundamentally flawed "conceptions of worship" (11.2.1, *tōn thrēskeiōn hypo-noias*).[51] This corrupt reasoning, in turn, leads to unnatural behaviors that produce all manner of suffering and disease in the present life and will ultimately necessitate eternal punishment in a next one.[52]

Human diversity, in the view of the Homilist, was a direct consequence of this new demonic race. What had originally been a unified and peaceful monarchy of the one true God devolved into a chaotic polyarchy in which worshippers of multiple gods, inspired by demonic reasonings, each sought their own kingdoms. Noah was "a king according to the image of the one God"; but after his death Zoroaster of the family or race (*genos*) of Ham, desiring his own kingdom, became a powerful practitioner of magic and introduced still more practices opposed to God. The fire-worshipping tribes (*phyla*) of the Egyptians, Babylonians, and Persians, in turn, each branched off from him, developing their own characteristic perversions. Thus arose the "many partitions of the one original kingdom" (9.6.1) into the social diversity and ethnic rivalries the Homilist observes in his own day.[53] Egyptians and Phoenicians—quite ironically from the point of view of the *Homilies*—mock the absurdities of each other's piety (10.16–18), while Greeks scoff more generally at the ignorance of "Barbarians" (e.g., 1.11). Greek culture—that is, what the text calls "the patrimonial customs of the Greeks" (4.8.2, *ta patria ethē . . . ta Hellēnōn*)—is singled out for particular censure. This includes not only Greek myths (*mythoi*) and shows (*theatra*), but ethical practices, books, and not least philosophy (4.19). In short, "the whole learning of the Greeks [*tēn pasan Hellēnōn paideian*] is a most dreadful fabrication of a wicked demon" (4.12.1). Such is its special perversion, in fact, that the greater one's Greek education, the further one gets from "thinking in accord with nature" (*tou kata physin . . . phronein*); rustics and Barbarians, therefore, actually sin less by "not having been instructed by Greeks" (4.19).[54] Greek culture is all the more insidious, in the view of the Homilist, because of its spread beyond the Greek *ethnos* to people of other nations—people, indeed, who as a result can be considered "Greeks" themselves in some sense.[55] Youths in particular are thus counseled to avoid exposure to Greek culture, and even Greek cities, as far as possible.[56]

While the *Homilies* understand that Judeans are in several respects comparable to other peoples, their culture—what the Homilist summarily calls "the things of the Judeans" (e.g., 4.7.2, *ta Ioudaiōn*)—is said to be different not merely in content but in kind from all others. Judeans, to be sure, are themselves described variously as an *ethnos* (e.g., 2.16.5) and a tribe (14.5.2, *phylon*). Like other peoples, moreover, they are correlated both with a particular land (Judea; e.g., 1.7–9) and with patriarchal ancestors from whom they received distinctive customs, books, and above all piety.[57] The various names used of this people in the *Homilies*—most commonly *Ioudaioi*, but also Hebrews and sons of Israel—apparently reflect various of these aspects.[58] More fundamentally, the Homilist is quite explicit regarding the underlying human nature common to Judeans and others. Nevertheless, the text is equally emphatic in its assertion of an essential and far-reaching difference between the Judeans and the collectivity of other Nations—what it calls *ta ethnē*—and precisely at what we might term the cultural or arguably even religious level: "Do not conclude," it cautions in 9.20, "that we [Judeans] are of a different nature [*allēs physeōs ontes*]. For we are of the same nature as you [Nations], just not of the same piety [*tēs gar autēs hymin esmen physeōs, all' ou thrēskeias*]." This difference, moreover, is articulated not merely on a quantitative scale of greater and lesser value, but qualitatively: Judeans, it continues, are "not only much but altogether superior to you [Nations]." While the characteristic customs of all other peoples are demonic contrivances so ingrained as to have become an artificial and wholly corrupt "second nature," Judean culture is simply a direct reflection of the primal human nature originally created by God. More specifically, God's eternal law, unwritten in the earliest eras of human history, was revealed in written form to Moses in the wake of the unnatural practices inspired by demonic reasonings—and precisely to clarify the genuine dictates of right reason: "there would have been no need of Moses ... if of themselves they would have understood what is rational (*to eulogon*)."[59] Not only this law but also its authoritative interpretations were initially entrusted, by divine fiat, to seventy authorized teachers, and eventually to the "scribes and the Pharisees" as the current holders of the "Chair of Moses."[60] Unlike the books of the Greeks, then, the "books current among the Jews" represent a divine disclosure of discourses and behaviors properly consistent with rational human nature.[61] Judeans, consequently, are subject neither to the irrational phantasms experienced by the Nations nor to the variety of other infirmities that result from an unnatural, demonic diet. Nor, in the end, will their souls be subject to eternal punishment when finally separated from the body at death.[62]

What makes the Judeans different in kind from the collective "Nations" of the world, in short, is their defining "polity of piety" (*tēs hēmeteras thrēskeias tēn politean*).[63] Indeed, in the Homilist's view, being Judean, much like being Greek, is less a matter of descent than of participation in a cultural praxis:

> For the worshipper of God [*theosebēs*] is the one ... who is actually a worshipper of God; not who is only said to be such, but who actually carries out the commandments of the law that has been given to him ... In just the same way, if someone from another tribe should practice the law, he is a Judean, but by not practicing it is a Greek [*ean ho allophylos ton nomon praxē, Ioudaios estin, mē praxas de Hellēn*]. For the Judean, believing in God, does the law [*ho gar Ioudaios pisteuōn theō poiei ton nomon*], by which belief he also removes the other sufferings [or passions, *pathē*] ... But one who is not doing the law [*ho de mē poiōn ton nomon*] is clearly, due to his failure to believe in God, a deserter—and thus not as a Judean [*kai houtōs hōs ouk Ioudaois*] but as a sinner is subjected, because of his sin, to those sufferings [or passions, *pathōn*] established for the punishment of sinners. (11.16.2–4)

From this point of view, "worshipper of God" and "Judean" are virtual synonyms.[64] In fact, while the Judeans on one level represent a particular and particularly "God-beloved" *ethnos* (2.33.3, *tou theophilous hēmōn ethnous*), on another, more profound level they are less one more people among others than the instantiation of generic humanity itself, living alongside the less-than-fully-human "ethnic ones" whose customs diverge variously and tragically from the divine (Judean) order. To be Judean, in other words, is simply to be fully human. Those from "other tribes" can recover their degraded humanity by adopting Judean customs and becoming, in effect, Judeans themselves.[65] This, according to the Homilist, is precisely why God sent Jesus.

Jesus and Judeans "from the Nations"

At a fundamental level, the Jesus of the *Homilies* functions much like its Moses. He is a prophet who provides an inerrant guide to the rational for those unable to discern it for themselves, and thus the "saving truth" to those who would be otherwise unable to grasp it firmly.[66] His teaching is essentially identical to that of Moses, to the point that a given individual needs only one or the other, not both, in order to live in accord with the will of God. "For there being one teaching by both, God accepts him who has believed either of these. But believing a teacher is [only] for the sake of doing the things spoken by God."[67] To be sure, Jesus also taught his disciples to discern corrupting emendations inserted into the books of Moses in the era after the Seventy; still, he is neither essential nor necessary for Judeans, who have long had his basic teaching within that revealed law in any case.[68] Those like Peter who recognize both Moses and Jesus, therefore, are not practicing a piety that transcends that of the Judean people—for nothing does!—but are simply Judean scribal elites, in the know not only about Jesus but about text-critical problems in the Torah.[69] Indeed, they are themselves still subject to the authority of the "scribes and Pharisees" as rightful occupiers of the "Chair of Moses," even if some of these latter merit criticism, particularly with respect to their reticence in sharing Judean salvation with the Nations.[70]

The central difference between Moses and Jesus, in fact, is simply their target audience. While Moses was sent as a prophet to the Judean people, Jesus, in fulfillment of ancient prophecy, was sent first and foremost for the sake of the Nations, who, unlike the Judeans, remain yet "ignorant of what they ought to do."[71] More specifically, Jesus appeared in Judea, which is to say among those "pious" already accustomed to his basic message, to find disciples to send "to the uneducated Nations" (17.7.1, *eis ta amathē ethnē*).[72] Peter in particular is at the forefront of this effort, and it is precisely his initial foray among the Nations that the *Homilies* purport to report.[73] What Peter brings to these ignorant and suffering Nations is described among other things as a teaching on "the whole matter of piety" (1.19.4, *holon to tēs eusebeias ... pragma*), a polity based on worship (13.4.1, *tēs hēmeteras thrēskeias tēn politeian*), a prophetic principle (1.21.2, *tēs prophētikēs hypotheseōs*), and a God-willed dogma (1.21.3, *tō theoboulētō dogmati*) or simply "the true *logos*" (1.13.3, *tou alēthous logou*). To put it in our terms, then, it is a cultural complex—albeit one framed as being uniquely authoritative by virtue of its grounding in the transcendent realities of divine revelation and natural law. While correlated with universal human nature, the discourse and praxis constituting this "polity of worship" are also identified, as we have seen, specifically with the ancestral customs of the Judeans.[74] Accordingly, ritual initiation of Gentiles into the group—an elaborate rite involving a period of instruction followed by fasting, ritual washing, and perhaps even public self-shaming—is seen simultaneously as a "regeneration" of the corrupt soul into something more akin to its primal rational nature and as integration into an imagined divine monarchy represented by the Judean people.[75] It is, in other words, to begin to live like a Judean—and indeed, from the point of view of the text, to become one: "if someone from another tribe should practice the law, he is a Judean" (11.16.3, *ean ho allophylos ton nomon praxē, Ioudaios estin*).

The point is well illustrated by the *Homilies'* iteration of the story of Jesus and the Canaanite woman (2.19–20; cf. Matt 15:21–27). The woman, who is here named Justa, is identified as a Syro-Phoenecian and a Canaanite by race (*to genos Chananitis*). As in Matthew, the grounds for Jesus's initial refusal to heal her daughter is her status as a Gentile "dog," though here the matter is explained more fully in light of the *Homilies'* own theory of human diversity: "It is not lawful to heal the Nations [*ta ethnē*], who are like to dogs on account of their indiscriminate use of meats and practices, while the table in the kingdom has been given to the sons of Israel [*tois hyiois Israēl*]." Jesus relents, moreover, not simply as a result of the woman's acceptance of her subordinate, subhuman status as in Matthew, but specifically because she exchanged her own "ethnic" customs for the practices of these children of Israel—a move that represented not only a change of *politeia*, but of her very identity: "Having changed what she was, by living like the sons of the kingdom [*metathemenē hoper ēn, tō homoiōs diaitasthai tois tēs basileias hyois*] she obtained healing for her daughter, as she asked. For had she been a Gentile [*ethnikēn ousan*] and remained in her polity [*politeia*], he would not have healed her since it is not permitted to heal someone as a Gentile who remains a Gentile [*hōs ethnikēn <ethnikēn meinasan>*]."[76] If no longer a Gentile, what Justa became was not a Christian, but "a proselyte of the Judeans" (13.7.3, *Ioudaiois prosēlytos*). Her adoptive sons grow similarly attached to their mother's newly adopted worship (13.4, *thrēskeia*) and eventually become key disciples of Peter. Their own Gentile background, early exposure to Simon Magus, and extensive Greek education, in fact, make them particularly useful both as advanced spies in Peter's incursion into Gentile territory (3.73–4.6) and as effective champions of the Judean way of life over against the culture of the Greeks (13.7; cf. 15.4).[77]

The parade example of what the Homilist sees as the transfer of a person of "ethnic" origin into the "natural" Judean polity is Clement himself. Unlike the Canaanite woman, Clement is no barbarian, but a Roman nobleman of the *genos* of Tiberius Caesar, equipped with a "full Greek education."[78] Much like Justin, the pseudonymous Clement portrays himself as unable to find satisfaction in Greek philosophy, which as mere "opinion" provides neither intellectual certainty nor sufficient ethical motivation (1.1–4; cf. Justin, *Dial.* 2–8). But whereas Justin found ultimate solace in the teachings of the Christians, Clement found it in the teachings of the Judeans.[79] According to the story, he had been considering searching for answers among the Egyptian magicians when he caught wind of a Judean wonder-worker instead: "a certain one in Judea . . . proclaiming good news to the Judeans of the kingdom of the invisible God, saying that any of them who set their *politeia* right would enjoy it," and working miracles as proof of his authenticity (1.6.2–4). Clement thus resolves to go not to Egypt, but rather to Judea; and though his plan is initially thwarted by adverse winds that leave him, ironically, in Alexandria after all, his zeal to get to Judea is only heightened by an encounter in Egypt with someone who was not only acquainted with Jesus, but "from that very land" (*tēs ekeithen gēs*) himself, namely a "Hebrew" called Barnabas (1.9.1).[80] When this Barnabas, out of a desire to be among his own *ethnos* (*tois heautou homoethnesin*), decides to return to Judea for a festival (1.13.4), Clement secures directions to his home and soon follows. Upon arriving he meets Peter, who immediately promises that Clement, though a "foreigner" (*xenon*), would soon become a "citizen of [truth's] own city" and an "heir of the blessings which are both eternal and cannot possibly be taken from you" (1.16.3). Sure enough, Clement immediately attaches himself to Peter and, after several months of instruction, experiences formal "regeneration" by means of ritual fasting and washing (11.35.1–2, *anagennēsei*).[81]

Meanwhile, the resulting change in Clement's behavior is said to rekindle an earlier tension between Clement and an old family friend named Appion—as it happens, the famed anti-Judean writer against whom Josephus too polemicized—about the merits of the Judeans and their culture.[82] When the two men happen to run into each other in Tyre, Appion is distressed that Clement, despite his Roman nobility and Greek education, "has been seduced by a certain barbarian [*hypo barbarou tinos*] called Peter to practice and to speak the things of the Judeans [*ta Ioudaiōn poiein kai legein*] . . . forsaking his ancestral ways [*ta patria*], and falling away to the customs of the barbarians [*eis ethē barbara*]."[83] His expression of concern touches off an extended discussion about whether abandoning the cultural heritage of one's own ancestors in favor of that of another people—specifically, in this case, abandoning Greek things in favor of Judean ones—can be considered in any way pious (4.7–25; cf. 6.1–26).[84] Clement's general answer is that the essence of piety is not "to observe the customs of one's fathers [*ta patria*]; but to observe them if they be pious, and to shake them off if they be impious" (4.8.3). Regarding the specific question of Greek versus Judean culture, the matter stands thus: while "the whole learning of the Greeks [*tēn pasan Hellēnōn paideian*] is a most dreadful fabrication of a wicked demon ... the doctrine of the barbarous Judeans [*ho de tōn . . . barbarōn Ioudaiōn logos*], as you call them, is most pious" (4.12.1, 4.13.3). "On this account," he concludes, "I took refuge in the holy God and law of the Judeans" (4.22.2). Appion's fears are thus confirmed: "I knew, ever since I heard that you were consorting with Judeans, that you had alienated your judgment" (4.24.1). Clement and his brothers, as Appion will put it at the close of the *Homilies*, had "become Judeans" (20.22.2, *Ioudaious gegenēmenous*).[85]

The Pseudo-Clementine *Homilies* give expression to a form of group identity in which Jesus figured centrally but that nonetheless differed fundamentally from that of the social network to which Ignatius and Irenaeus belonged. The difference between them is not resolvable into a distinction between particularism and universalism, nor is it attributable to especially "syncretistic" developments in the *Homilies*. The self-understanding of the Homilist is every bit as universalistic as Irenaeus's, and indeed on much the same grounds. In both cases a theory of racial and cultural diversity, formulated from a blend of Judean and Greek philosophical traditions, provides the basis for positing a stark and qualitative difference between the writer's own group and all other peoples of the world.[86] Both writers portray their own defining habits of practice and discourse not so much as one more culture among others, but as the instantiation of a primal, generic human nature created by God. All others, insofar as they are different, represent so many demonic devolutions from that primal humanity. Both, moreover, imagine that God revealed a written law to Israel precisely to counter human deviance from the natural law he intended for them, and that the apostles were sent particularly to "the Nations" with a message and means of regeneration to restore them to their lost, primal nature. The central difference between Irenaeus and the *Homilies*, rather, is the underlying social taxonomy in whose service this racial theory is enlisted: the identification of the universalized "us" in relation to the Judeans on one hand and the Nations on the other.

While Irenaeus uses this theory to valorize a new race of Christians over against both Judeans and the Nations, there is no such third term at work in the *Homilies*. The only "new race" (*kainon genos*) reckoned with here is the one created by demons that led to human diversity in the first place (8.18.1). The only "parting of the ways" (cf. 8.22.4, *tas diexodous tōn hodōn*), in a striking turn of phrase, is the one that occurred long ago, when those "ignorant of the foreordained law" became "polluted in body and soul" by demonic practices and formed themselves into the Nations, which is to say the subhuman "ethnic ones." In the view of the Homilist, in fact, Jesus came into this ancient breach as the Prophet of Truth, precisely to overcome it.[87] He does this not by establishing yet another new race, let alone a religion inclusive of both Jews and Gentiles, but by sending apostles from Judea to persuade the Nations to give up their ethnic heritages in favor of the ancestral customs of the "God-beloved *ethnos*," the Judeans (2.33.3), and in this way to regenerate their degraded humanity. While concerned first and foremost to call people "from the Nations" (*apo ethnōn*), then, the *Homilies* has no comparable notion of disciples *from* the Judeans. Faithful Judeans, already embodying the "natural" practices of a generic humanity, require no such call to a new people, polity, or piety. Indeed, what the Nations are called to is nothing other than the people and culture of Judea. There are, in short, neither Christians nor Christianism in the *Homilies*, only the Judeans and their ancestral customs on one hand and the collective Nations and theirs on the other.[88] More specifically, there are two types of Judeans envisioned here: born ones and made ones, "Hebrews" and those "called from the Nations" to restore their full humanity as Judean proselytes (cf. 13.7.3, *Ioudaiois prosēlytos*).[89]

The Pseudo-Clementine *Homilies*, in sum, do not articulate a distinctly Jewish form of Christianity. To redescribe the *Homilies* with reference to "Christianity" at all, Jewish or otherwise, is not to recover its historical self-understanding. On the contrary, it is to overwrite it with terms manufactured pointedly by one of its more historically successful rivals. Translated into the modern English idiom of "isms," the *Homilies* do not represent a Jewish Christianism, but a Judaism seeking Gentile converts.[90] To analyze this text as a combination of "Christian" and "Jewish" traits at all is to relocate it within a (now naturalized) taxonomic framework invented specifically by the makers of Christianity—and, in the process, to fundamentally misrepresent its own understanding of its relationship to what 2 Maccabees, at least, would have called *Ioudaïsmos*.[91] Whatever other purposes the interpretive construct "Jewish Christianity" might serve for the modern reader, then, it is very much at odds with the historical task of elucidating the role played by social constructions of identity in the historical separation of Christianity and Judaism, at least where the *Homilies* are concerned. The same, in fact, appears to be true of the ancient group with whom the *Homilies* have frequently been associated, the Ebionites.

Ebionites

Portions, at least, of the Pseudo-Clementine literature have often been attributed to a group first known to us from Irenaeus called the Ebionites.[92] While already apparent in the account of Epiphanius, this attribution is questionable, not least given our scant knowledge of the group. Even more than the Pseudo-Clementines, the Ebionites in any event have been all but synonymous with Jewish Christianity in the scholarly imagination since the very inception of the category. It was precisely Toland's interest in reinterpreting what had long been considered the Ebionite heresy as "original Christianity" that led him to introduce the idea of an early Jewish Christianity in the first place.[93]

As the new concept "Jewish Christianity" became mainstreamed in nineteenth- and twentieth-century scholarship, the relationship of these Ebionites to the apostolic community became a generative problem. As we have seen, concerns to distance them from the apostles led to the postulation of subcategories of Jewish Christianity, which in turn produced the methodological problems of terminology and definition.[94] The question of the genealogical relationship of the Ebionites to the apostles, which is deeply rooted in a Christian anxiety to imbue contemporary values with all the authority of an original, apostolic Christianity—or, conversely, to divest them of it—matters little for my purposes. No doubt the Ebionites claimed the same essential continuity with Jesus and the apostolic community that the propagators of Christianism and the Pseudo-Clementine *Homilies* were each claiming. And no doubt the reality was in all cases a complex combination of historical continuities and discontinuities, and of morphological similarities and dissimilarities, with respect to any number of variables.[95] My interest here, as in the earlier sections of this chapter, is limited to recovering, as far as possible, how the members of the group in question understood themselves in relation to others, particularly where Judeans and their characteristic culture were concerned.

Significant challenges complicate this project. In the first place, the only secure evidence we have for Ebionites comes in the form of reports by their hostile and frequently unreliable detractors.[96] None of the texts that have been attributed to the group by one author or another clearly self-identifies as Ebionite in a manner analogous to the self-identifying Christian works produced by Ignatius, Irenaeus, and others in their orbit. Most such texts, moreover, involve significant interpretive complications of their own.[97] Second, the heresiological accounts of the Ebionites raise as many questions as they answer about the nature and history of the group, not least in relation to another purported group called Nazoraeans.[98] Third, and most immediately relevant for our present purpose, are problems resulting from the strategic importance of naming in heresiological rhetoric. Assigning names to and constructing genealogies of one's competitors are essential and interrelated components of the heresiological project. Christian heresiology, then and now, is driven by several basic assumptions: that the Christianism of the heresiologist represents an essentially stable, ontological reality existing somehow beyond the vagaries of cultural history; that this reality manifested itself primally and authoritatively in Jesus and (at least some segment of) the apostolic community in the past; that the heresiologist's own group stands in essential continuity with the latter as the authoritative repository of the original, apostolic Christianism in the present; that others who make analogous claims, regardless of what they might say about themselves, can only have derived their salient habits of discourse and practice from somewhere other than Jesus and the apostles; and that such rivals, therefore—again, whatever they might say about themselves— cannot be considered straightforward examples of Christianity. In short, the name of the heresiological game is to construct histories that show where such competing views and values "really" came from, and to name the groups that espouse them accordingly. The central aim of the genre, in other words, is precisely to displace the self-understanding of one's competitors by means of an identity constructed *for them* in the service of the heresiologist's own apologetic agenda. The fundamental question facing the critical historian, then, is the extent to which it is possible to recover, from one group's efforts to construct taxonomies of heretical others, the social taxonomies at work among the so-called heretics themselves.

Epiphanius's treatment of the Ebionites well illustrates the complex dynamics of naming as heresiological strategy.[99] It is to be recalled at the outset that Epiphanius is unwilling to grant any of his rivals, Ebionites or otherwise, that name which he himself holds most dear—Christian— regardless of the extent to which they themselves might want or at least tolerate it. "Even today," he says, "people call all the sects [*haireseis*], I mean Manichaeans, Marcionites, Gnostics and others, by the common name of 'Christians,' though they are not Christians. However, although each sect [*hairesis*] has another name, it still allows this one with pleasure, since the name is an ornament to it" (*Pan.* 29.6.6). Epiphanius, accordingly, approaches naming with a subtle asymmetry. Competing Jesus groups are frequently named after some purportedly deviant teacher said to have authored their salient features; Cerinthians and Ebionites, for example, are people whose heretical ideas came from Cerinthus and Ebion, respectively—not from Christ and the apostles. Epiphanius, on the other hand, does not call himself, say, a "Paulianist"—a name reserved for disciples of Paul of Samosata (not those of Paul of Tarsus!) in *Anacephalaeosis* 5.65—but simply a Christian. Nor does he hesitate to assign his competitors names they may not use or even want for themselves if it can help distance them from the apostles. The term *hairesis* ("heresy") is an obvious, generic example. But this can also involve more specific names meant to highlight the derivation of competitors' salient features from somewhere (anywhere!) other than Jesus and the apostles.[100] Thus Epiphanius tells his readers, for example, that Ebion "is a Samaritan" even while reporting that Ebion himself "rejects the name with disgust" (*Pan.* 30.1.5). A different tack is taken when Epiphanius denies the Ebionites any place in his taxonomy at all: since Ebion, he says, "is midway between all the sects ... he amounts to nothing" (*Pan.* 30.1.4).[101]

It is reasonably clear at any rate that the name "Ebionite" reflects a term of self-identification by some actual ancient Jesus group. To be sure, even here the sources are not univocal. Eusebius claims it was a name of derision bestowed on the group from the outside: "The first Christians gave these the suitable name of Ebionites because they had poor and mean opinions concerning Christ" (*Hist. eccl.* 3.27.1). If seemingly at odds with reports of a founder called Ebion—of whom Eusebius seems to know nothing—this claim does show awareness of both the etymological derivation of the name from the Hebrew term for "poor" or "needy" (*ebion*, perhaps as Carleton Paget suggests "via its Aramaic equivalent, 'ebionaya'"), as well as the apparently common practice of mocking that name by giving it a demeaning interpretation.[102] Of course this latter strategy—yet another in the heresiological arsenal—would have had that much more bite if used to undermine a name a group had actually used of itself. Epiphanius, in fact, provides at least one alternative interpretation of the name apparently offered by the group: "They themselves ... boastfully claim that they are poor because they sold their possessions in the apostles' time and laid them at the apostles' feet, and went over to a life of poverty and renunciation; and thus, they say, they are called 'poor' by everyone" (*Pan.* 30.17.2; cf. Acts 4:32–37). The fact that Epiphanius feels compelled to deny this, countering that the name really derived from their founder Ebion, suggests that this claim was made by the group itself.[103] Certainly Epiphanius would have had little reason to supply his rivals with such a convenient claim of continuity with the apostolic community.

A self-designation as "the Poor," moreover, is anything but surprising for a group correlated so closely with Judean piety.[104] It has long been noted that this is a highly charged term in the Jewish scriptures, where it is used frequently and in a variety of texts to refer particularly "to those within Israel who are suppressed and oppressed by other Israelites—those who have their legitimate rights taken away from them by the rich and powerful," but who can also, for precisely this reason, expect divine vindication.[105] The term was thus ripe for the picking by dissident Judean groups who wished to valorize themselves over against more powerful rivals. The Dead Sea sect did precisely that, identifying themselves as both "the congregation of the poor" (*edat ha-ebionim*) and "the meek" who would "inherit the land" in their commentary on Psalm 37.[106] Whether or not the first-generation Jesus group in Jerusalem did the same (cf. Gal 2:10, Rom 15:26), the complex of ideas was clearly picked up in circles of Jesus's followers, most notably in texts arguably reflecting a sectarian Jewish outlook.[107]

There can be little doubt that the self-described "Poor" underlying these ancient reports about Ebionites claimed precisely the sort of essential continuity with Jesus and the apostles that their critics wished to claim. Beyond the matter of the apostles' economic practice as reported by Epiphanius, a variety of sources indicate that the group explained its Torah observance in particular—apparently in answer to criticism from the nonobservant propagators of Christianism—by appealing to the example of Jesus.[108] It is easy to imagine, in fact, that their widely reported rejection of Paul served a function structurally analogous to the heresiological invention of Ebion, allowing them to assert that their Christian critics were really disciples of Paul, not of Jesus and the apostles.[109] But how did their own claim on the latter translate into group identity? Our hostile witnesses deny them any unqualified claim on the name "Christian," but did they actually use or even want that name at all? Epiphanius at one point seems to imply that they did, saying that Ebion "wants to have only the Christians' name [*Christianōn bouletai echein to epōnymon monon*]" but "most certainly not their behavior, opinion and knowledge, and the consensus as to faith of the Gospels and Apostles" (*Pan.* 30.1.3). This framing of the matter, however, sounds suspiciously like the blanket generalization he registers at the outset of the *Panarion* regarding all the postincarnation heresies; namely that "they have Christ's name only [*onoma monon Christou*] but not his faith" (Proem I, 4.2). As applied to the Ebionites, then, the extent to which it reflects a specific self-understanding as "Christians" as opposed to simply a claim on the authority of Jesus is less than clear.[110] Did these "Poor Ones," like Epiphanius and those examined earlier in this chapter, use "Christian" as a primary term of self-identity? Did they merely tolerate it as a term applied to them by outsiders? Or did they associate it primarily with a heresy propagated by Gentiles who claimed to follow Christ while ignoring Mosaic law? We simply do not know.[111]

The substantive question for our purpose in any event is how these "Poor," by whatever name, understood themselves in relation to Judeans. Whatever their feelings regarding the name "Christian," did they consider alignment with Jesus and the apostles to be in any way extraneous to Judean culture? Did they, in other words, assume a social taxonomy analogous to the one articulated by their self-described Christian critics and consider themselves as a group who had come "from the Judeans" to something other than a Judean way of life? Or did they, more like the Pseudo-Clementine Homilist, see themselves more straightforwardly as faithful Judeans? Did calling themselves "the Poor" imply much the same for them as it did for the Dead Sea sect—namely, that they were the oppressed but soon-to-be-vindicated elect among the elect? Here again we must be wary of reading our sources too naïvely. The uncomfortable fact is that "Judean" and "Judaism" are sometimes used as slurs in the heresiological literature: names with which one can saddle opponents in order to debase them.[112] Thus when Pseudo-Tertullian says that Ebion "brings to the fore ... the Law, of course for the purpose of excluding the gospel and vindicating Judaism," we are encountering first and foremost the terms of the heresiologist's own taxonomy—one in which "the gospel" and "Judaism" represent separate classes. The extent to which we are also glimpsing the social taxonomy assumed by "the Poor Ones" themselves is far from obvious.[113]

Nonetheless, a few pertinent observations can be made. As we have seen, propagators of Christianism, in contrast to the Pseudo-Clementine *Homilies*, incorporated the traditional Judean dichotomy between Israel and "the Nations" into their "new race" theory, portraying Christians as being either "from the Jews" or "from the Nations." Origen's repeated description of "Ebionites" as "those from the Jews [*hoi apo Ioudaiōn*] who accepted Jesus as Christ" reflects this point of view, anticipating something along the lines of what modern interpreters would come to imagine as "Jewish believers" or "Jewish Christians" in an "ethnic" sense.[114] There is little reason to believe, however, that these Poor Ones themselves were drawing any such distinction between piety and ethnicity—between a people and culture they came *from* and a new people and culture they came *to*—and every reason to conclude, on the contrary, that they did not. Epiphanius, in marked contrast to his treatment of the Nazoraeans, has Ebion positively "professing to be a Judean"; and the fact that, ever the contrarian, he feels compelled to deny even this name to the group—to the point, indeed, of declaring Ebion "the opposite of Judeans"—strongly suggests not only that the group did in fact claim the name for themselves, but that they did so with much more than the bare facts of derivation at stake.[115] Irenaeus, in the first extant account of the group, defines them entirely in cultural terms summarized as "a Jewish way of life" (*iudaico charactere vitae*), citing a number of specific practices that would become staples of subsequent reports (*Haer.* 1.26.2 [Klijn and Reinink, *Patristic Evidence*, 105–6]). Origen, moreover, faults the Ebionites for an all-too "fleshly" interpretation of Jesus's declaration in Matthew that he "was sent only to the lost sheep of the house of Israel," complaining (à la Paul) that they fail to recognize that "the children of the flesh are not the children of God."[116] If this is so, one can scarcely imagine that these "Poor Ones" understood Jesus and the apostles to have initiated a form of piety anything other than Judean. Indeed, if Epiphanius is to be trusted on the point, the Ebionite rejection of Paul included the charge that he was not actually Judean at all, but rather a jaded Greek proselyte—a claim that is suggestive of a decidedly Judean form of "othering."[117]

The self-described "Poor Ones" critiqued by Christian heresiologists, in sum, seem not to have considered the salient features of their culture to be extraneous to Israel's piety any more than the self-described Poor at Qumran did. The evidence, though challenging, strongly suggests a group that operated with a social taxonomy more akin to the one found in the Pseudo-Clementine *Homilies* than to the one propagated by the disseminators of Christianism. Whatever their feelings about the name "Christian," one can only imagine that these "Poor" would have considered the Christianism-Judaism distinction drawn by Ignatius and others in his network a clear mark of heresy.

The "Nazoraean" Commentary on Isaiah

Since late in the fourth century, the Ebionites have been closely associated with another group identified by Epiphanius and Jerome as "Nazoraeans." The problems involved in the historical analysis of this supposed

group are even greater than those surrounding the Ebionites. Epiphanius, who is the first to identify a distinct heresy by this name, portrays
Nazoraeans as historically related to but ultimately separate from the
Ebionites. The eponymous founder of the latter, he tells us, began as part
of the Nazoraean heresy but then created his own distinct sect by adding
elements from a variety of other heresies as well (*Pan.* 30.1.1–4). In itself,
this genealogy must be considered most doubtful, not least since the whole
idea of a founder called Ebion is almost certainly a heresiological fabrication. Jerome, writing around the same time as Epiphanius, seems to treat
"Ebionite" and "Nazoraean" as interchangeable names for the same heresy,
while others, including already Luke-Acts, knew "Nazoraean" simply as another name for Christians more generally (Acts 24:5, *Nazōraioi*; cf. 11:26,
Christianoi).[118]

The question is further complicated by the fact that Christian writers
of earlier centuries, while apparently unaware of any distinct "Nazoraean"
heresy, sometimes formulated their own distinctions regarding Judeans
who aligned themselves with Christ. Justin, using neither the name "Ebionite" nor "Nazoraean," divides Judeans who "profess their belief in Christ"
and observe Jewish law into two categories: those who refuse to share meals
or otherwise interact with nonobservant Gentile Christians, and those who
do not require Gentile observance. Unlike other Christians he knows, Justin considers the latter to be simply "weak-minded" ones whom "we Christians should receive . . . and associate with . . . in every way as kinsmen and
brothers." The former, on the other hand, will not be saved.[119] Origen, for
his part, used a Christological criterion in order to distinguish one type
of Ebionite from another.[120] After Baur identified the Ebionites with the
apostolic community, his critics found it expedient to correlate these disparate distinctions within a newly rehabilitated Epiphanian historiography,
with the Nazoraeans as the moderate, orthodox descendants of an apostolic
Jewish Christianity from which the radical and heretical Ebionites had de-
viated.[121] Recent interpreters, however, are rightly skeptical about whether
a distinct "Nazoraean" group ever existed at all. To be sure, the fact that
both Epiphanius and Jerome identify a Nazoraean presence specifically in
Beroea—a region where Jerome had spent some time—suggests the existence of some group of Jesus adherents there whom these writers found
suspiciously "Jewish." However, the sketchy and sometimes muddled character of their accounts—not least where their relationship to the Ebionites is concerned—raises the very real possibility that Epiphanius's notion

of a distinctly "Nazoraean" heresy was the product of his own overactive imagination.[122]

The sparse reports of Epiphanius and Jerome are in any event so shot through with their own polemical rhetoric as to be all but useless for reconstructing the self-understanding of whatever group might underlie them. Jerome, taking a tack reminiscent of Epiphanius's comment on the Ebionites, denies them any place in his social taxonomy at all: "since they want to be both Jews and Christians, they are neither Jews nor Christians" (*Ep.* 112.13). While this might seem to imply on the face of it that the group laid claim to both names, it is primarily a reflection of Jerome's own assumptions: "Judean" and "Christian" are separate categories; therefore, groups like the Nazoraeans that he cannot fit neatly into this conceptual framework are in effect nothing at all.[123] Epiphanius, in fact, creates quite a different impression. They neither "kept the name of Judeans, nor termed themselves Christians," he reports, but called themselves simply "'Nazoraeans' supposedly from the name of the place 'Nazareth'" (*Pan.* 29.7.1). But neither can this be taken at face value. Epiphanius's central concern is to drive a historical wedge between a heresy and the apostolic community that, according to Acts, was once called by the very same name—an apostolic community whose authority Epiphanius wishes to claim exclusively for his own values. To this end, he portrays the heresy as attaching a different meaning to the name than it had for the apostles. Before becoming known as Christians, he tells us, the apostles had preferred to call themselves simply "disciples of Jesus . . . as indeed they were," while only tolerating "Nazoraean" when termed such by outsiders. The heretics, in contrast, having "seceded" from the apostolic community, *deliberately* chose the name Nazoraean—and this in blatant disregard for the name of Jesus![124] What's more, Epiphanius says, regardless of their own self-understanding, "they are Judeans in every way and nothing else" (*Pan.* 29.7.1, *ta panta de eisin Ioudaioi kai ouden heteron*). In short, where Jerome treats "Judean" as a name to which the group laid claim in order to deny it to them, Epiphanius frames it as a name they didn't want in order to saddle them with it. If all this tells us a great deal about the important role of naming in heresiological rhetoric, it also entirely obscures the self-understanding of whatever group these Christian writers purportedly have in mind.

More potentially productive for our purposes are the fragments of an interpretation of Isaiah quoted by Jerome from a work he identifies as Nazoraean in his commentary on Isaiah.[125] Composed in Hebrew or

Aramaic, the text was produced no earlier than the late second century and more likely in the third.[126] Whether actually representative of a distinctly "Nazoraean" faction or not, the fragments provide a more direct glimpse at the self-understanding of the kind of group Jerome, at least, had in mind when writing about Nazoraeans.

Among the most characteristic and recurring features of the fragments is their running polemic against the rabbis. Significantly, the same weaponization of genealogy and naming at work in the Christian construction of Ebionite and Nazoraean heresies is also found here—but now in the service of the supposed heretics' own critique of the self-described sages of Israel. Despite the rabbis' apparent disinterest in claiming the name "Pharisee," the fragments identify them pointedly, relentlessly as precisely that: "the Scribes and Pharisees."[127] An interpretation of Isa 8:11–15 traces their origins to two corrupt founders, Hillel and Shammai. Derisive Hebrew puns on the names of these teachers render them a "scatterer" and an "unholy" one, respectively—deviants whose invented "traditions and *deuterōseis*" "scattered and defiled the prescripts of the Law."[128] In what amounts to its own heresiological genealogy, the text proceeds to construct a (historically inaccurate) line of descent from Hillel and Shammai to, among others, Yohanan ben Zakkai, R. Akiva, and R. Meir in order to frame the rabbis in general—and by implication the Mishnah in particular—as the present-day legacy of a sectarian, Pharisaic perversion of the Torah.[129] The fragments' interest in Jesus is tied directly to its rise. Isaiah 9:1–4 is interpreted with reference to the coming of Christ precisely to free "Zebulon and Naphtali"—here apparently taken to represent the land of Israel more generally—"from the errors of the Scribes and Pharisees."[130]

Particularly striking in this connection is the correlation of these "Scribes and Pharisees" with the cultural practices of non-Israelites. The fragment on Isa 8:19–22 interprets the words of the prophet ("Now if people say to you, 'consult the ghosts and the familiar spirits that chirp and mutter'") with reference not only to a purported rabbinic magic, but to a more general rabbinic "idolatry." Another central and recurring theme of the fragments, this notion of idolatry is used to sum up both the culture of the "distant tribes" beyond Israel—those traditionally called "the Nations"—and that of the rabbis as having been tainted by them. Much as in the reported Ebionite claim that Paul was really a Gentile, in other words, the perceived "otherness" of the rabbis is chalked up to their adoption of Gentile practices. The coming of Jesus is interpreted not only as a divine answer to the idolatry of Hillel and Shammai, but as the beginning of a long-predicted purge of the world more generally from Gentile impiety: "Later . . . the preaching was multiplied through the Gospel of the apostle Paul, who was the last of all the apostles. And the Gospel of Christ shone to the most distant tribes . . . Finally the whole world, which earlier walked or sat in darkness and was imprisoned in the bonds of idolatry and death, has seen the clear light of the gospel" (*Comm. Isa.* 9.1).

While the fragments clearly assume a self-definition over against these distant, non-Israelite "tribes," it is equally clear that the rabbis are the ones who represent their most immediately distressing "other."[131] The rabbis, notably, are not treated as the functional equivalent of Israel as a whole, but as rival, scribal authorities of a people to whom both otherwise belong—not, as in the fourth gospel, the functional equivalent of "the Judeans," but rather a sinister enemy within.[132] Hillel and Shammai are interpreted, via Isa 8:14, as "two houses that did not accept the Savior" (*Comm. Isa.* 8.11–15). The Scribes and Pharisees who follow them, in turn, are portrayed as those who "deceived the people with very vicious traditions"; who "watch day and night to deceive the simple ones"; "who made men sin against the Word of God in order that they should deny that Christ was the Son of God" (*Comm. Isa.* 29.17–21). It is clear from the comment on Isa 8:19–22, moreover, that their machinations among "the people" are not imagined as a decisive fait accompli, but as a live and ongoing problem faced in the here and now: "When the Scribes and Pharisees tell you to listen to them," one text says, "you must answer them like this: 'It is not strange if you follow your traditions since every tribe consults its own idol'" (*Comm. Isa.* 8.19–22). Indeed, the fragment on Isa 31:6–9 indicates that the voice behind this interpretation of Isaiah still sees itself very much in competition for the hearts and minds of those "simple ones" of "the people" whom the rabbis actively "deceive." "O Sons of Israel, who deny the Son of God with a most vicious opinion," it pleads, "turn to him and his apostles. For if you do this, you will reject all idols which to you were the cause of sin in the past and the devil will fall before you" (*Comm. Isa.* 31.6–9).

The overall impression created by these fragments, then, is that they were produced by a dissident Judean group that was resisting the authority of the rabbis by, among other things, portraying them effectively as heretics: followers of a pair of deviant teachers who had set aside Israel's divine law in favor of traditions derived from the magic and idolatry of foreigners.[133] The group fantasized not only about displacing the rabbis' influence over "the people," but about the wider spread of their own defining values into "the whole world." Interestingly, the latter is understood already to be happening, not least through the agency of the apostle Paul.[134] But within what taxonomic framework did they make sense of all of this? Did they, like their Christian critics, imagine themselves and such converted Gentiles as analogous members of a new people that had replaced the Judeans as God's elect? Or more like the Pseudo-Clementine Homilist, did they interpret all this simply in terms of a division between Judeans and the Nations, with themselves as the rightful authorities ensuring not only a true Judean piety in Israel, but one that would radiate out to all the Nations just as prophets like Isaiah had long predicted?[135]

The only suggestion that the former may be the case comes as Jerome reports the "Nazoraean" interpretation of Isa 9:1: "When Christ came and his preaching shone out, the land of Zebulon and the land of Naphtali first of all were freed from the errors of the Scribes and the Pharisees and he shook off their shoulders the very heavy yoke of the Jewish traditions [*gravissimum traditionum Iudaicarum iugum*]. Later, however, the preaching became more dominant . . . and the Gospel of Christ shone to the most distant tribes . . . Finally the whole world, which earlier walked or sat in darkness and was imprisoned in the bonds of idolatry and death, has seen the clear light of the gospel" (*Comm. Isa.* 9.1). The usage of the term "Judean" here is striking, particularly in comparison with the other extant fragments. While the exegesis elsewhere seems to channel rather emphatically the targeted critique of "the scribes and the Pharisees" found in the Gospel of Matthew—a Hebrew version of which Jerome attributes to these same "Nazoraeans"—this particular passage is more reminiscent of the conflation of the Pharisaic "traditions of the elders" with those of "all the Jews" in the Gospel of Mark than with Matthew's subsequent correction of it (Mark 7:3; cf. Matt 15:1–9).[136] Taking the passage in isolation, then, one might conclude that "Judean tradition" and rabbinic "idolatry" are essentially one and the same—and that the group's own "gospel," therefore, is something other than Judean. One possible interpretation, then, would be that the group who produced this interpretation of Isaiah had effectively disavowed Judean piety per se as much as Jerome himself had. However extensive its social and cultural overlaps with Judeans in practice, in other words, the group on this reading would have postulated in theory—under whatever particular nomenclature—something analogous to a taxonomic distinction between Judaism and Christianism.

The problem, though, is how such an interpretation would square with the very different impression, otherwise created by the fragments, of a group who imagined itself in contrast not with the Judean people per se, but with the rabbis as rival influencers of its hearts and minds. Other interpretations are thus not only possible but more likely within the wider context of the fragments. First, it is tempting to speculate that the singular description of the offending traditions as "Judean" was introduced only as the underlying Hebrew or Aramaic text was rendered into Latin by a translator who assumed a Christianism-Judaism distinction.[137] On the other hand, the conundrum is not altogether different from the one presented already by the Gospel of Matthew, which contains one singularly puzzling reference to "Judeans" in what otherwise reads very much like a sectarian Jewish composition.[138] In any event, in the absence of the Hebrew or Aramaic original, this possibility remains entirely speculative.

If we take the identification of the offending traditions as "Judean" as reflecting the Hebrew or Aramaic original, two alternatives remain. One is that the term "Judean" is not a point of emphasis at all, let alone an especially negative one. Elsewhere the emphasis is plainly on the matter of *tradition* itself—specifically, in the context of a contrast between what the group apparently takes to be its own divinely ordained practices on one hand and the mere (human or demonic) "traditions" of its rivals on the other. Thus Hillel and Shammai "scattered and defiled the precepts of the Law" with their "traditions and *deuterōseis*" (*Comm. Isa.* 9.1–4; cf. Matt 15:1–9, similarly citing Isaiah). Similarly, the fragments imagine rebuffing the authority claims of the "Scribes and Pharisees" who follow them by pointing out that they "follow [their own] traditions" just like "every tribe consults his own idols" (*Comm. Isa.* 8.19–22; cf. 29.17–21, "very vicious traditions"). One might conclude, therefore, that the singular characterization of the offending traditions as "Judean" in this particular fragment is to be correlated above all with the fact that in this instance the spread of the gospel to the Gentiles is also invoked—a context that immediately renders "Judean" a salient category. The characterization of rabbinic traditions as "Judean" may have simply reflected a widespread perception of the rabbis' pervasive influence on the Judean people.[139]

The other possibility, finally, is that "Judean" is to be taken straightforwardly as an effective synonym for what we would today call "rabbinic" and thus used with as decidedly negative a valence as by Jerome and Epiphanius. To be sure, this line of interpretation comes with complications of its own. As noted above, the heresiological historiography constructed by the fragments identifies Hillel and Shammai as the ultimate authors of the offending traditions and correlates the appearance of Jesus closely with their activity. If this would imply that Judean things are precisely what Jesus came to do away with (much as for Thomas Morgan centuries later; see Chapter 2), it would also thereby imply that Judean tradition per se did not exist at all until right around the time of Jesus's birth. Such a usage of "Judean," it must be pointed out, would have been remarkably idiosyncratic in the context of the ancient world. While a variety of writers historicize the name "Judean," it is typically correlated with much earlier events, in a manner more consonant with its widespread usage in the ancient literature.[140] Josephus, for his part, links it to the Babylonian exile: "This name [that is, *hoi Ioudaioi*], by which they have been called from the time they went up to Babylon, is derived from the tribe of Judah . . . both the people themselves and the country have taken their name from it" (*A.J.* 11.173). Eusebius and Epiphanius, both of whom historicized "Judean" in order to distinguish it from a more primordial Abrahamic piety they wished to claim for themselves, correlated it, respectively, with the corrupting sojourn of "the Hebrews" in Egypt or, earlier still, with the institution of circumcision late in Abraham's life.[141] Who and what, then, would the prerabbinic *ethnos* and customs referred to as "Judean" by Josephus and in the other ancient sources more generally have represented in the minds of the author(s) of this interpretation of Isaiah? The people are directly addressed at one point as "children of Israel" (*Comm. Isa.* 31.6–9). Does this imply a taxonomy in which "Judean" represents a Pharisaic perversion of "Israel"? Even if this were so, Israel would refer plainly to the people whom others routinely called "Judean"—a people whose way of life had properly distinguished them from the idolatrous (Gentile) "tribes" until Hillel and Shammai came along and blurred the distinction. Even on this reading, in other words, Jesus would not be imagined as having come to create a new people and way of life, but to purge Israel and its Torah of the Gentile magic and idolatry recently imported into it in the form of Pharisaic-*cum*-rabbinic traditions. While this was imagined as the beginning of a more comprehensive purge of idolatry even from those "distant tribes" themselves, there is no new *genos* envisioned here, nor anything comparable to a Christianism distinct from Israel and its law. There is only Israel, the idolatrous "Judean" heretics within it, and those from the "distant tribes" who either have given up or still yet should give up their idolatry in favor of Israel's God.

I leave it to the reader to decide which of these possibilities is most likely. The central point I am concerned to make is that on any of these three interpretations, there is no "new people" envisioned in these fragments' interpretation of Isaiah. At most, there is a disavowal of "Judean" as a term so associated with the rabbis as to have become reinterpreted with specific reference to them as a Gentile perversion of ethnic Israel and its long-standing law. Unfortunately, we do not know how exactly the fruits of Paul's labors among the "distant tribes" were imagined in relation to Israel. The sheer fact that Paul was embraced suggests that they were not expected to observe Israel's law themselves. If this implies that they had not become Israelites in a manner analogous to the Pseudo-Clementine *Homilies'* "Judeans," it hardly implies, conversely, that the Israelites had themselves become something else. More likely, the general dynamic was simply interpreted along the lines of Isaiah's predictions that the Nations would one day finally acknowledge Israel's God (e.g., Isa 49)—a hope that, if universalistic in an imperialistic sense, scarcely implies in and of itself that the distinction between Israel and the Nations would thereby be abolished.[142] Even on this reading, in other words, there is no Jewish Christianity and Gentile Christianity here, or indeed any distinct Christianism at all. There are only the children of Israel who reject the heretical innovations of idolatrous, Pharisaic "tradition," and those from the Nations who have at last given up their own long-standing idolatry in solidarity with them.

Made, Not Begotten

At some point in the first or second century of the Common Era, someone began to claim that Jesus and his apostles were the authoritative embodiment of values categorically other than Judean. Ignatius of Antioch formulated this claim under the rubric of a "Christianism" that was not only separate from "Judaism" in theory, but that had actively to be kept separate from it in practice. This taxonomic division was disseminated through a translocal network spanning the northern Mediterranean, a network whose members also frequently identified themselves as the "universal," or Catholic, Church. Where exactly the social and cultural boundaries between Judaism and this Christianism lay inevitably became matters of dispute, and this in turn led to schisms within the network itself. In Rome, different lines in the sand drawn respectively by figures like Valentinus, Marcion, and Irenaeus gave rise to mutual recriminations in a debate as to who and what "really" represented Christianism. From this debate arose the new genre of

Christian heresiology, the object of which was to portray one's own values as being in essential continuity with a supposed original Christianity of Jesus and his apostles, and the salient values of one's rivals as having been derived from mere human or even demonic imagination.

Underlying that debate was a shared apologetic assumption: that the network's Christianity, however precisely articulated, was not the product of any analogous imaginative activity, let alone the invention of the group itself; that it had been, rather, hierophanically revealed through Jesus and (at least one of) his apostles as a divine reality essentially and indeed quali-tatively different from the cultures of all other peoples in general and from Judaism in particular. Christians, to be sure, came either *from* the Judeans or *from* the Gentiles; but the Christianity they came *to* was neither Judean nor Gentile. The ability of this fragmenting network to disseminate and naturalize both this notion of a transcendent Christianity and the new social taxonomy that went along with it took a quantum leap forward when the emperor Constantine aligned himself with a particular segment of the group in the fourth century.

Meanwhile, alongside these developments, a significantly different so-cial taxonomy was operative among other claimants on the authority of Jesus and the apostles. The work now known as the Pseudo-Clementine *Homilies* makes analogous claims not only regarding the unique transcen-dence of its own defining values over against those of the world's other peoples, but on Jesus and the apostles as an authoritative articulation of them. It does not, however, appeal to any comparable notion of a Chris-tianism. The central human division it postulates, rather, is one between the Judeans and their divinely ordained way of life on one hand and the eth-nic "Nations"—most especially the Greeks—and their demonic traditions on the other. Jesus and the apostles, accordingly, were sent by God from the Judeans to the other Nations not with any Christianity, but simply with "the things of the Judeans," or what others in antiquity sometimes called *Ioudaïsmos*, "Judaism." Those "from the Nations" who embraced this prophetic message, therefore, became not Christians but proselytes of the Judeans, even Judeans themselves. Those who already were Judeans, natu-rally, required no such movement at all. Analogous taxonomic frameworks, if not the same specific nomenclature, seem to be reflected as well in early Christian reports about Ebionites and Nazoraeans.

It is difficult, given the nature of the evidence, to determine the ex-tent to which a separate translocal network analogous to the Catholic one underlies the *Homilies,* the so-called Nazoraean commentary on Isaiah, and accounts about Ebionites. To be sure, the narrative of the *Homilies* posits just such a network of communities founded by Peter, centered not in Rome but rather in the East, stretching from Caesarea Maritima to Antioch. Epiphanius's account of the Ebionites and Nazoraeans postulates the fragmentation of a group analogous to what we find among the self-described Christians: Ebion parted ways with a Nazoraean group centered in Cocabe over differences of opinion, he says, and continued developments among Ebion's followers led to what we now call the Pseudo-Clementine literature.[143] Epiphanius's account, however, is shot through with major problems, and the evidence is otherwise unclear. It is difficult at any rate to imagine that the significant variations on the underlying taxonomic scheme of the *Homilies* and the "Nazoraean" interpretation of Isaiah—how exactly the rabbis and those "from the Nations" figured in, and perhaps even the significance of the name "Judean" itself—would not have had concrete implications for social interaction among whatever group or groups produced them.

As we have seen, those ancients who assumed that Christianism had been there from the beginning struggled to make sense of such groups. Christian writers interpreted them in a variety of ways, though always, of course, through the lenses of, and in the terms of, their own taxonomic assumptions. Accordingly, groups like the Ebionites and Nazoraeans were analyzed as so many odd and ultimately disqualifying combinations of Christianism and Judaism. Propagators of Christianism explained these supposed combinations within the same historiographical paradigm they used to account for differences among themselves: later teachers, they said, had added foreign (in this case Judean) values to the supposed original Christianism of Jesus and the apostles.

The profound success of these Christians' efforts to disseminate their own social taxonomy is evident not least in the perdurance of their interpretive framework, centuries later, in European and North American scholarship on early Christianity and its relationship to Judaism. Even as critical scholars came increasingly to recognize the rootedness of Jesus and the apostles in ancient Judean society and culture, the sense that there was nonetheless something about them—indeed, at their very essence—that was somehow other than or more than "merely" Jewish remained the routine assumption. In the Enlightenment era, discomfort with traditional appeals to supernatural revelation to explain that unique "something else" led some intellectuals to reconceptualize Christianity's transcendence more exclusively along the lines of another long-standing way of imagining it: a claim that Christianity represented a divinely wrought, spiritual law latent in the rational nature of humanity itself. The incarnation traditionally posited at the origins of Christianity was thus reconceived in more thoroughly humanistic terms: not the sudden visitation of a preexistent God in the flesh of an otherwise Jewish man, but the sudden and perfect instantiation of an immanent natural religion within the otherwise Jewish culture of Jesus and his apostles. "Jesus," Wellhausen famously declared, "was not a Christian, but a Jew"; nonetheless, Wellhausen hastened to add, "what is un-Jewish in him, what is human, is more characteristic than what is Jewish."[144] This new theory gave rise to the new idea of an early Jewish Christianity—a transcendent religion expressed in, and sometimes obscured by, the Jewish culture whose forms it had initially assumed.

Apologetic theories regarding such a transcendent Christianity, whether in the traditional or this more humanistic variety, were increasingly set aside as critical scholarship on Jewish and Christian antiquity continued to disentangle itself from Christian theology over the course of the late twentieth and early twenty-first centuries. Through it all, however, the underlying assumption of a Christianity there from the beginning—even if somehow "within Judaism"—has remained largely intact, neatly encapsulated in the enduring idea of an early Jewish Christianity. Generations of scholars have thus continued to wrestle with the problem of isolating the various ways this assumed Christianity might also be said, at least at first, to have been Jewish as well, and to understand how it gradually became separate from the Judaism "within" which it first appeared.

To persist in interpreting the Pseudo-Clementine *Homilies* and other analogous texts and groups as "Jewish Christian" is to continue to make sense of them through decidedly Christian eyes within a decidedly Christian interpretive framework. Apologetic intentions or not, it is to carry on analyzing them much as Christian heresiologists have always done, as so many peculiar combinations of a categorical distinction manufactured pointedly within the heresiologists' own social network for its own rhetorical ends. Redescribing such groups as Jewish Christianity means overwriting their own terms of identity with the now-naturalized categories invented by their Christian rivals—relocating them, regardless of their own historical self-understanding, from Judaism to Christianism. More consequentially, such redescription continues to reinforce, even if unintentionally, the sense that Christianity is in the end something more than an artifact of one particular people's ongoing efforts at social and cultural differentiation. To analyze the ancient Jesus movement in terms of Jewish Christianity is to renew yet again the fundamental, generative assumption of Christian apologetics: that Christianity was, in some sense at least, already there "in the beginning," begotten not made.

Abbreviations

Citations of ancient sources follow the abbreviations found in *The SBL Handbook of Style,* 2nd ed. (Atlanta: SBL Press, 2014).

ANF	*Ante-Nicene Fathers*
ANTZ	Arbeiten zur neutestamentlichen Theologie und Zeitgeschichte
AYBRL	Anchor Yale Bible Reference Library
BTB	*Biblical Theology Bulletin*
CSHJ	Chicago Studies in the History of Judaism
HBS	History of Biblical Studies
JSJ	*Journal for the Study of Judaism in the Persian, Hellenistic, and Roman Periods*
LCL	Loeb Classical Library
NovT	*Novum Testamentum*
NovTSup	Supplements to Novum Testamentum
NTS	*New Testament Studies*
PL	Patrologia Latina (= *Patrologiae Cursus Completus*: Series Latina)
RAC	*Reallexikon für Antike und Christentum.* Edited by Theodor Klauser et al. Stuttgart: Hiersemann, 1950–
RSR	*Recherches de Science Religeuse*
TDNT	*Theological Dictionary of the New Testament.* Edited by Gerhard Kittel and Gerhard Friedrich. Translated by Geoffrey W. Bromiley. 10 vols. Grand Rapids: Eerdmans, 1964–2006.
TRE	*Theologische Realenzyklopädie.* Edited by Gerhard Krause and Gerhard Müller. Berlin: de Gruyter, 1977–
TSAJ	Texte und Studien zum antiken Judentum
VC	*Vigiliae Christianae*
WUNT	Wissenschaftliche Untersuchungen zum Neuen Testament

Notes

Introduction

1. See esp. Lieu, "'Parting of the Ways'"; Boyarin, *Dying for God* (esp. 1–21) and *Border Lines* (esp. 1–33); also the introductory essay in Becker and Reed, eds., *Ways That Never Parted*, 1–33. Martin Goodman's essay in the latter volume ("Modeling the 'Parting of the Ways'") depicts graphically no fewer than nine different historical models of the separation. As pointed out in my review of *The Ways That Never Parted*, even the sense in which Judaism and Christianity are said to part—socially or taxonomically, as social identities in general or as separate religions in particular—now varies from study to study.
2. For Jewish Christianity as a transitional phenomenon see, e.g., Hort, *Judaistic Christianity*; cf. in this respect the more recent (but otherwise significantly different) "Judaeo-Christianity" theorized by Daniel Boyarin in *Dying for God* and *Border Lines*. For Jewish Christianity as evidence of ongoing contacts between a separated Judaism and Christianity, see, classically, Simon, *Verus Israel*, 237–70.
3. Boyarin, *Dying for God*, 17; Reed, "'Jewish Christianity' after the 'Parting of the Ways,'" 191 n. 5.
4. Strikingly symptomatic of the definitional problem is the fact that the three principal English-language monographs on Jewish Christianity produced before the 1980s—namely, Hort, *Judaistic Christianity*; Schoeps, *Jewish Christianity*; and Daniélou, *Theology of Jewish Christianity*—overlap minimally if at all in their actual subject matter; see my Introduction in Jackson-McCabe, ed., *Jewish Christianity Reconsidered*, 1–3, and further, in the same volume, "What's in a Name?"
5. Saldarini's *Matthew's Christian-Jewish Community* is an early example; for a more recent analysis of Matthew along analogous lines, see Kampen, *Matthew within Sectarian Judaism*. Cf. also among others the treatment of the Apocalypse of John in Marshall, *Parables of War*, and of the early Antioch community in Zetterholm, *Formation of Christianity*.
6. For this development in the study of Paul, see among others Gager, *Reinventing Paul*; Eisenbaum, *Paul Was Not a Christian*; and Nanos and Zetterholm, eds., *Paul within Judaism*.

7. See esp. Mimouni, *Le judéo-christianisme*; Broadhead, *Jewish Ways of Following Jesus*; Luomanen, *Recovering Jewish-Christian Sects and Gospels*; Jones, *Pseudo-clementina*; Carleton Paget, *Jews, Christians and Jewish Christians in Antiquity*; and Reed, *Jewish-Christianity and the History of Judaism*. Note also the inclusion of chapters on Jewish Christianity in both the *Cambridge History of Judaism* and the *Cambridge History of Christianity* by James Carleton Paget and Joel Marcus, respectively.

8. So, e.g., Brown, "Not Jewish Christianity." Oskar Skarsaune uses the category "Jewish believers" alongside Jewish Christianity as related but distinct phenomena in "Jewish Believers," 9–10.

9. A tentative step in this direction is taken already by Lemke, *Judenchristentum*, 307, who concludes her lengthy study of the rise of the concept by wondering aloud whether it might be too general to be of use for future historical and exegetical research. Carleton Paget takes the point a step further by imagining how an argument against the category might run ("Definition," 51–52). A more decisive step was taken by Boyarin ("Rethinking Jewish Christianity"), who argues forcefully on theoretical grounds that the category "Jewish Christianity" should be entirely abandoned.

10. See esp. Colpe, *Das Siegel der Propheten*, 35–58; cf. Lemke, *Judenchristentum*, 306: "Daß es sich bei unserem Begriff um ein historisches Erklärungsmodell und bei diesen Beurteilungen um interpretierende Wertungen und nicht um historische 'Tatsachen' handelt sollte nicht in Vergessenheit geraten."

11. Cf., e.g., Hoennicke's 1908 survey of German scholarship on Jewish Christianity after Baur in *Das Judenchristentum*, 1–19, and Carleton Paget's recent analysis of the same period in England in "Reception of Baur in Britain." On the era before Baur, see now esp. Lemke, *Judenchristentum*, and Jones, ed., *Rediscovery of Jewish Christianity*. For a good synthetic overview, see esp. Carleton Paget, "Definition"; cf. Jackson-McCabe, "What's in a Name?"; and Broadhead, *Jewish Ways of Following Jesus*, 6–27. Cf. the bibliographies on Jewish Christianity compiled in Manns, *Bibliographie du Judéo-christianisme*; Malina, "Jewish Christianity"; and most recently Reed, *Jewish-Christianity*, 444–73.

12. This apologetic strategy, interestingly, is common among Christian writers who also had pronounced heresiological interests; so, e.g., Justin, Irenaeus, Tertullian, and Epiphanius. See further Chapter 1. For context, including both the Greek philosophical idea of natural law and its various adaptations by early Judean and Christian writers, see Jackson-McCabe, *Logos and Law*.

13. See Chapters 1 and 2 below.

14. For a recent treatment of the history of the modern concept "religion," see Nongbri, *Before Religion*.

15. Cf. the insightful treatment "On the Origins of Origins" in Smith, *Drudgery Divine*, 1–35.

16. Albert Schweitzer's *Quest of the Historical Jesus* remains a profoundly insightful analysis of this dynamic as it applies to Jesus and the gospels in particular.

17. The point is widely recognized. See in detail Lemke, *Judenchristentum*, 57–104, which can be fruitfully compared with Myllykoski, "'Christian Jews' and 'Jewish Christians.'" See further Chapter 1 below.

18. See Chapter 1.

19. See Chapter 2.

20. Hoennicke, *Judenchristentum*, 16. See Chapter 3 below.

21. See Chapter 4. Specification of what makes it "Christian," in contrast, has traditionally been considered relatively straightforward if requiring explicit discussion at all. Broadhead, while rightly critical of the Parting of the Ways paradigm, remains representative in this respect: "The difficulties of defining Jewish Christianity are common to much of the religious landscape of antiquity. The more difficult side of this equation, however, is presented by the complexity of what it means to be Jewish" (*Jewish Ways of Following Jesus*, 46).

22. For a recent analysis of the term "Christian," see Townsend, "Who Were the First Christians?"; cf. Runesson, "Question of Terminology"; cf. notes 5 and 6 above. On "Jew" and "Judaism," see esp. Mason, "Jews, Judaeans, Judaizing," and the responses collected in Law and Halton, eds., *Jew and Judean*; further Collins, *Invention of Judaism*, 1–19. On "religion," see Nongbri, *Before Religion*; and Barton and Boyarin, *Imagine No Religion*.

23. Cf. in this respect Lemke's concluding thoughts regarding the category's potential use for modern Christians in *Judenchristentum*, 307: "Heute könnte er auf Verbindungen zwischen Judentum und Christentum aufmerksam machen und sie stärken, und gleichzeitig den gemeinsamen Grund des vielfältigen Christentums benennen und hervorheben." Jewish Christianity and related terms may also be relevant for historical analysis of the modern era insofar as they have sometimes been appropriated as terms of identity; e.g., Schonfield, *History of Jewish Christianity*; Sobel, *Hebrew Christianity*; and Fruchtenbaum, *Hebrew Christianity*.

24. Reed, *Jewish-Christianity*, xxiv.

25. My central concern is the invention of Christianity and the Christianity-Judaism division as a new social taxonomy in the ancient world. It matters little for my purposes whether this taxonomy was imagined already in antiquity specifically as a division of "religions" as opposed to a more general division of peoples and their respective ways of living (which typically included interacting with gods). That being said, I consider the latter a much more defensible interpretation of the evidence than the view that the ancients were already thinking in terms of "religions."

26. Cf. the balanced treatment in Collins, *Invention of Judaism*, 1–19.

Chapter 1. The Invention of Jewish Christianity

1. When Skarsaune says this is only "partly true," the ancient precedents he has in mind are solely identifications of the ethnic derivation of particular people,

not any abstract notion of a Jewish *Christianity*; see "Jewish Believers," 5–7; cf. Carleton Paget, *Jews, Christians and Jewish Christians*, 289; and Reed, *Jewish-Christianity*, xv n. 2. Lemke's extensive survey of ancient terms yields "no synonym for the *wissenschaftsprachlichen* concept 'Jewish Christianity'" (*Judenchristentum*, 293, cf. 57–81).

2. Toland, *Nazarenus* (1718), an earlier (1710) French draft of which was titled *Christianisme Judaique et Mahometan*. In what follows, citations of *Nazarenus* refer to the second, revised edition, a facsimile of which is available on the Gallica digital library of the Bibliothéque Nationale de France (http://gallica .bnf.fr/ark:/12148/bpt6k67828g). Citations of the French version refer to Claus-Michael Palmer's edition of *Nazarenus*, published as an Anhang in Palmer, *Freispruch für Paulus*. Following Palmer's conventions, I abbreviate citations of *Nazarenus* as *N.* and refer to the French version as *C.* I owe thanks to Stanley Jones for pointing out problems with the editions of *N.* and *C.* in Justin Champion's otherwise indispensable *John Toland: Nazarenus*.

3. Jones, ed., *Rediscovery of Jewish Christianity*. Reed's analogously titled chapter "The Modern Jewish Rediscovery of 'Jewish-Christianity'" signals the ambivalence of the matter by setting the category in quotation marks (*Jewish-Christianity*, 361–87).

4. *N.*, 68.

5. For Paul's use of *ioudaïzein*, see Gal 2:14, where the distinction is between living *ethnikōs* or *ioudaikōs*; cf. 1 Cor 9:20–21; further Cohen, *Beginnings of Jewishness*, 182; and Reed and Vuong, "Christianity in Antioch," 114–16.

6. What would come to be known as the "Antioch incident" was an ongoing problem for early Christian interpreters. See Tertullian, *Praescr.* 23–24; cf. the testy exchange of letters between Jerome and Augustine on the subject, on which, see White, ed., *Correspondence*; further Myers, "Law, Lies and Letter Writing." Making matters worse, Porphyry made sport of the incident in *Against the Christians*; see Jerome's preface to his commentary on Galatians (Cain, ed., *St. Jerome*, 60).

7. On the evolving valence of the term *ioudaïzein*, see Cohen, *Beginnings of Jewishness*, 175–97; further Mason, "Jews, Judaeans, Judaizing," which helpfully contextualizes its negative connotations.

8. Ign. *Magn.* 10.1–3; cf. 8.1, *kata Ioudaïsmon zōmen*; also Ign. *Phld.* 6.1. See further on this below, Chapter 6.

9. Cf. Jones, *Pseudoclementina*, 513: "There is no doubt that the heresiologists are in part responsible for the application of the name 'Ebionites' more broadly to all Jewish Christians. Thus Irenaeus, following his source, lumps all Jewish Christians under the title."

10. Unlike Irenaeus's "gnosis, falsely so-called," Epiphanius and Jerome develop no special category for Ebionites and Nazoraeans beyond the generic notion of heresy. Epiphanius conceived the relationship between them in genealogical

terms, with "Ebion" beginning as a Nazoraean. Jerome's understanding of the relationship is more puzzling. Sometimes he seems to treat them as separate groups, but other times he uses the names seemingly interchangeably. See further on this below, Chapter 6.

11. Jerome, *Ep.* 112.13; text and translation from Klijn and Reinink, *Patristic Evidence*, 200–201.

12. Epiphanius, *Pan.* 29.6.6. Translations of Epiphanius are based on Williams, *Panarion*, though I have periodically altered them when it seemed useful to do so. Angle brackets, which represent suggested emendations, are his. Here and elsewhere I cite the Greek edition of Holl, *Epiphanius.*

13. See also Tertullian, *Praescr.* 37.2, *si enim haeretici sunt, christiani esse non possunt*; cf. 14.10, *non sunt christiani*; also 14.13, 16.2; also 36.8: "heresies are of our plant, but not of our kind" (*haereses de nostro frutice, non nostro de genere*). Here and elsewhere, citations of Tertullian's *Prescription against Heretics* refer to the Latin edition of Rauschen and Martin, *Quinti Septimii Florentii Tertulliani.* L. Michael White (*From Jesus to Christianity*, 433) argues that, at least through the second century, "there is no evidence" that Christians "used the term 'Christian' as a polemical tool in dealing with those holding divergent beliefs or practices. They might call such people false prophets, apostates, or heretics . . . But they were still Christians." He cites in this connection Eusebius's quotation of Justin (not Hegesippus, *pace* White) regarding Marcion in *Hist. eccl.* 4.11.9: "by the instigation of demons [Marcion] has made many to speak blasphemously and to deny that the Maker of this universe is the Father of Christ . . . All those who begin from them, as we said, are called Christians [*Christianoi kalountai*] just as the name of philosophy is common to philosophers though their doctrines vary." The comment is taken from Justin's *1 Apology* (26.6), and alludes ("as we said") to 7.1–5, where Justin had argued that people should not be convicted simply because they are called Christians since the name is used indiscriminately among "Barbarians," much as "philosopher" is among Greeks—that is, with respect to both "those who are and those who seem wise" (*tōn en Barbarois genomenōn kai doxantōn sophōn*). While thus acknowledging the fact that those he considers heretics are commonly *called* "Christians," this hardly indicates that Justin would himself consider them really to be such any more than Tertullian, Jerome, or Epiphanius would. Cf. Le Boulluec's conclusion regarding Justin: "s'il rapproche 'hérésies' et écoles philosophiques, c'est sous la forme d'une simple analogie, qui a pour fin de priver du titre de 'Chrétiens' ceux qui ne professent pas le mêmes doctrines que le parti ecclésiastique" (*La notion d'hérésie*, 91; cf. 110, 111); cf. Lampe, *From Paul to Valentinus*, 190. Cf. already Ign. *Trall.* 6.1–2: "make use only of Christian food [*monētē christianē trophē*] and abstain from a foreign plant, which is *hairesis*. Even though such persons seem to be trustworthy, they mingle Jesus Christ with themselves, as if giving a deadly drug mixed with honeyed wine." The clear implication is that *hairesis* per se is not to be counted as "Christian."

14. H. Schlier, "*haireomai, hairesis, ktl.*," *TDNT* 1:180–85; Iricinschi and Zellentin, "Making Ourselves and Marking Others," 3–5; further Le Boulluec, *La notion d'hérésie*, 36–91. Note in this connection Williams's observation that "Epiphanius is writing, not simply of heretical ideas as such but of heretical ideas in the context of the sects which hold and teach them." That is, while "Epiphanius does occasionally use *hairesis* to mean 'heresy,'" it refers "most often . . . to the party or faction—the 'sect'—which holds a particular error" (*Pan.* 1.xxi).

15. Josephus, *Life* 10–12; *Ant.* 13.171–73; cf. *J. W.* 2.119; cf. Acts 5:17, 15:5, 26:5, noting its somewhat more ambivalent use of the same term with respect to the "sect" of the "Nazoraeans" or "the Way" in 24:5, 14 and 28:22.

16. Cf. Schlier, "*haireomai,*" 183: "*ekklēsia* and *hairesis* are material opposites. The latter cannot accept the former; the former excludes the latter." Cf. Le Boulluec, *La notion d'hérésie*, 110: "Justin est en effet le premier à utiliser le terme *hairesis* pour designer les tendances divergentes à l'intérieur du christianisme en se référant explicement aux 'écoles' de la philosophie grecque. Il exploite cette analogie pour priver l'adversaire du titre de 'Chretien' en rapportant ses opinions à l'inconstance de la fantaisie humaine. L'exclusion qui peut être ainsi prononcée est d'autant plus redoutable que cette fantasie est condamnée de surcroît comme l'instrument de Satan contre Dieu et son Christ."

17. See the Proemium to book one. All translations of Hippolytus are from *ANF* unless otherwise noted.

18. Tertullian, *Praescr.* 7.1–2: Heresies "are the doctrines of men and of demons, produced for itching ears of the spirit of this world's wisdom . . . For (philosophy) . . . is the material of the world's wisdom . . . Indeed heresies are themselves instigated by philosophy [*haereses a philosophia subornantur*]." Tertullian proceeds to develop the point, citing several examples.

19. See further on this immediately below. Cf. the passing reference to "Judaism's heretics," including esp. the Samaritan Dositheus, the Sadducees, the Pharisees, and the Herodians in the first book of Pseudo-Tertullian's *Against All Heresies*. The consternation registered by some modern scholars regarding Epiphanius's inclusion of pre-Christian groups under the heading *hairesis* thus seems to me unnecessary; see, e.g., Young, "Did Epiphanius Know What He Meant by Heresy?"; contrast Schott, "Heresiology as Universal History."

20. Thus, succinctly, Tertullian, *Praescr.* 37.2, *si enim haeretici sunt, christiani esse non possunt.*

21. See, e.g., Tertullian, *Praescr.* 7.1: "the doctrines of men and of demons"; cf. Le Boulluec, *La notion d'hérésie*, 26–34.

22. Cf. Shott's apt characterization of Epiphanius in "Heresiology as Universal History," 547: "heresy exists in radical opposition to an a-historical orthodoxy that is entirely dissociated from historical processes of cultural development"; thus "the history of human civilization serves primarily as a foil to an orthodoxy that stands above and outside history" (563). The same applies equally well to

Tertullian and Hippolytus, who are quoted above, and to Irenaeus, who is discussed more fully in Chapter 6. So too, Justin, who, while coming at the matter from a somewhat different angle, can declare Christian doctrine to be "greater than all human teaching" (*megaleiotera . . . pasēs anthrōpeiou didaskalias*), even while conceding that glimpses of it are already found in philosophy as a result of humanity's natural possession of the seeds of a reason (*logos*) that was fully embodied in Christ (*2 Apol.* 10.1). Cf. also already the characterization of *Christianoi* in *Epistle to Diognetus* in 5.3: "They have not discovered this teaching of theirs through reflection or through the thought of meddlesome people, nor do they set forth any human doctrine, as do some."

23. See, e.g., Irenaeus, *Epid.* 1: "For the way of all those who see is single and upward; illuminated by the heavenly light, but the ways of those who do not see are many, dark, and divergent." Tertullian returns to this theme repeatedly in *Prescription against Heretics*, ironically quipping that it is precisely a tendency to schism that unifies the heretics (42.6, *schisma enim est unitas ipsa*). Their instability is such that they "swerve even from their own regulations, forasmuch as every man, just as it suits his own temper, modifies the traditions he has received after the same fashion as the man who handed them down did, when he moulded them according to his own will" (42.7; cf. 38). Note esp. the clever logic in *Praescr.* 14: "For since [heretics] are still seekers, they have no fixed tenets yet; and being not fixed in tenet, they have not yet believed; and being not yet believers, they are not Christians." In *Praescr.* 28, this (by definition not-Christian) multiplicity is contrasted with a singular tradition said to underlie all the genuinely apostolic churches, whose stable truth is guaranteed by the Holy Spirit. See also Epiphanius's interpretation of Jesus's commissioning of the disciples in Matt 27 in *Incarn.* 3.5: "'Make disciples of the nations'—that is, convert the nations from wickedness to truth, from sects to a single unity [*apo haireseōn eis mian henotēta*]." Cf. Le Boulluec's (*La notion d'hérésie*, 35) insightful observation regarding the earliest Christian discourse on *hairesis*: "C'est le fait des divisions, plus que leur nature, qui est un obstacle."

24. On the sources used by Epiphanius, see Williams, *Panarion*, xxv–xxvii.

25. See further Kim, *Epiphanius*, 44–80; Schott, "Heresiology as Universal History"; and Flower, "Genealogies of Unbelief." Cf. in this respect Irenaeus, *Haer.* 1.22.2: "Since, therefore, it is a complex and multiform task to detect and convict all the heretics, and since our design is to reply to them all according to their special characters, we have judged it necessary, first of all, to give an account of their source and root, in order that, by getting a knowledge of their most exalted Bythus, thou mayest understand the nature of the tree which has produced such fruits." Cf. the genealogical interests in Tertullian's *Prescription against Heretics*, which traces post-Christ heresies to particular philosophical schools—linking Valentinus to Plato and Marcion to Stoics and Epicureans, among others (7)—and apparently, as well, to the Sadducees (33.3–4); cf. Pseudo-Tertullian, *Against All Heresies* 2.

26. The categories are derived from Col 3:11; cf. *Anacephalaeosis* 1.4.

27. This concept was widespread long before Epiphanius. See esp. Irenaeus's theory of history, which is similarly built around a notion of natural law; see Chapter 6 below and, for further discussion of Irenaeus's natural law theory in particular, Jackson-McCabe, "Letter of James and Hellenistic Philosophy," 68–69. Cf. Tertullian, *Adv. Jud.* 2. Justin puts natural law theory to a rather different use in *Second Apology*, on which, see Jackson-McCabe, *Logos and Law*, 123–27.

28. Hellenism, for Epiphanius, begins historically with Serug (Gen 11:22) and is associated with Egypt, Babylon, Phoenicia, and Phrygia before being brought to Greece (*Pan.* 3 and 4.2.6–8). Epiphanius also correlates the rise of mystery cults with this era.

29. Epiphanius is emphatic that *hairesis* in the strict sense arises only with the Greeks; cf., e.g., *Pan.* 1.9, 2.3, and 3.3.9 with 4.2.6–9. The fact that he nonetheless includes the earlier "Barbarism" and "Scythianism" within his taxonomy of eighty *haireseis* reveals that the core dichotomy with which he is ultimately concerned is human invention as opposed to divine or natural derivation.

30. Cf. Hippolytus *Haer.* 1, Proem.: "their doctrines have derived their origin from the wisdom of the Greeks, from the conclusions of those who have formed systems of philosophy, and from would-be mysteries, and the vagaries of astrologers ... [T]he earliest champion of the heresy availing himself of these attempted theories, has turned them to advantage by appropriating their principles, and ... has constructed his own doctrine"; cf. Tertullian, *Praescr.* 7.

31. Cf. in this respect already Justin, whose similar correlation of Christianism with right reason and natural law allowed analogous claims not only about Abraham and biblical heroes, but about revered figures of the Greek past like Socrates and Heraclitus (*1 Apol.* 46.3); see further Droge, *Homer or Moses?*, 65–72.

32. In addition to the following discussion of Epiphanius, cf. Irenaeus, on whom, see further Chapter 6. See more generally Cameron, "Jews and Heretics."

33. Tertullian similarly interprets circumcision as both temporary and meant for Abraham's descendants in particular, but with a less prophylactic and indeed more sinister motive: "This, therefore, was God's foresight,—that of giving circumcision to Israel, for a sign whence they might be distinguished when the time should arrive wherein their ... deserts should prohibit their admission into Jerusalem ... [T]he carnal circumcision, which was temporary, was inwrought for a 'sign' in a contumacious people" (*Adv. Jud.* 3).

34. Epiphanius, while conceding that "it is obviously impossible to say distinctly what the regimen of the children of Israel was until this time, other than simply that they had the true religion and circumcision," nonetheless interprets the summary report in Exod 1:7 about the multiplication and abundance of the children of Israel in Egypt as having "surely ... been due to laxity" in "the period of their sojourn and intercourse (with gentiles)" (8.5.1). This line of interpretation is developed with gusto in Thomas Morgan's *Moral Philosopher* (236–44, 247–49), on which see Chapter 2 below.

35. Epiphanius attributes the rise of Samaritanism to non-Jewish nations attempting to interpret Jewish law (8.9.3). The Sadducean *hairesis*, in turn, is "an offshoot of Dositheus" the Samaritan (14.2.1; cf. 13). Cf. Pseudo-Tertullian, *Against All Heresies* 1.

36. Cf. Kim, *Epiphanius*, 76–77: "The failure of the Jews—and hence the heresy of Judaism—was [for Epiphanius] their denial of the prophesied Christ," and thus their inability to recognize the true meaning of things like circumcision and Sabbath; cf. Cameron, "Jews and Heretics," 354–59.

37. Skarsaune, "Jewish Believers," 5–7. See further on this point in Chapter 6.

38. Myllykoski, "'Christian Jews' and 'Jewish Christians.'"

39. Observed already in 1877 by Patrick, "Two English Forerunners." For more recent treatments of Toland's concept of Jewish Christianity, see esp. Palmer, *Freispruch für Paulus*; Lemke, *Judenchristentum*, 105–48; and the essays collected in Jones, ed., *Rediscovery of Jewish Christianity*. An earlier version of the analysis of Toland presented here was published in the latter volume under the title "The Invention of Jewish Christianity in John Toland's *Nazarenus*."

40. *N.*, iii. All use of italics, capitals, small capitals, and other forms of emphasis in quotations from Toland's writings reflect the original text unless explicitly noted otherwise. It should be noted in this connection that where quotations from the Preface are concerned (evident by Roman numeral pagination), italic font is the norm, with Roman font (with or without capitals) used for emphasis.

41. Lemke, while finding no instances of the term before Toland, concludes from what she takes to be Toland's lack of explanation of the term that he assumed "Jewish Christianity" was a concept already known to his readers (*Judenchristentum* 104, 142, 293). This seems to me to be quite far from certain. It is equally if not in fact more likely that he assumes the knowledge of Jewish *Christian* as a category of *people* but took the step of inventing the idea of Jewish *Christianity* as a category of *religion* himself.

42. See *N.*, 5: "And tho for the most part I am only a historian, resolv'd to make no Reflections but what my facts will naturally suggest . . . yet I am not wanting, when there's occasion for it, to chalk out the methods, whereby the errors of simple or designing men may be seasonably confuted."

43. E.g., *N.*, vi: "*These* [converts from the Gentiles] *did almost wholly subvert the TRUE CHRISTIANITY, which in the following Treatise I vindicate; drawing it out from under the rubbish of their endless divisions, and clearing it from the almost impenetrable mists of their sophistry.*"

44. The sincerity of Toland's Christian profession has been a matter of debate from his day to our own. Most recently, Justin Champion, in a series of publications, has argued forcefully for the genuineness of Toland's attempt to reform Christianity; see esp. "John Toland" and *Pillars of Priestcraft Shaken*; also *Republican Learning*. The most recent and perhaps most intriguing argument for the contrary position is that of Daniel C. Fouke, *Philosophy and Theology in a Burlesque*

Mode. Fouke contends that Toland merely *"pretended* to engage in theology and to operate within its framework of assumptions but constructed burlesques that exposed the inconsistencies and weaknesses of its framework" (25). "The whole thrust of his literary manner," in other words, "was to deconstruct the discourses of the establishment and to disrupt their ideological functions" (23). For Fouke's treatment of Toland's reconstruction of early Christianity in particular, see in the same work pp. 215–68. While Fouke's analysis of Toland's rhetoric is illuminating in many respects, I am inclined to think that Toland really did idealize Jesus, at least as an embodiment of his own values. The question, though, is immaterial to the present concern, which is simply the rhetoric itself.

45. Cf. Lemke, *Judenchristentum*, 144–45: "Der untersuchte Begriff besitzt als historischer Beleg für die Angemessenheit des deistischen Denkens und der deistischen Kirchenkritik eine zentrale Bedeutung und Funktion ... ist Produkt seiner [i.e., Toland's] Projektion des eigenen Religionsverständnisses auf die vermeintlich früheste historische christliche Gruppe."

46. *N.*, 4; cf. the summarizing conclusion in *N.*, 84–85: "You perceive by this time ... that what the Mahometans believe concerning CHRIST and his doctrine, were neither the inventions of MAHOMET, nor yet of those Monks who are said to have assisted him in the framing of his *Alcoran*; but that they are as old as the time of the Apostles, having been the sentiments of whole Sects or Churches."

47. The full title as anticipated in BL 4465 f.64v is "Mahometan Christianity: or an Acco[un]t of ye ancient Gospel of Barnabas, and the modern Gospel of the Turks; with some reflections on the Contest between Peter and Paul about the observation of the Law of Moses by Christian Believers." I follow Champion's reading with respect to the words "Account" and "ye" (*John Toland*, 58), both of which are difficult to make out in the manuscript. What Champion transcribes as "contexts," however, seems to me to read "Contest"—a reading, moreover, that not only makes better grammatical sense, but also finds support in the subsequent French version of the title: "Des Reflections sur le demelé entre Pierre et Paul, touchant l'observation perpetuelle de La Loy de Moyse par les Chretiens d'entre les Juifs" (Palmer, *Freispruch für Paulus*, Anhang, 9).

48. Palmer, *Freispruch für Paulus*, Anhang, 9, giving the full title as "Christianisme Judaique et Mahometan. ou RELATION de l'ancien Evangile de Barnabas, et de l'Evangile moderne des Mahometans: avec Des Reflections sur le demelé entre Pierre et Paul, touchant l'observation perpetuelle de La Loy de Moyse par les Chretiens d'entre les Juifs, de meme que des preceptes Noachiques par les Chretiens d'entre les Gentiles; où l'on prouve que toutes les deux doivent etre d'obligation indispensable, selon le plan originel du Christianisme: comme aussi Une Difficulté proposeé touchant deux sortes de Christianisme, qui ont continué depuis le temps des Apotres jusqu'à nous; où l'on donne un veritable recit des Nazareens et Ebionites. Le tout dans une lettre à Megalonymus."

49. Note, however, that this tripartite scheme only makes explicit what was already implicit in the French title, where the "two sorts of Christianity" that existed from apostolic times are plainly to be correlated with "les Chretiens d'entre les Juifs" and "les Chretiens d'entre les Gentiles." See further Palmer, *Freispruch für Paulus*, 45–46 (n. 90) and 50.

50. This is also clear from the fact that Toland argued that this new classification scheme—particularly where Mahometan Christianity was concerned—should lead to sociopolitical changes in Christian Europe. See below.

51. All quotations from BL 4465 f63–64 represent my own reading of the manuscript unless otherwise noted; cf. the transcriptions in Champion, *John Toland*, 300–301. The date of the manuscript is something of a puzzle. The notation "1698" is given at the top of f64r but was later struck through in pencil and replaced by "1718"—i.e., the publication date of *Nazarenus* itself. (Note that Toland's original numbering of these manuscript pages as "34" and "35" on f63r and 64r, respectively, was similarly struck through and replaced by their current folio designations in pencil. Whether this was all done by the same hand, however, is not immediately clear.) Champion, accordingly, appears to date them to 1698 (*John Toland*, 56–57 and 300). Such an early dating, however, does not seem to square with its references to the Gospel of Barnabas, which Toland elsewhere says he found only in 1709 (*N.*, ii). That these pieces of text in any case predate the French version of 1710 is clear from the fact that they assume a title of "Mahometan Christianity" in a passage that will be revised in the French version to account for the title "Christianisme Judaique et Mahometan," and finally again in the published version to account for the tripartite subtitle "*Jewish, Gentile,* and *Mahometan* CHRISTIANITY." Cf. f63v (cf. Champion, *John Toland*, 300) with *C.*, 2, and *N.*, 4.

52. BL 4465 f63v (cf. Champion, *John Toland*, 300). It is plain from the manuscript page that the phrase "and reckon'd a sort of" was a secondary insertion into the sentence by Toland. The first draft of the line thus stated even more straightforwardly that "the Mahometans may not improperly be call'd Christians."

53. BL 4465 f64r and f63v (cf. Champion, *John Toland*, 300–301). The "Doctor" is identified by name in the corresponding passage in the French version (*C.*, 2); see further Champion, *John Toland*, 55–56.

54. For a very helpful treatment of this wider context, see Champion, *Pillars of Priestcraft Shaken*, esp. 99–132.

55. For a cogent treatment of ambiguity—an oft-noted aspect of Toland's writing in general—as rhetorical strategy for Toland, see Champion, "John Toland"; further Champion, *Pillars of Priestcraft Shaken*, 259–80.

56. BL 4465 f64r (cf. Champion, *John Toland*, 301): "The reason of this odd complement I am yet to learn, unless it be that I can't drink wine enough to pass for orthodox with some Doctors: for I am by no means for propagating Religion by force, in which respect the Doctor is a very good Mahometan, how ill a Christian soever he may be. Neither am I for passive obedience or nonresistance a

fundamental article among the Turks, and what was formerly preach'd with the greatest warmth of any Disciple they have in England by the Doctor." The insertion of the word "odd" is one of several secondary revisions evident in the manuscript. The characterization of Islam on which Toland's critique depends was typical of the era; see Champion, *Pillars of Priestcraft Shaken*, 99–132.

57. *N.*, iii, speaking of "Mahometan Christians"; cf. the earlier sentiments in f63v: "I need not assure you ... that their Christianity is none of mine"; also *C.*, 4. Cf. *Mangoneutes*, 157, where, following up on this comment, Toland says that Muslims are "better than Idolatrous Christians, than tritheistical Christians, than persecuting Christians, than several other sorts of false Christians I cou'd easily specify." Here and elsewhere I cite the Elibron Classics facsimile edition of Toland's posthumously published collection *The Theological and Philological Works of the Late Mr. John Toland*.

58. *N.*, 5; cf. 61, where he says that, even if Islam should be considered a Christian heresy, "I still inferr, that, whether upon a prospect of advantaging Traffic, or of putting them in the way of conversion to a better Christianity, the Mahometans may be as well allow'd Moschs in these parts of Europe, if they desire it, as any other Sectaries."

59. Cf. *N.*, iii: "*therefore upon this occasion* [i.e., the discovery of the Gospel of Barnabas] *I have given a clearer account, than is commonly to be met, of the Mahometan sentiments with relation to Jesus and the Gospel; insomuch that it is not (I believe) without sufficient ground, that I have represented them as a sort of Christians, and not the worst sort neither, tho farr from being the best*"; and again, in section II (also iii): "*I was naturally led by the Gospel of Barnabas to resume some former considerations I had about the* NAZARENS; *as being the Primitive Christians most properly so call'd, and the onely Christians for some time.*" On the relation of *Nazarenus* to *Christianity not Mysterious*, see Champion, *John Toland*, 55–60.

60. *N.*, 20 and 21. Toland's ambiguity regarding the origins of this gospel is intriguing. In line with the remark quoted here, he repeatedly works to create a sense of its antiquity: its opening is "Scripture-stile to a hair" (*N.*, 15); the fact that it is twice as long as the known Christian gospels is said to be at least potentially in favor of its authenticity (16); Muslims are known for their special care in preserving texts (10–11), etc. On the other hand, he does assume at the very least some Islamic redaction (e.g., 20, 61) and at one point even suggests that Acts 9: 26–27 may have provided an occasion for "Impostors" to write a gospel critical of Paul in the name of Barnabas (34). There is a similar ambivalence regarding its identification with the ancient Gospel of Barnabas. Note in this connection the apparent distinction drawn between the "antient" and "modern" gospels of this name in the subtitle of *Nazarenus* ("The history of the antient GOSPEL OF BARNABAS, and the modern GOSPEL OF THE MAHOMETANS, attributed to the same APOSTLE"); and cf. *N.*, 20, where he makes the (rather sketchy) point that a saying attributed to Barnabas in the Barrocian manuscript, but otherwise

unknown, is also found in the Gospel of Barnabas: "I found it almost in terms in this *Gospel*, and the sense is evidently there in more than one place; which naturally induces me to think, it may be the *Gospel* anciently attributed to BARNABAS, however since (as I said) interpolated." Standing in a certain amount of tension to this comment, however, is the rather less committed statement of the preface: "*I have shown by unexceptionable authorities, that Ecclesiastical writers did antiently attribute a* Gospel *to* BARNABAS, *whether there be any remains of it in this new-found* Gospel, *or not*" (*N.*, ii–iii). His ambiguity on these matters was such that his critics, at any rate, took him to be claiming it was an authentic text and thereby challenging the very canon itself. Champion (*John Toland*, 95) finds Toland's disavowal of the former charge in his subsequent rebuttal in *Mangoneutes* to be "less than honest." It is hard to believe at any rate that he is not being deliberately slippery. From the perspective of Fouke (*Philosophy and Theology*, 249–59), it represents another aspect of Toland's "burlesque" mockery of the whole project of ecclesiastical history writing.

61. *N.*, 5, explicitly rejecting the view that such ideas can be traced to "SERGIUS the Nestorian monk"—a figure that seventeenth-century Christians had identified as Muhammad's collaborator in the composition of the Qur'an (Champion, *Pillars of Priestcraft Shaken*, 105, 115). Cf. the concluding summary, at the close of the discussion of this gospel, in *N.*, 84–85: "You perceive by this time … that what the Mahometans believe concerning CHRIST and his doctrine, were neither the inventions of MAHOMET, nor yet of those Monks who are said to have assisted him in the framing of his *Alcoran*; but that they are as old as the time of the Apostles, having been the sentiments of whole sects or Churches: and that tho *the Gospel of the Hebrews* be in all probability lost, yet some of those things are founded on another *Gospel* anciently known, and still in some manner existing, attributed to BARNABAS."

62. Note that Toland considered Ebionites and Nazoraeans to be essentially "the same people" (*N.*, 25). To be sure, the group was not entirely uniform: "There were diversities of opinion among 'em, no doubt, no less than among other societies" (28); but Toland does not seem to correlate such differences with the names "Ebionite" and "Nazoraean," which for him are thus basically interchangeable.

63. See *N.*, 16–17, noting that this "System" "agrees in every thing almost with the scheme of our modern Unitarians"; cf. *N.*, 28, where Toland describes the patristic reports regarding the Nazoraean and Ebionite understanding that Jesus was "a mere man" as being "just the Socinianism of our times."

64. This, then, is the section that develops a second major thesis of *Nazarenus* as identified in its first chapter, namely, that concerning "THE TRUE AND ORIGINAL CHRISTIANITY," and specifically, the point "that JESUS did not, as tis universally believ'd, abolish the Law of MOSES (Sacrifices excepted) neither in whole nor in part, not in the letter no more than in the spirit" (*N.*, 5).

65. This is interesting not only because the intended slur "Mahometan Christian" arose precisely in connection with the Trinitarian-Unitarian debate, but also because the Gospel of Barnabas, as Toland well knows, is critical of Paul specifically on the matter of Christology, especially with respect to the identification of Jesus as "Son of God"; see *N.*, chap. 8, esp. 22–23. Note also in this connection Palmer's observation regarding the diminished role of the issue in *Nazarenus* as compared with the early French version (*Freispruch*, 79–80 with n. 190).

66. *N.*, 31–32. According to Toland, it was precisely this reading of Paul's account that led to the composition of the letter from Peter to James preserved in the Pseudo-Clementine literature.

67. See *N.*, chap. 12, here 38 (on the Jewish view of the law) and 42 (on those few, as in Acts 15, who would compel Gentiles to be circumcised). Toland further contextualizes this understanding of the law by citing an analogous sentiment from Maimonides (*N.*, 38–39).

68. E.g., *N.*, 39–40; cf. the statement of this position as a general thesis of *Nazarenus* in *N.*, 5. Apparently anticipating the counterargument that Peter ate with Gentiles according to Acts 10, Toland suggests that "it does not appear that he ate any thing prohibited by the Law" (44).

69. Notably, however, Toland never does get around to explaining why this supposed agreement suddenly erupted in conflict in Antioch.

70. See esp. *N.*, chap. 16. For a brief account (and example) of the rise of this reading in our own era, see Gager, *Reinventing Paul*.

71. The decree is discussed at length, esp. in chaps. 12–13. Noting that it is precisely the matter of diet "that makes society so difficult a thing" between Jews and Gentiles (*N.*, 43), Toland argues that the decree served the purely pragmatic purpose of facilitating social interaction. He argues further that though it was to remain in force forever, it does not apply "out of Judea, or any place where the Jews and Gentiles don't cohabit in one society" (*N.*, 47–48).

72. On the social dimension, see, e.g., *N.*, 59, where Toland mocks the "hotheaded raving monk" Jerome for his concern that Gentiles might adopt Jewish practices: "as if the Jews and Gentiles were not to have their Churches apart, and as if the former wou'd not perform their peculiar ceremonies in their own Churches."

73. Note in this connection his pointed comment regarding the subsequent fate of the Nazoraeans, namely, that they were excluded on account "not only of their Judaism, but I may say of their Christianity too" (*N.*, 56).

74. As we have seen, Toland works primarily to correlate the Gospel of Barnabas with the Nazoraeans. The fact that Muslims are neither Jews nor practice Jewish law, however, is never addressed. The implication would seem to be that "Mahometan Christianity" stems from Gentile Christianity as practiced in Judea (note esp. his emphasis on the relation of Islamic dietary practice to

the Apostolic Decree in *N.*, 61). But if so the point is never made explicit, nor is the issue addressed of the continued observance of dietary directives in the Apostolic Decree in places like Turkey (i.e., beyond Judea). With respect to the latter point, however, note also that Toland does not idealize Islam but, as pointed out above, maintains a certain critical distance from it.

75. Fouke (*Philosophy and Theology*, 218) notes that Charles Leslie, in this same era, "thought he had sufficiently discredited Socinianism, which denied the divinity of Christ, by showing its similarity to Islam."

76. *N.*, 85. Cf. the work's full title: "The history of the antient GOSPEL OF BARNABAS, and the modern GOSPEL OF THE MAHOMETANS, attributed to the same APOSTLE: this last GOSPEL being now first made known among CHRISTIANS. ALSO, the ORIGINAL PLAN OF CHRISTIANITY occasionally explain'd in the history of the NAZARENS, whereby diverse CONTROVERSIES about this divine (but highly perverted) INSTITUTION may be happily terminated."

77. Cf. in this respect, a few decades after Toland, Thomas Morgan's remarkable characterization of Paul in particular as "the first and purest Part" of "the Apostolick Age" (*Moral Philosopher*, 395). Cf. more generally Champion, *Pillars of Priestcraft Shaken*, 11–12: "The Christian past was a necessary determinant (for the Christian) of the morality or truth of the present. For the seventeenth-century Christian an essential part of religious experience was the continual re-evaluation of the present in terms of the past ... I wish to argue that the developments in the writing of history were perceived as a means to securing a credible defence of ideological opinions rather than forging modern ways of writing history."

78. Cf. Fouke, *Philosophy and Theology*, 221–51. As noted above, Fouke argues that Toland's participation in this discourse was the result of a deliberate attempt to mock it. For a different view, see Champion, *Pillars of Priestcraft Shaken*, and, more concisely, "John Toland."

79. E.g., *N.*, 71; cf. vii and, with respect to Robert South in particular, the earliest draft of the introduction: "in which respect the Doctor is a very good Mahometan, how ill a Christian soever he may be" (BL 4465 f64r; cf. Champion, *John Toland*, 301). This move is the obverse of redescribing the Nazoraeans as "Jewish Christianity."

80. Note the repeated juxtaposition of the terms "original" and "true" or "genuin" in, e.g., *N.*, 5, 33, 52, 65. Note also that in the very passages where Toland denies the term "Christianity" to his adversaries, he simultaneously aligns his own position—using a phrase reminiscent of 1 Cor 2:16—with that of Jesus and the apostles; thus *N.*, vii: "*I do here teach a very different doctrine, more consonant (I am persuaded) to the mind of* CHRIST *and his* Apostles, *as tis more agreeable to the Law of nature and the dictates of Humanity.*" Cf. further *N.*, 70–71, where, decrying the "Antichristianism" of his opponents, Toland identifies "the articles of their belief and the rubric of their practice" as "manifestly the very things

which JESUS went about to destroy" and asks: "what can be less Christian, I say, or more contrary to the design of JESUS CHRIST, than all these things I have here enumerated?"

81. E.g., *N.*, 81: "In short, every side and sect pretended they were the onely true Christians, and each did peremtorily (as many persons now do with as little ground yet equal confidence) appeal to APOSTOLICAL TRADITION AND SUCCESSION . . . Just so it is at this day between some of the Protestants and all the Papists (not to speak of the Greecs) each of 'em boasting I know not what *uninterrupted Tradition and Succession,* which are the most chimerical pretences in nature."

82. *N.*, 68. Cf. his discussion in the Preface of the rhetorical strategies "*corrupt Clergymen*" (xvii) employ against anyone (like Toland!) who offers alternative views: "*They never fail to accuse him of Innovation, which, if not his greatest merit (as new Reformations ought to be substituted to old disorders) yet his greatest crime is many times the reviveing of some obsolete unfashionable Truth, a novelty not to be endur'd by men who live upon error*" (xix).

83. Cf. the synthetic treatments of Toland in Daniel, *John Toland*; and, more briefly, Duddy, *History of Irish Thought,* 82–98.

84. Cf. in this respect, e.g., Epiphanius's notion of Adam's primordial Christianism, on which see above, and Irenaeus, on which see Chapter 6 below. Analogous apologetic adaptations of the Stoic theory of natural law are made by Justin and Methodius, as well as by early Judean apologists like the author of the Pseudo-Clementine *Homilies* (on which see Chapter 6); see further Jackson-McCabe, *Logos and Law.*

85. The context is helpfully elucidated in Byrne, *Natural Religion*; see further Stroumsa, *New Science.*

86. See esp. *N.*, chap. 17 (here 66–67), where Toland cites Cicero's account of natural law at length.

87. E.g., *N.*, v–vi, speaking of Judaism in particular; cf. *N.*, 38.

88. *N.*, xv; for further on this notion of "mystery," see Champion, *Pillars of Priestcraft Shaken,* 165–69; also Nicholl, "John Toland," 60–65.

89. Cf. *N.*, v–vi: "*But the Jews generally mistook the means for the end: as others, who better understood the end, wou'd not onely absurdly take away the means; but even those other civil and national rites which were to continue always in the Jewish Republic . . . thus confounding political with religious performances.*" Cf. *Mangoneutes,* 217: "a great many of the observances in the *Old Testament,* tho generally mistaken for Religion, were only national and commemorative Ceremonies." See further on Toland's understanding of Judaism Lemke, *Judenchristentum,* 127–41. While Lemke correctly observes "Das jüdische Gesetz sieht Toland in erster Linie als eine nationale, politische Größe," the point that "Daneben ist es auch religiös und heilig" must be carefully nuanced, particularly where *Nazarenus* is concerned (126; cf. 138–40).

90. In this sense Reventlow's characterization of Toland as having gone "so far as to see the three monotheistic religions [of Judaism, Christianity, and Islam] on the same level" is misleading ("Judaism and Jewish Christianity in the Works of John Toland," 113). To be sure, Toland elsewhere gives Mosaic law a very high appraisal, but precisely as a "political System": Moses was an "incomparable legislator," who instituted a theocracy that was "the most excellent and perfect" of all forms of commonwealth (*Hodegus*, 6; cf. p. i of the Preface to *Hodegus* and other works collected under the title *Tetradymus*; I rely in both cases on the facsimile edition in Toland, *Theological and Philological Works*). Christianity, however, is qualitatively different precisely in its unique status as religion in Toland's strict sense of the term. Cf. Lemke, *Judenchristentum*, 139–41, esp. 139: "Trotz aller Kritik am bestehenden Christentum bezeichnet er [i.e., Toland] die wahre, natürliche Religion immer als 'christliche.' Die drei monotheistischen Religionen entsprechen sich hinsichtlich ihrer aktuellen Form: Sie stellen alle drei Verfälschungen der wahren, natürlichen, christlichen Religion dar."

91. See *N.*, chap. 14 (51–56); cf. v–vi.

92. The model is encapsulated in Toland's interpretation of the Letter of James, which he takes to be an authentic writing of James and thus an articulation of original Jewish Christianity. Interpreting the discursive transition from *logos* to law in Jas 1:21–25, Toland writes that "*Christianity is by the same Apostle . . . most properly stil'd* the engrafted word able to save their souls, *engrafted I say on the* Law of Moses, *not sanctifying the inward man; yet for most wise reasons to be perpetually observ'd by the Jews, and wherof Christianity is the spirit*: for as the body without the breath is dead, so Faith without Works is dead also [Jas 2:26]" (*N.*, xiii). Here it is Jewish law itself, not merely individual Jews, that is understood to be lacking religion apart from Christianity.

Chapter 2. Jewish Christianity, Pauline Christianity, and the Critical Study of the New Testament

1. Baur recognized that German rationalism "was only a different form of the same thinking that had already emerged in the previous period in England under the name of deism" (*History of Christian Dogma*, 327). Reconstruction of the path by which the particular concept "Jewish Christianity" made its way to him, however, is complicated by the fact that English Deists, as *personae non gratae* in the German theology of the time, were not generally directly cited as influences. Mosheim and Semler, however, seem likely to have been key links in the chain. See on this esp. the impressive sleuthing in Jones, "From Toland to Baur," and the extensive survey of German scholarship from the late seventeenth to early nineteenth centuries in Lemke, *Judenchristentum*, 171–255; further Lincicum, "F. C. Baur's Place."

2. Jones's attempt to trace "a distinctive set of ideas . . . like a red thread" between Toland and Baur does not account for influence by Morgan, whose ideas he

considers "quite distinct" from it ("From Toland to Baur," 123 n. 2). If Jones is correct, and Baur came to his redeployment of Toland's notion of Jewish Christianity independently of any analogous influence by Morgan, the similarities between them only become more interesting, suggesting something about a deeper structural dynamic at work in the liberal Christian apologetics of the era.

3. See already in the eighteenth century Leland, *View of the Principal Deistical Writers*, 1:131–50; and in the nineteenth century Stephen, *History of English Thought in the Eighteenth Century*, 1:140–42. More recent accounts of Morgan's life and legacy are found in the introductions to the respective editions of *The Moral Philosopher* by John Vladimir Price (v–xvii) and Günter Gawlick (*Thomas Morgan*, 5–30). On his concept of Jewish Christianity in particular, see esp. Lemke, *Judenchristentum*, 148–67; also Patrick, "Two English Forerunners." The present analysis draws liberally on my earlier treatment of Morgan in Jackson-McCabe, "'Jewish Christianity' and 'Christian Deism.'"

4. For Morgan's use of the actual term "Jewish Christianity," see *Moral Philosopher*, 369, 374, 382; also 377, "Jewish and Gentile Christianity." Cf. Patrick, "Two English Forerunners," 587: "In all the then extant theological literature, no one work is so likely to have given Morgan materials for his view of the apostolic Church as a once notorious dissertation by John Toland."

5. Patrick, "Two English Forerunners," esp. 581–83.

6. Morgan, *Moral Philosopher*, viii; cf. the title page, which presents the work as a "DIALOGUE ... IN WHICH The Grounds and Reasons of RELIGION in general, and particularly of CHRISTIANITY, as distinguish'd from the Religion of Nature ... are fairly considered, and debated, and the Arguments on both Sides impartially represented." I cite the facsimile of the second edition (1738) of *The Moral Philosopher* published in the History of British Deism series by Routledge/Thoemmes. Further citations will be to this edition and given parenthetically in the text. All capitals, small capitals, italics, and other forms of emphasis reflect the original text unless otherwise noted.

7. So the title page (and in slightly different font, p. 13) of *The Moral Philosopher*. Morgan describes the gentleman's society in his Preface (vii–xi).

8. See Morgan, *Moral Philosopher*, 14–15.

9. Morgan, *Moral Philosopher*, 85–86; the words are repeated almost verbatim in the Preface (viii–x); see further 99, 198, 256, 443–44.

10. Morgan, *Moral Philosopher*, 392. These are running themes in the work as a whole.

11. Morgan, *Moral Philosopher*, 416, here defining "true Religion," which, however, is synonymous with true Christianity in the context of the work; cf. 96–97: "I take Christianity to be that most complete and perfect Scheme of moral Truth and Righteousness ... This Definition, as I imagine, takes in all that is essential to Christianity, or that can be receiv'd and allow'd as a constituent Part of it."

12. Morgan, *Moral Philosopher*, 412. The historical claim is registered repeatedly in the *Dialogue*, e.g., 96–97: "I take Christianity to be that most complete and perfect Scheme of moral Truth and Righteousness, which was first preach'd to the World by Christ and his Apostles, and from them convey'd down to us under its own Evidence of immutable Rectitude, Wisdom, and Reason"; 439: "By Christianity, I mean that complete system of moral Truth and Righteousness, Justice and Charity, which, as the best Transcript of the Religion of Nature, was preach'd to the World by Christ and the Apostles, as the Rule of Equity and Rectitude, by which Men were to be rewarded or punished in the final Judgment by God himself, as the most powerful, wise, and righteous Creator, Governor, and Judge of the World. This I take to be original, real, and indisputable Christianity"; 392: "I am a profess'd Christian Deist. And, therefore, I must take Christianity, as to the Substance and doctrinal Parts of it, to be a Revival of the Religion of Nature; in which the several Duties and Obligations of moral Truth and Righteousness are more clearly stated and explained, enforced by stronger Motives, and encouraged with the Promises of more effectual Aids and Assistances by Jesus Christ, the great Christian Prophet, than ever had been done before by any other Prophet, Moralist, or Lawgiver in Religion."

13. Stephen (*History of English Thought*, 1:141) notes that the "one peculiarity" that makes Morgan stand out from earlier Deists is that "his book is more historical than his predecessors' writings," though with one notable exception: "some of the points raised by him are touched on in Toland's later writings." Stephen perceptively observes that this attempt by Morgan (and by implication, Toland) to "support . . . doctrine by a distinct historical theory" is "symptomatic of the coming change" in the intellectual discourse of the era.

14. See Smith, *Drudgery Divine*, 1–35 and passim.

15. Morgan, *Moral Philosopher*, 412 (emphasis mine); see also 96–97 and 439.

16. Morgan, *Moral Philosopher*, 373. On Morgan's understanding of Jesus's relationship to Judaism, see below.

17. Contrast, e.g., Luther's logic in dealing with the Letter of James: if true Christianity is the (Pauline) gospel, and if the promulgation of that gospel is the heart of the apostolic office, then the absence of that gospel from the Letter of James means that it is not properly apostolic, no matter who wrote it. See further Jackson-McCabe, "Politics of Pseudepigraphy," 609–10.

18. Morgan, *Moral Philosopher*, 21 and 24. Note, e.g., the subtle shift as Philalethes, questioning Theophanes, nods to the latter's traditional rhetoric before issuing a caveat more characteristic of his own: "Do you think, that Christ and the Apostles, particularly St. *Paul*, might not argue against the *Jews* upon their own Principles?" (50).

19. So, e.g., Theophanes: "For the main Question between us, is, whether this be not a Scripture Doctrine, and a Doctrine taught by St. *Paul*; and if it is, you must either some Way or other reconcile the Doctrine to Reason, or give up your

great Apostle *Paul*, which yet you seem very loth to do" (Morgan, *Moral Philosopher*, 213–14). Morgan, for his part, claims that "the Account I have given of St. *Paul* is exactly agreeable to all the Memoirs of his Life, which are still extant in his own genuine Epistles, and the History of the *Acts*" (70). See further, e.g., 37, 42–43, 265, 330.

20. Morgan here anticipates the full-blown rationalist lives of Jesus famously critiqued in Schweitzer, *Quest of the Historical Jesus*.

21. Morgan, *Moral Philosopher*, 441; cf. 394: "I am a Christian, and at the same Time a Deist, or, if you please, this is my Christian Deism; but as for *Moses* and the Prophets, though I admire them, as Politicians, Historians, Orators, and Poets, I have nothing to do with them in Religion, as I cannot possibly be of their Religion." Morgan's understanding of Judaism became still more negative after the initial publication of *The Moral Philosopher*; see Lemke, *Judenchristentum*, 150–60.

22. See esp. the extensive discussion of preexilic Israel in Morgan, *Moral Philosopher*, 266–322, particularly in light of the treatment of Egyptian "Priestcraft" and hierarchy on 237–44 and 247–49.

23. Morgan, *Moral Philosopher*, 258–63; cf. his treatment of the messianic interpretation of Jesus, esp. 325–29 and 349–54.

24. Morgan, *Moral Philosopher*, 255; cf. 322: "this [Jewish] Nation, I believe, have been set up by God and Providence, as an Example and Warning to all other Nations." The background here is likely 1 Cor 10 (esp. 10:6).

25. For the characterization of Jesus as prophet, see, e.g., 394: "Jesus Christ came into the World, and was sent by God to restore, revive, and republish this Religion [i.e., the rational, natural one]"; cf. 167, 327, 392, 439.

26. Morgan's understanding of revelation and miracle is complex. He doesn't reject them as fact where Jesus and Paul are concerned so much as simply their use as criteria of truth; see esp. *Moral Philosopher*, 85–87, 98–100, 393–95. Thus Paul too, he claims, did not stake his argument against Jewish law on a revelation, but on the rational superiority of his own religion (50–53).

27. This, of course, is new only in a relative sense. Structurally speaking, Morgan's strategy is not all that different from the one already proffered by Marcion in the second century.

28. See on Toland Chapter 1 above. Cf. Lemke's comparison of Toland and Morgan in *Judenchristentum*, 167–70.

29. Morgan, *Moral Philosopher*, 54; cf. 71. Cf. in this respect Toland's understanding of Jewish law as a "political system" (*Hodegus* 6, in Toland, *Theological and Philological Works*) that Jews—with the exception of Jesus and the apostles!—generally confused with religion (see further Chapter 1). Morgan differs from Toland in ascribing different motives for observance to the Jerusalem apostles on one hand and to Paul on the other. This distinction between religious and merely civic observance will come to play a crucial role in later attempts to

defuse Baur's (and by implication, Morgan's) understanding of Paul's relationship to the Jerusalem "Pillars"; see on this Chapter 3 below.

30. Morgan, *Moral Philosopher*, 71–72.

31. Morgan, *Moral Philosopher*, 441. Morgan routinely uses the terms "Judaizers"
and "Judaizing" as virtual synonyms for "Jewish Christians," as on 377: "the
Judaizers, or circumcised Christians of the world." When discussing the apostolic era Morgan associates these terms esp. with Peter (e.g., 364, where Peter
is named as "Head and Ring-Leader" of "these *Judaizers*, or Christian *Jews*")
and James (e.g., 363, "*Judaizing* Zealots . . . from James"). When discussing the
postapostolic era he correlates them particularly with early Catholicism; see
esp. 396: "the *Judaizers* prevailed, upon St. *Paul*'s Death, and assum'd the Name
and Dignity of the *Catholick Church*"; 389: "these pretended Catholicks were
the true *Judaizers*."

32. Regarding the latter, Philalethes thinks particularly of the Gnostics, whom
he identifies as "truly primitive Christians, who maintained Liberty of Conscience, and the Right of private Judgment" (Morgan, *Moral Philosopher*, 381;
cf. 386–91); cf. Lemke, *Judenchristentum*, 155–56.

33. Hoennicke, *Judenchristentum*, 16, "eines der Hauptprobleme der Geschichte des
Urchristentums."

34. Cf. Harris, *Tübingen School*, 1: "No single event ever changed the course of Biblical Scholarship as much as the appearance of the Tübingen School. All New
Testament criticism and, derivatively, much Old Testament criticism from the
mid-nineteenth century onwards finds its origin, consciously or unconsciously,
in this School."

35. Baur was at least generally aware of Toland by the time he published the first
edition of *Lehrbuch der christlichen Dogmengeschichte* in 1847 (see p. 212); by the
second (1858) and identical third (1867) editions, *Christianity not Mysterious* is
cited by name (*History of Christian Dogma*, 286). I have yet to find any reference
either to *Nazarenus* or to Thomas Morgan in Baur's writings. See further on
this notes 1 and 2 above.

36. So, e.g., Ellis in his Foreword to the second edition of Harris, *Tübingen School*,
(xii–xv); cf. Slater, "Hort's Lectures on 'Judaistic Christianity,'" 129; and cf.
the comments at the conclusion of Hoennicke's 1908 survey of scholarship
on Jewish Christianity after Baur (*Judenchristentum*, 16–17). O'Neill, in contrast, correctly observes that the "leading idea" of nineteenth-century German
scholarship—namely, that "Catholic Christianity was a late synthesis which
more or less seriously misrepresented the historical process that produced it"—
"had been imported from England" ("Study of the New Testament," 143).

37. Part of the problem is the fact that Baur himself, as Harris points out, "never
gave a systematic account" of his own theology (*Tübingen School*, 160). See esp.
the competing reconstructions by Harris, *Tübingen School*; Hodgson, *Formation*; and more recently Zachhuber, *Theology as Science*, 25–72, who finds the

programmatic "heart of Baur's project" (p. 26; cf. 48) in Baur's early work *Die christliche Gnosis.*

38. See Hodgson, *Formation*, 86–88.

39. Hodgson, *Formation*, 39.

40. Hodgson, *Formation*, 41.

41. See esp. Baur, *History of Christian Dogma*, 324–38. See further Hodgson's outstanding analysis of the matter in *Formation*, 37–89.

42. On Baur's relation to Schleiermacher, see Harris, *Tübingen School*, 19–20, 146–54, 163; Hodgson, *Formation*, 43–54; further Zachhuber, *Theology as Science*, 38–41.

43. Quoted from Harris, *Tübingen School*, 148.

44. See Hodgson, *Formation*, 43 (quoting Baur, *Church History*, 5 and 112–13); cf. 51: "For the young Baur, the most exciting aspect of Schleiermacher's thought had been the primacy he afforded to religious consciousness as a new starting place for Christian dogmatics, one which could free the believer from the external authority of Protestant scholasticism."

45. Baur's early *Symbolik und Mythologie oder die Naturreligion des Alterthum* (1824) already assumes such a "consciousness" as the essence of religion more generally; cf. Harris, *Tübingen School*, 19–20. Regarding Christianity in particular, see further below.

46. Harris, *Tübingen School*, 150–54; Hodgson, *Formation*, 47–54.

47. Hodgson, *Ferdinand Christian Baur*, 22, from which the earlier quotations in this paragraph also come; see further 17–24; cf. Hodgson, *Formation*, 64: "Baur discovered in Hegel's doctrine of God and his philosophy of history an objective basis for interpreting Christianity as a historical process and for understanding speculatively the meaning of reconciliation"; further 37–89 (esp. 54–58), 93–97, 127–31. See also Zachhuber, *Theology as Science*, 42 and 61; and Harris, *Tübingen School*, 164–67, which includes a discussion of "diremption." Cf. Baur's own condensed reflections on the matter in *History of Christian Dogma*, 334–35.

48. I cite the English translation of the lengthy introduction to this work in Hodgson, *Ferdinand Christian Baur*, 259–366, here 298.

49. Cf. Hodgson's formulation of the matter (*Ferdinand Christian Baur*, 27): "Baur's conception of dogma in relation to Spirit can perhaps best be summarized by saying that it is the fundamental means by which human Spirit assimilates into consciousness the absolute truth of Infinite Spirit, a truth that is mediated, according to Christian faith, by a historical revelation with its source and center in the person of Christ." Harris (*Tübingen School*, 19–20) finds such a redefinition of revelation at work already in Baur's *Symbolik und Mythologie.*

50. Cf. Hodgson, *Ferdinand Christian Baur*, 33: "The Idea of Christianity is to be understood as the Idea of reconciliation or of divine-human unity and union, the Idea of God-manhood, as perceived originally and definitively in the person of Christ, in the fullest perfection conceivable for a single individual."

51. See Baur, *History of Christian Dogma*, 50, and further Hodgson's comments in the introduction to his translation, 18–21.

52. See, e.g., Baur, *History of Christian Dogma*, 91: "Since dogma lays out its substantial content initially from itself [i.e., as revelation in Baur's sense], and brings it to consciousness, dogma is an object open to various possible interpretations; and the forms in which its inherently still-indefinite content first obtain more precise definition can derive only from the sphere of thoughts and religious representations in which the consciousness of the age was accustomed to operate." Cf. also his comments in *Epochs of Church Historiography*: "To assume its vantage point, dogmatics can only place itself in the movement of the history of dogma. It does this, however, by attempting as far as possible to bring to a halt the ever elapsing movement of dogma; it does so in order to arrive at a clear awareness of the constant element in the true Christian consciousness, of its immanent substantial content within the variable forms of the changing consciousness of the times" (trans. Hodgson, *Ferdinand Christian Baur*, 263).

53. Hodgson, *Formation*, 93–97; cf. Hodgson, *Ferdinand Christian Baur*, 27: "Religion, and above all Christianity as the absolute religion, transcends the subjectivism of philosophy in its claim that truth is not simply immanent to man but is rather given to him by God in a revelatory historical event that stands outside subjective consciousness, confronting the latter with the truth of its own being."

54. Baur, *Church History*, 6, 9, 12 (*Kirchengeschichte*, 5–6, 9, 12); see further 6–37, esp. 17 (16, *die absolute Religion*), 18 (17, *für das Christenthum auf seinem universellen und absoluten Standpunkt die adäquate Form des religiösen Bewusstseins*), 32 (31, *jenes Absolute des christlichen Bewusstseins*), 33 (32, *In dem sittlichen Bewusstsein spricht sich demnach der absolute Inhalt des christlichen Princips aus*), and 34 (32, *das Absolute des christlichen Princips*). See also Baur's *History of Christian Dogma*, 58–59 and 98–100.

55. Hodgson, *Ferdinand Christian Baur*, 27.

56. Cf. Baur's characterization of dogma as "something self-moving, shaping itself this way or that, becoming determinate in a multiplicity of forms" in the methodological statement at the beginning of *History of Christian Dogma*, 52. Cf. Hodgson's comment in his Introduction to the work: "The 'operative' character of dogma is one of the distinctive features of Baur's history ... Baur speaks of dogma as though it were an active agent in history, a moving power" (20). For the broader philosophical context of this assumption, see Zachhuber, *Theology as Science*, 7–10, 67–72, who traces it above all to Schelling.

57. Baur, *Church History*, 37; cf. 23–24, where the "true core and centre," the "substantial essence" of Christianity must also be its "original" core, thus rendering the normative question one with the historical. Cf. also *History of Christian Dogma*, 50–51: the discipline of the history of dogma "must accept as the unshakable ground of all historical movement the substantial content of Christian consciousness that is connected to and identical with the person of Jesus."

58. Baur, *Church History*, 37.

59. Baur, *Church History*, 37. In Baur's *History of Christian Dogma*, the "original and as yet undivided one dogma" correlated with the origin of Christianity (51) is imagined as driving ever after the whole history of dogma—and thus indeed the whole of Christian history more generally insofar as the "external world and political life" of church history presupposes dogma as its "inner world of thought" (48).

60. Cf. Hodgson, *Ferdinand Christian Baur*, 36: "Church history [according to Baur] is to be viewed as the process of the self-actualization of its *Sache*, the Idea of Christianity, the Idea of divine-human unity as perceived in the fullest perfection possible for a single individual in the person of the church's 'founder,' Jesus of Nazareth. The speculative conception of church-historical development must show the essential connection between this originative event and the church's subsequent historical forms."

61. Baur, *Church History*, 1; cf. his comments in the introduction to *Epochs of Church Historiography*, translated in Hodgson, *Ferdinand Christian Baur*, 47–48.

62. See Baur, *Church History*, 1–23, esp. 22–23: "As this process gradually moves forward [in Greek philosophy and Hellenistic, esp. "Essene," Judaism], and eliminates more and more completely all that bears the stamp of particularism and subjectivity, we see that it can have no other issue than at the point where the origin of Christianity is found. On what grounds then can we regard Christianity itself as a phenomenon purely supernatural, as an absolute miracle introduced into the world's history without the operation of natural causes, when we find in every direction, wherever we turn, numerous points of contact and affinity in which it is linked with the most intimate bonds to the whole history of the development of mankind? It contains nothing that was not conditioned by a series of causes and effects going before." See further on Baur's "absolute beginning" problem in Zachhuber, *Theology as Science*, 36–37.

63. The question of whether the essential principle of Christianity can be considered "new or peculiar to Christianity" is explicitly addressed—and answered in the affirmative—in Baur, *Church History*, 29–30; cf. the extended discussion of "Christianity as a New Principle in the World's Historical Development" in Baur, *Paul*, 2:212–27. Indeed, note in this connection Baur's own appeal to "miracle" where Paul's conversion is concerned, on which see further below.

64. Baur, *History of Christian Dogma*, 91.

65. Zachhuber, *Theology as Science*, is particularly perceptive on this point. Cf. his analysis of Baur's "perpetual dilemma" (41; cf. 58–59), namely, the fact that "no absolute point of reference can be found within history" from Baur's critical, historical perspective (49). "From a historical perspective, there could only ever be a relatively best, relatively most perfect individual: 'but between the relatively best and the absolutely perfect, there is a chasm which history can never cross'" (40 [quoting Baur, *Die christliche Gnosis*, 638]). Zachhuber thus finds two ultimately irreconcilable programs coexisting in Baur's project, an idealist one and the historical-critical ("neo-rationalist") one (47–72).

66. Baur, *History of Christian Dogma*, 356. See further Harris, *Tübingen School*, 148–49 and 150–51: "Schleiermacher was never able to bridge the gulf between the Christ of speculation and the Jesus of history. His Christ always remained a product of his own analysis of the religious consciousness, a production which in Baur's opinion had no connection with historical reality" (151).

67. Zachhuber, *Theology as Science*, 45: "Baur . . . finds in Hegel the same unresolved duality between the historical and the ideal Christ that he had detected previously in Schleiermacher and the ancient Gnostics." See further Hodgson, *Formation*, 58–64; Hodgson, "Hegel's Christology"; and Harris, *Tübingen School*, 168–72.

68. Baur, *Die christliche Gnosis*, 717. The passage is quoted from Harris, *Tübingen School*, 171, who essentially reproduces (at least with respect to the sentence quoted here) the translation in Hodgson, *Formation*, 62.

69. Baur, *Die christliche Gnosis*, 717, cited from Hodgson, *Formation*, 62.

70. Cited in Harris, *Tübingen School*, 151.

71. Cf. the summary statement of Baur's broad project in Baird, *History of New Testament Research*, 1:259–60: "Historical criticism can establish the credibility of Christianity and explicate Christian truth."

72. Note esp. Strauss's incisive point, in a letter detailing his "plan for a course of lectures on the life of Jesus" written in 1832, about "the more elegant supernaturalism of Schleiermacher, who permits criticism in itself . . . but marks out one holy circle in the name of faith over which criticism shall have no power—namely, that this historical individual was the absolutely perfect one" (Harris, *David Friedrich Strauss*, 32–34). The work was published in successive editions beginning in 1835, and its fourth edition was translated into English by George Eliot (Mary Anne Evans). See further on Strauss's critique Baird, *History of New Testament Research*, 1:246–55; and Keck's Introduction to his English translation of Strauss, *Christ of Faith and the Jesus of History*. Harris's suggestion (*Tübingen School*, 173) that Baur was silent on the question of Jesus because "it was really of no consequence to him who Jesus was" is far from persuasive; that Baur felt that "Strauss had said all that was worth saying on the subject" is equally dubious given Baur's comments on Strauss in *Paul*, 1:2; see note 74 below.

73. Schwegler, *Das Nachapostolische Zeitalter*, 148. Schwegler suggests in passing that Paul "brought to general consciousness" views that "the inner, spiritual life of Jesus himself had achieved," with this footnoted caveat: "Wir haben es vermieden, über die Person Christi, namentlich über dasjenige, was man seinen 'Plan' zu nennen pflegt, genauere Bestimmungen aufzustellen, da die Geschichtsquellen . . . keine völlig sicheren Aussagen hierüber zulassen." He is careful to point out, however, that the disputes between Paul and the *Urgemeinde* demonstrate that Jesus had articulated no formal doctrine regarding the relationship of Christianity to either the Gentile world or to Mosaic law—but

"not, however, that [Jesus] himself still thought about such things in a Jewish manner [*nicht aber, das er selbst hierüber noch jüdisch dachte*]."

74. The quotation comes from a letter Baur wrote to L. F. Heyd regarding Strauss's work, translated in Harris, *David Friedrich Strauss*, 86–88 (here 87–88); cf. Baur, *Paul*, 1:2 (*Paulus*, 1:4–5), which frames Strauss's "negative" results and their impact on the "consciousness of the age" (*dem Bewusstsein der Zeit*) as both "a decided need in the education of the age" and "a challenge to us to go still deeper and more thoroughly into the critical process begun by him."

75. See Baur, *Church History*, 26–43. The quotations given here are taken from 28–29, 33, and 37.

76. Baur, *Paul*, 1:3. This sentiment, which was substantially the same from the first edition of *Paulus* (1843, pp. 3–4) through Zeller's second edition (the 1873 English translation of which is quoted here), was written long before the publication of the account of Jesus found in Baur's *Church History*.

77. Baur, *Church History*, 47; cf. 32 (*Kirchengeschichte*, 30): Jesus felt "that it was unnecessary for him to set forth the antagonism of principle [*principielle Gegensatz*] expressly . . . sure that, as the spirit of his teaching came to be understood and realised, it would be worked out to all the results which it necessarily involved . . . [H]e himself was thoroughly aware not only of the antagonism of principle [*des principielles Gegensatzes*], but of the consequences to which it could not fail to lead." Cf. the statement in his posthumously published "Vorlesungen über Neutestamentliche Theologie," cited in Lemke, *Judenchristentum*, 265: "Jesus ist Stifter einer neuen Religion; was aber das Wesen einer Religion an sich ausmacht, ist nicht ein dogmatisch ausgebildetes Religionssystem, ein bestimmter Lehrbegriff, es sind nur Grundanschauungen und Principien, Grundsätze und Vorschriften, als unmittelbare Aussagen des religiösen Bewusstseins."

78. Baur, *Paul*, 1:3.

79. Baur, *Church History*, 46 and 49.

80. Baur, *Paul*, 2:123–24; cf. 2:146: "We have therefore a right to say that no one ever felt so truly this disunion of man with himself—this division which prevails at the standpoint of law—as the apostle, who, when he felt it, had already overcome it." Indeed, so great is Baur's emphasis on Paul's revelatory experience that, in *Church History*, he is forced to reckon with the possibility that it was actually Paul himself who originated Christianity: "But the apostle takes up an attitude of so great freedom and independence not only towards the other apostles, but towards the person of Jesus himself, that one might be inclined to ask whether a view of his relation to the person of Christ can be the right one which would make the apostle Paul the originator and first exponent of that which constitutes the essence of Christianity as distinguished from Judaism." He quickly turns back this problem, however, by invoking his earlier argument regarding the "moral universalism" of Jesus; see Baur, *Church History*, 49.

81. Baur, *Church History*, 46–47 (*Kirchengeschichte*, 44–45); cf. 48: "In what other way can he have overcome his hatred and repugnance towards Christianity but

being plunged, almost against his will [!], in a high-wrought and intense frame of spirit, into contemplation of [Jesus's] death."

82. See Baur, *Paul*, 2:115–18, esp. 118: "It is not possible to maintain order, connexion, and unity in our view of the whole [of Pauline doctrine], and to give the respective doctrines their proper place, except in this way: that the apostle's doctrine of justification with all that belongs to it be recognized as constituting his representation of the subjective consciousness, and kept separate from his view of the objective relation in which Christianity stands to Judaism and Heathenism in the religious development of mankind."

83. See Baur, *Paul*, 2:123–33 (*Paulus*, 2:133–45). The quotation is taken from 124, 125–26, 127, 128–29, and 133.

84. Baur, *Paul*, 2:169, restating the basic thesis found on p. 118 and again on 182. The negative (not from works of the law) and positive (through faith) sides of this doctrine are treated respectively in Chapters 2 and 3.

85. See Baur, *Paul*, 2:169: "The Christian consciousness which is awakened and inspired by faith in Christ is necessarily also the consciousness of a communion of believers"; further 169–81.

86. See Baur, *Paul*, 2:182–211: "Now this contrast [between law and faith, division and atonement], which is found deepest and most intense in the individual human consciousness, presents itself also as a great historical contrast in the relation of Judaism and Christianity. It was through a breach with Judaism that the apostle's Christian consciousness first took shape" (182). Nonetheless, "the Jew stands at a higher stage of religious consciousness" than the pagan (210), insofar as "the essential conception of heathenism is . . . a denial and perversion of the original consciousness of God" (205).

87. See Baur, *Paul*, 2:212–27, esp. 222: "As Adam represents this [sensual, earthly, sinful] side of human nature . . . so we behold in Christ the principle of the other, spiritual side of human nature. This contrast of the two principles . . . shows us that it is something more than the resurrection . . . that Christ is regarded as procuring. What is obtained through him is the higher spiritual consciousness of man, awaked by Christ and invested with permanent authority and power. Christ is the principle of consciousness."

88. Baur, *Paul*, 2:233: "Faith, love, and hope are the three momenta of the Christian consciousness, the three essential forms in which it finds expression; but while to faith and hope that infinity of the subject which Christianity promises is reserved for the transcendent hereafter, and is unattained here, love possesses that infinity here and now as her own immanent virtue . . . Love, therefore, or faith in the form of love, is a greater thing than hope." The discussion is wrapped up with a "Special Discussion of Certain Minor Points of Doctrine" in chap. 8, and "On Certain Features of the Apostle's Character" in chap. 9.

89. E.g., Baur, *History of Christian Dogma*, 91–92, singling out Greek philosophy as the main factor in "paganism."

90. Baur, *Paul*, 1:3; cf. Baur, *History of Christian Dogma*, 91–96.

91. Baur, *History of Christian Dogma*, 93, and *Church History*, 48.

92. Baur, *Paul*, 1:3.

93. E.g., Baur, *History of Christian Dogma*, 96: "Pauline antinomianism and the doctrine of justification that rests on it were too blunt and abstract [as doctrines] for the popular consciousness to be able to embrace them readily. The customary way of looking at things based on the legal authority of the Old Testament made it natural to position law and gospel, faith and works, Old and New Testaments, alongside each other with equal justification. More time was needed before it was possible to come to terms with the originally so sharp antithesis of Pauline thought."

94. Baur, *Church History*, 37, drawing a particular contrast with the insistence on such faith in the Gospel of John: "In the original Christian doctrine no such requirement is put forward." This claim no doubt had special resonance in the post-Strauss era.

95. Baur, *Church History*, 38–39 (*Kirchengeschichte*, 36). Menzies's appeal to the image of clothing to translate "Durch die Messiasidee erhielt erst der geistige Inhalt des Christenthums die concrete Form," if somewhat interpretive, captures the thrust of Baur's paradigm quite effectively. Just as in traditional Christian myth, a transcendent, divine reality had to assume a temporal Jewish form in order to change the world; in this case, however, the "incarnation" is immanent and idealistic rather than supernatural and fleshly.

96. Baur, *Church History*, 41 and 42; cf. 35, where Jesus's "Kingdom of God" idea is interpreted as "the Old Testament notion of theocracy in a spiritualised form."

97. Baur, *Church History*, 32, where Menzies renders the twice-appearing phrase "principielle Gegensatz" (*Kirchengeschichte*, 30) with effective sharpness as "antagonism of principle." See further note 77 above.

98. Baur, *Paul*, 2:134.

99. Note in this connection that Baur considered even Paul's "forms" to have been limited in their ability to capture the true spiritual reality he found behind them. A particularly striking example is found in the comparison of Paul with Ebionite doctrine: "The limitation of Ebionitism was that it posited the divine in Christ only in the *pneuma*, the Spirit, and thus for Ebionites Christ was essentially only a human being. But even Pauline thought still had not gotten beyond such a view. Over against this standpoint that still depended on Judaism, Christian consciousness found its nobler ascent to its absolute idea in the Johannine idea of the Logos"—which was derived not from Judaism but from Greek philosophy (*History of Christian Dogma*, 105). Note also in this respect Baur's ambiguous comments regarding Paul's apparent expressions of "patriotism" in Romans in *Church History*, 68: while the question of the status of the Jewish people vis-à-vis Christian salvation "sums up the claim to which Jewish particularism still clung . . . [i]t was not a question of material rights so much

as a question of faith, and the apostle would have been stifling his own feelings of patriotism in an unnatural way, had not this question moved him to the very depths of his heart."

100. Baur formulated his initial understanding of this matter in 1831 in the now-classic "Die Christuspartei in der korinthischen Gemeinde." It was subsequently developed over a variety of publications, including most especially *Paul* and *Church History*. For a brief analysis of his evolving understanding of the conflict, see Lemke, *Judenchristentum*, 276–79.

101. Cf., e.g., *Kirchengeschichte*, 51: "die Zähigkeit, mit welcher die älteren Apostel an ihrem Judaismus festhielten" (*Church History*, 54); *Paulus*, 1:281: "Wir begegnen hier [in Galatians] judaisirenden Gegenern … und zwar tragen sie hier noch ganz das schroffe judaistische Gepräge an sich, das sie as Gegner des paulinischen Christenthums bezeichnet" (*Paul*, 1:261); 1:326: "ein antipaulinisches judaisirendes Christenthum" (*Paul*, 1:305); cf. 1:271 on "das paulinische Christenthum" versus "das ihm gegenüberstehende Judenchristenthum" (*Paul*, 1:251); and 1:137, "der Conflict des paulinischen Christenthums mit dem judenchristlichen" (*Paul*, 1:125). See also Lemke, *Judenchristentum*, 273–74.

102. Perhaps the closest Baur comes to a definition is the summary characterization of Ebionites in *History of Christian Dogma*, 97: "what counted in Ebionitism was the Christian consciousness adhering to the religious traditions and institutions of Judaism." Note in this connection that "Jewish Christianity in general," according to Baur, "was a kind of Ebionitism" (*Church History*, 182 [*Kirchengeschichte*, 174: "es wenigstens kein unberechtigter Gebrauch des Namens ist, wenn man das Judenchristenthum überhaupt in gewissem Sinne as Ebionitismus bezeichnet"]). Cf. his assessment of the Letter of James in *Paul*, 2:304 [*Paulus*, 2:330]: "The absolute standpoint of Christian consciousness which Paul took up in his doctrine of faith is degraded again to that of Judaeo-Christianity [*Der absolute Standpunkt des christlichen Bewusstseins … wird wieder zu dem judenchristlichen degradirt*]." Cf. Lemke, *Judenchristentum*, 274–79.

103. Baur, *Church History*, 46; cf. *Paul*, 1:61 on "the Jewish monopoly of religion," in contrast to the "universal system" of Christianity.

104. Baur, *Paul*, 1:261–62, saying that Paul's "Judaising opponents" had "placed this principle in the highest place of all." While this did not mean that Gentiles were denied "participation in the Messianic salvation," it did mean that they were to be not "so much converted to Christianity as to Judaism"; cf. 1:332: "as Jewish Christians they would not renounce the precedence which as Jews they claimed over Gentiles"; cf. *History of Christian Dogma*, 93–94.

105. Baur, *Church History*, 57, and *Paul*, 2:199.

106. Baur, *Paul*, 1:125.

107. Cf. Baur, *Paul*, 1:321 (*Paulus*, 1:344): Paul "had not fulfilled his mission as the Apostle to the Gentiles, whilst the absolute importance which Judaism, and the Jewish Christianity identified with it, claimed for themselves [*welche*

*das Judenthum und das mit demselben identische Judenchristenthum für sich an-
sprach*], . . . was not separated from them, and reckoned according to its merely
relative value"; cf. 1:133: the stricter class of Jewish Christians who actively opposed Paul at the time of the so-called Jerusalem conference "saw perfectly
well that if the necessity of the law was not recognized in the case of Gentile
Christians, its absolute importance to Judaism was at an end."

108. Baur, *Church History*, 57.

109. Cf. Lemke, *Judenchristentum*, 286: "Die Kategorie 'judasistisch'/'judenchristlich' dient [for Baur] unversehens zur Bestimmung dessen, was nicht eigentlich
christlich, insbesondere nicht Jesu Lehre entsprechend ist."

110. Hodgson's work on Baur is indispensable here. See the introductory comments
in his edition of Baur's *History of Christian Dogma* (esp. 18–21) and in *Ferdinand
Christian Baur* (esp. 17–36); further *Formation*, 90–141.

111. In Baur's view, even Ebionism represented "the Christian consciousness," albeit "adhering to the religious traditions and institutions of Judaism" (*History of Christian Dogma*, 97). Thus, for Baur, does the traditional distinction
between orthodoxy and heresy—like canonical and noncanonical—dissolve
into a broader continuum of more and less obscurant vehicles of Christian
consciousness. Indeed, even Paul is said to be subject to certain Jewish limitations, as noted above (note 99). Thus too the "relatively [!] positive view of
Jewish Christianity" Lemke finds in Baur (*Judenchristentum*, 288): whatever its
imperfections, it is still Christianity.

112. Baur, *Church History*, 42, elaborating that "to believe in him as the Messiah
after his dying such a death involved the removal from the conception of the
Messiah of all the Jewish and carnal elements which were associated with it."

113. Baur, *Church History*, 42.

114. The preceding quotations are all from Baur, *Church History*, 43.

115. Baur, *Church History*, 49; cf. *Paul*, 1:43: "The only thing that divided [the first
disciples of Jesus] from the rest of the Jews was the conviction . . . that the
promised Messiah had appeared in Jesus of Nazareth. They saw nothing an-
tagonistic to their national consciousness in this belief in Jesus as the Messiah.
And yet this simple undeveloped belief contained, on the Jewish side of its
consciousness, an element of discord which necessarily widened the division
between Judaism and Christianity."

116. See, e.g., Baur, *Church History*, 46–51; cf. *Paul*, 2:124, which lays particular emphasis on Jesus's resurrection as "the most essential element in the apostle's
conviction of the Messianic dignity of Jesus" since this is what resolved the
contradiction of a crucified messiah. Stephen and the Hellenists are identified
as the specific precursors of Paul; see below.

117. See esp. Baur's survey of New Testament literature, the apostolic fathers, and
Justin in *Church History*, 99–152.

118. Baur, *Church History*, 49–50.

119. The quotations come from Baur, *Paul*, 1:43, and *Church History*, 45. See further *Paul*, 1:43–62, esp. 59–60: "This inevitable rending asunder of Christianity from Judaism, whereby Judaism would be rendered negative as an absolute religion, and by which its final extinction was threatened, had been realized by Stephen . . . [through] the high, liberal standpoint which he assumed . . . This spirit of Christianity, asserting itself all at once in its full power and importance in Stephen, is an astonishing phenomenon, as we are accustomed to see him take a very subordinate standpoint with regard to the Apostles . . . whilst he considers the temple worship with all its outward forms as something already antiquated and dying out of itself—the Apostles always remain immoveably true to their old adherence to the Temple." Stephen nonetheless was only "the first to draw public attention" to an "opposition to Judaism" that "seems to have existed in the Church of Jerusalem for some time" in the distinct "party" of Hellenists to which Stephen belonged (*Church History*, 45). The implication would seem to be that the universalizing ideas furnished by Hellenistic discourse provided a less cramping vehicle for the new Christian consciousness than traditional Jewish ones; cf. *Church History*, 2–6, 11–17.

120. Baur, *Paul*, 1:39–40, 60 (*Paulus*, 1:45–47, 67–68).

121. See Baur, *Paul*, 1:60–62. The tension in Baur's interpretation between Paul's historical dependence on Stephen and ultimate authoritative independence is fascinating—and telling. He concludes, on one hand, that we can see in Stephen's speech reflections of an early development of "the original ideas of Pauline Christianity" and thus "the forerunner of the Apostle" (61 [*Paulus*, 1:68]). On the other hand, the fact that Paul nowhere mentions Stephen is taken as evidence of the ultimate "originality of [Paul's] religious ideas—the immediacy of the revelation he received [*der Unmittelbarkeit der ihm gewordenen Offenbarung*] (Gal 1:16). These of themselves exclude the idea of any preparatory means for his adoption of Christianity" (1:62 [1:70], with my own rendering of the cited German phrase).

122. Cf. Baur, *Church History*, 48–49 (here 48) and *Paul*, 1:112–15 (here 113), noting that Paul's design was "to enter on his apostolic mission under the influence of a revelation vouchsafed to him alone, in a perfectly free and independent manner, unbiassed by any human interposition."

123. Baur, *Paul*, 1:117.

124. Baur discusses the so-called Jerusalem conference at length in *Paul*, 1:116–51. See esp. *Paul*, 1:128 n.: "Here first in the history a decided contest presents itself between Jewish and Gentile Christianity"; cf. 1:125, "a conflict between the Pauline and Jewish Christianity." Note in this connection the repeated framing of the conflict as a matter of "principle" (*Grundsatz*) rather than merely practice (esp. 1:132–33 [*Paulus*, 1:144–46]); cf. 1:131: "fourteen years after the conversion of the Apostle Paul, [the original apostles'] circle of vision did not extend beyond Judaism"; cf. *Church History*, 54: "the older apostles [were] clinging tenaciously

to their Judaism. During the long period of years which had elapsed they had not made a single step that would have carried them beyond their Jewish particularism."

125. Baur, *Paul*, 1:126, 129.

126. Baur, *Paul*, 1:132.

127. Baur, *Paul*, 1:132–33 (*Paulus*, 1:145): "We have here presented to us the exact origin of those two sections of Jewish Christianity [*zwei Fractionen des Judenchristenthums*] with which we become more nearly acquainted in the history of the succeeding period. There grew up within Jewish Christianity itself a strict and a liberal party [*Es gab innerhalb des Judenchristenthum selbst eine strengere und mildere Ansicht und Partei*]." Note that Baur is clear that "the more liberal party was in principle [*in dem Grundsatz*] in harmony with the stricter one, only after the concessions made by the Jewish Apostles to the Apostle Paul, they could not in practice [*praktisch*] act against him" (133 [146], with my translation of *praktisch*). The role of James in all of this is not developed in the main discussions of the Antioch incident (*Paul*, 1:133–51; *Church History*, 54–56); see, however, the appendix on the Letter of James in *Paul*, where Baur comments in passing on "the Judaeo-Christianity [*Judenchristenthum*] of James, a man we know from Gal. ii to have been impregnated with all the obstinacy of traditionary Judaism, and to have been the uncompromising upholder of every Jewish institution, even of circumcision" (2:309–10 [2:337]).

128. Baur, *Church History*, 84–87.

129. See esp. Baur, *Church History*, 54–98; also *Paul*, 1:132–36.

130. E.g., Baur, *Church History*, 99: "Some process of this sort there must have been: otherwise we could not understand how a Catholic Church . . . which united opposites within itself, ever came to exist at all"; cf. 76–77. Baur attributes this tendency to both sides "feeling more or less distinctly that they belonged together" (105).

131. Baur, *History of Christian Dogma*, 96; further *Church History*, 181–83, esp. 183: "Jewish Christianity in general was a kind of Ebionitism. In the ordinary and narrow sense of the name, however, it denotes that form of primitive Christianity which . . . came to be detached from the community of the Catholic Church, because its adherents were unable to keep pace with the development of the Christian consciousness in its advance beyond Jewish Christianity."

132. See Baur, *Church History*, 106–11. According to Baur, baptism was initially only a Gentile requirement; but as the number of Jews joining Christianity decreased, it "came more and more to be the universal form of making the Christian confession, and to be considered the characteristic mark of the Christian . . . religion" (108). Cf. his comments on the Pseudo-Clementine *Homilies*— which Baur attributes to "Hellenistic Jewish Christians" (*hellenistischen Judenchristen*)—in *Paul*, 1:144–45 (*Paulus*, 1:158–59).

133. Baur, *Church History*, 113–14: "This, however, is not to be regarded as a renunciation of Pauline principle" so much as a deemphasis resulting from circumstance:

"Paulinism only presents its sharp doctrine of justification by faith in its most incisive mode of statement when it has to contend with Jewish Christianity for the ground of its existence, and for its warrant on grounds of principle … But as soon as this end had been attained, Paulinism was quite at liberty to concede to works their proper place by the side of faith."

134. Baur, *Church History*, 131–36, 147–52.

135. Baur, *Church History*, 151–52.

136. Baur, *Church History*, 112–13, correlating the "theocratic institutions and aristocratic forms" of Catholicism—i.e., the episcopate and eventually the papacy—with "the Jewish messianic idea."

137. Baur, *Church History*, 148–49 (*Kirchengeschichte*, 142: *der Kanon der neutestamentlichen Schriften, als die wesentliche Grundlage der sich constituirenden katholischen Kirche*).

138. Baur, *Church History*, 136.

139. See Baur's survey of the ancient literature in *Church History*, 114–47. Each text is classified as either basically Jewish Christian (Hebrews, James, 1 Peter, *Epistle of Barnabas*, Letters of Ignatius, Hermas) or Pauline Christian (canonical Pseudo-Pauline texts, Acts, 1 Clement, Polycarp), with its peculiar reconciling tendencies isolated. Cf. the discussion of more hostile forms of Pauline Christianity (Luke, Marcion) and Jewish Christianity (Revelation, Papias, Hegesippus, Pseudo-Clementines) on 84–97. The treatment of Justin—who according to Baur was deliberately silent on Paul—is somewhat ambiguous; Baur initially discusses him in connection with the hostile Jewish Christians (88) before treating him as the last step in the "transition," from the Jewish Christian side, "to Catholic Christianity" (142–47 [here 147]).

140. In the end, the purest expressions of Christian consciousness in the New Testament according to Baur are four Pauline texts (1–2 Corinthians, Galatians, and Romans) and the Sermon on the Mount, with allowances even here for later adulterations as, e.g., in the case of Romans 15–16 (see *Paul*, 1:369–81) and Matt 5:17–19 (Lemke, *Judenchristentum*, 285–86). Philippians, 1 Thessalonians, and Philemon are treated—quite literally!—as "second class" (*zweite Klasse*) texts (*Paul*, 2:1–111).

141. Note here Baur's critique of the traditional Protestant emphasis on the New Testament in *History of Christian Dogma*, 268 and 270: "when it had become clear for the first time that the whole shape of the church, even in its dogma, was nothing other than an enormous mistake, the Reformation set out precisely to return to the earliest period and to renew dogma from the primary sources of the gospel. It is fruitless, however, to bring a now-vanished form of consciousness [i.e., "the consciousness of an age" reflected in the New Testament] back into existence in the same shape that it once assumed … [N]othing can be more erroneous and false than the view that the essence of Protestantism can be grasped from the circle of its first appearance, and defined, more or less narrowly, from its so-called sources."

Chapter 3. Apostolic vs. Judaizing Jewish Christianity

1. For a detailed analysis of the principal figures, see esp. Harris, *Tübingen School*. Much of the work of those figures was published in *Theologische Jahrbücher*, "the literary organ of the School" (5), founded and edited by Eduard Zeller. The most exhaustive elaboration was Albert Schwegler's massive *Das Nachapostolische Zeitalter in den Hauptmomenten seiner Entwicklung* (1846).

2. Ritschl, *Entstehung,* esp. v–vi. Baird calls Ritschl "the architect of modern liberalism" (*History of New Testament Research*, 2:86). For a thorough analysis of Ritschl's theological-historical project in relation to Baur's, see Zachhuber, *Theology as Science,* 131–285, esp. 131–74.

3. Carleton Paget, "Reception," 368. See esp. Lightfoot's extensive engagement with basic theses of the Tübingen School regarding the relationship of Jewish and Gentile Christianity in the dissertation on "St Paul and the Three" appended to his commentary on Galatians (*Epistle of St. Paul to the Galatians* [hereafter *Galatians*], 292–374). Lightfoot acknowledges a special debt to Ritschl (295 n. 1).

4. See further on the decline of the school Harris, *Tübingen School,* 238–48. By the end of the century, Slater considered "the theory of Baur and Schwegler" to have been "so completely refuted" that it seemed to him "remarkable that its effects should have been so wide and extensive" ("Hort's Lectures on 'Judaistic Christianity,'" 129).

5. Lightfoot, *Galatians,* 311 and 293, framing the central question as follows: "What were the relations existing between St Paul and the Apostles of the Circumcision? How far do the later sects of Ebionites on the one hand and Marcionites on the other ... represent opposing principles cherished side by side in the bosom of the Church and sheltering themselves under the names, or (as some have ventured to say) sanctioned by the authority, of the leading Apostles? What in fact is the secret history—if there be any secret history—of the origin of Catholic Christianity?" Lightfoot is quite aware that the apostolic era is "an age which, closing our eyes to facts, we are apt to invest with an ideal excellence" (374). See further Carleton Paget, "Reception," 363–64.

6. See his extensive treatment of Jewish Christianity in *Entstehung,* 104–270.

7. Hilgenfeld, *Judentum und Judenchristentum,* 9 (emphasis mine): "Was die herrschende Theologie um jeden Preis abzuwehren suchte, war nur ein Dualismus des apostolisches Christenthums, welcher die Einheit des Urchristenthums zerreisse, die Ansicht, dass sämmtliche Urapostel in ihrer Denkweise über das Judenthum keineswegs hinausgekommen seien." Cf. Baird, *History of New Testament Research,* 2:87, 90: "Ritschl approaches theology from the perspective of history. He believes the essence of Christianity is to be found in Jesus, the founder of the church, and in the apostles, its first representatives ... In regard to Paul, Ritschl rejects the idea of a contradiction with the other apostles, and affirms both 'the originality of Paul' and 'his continuity with the early apostles'" [citing *Entstehung,* 52]."

8. Cf. Zachhuber's observation that Ritschl's theoretical shift away from Baur's developmental theory of Christian history "reflects Ritschl's theological interest not merely in the possibility but in the reality of an early phase of church history that is in principle perfect and can therefore permanently remain a normative point of reference . . . *One* purpose of his study of Primitive Christianity and its transition to Early Catholicism . . . was to argue *historically* for the plausibility of that possibility in the present case: Jesus' preaching and its reception by the apostles constitute the perfect foundation of Christian theology, and insofar as the writings of the New Testament reflect this reality, they have normative significance" (*Theology as Science*, 172, emphasis original). Zachhuber notes further that "Ritschl regards the apostolic era as a relatively enclosed historical period attested to by the writings of the New Testament canon" (174). As explained in the previous chapter, such a view stands in marked contrast to Baur's understanding of the place of the New Testament in the history of dogma.

9. Hilgenfeld, *Judentum und Judenchristentum*, 10: "Dass nun das Judenchristenthum die urapostolische Gestalt des Christenthums gewesen ist, können auch die Gegner Baur's nicht leugnen."

10. Ritschl, *Entstehung*, 128: "nur eine kleine Gruppe entschiedener Anhänger in der jerusalemischen Gemeinde"; Lightfoot, *Galatians*, 307, a "bigoted minority."

11. Ritschl, *Entstehung*, 127 ("unglaublich"), apparently referring to Mark 13:10 and 16:15 (cited on 126) and Matt 28:16–20.

12. Lightfoot, *Galatians*, 302.

13. Lightfoot, *Galatians*, 305; cf. Ritschl, *Entstehung*, 127–28: "Dagegen [i.e., the Pauline principle] verlangten Mitglieder der Gemeinde zu Jerusalem, welche früher der pharisäischen Sekte angehört, daß jene Heidenchristen um der Seligkeit willen sich der Beschneidung und dem ganzen mosiaschen Gesetze unterwerfen müßten." When Ritschl goes on to say that "Diese Forderung ist Merkmal des eigentlichen Judenchristenthum," he refers specifically to the nonapostolic form of Jewish Christianity whose core principle—that there is no essential difference between Christianity and Judaism—is the opposite of the apostolic one. See further on this below.

14. Ritschl, *Entstehung*, 128: "In diesen Worten [in Acts 15:7–11] bekennt sich also Petrus ganz zu den paulinischen Grundsätzen von der Unmöglichkeit der Gesetzeserfüllung, und von der Gerecht- und Seligmachung der Menschen durch die Gnade; und darin stimmt ihm auch Jakobus [cf. Acts 15:13–21]." Lightfoot (*Galatians*, 306) similarly frames the matter as a "question of principle" on which Paul and the Jerusalem "Pillars" agreed against the Pharisaic converts: "If the initiatory rite of the old dispensation were imposed on all members of the Christian Church, this would be in effect to deny that the Gospel was a new covenant; in other words to deny its essential character. It was thus the vital point on which the whole controversy turned. And the liberal decision of the council was not only the charter of Gentile freedom but the assertion of the

supremacy of the Gospel," i.e., over "the old dispensation." See further on this essential Christian "principle" inter alia 301–2 and 350–51. Like Ritschl—and, of course, Baur!—Lightfoot traces "the great principle" back to Jesus (295).

15. E.g., Ritschl, *Entstehung*, 147: "vorgeblich unter der Auktorität der Urapostel . . . so haben sie deren Namen mißbraucht"; cf. 142–43 ("in lügnerischer Weise"). Lightfoot (*Galatians*, 358) says this "disposition to sever" Peter from Paul by denying their "essential unity," evident already in the apostles' lifetimes in Corinth, only gets worse after their deaths "had removed all fear of contradiction."

16. Ritschl, *Entstehung*, 152: "Dagegen das eigentliche Judenchristenthum ist von apostolischer Auktorität entblößt, und bildet nicht den Grund eines dauernden Gegensatzes zwischen dem Apostel der Heiden und den unmittelbaren Jüngern Jesu." On Ritschl's technical distinction between *Judenchristenthum* and *Jüdische Christenthum*, see further below.

17. Lightfoot, *Galatians*, 374 and 306–7; cf. 371.

18. E.g., Ritschl, *Entstehung*, 124–25; Lightfoot, *Galatians*, 295–302.

19. See Ritschl, *Entstehung*, 126, 130–31, and 140–41.

20. Lightfoot, *Galatians*, 306.

21. Ritschl, *Entstehung*, 147.

22. Ritschl, *Entstehung*, 141: "daß Israel als ganzes Volk vor den Heiden in die christliche Gemeinde aufgenommen werden müsse."

23. Ritschl, *Entstehung*, 133, "nur rein relativer, nicht ein absoluter Vorrang der gläubigen Juden vor den gläubigen Heiden"; cf. 140: "Privilegium . . . nur in einem relativen Sinne."

24. Ritschl, *Entstehung*, 140–41 (140): "die Beobachtung des mosaischen Gesetzes mit der bei den Aposteln nachgewiesenen reinen Auffasung der christlichen Idee vereinbar war, weil auch Christus dieselbe hatte gelten lassen"; cf. 133, and further 33 and 125.

25. Ritschl, *Entstehung*, 129; for the distinction between the social and religious character of these practices as far as the Gentiles were concerned, see 132–33, 143, 150. Cf. in this respect already Toland, on whom see Chapter 1 above.

26. On the compatibility of the decree with Pauline principles, see Ritschl, *Entstehung*, 136–38.

27. Ritschl, *Entstehung*, 151.

28. Ritschl, *Entstehung*, 144; see further on James's role in this conflict esp. 132 and 142–46.

29. On Peter's role in the conflict, see Ritschl, *Entstehung*, 145–47, here 146: "Petrus, um die Einheit der Gemeinde zu erhalten, nachdem er an der frühern Praxis irre geworden war, den Heidenchristen außer den Enthaltungen des Proselytenthumes noch andere Pflichten des mosaischen Gesetz zugemuthet."

30. Ritschl, *Entstehung*, 146–47.

31. Lightfoot, *Galatians*, 294 and 295.

32. See the essay on "St Paul and the Three" in Lightfoot, *Galatians*, 292–374 (here 294, 295, and 302).

33. Lightfoot, *Galatians*, 350.

34. Lightfoot, *Galatians*, 306 (emphasis original).

35. Lightfoot, *Galatians*, 306; cf. 312: "The Apostles of the Circumcision . . . if conscious themselves that the law was fulfilled in the Gospel . . . strove nevertheless by strict conformity to conciliate the zealots, both within and without the church."

36. Lightfoot, *Galatians*, 306; cf. 310: "the decree was neither permanently nor universally binding."

37. Lightfoot, *Galatians*, 312.

38. For Lightfoot's analysis of James, see *Galatians*, 364–74 (here 370–71, 364–65, 368); cf. 306 n. 2 on the purpose of the "restrictive clauses" of the Apostolic Decree (against Ritschl). Lightfoot suggests that James's selection as local leader of Jerusalem was itself an accommodation to the Jewish environment, in two ways: "Among a people who set a high value on advantages of race and blood" the selection of a brother of Jesus was a natural choice; and "in a state of religious feeling where scrupulous attention to outward forms was held to be a condition of favor with God, one who was a strict observer of the law . . . might hope to obtain a hearing which would be denied to men of less austere lives" (365). In the end, then, while the "incidental notices" about James in the New Testament "throw much light on the practical difficulties and entanglements of his position," they "reveal nothing or next to nothing" about his "true principles" (373).

39. Lightfoot, *Galatians*, 365.

40. For Lightfoot's treatment of Peter, see *Galatians*, 352–59 (here 354–55, 356), noting esp. his appeal (as also by Ritschl) to a revelatory experience to explain how Peter went from being "as rigid and as scrupulous as the most bigoted of his countrymen" to holding "liberal principles, so entirely opposed to the narrow traditions of his age and country" (355). According to Lightfoot, it was only the brief lapse from his "normal principles" in Antioch that allowed the Pseudo-Clementine Homilist to claim Peter as the authority for his own position (352).

41. See Lightfoot's treatment of John in *Galatians*, 359–64 (here 360). Lightfoot explains the notorious differences among the canonical writings attributed to John with reference to this reported move: "The Writings of St John in the Canon probably mark the close of each period. The Apocalypse winds up his career in the Church of the Circumcision; the Gospel and the Epistles are the crowning result of a long residence in the heart of Gentile Christendom."

42. Thus, e.g., the very title of Ritschl's key work, *Die Entstehung der altkatholischen Kirche*; cf. Lightfoot's concern with the question of "the secret history—if there be any secret history—of the origin of Catholic Christianity" in the opening of his extended essay "St Paul and the Three" in *Galatians* (293).

43. Ritschl, *Entstehung*, 152–54, 178; Lightfoot, *Galatians*, 318–21.

44. Lightfoot, *Galatians*, 322, pointing out that "if Ebionism was not primitive Christianity, neither was it a creation of the second century." Regarding its

relationship to the Jerusalem "Pillars," cf. 352: "The author of the Clementine Homilies makes St Peter the mouth-piece of his own Ebionite views"; also 370: "the representation of St James in the canonical Scriptures differs from its Ebionite counterpart as the true portrait from the caricature." Cf. Ritschl, *Entstehung*, 154–56.

45. Lightfoot, *Galatians*, 323 (citing Ritschl), and more generally 322–31; cf. Ritschl, *Entstehung*, 204–34. The Elchasaites are said to be a further development of this Essene Ebionism; see Ritschl, *Entstehung*, 232 and 234–48, and Lightfoot, *Galatians*, 324–25.

46. Ritschl, *Entstehung*, 154: "die Nazaräer ... seit dem Jahre 69 fast außer Berührung mit der übrigen Kirche geblieben waren."

47. Ritschl, *Entstehung*, 252–59, interpreting Justin's distinction between Jews who do and do not think that Torah observance is required for Gentiles with reference to Ebionites and Nazoraeans, respectively.

48. Ritschl, *Entstehung*, 266: "Unsere Ansicht von der Ausscheidung des jüdischen Christenthums aus der Kirche, von den äußeren Bedingungen und inneren Motiven dieses Ereignisses macht die Annahme unmöglich, daß Judenchristenthum bis nach der Mitte des zweiten Jahrhunderts die herrschende Richtung in der Kirche gewesen sei." Ritschl, in fact, can correlate Hadrian's response to the Bar Kochba rebellion with the "fall of Jewish Christianity" (259, "den Sturz des jüdischen Christenthums").

49. Ritschl, *Entstehung*, 266 and 23: "wir ... dabei beharren, daß das katholische Christenthum nicht aus einer Versöhnung der Judenchristen und der Heidenchristen hervorgegangen, sondern daß es eine Stufe des Heidenchristenthums allein ist."

50. Lightfoot, *Galatians*, 311–14 (here 311, 312, and 314). "The Emancipation of the Jewish Churches" represents the third and final period in Lightfoot's "progressive history of the relations between the Jewish and Gentile converts in the early ages of the Church" (294–95).

51. Lightfoot, *Galatians*, 303–4; cf. 313.

52. Lightfoot, *Galatians*, 316–46 (here 316–17). According to Lightfoot, the Nazoraeans' "stubborn" refusal to live like Gentiles even in this new situation compromises their otherwise legitimate claim on apostolic authority: "while copying the letter, they did not copy the spirit of their model; for they took no account of altered circumstances" (319).

53. Ritschl, *Entstehung*, 108–24. It is noteworthy in this connection that Ritschl, in stark contrast to Baur, elevates trust in the relative authenticity of canonical over extracanonical Christian writings to the level of methodological principle: "Wenn es sich nun aber fragt, welcher Ausgangspunkt der Untersuchung der wahren kritischen Methode entspricht, so kann die Wahl zwischen den kanonischen Schriften mit den Apostelnamen und den Ueberlieferungen der Kirchenväter nicht schwer sein. Die protestantische Geschichtschreibung des

Urchristenthums kann sich nicht auf patristische Privattraditionen, sondern nur auf kanonische Schriften gründen" (108). Cf. Baird, *History of New Testament Research*, 2:88: "Ritschl held a high view of biblical authority . . . Ritschl rejected the orthodox doctrine of inspiration, but was conservative on critical issues."

54. Lightfoot, *Galatians*, 368–70; cf. Ritschl, *Entstehung*, 114–15.

55. Lightfoot, *Galatians*, 357.

56. Lightfoot, *Galatians*, 368 and 360.

57. See, e.g., Reuss's two-volume *History of Christian Theology in the Apostolic Age*, published in successive editions beginning with the original French in 1852, which includes both a multichapter analysis of "Judaeo-Christian Theology" (*"La théologie judéo-chrétienne"*) in Vol. 1 (345–424) and a more specific discussion of "Paulinism and Judaeo-Christianity" in Vol. 2 (220–28); cf. the chapter "Primitive Jewish Christianity" in McGiffert's *History of Christianity in the Apostolic Age* (1897); and that devoted to "Das Christenthum der Judenchristen" in the first volume of Harnack's *Lehrbuch der Dogmengeschichte* (3rd ed., 1894). For more specialized treatments, see in England Hort's posthumously published *Judaistic Christianity* (1894); and in Germany Hilgenfeld, *Judentum und Judenchristentum* (1886), and Hoennicke, *Das Judenchristentum im ersten und zweiten Jahrhundert* (1908), who provides a survey of German scholarship on the category from Baur through his own day (1–19).

58. Hoennicke, *Judenchristentum*, 16, "eines der Hauptprobleme der Geschichte des Urchristentums."

59. Thus, e.g., Hort, *Judaistic Christianity*, 39–83, noting esp. the explicit heading "No antagonism in principle with St. Paul" in the summary of his discussion of the so-called Antioch incident (x), which he explains as follows: Having initially been "weak-kneed" about their own policy, the Pillars immediately "confessed [Paul] to be in the right" when confronted by him and "were thenceforth doubly committed to concur heartily with the character of St Paul's work" (82; cf. 81 and 107). Thus those who continued to observe Jewish law after the temple had fallen represented "a real and really mischievous anachronism . . . at variance with the principles laid down by . . . authorities of the apostolic era . . . an unintelligent copying of [James's] policy under changed conditions" (179). Cf. Hoennicke, *Judenchristentum*, 177–247, esp. the extensive treatment of "Die Judaisten und die Urapostel," 211–25, which similarly rejects the idea that the opposition between Paul and Peter in Antioch was based on matters of principle (*auf bestimmte Prinzipien*): "Denn auch Petrus erkannte, daß die Beobachtung der jüdischen Volkssitte für die christliche Gemeinschaft an sich gleichgültig sei . . . Die Einheit der apostolischen Verkündigung erscheint also nicht durch eine eingetretene Spannung zwischen Paulus und den Uraposteln verdunkelt" (217, 221); cf. Reuss, *History of Christian Theology*, 1:283–315 and 2:220–28; also Harnack, *What Is Christianity?*, on which see the following note.

60. Harnack, *What Is Christianity?*, 173–74. In a manner reminiscent of Baur, Harnack identifies "the essence of Christianity"—a more literal rendering of the book's German title, *Das Wesen des Christentums*—with "*an actual experience*" "in every individual member of the new community" of "the consciousness of a living union with God," which in turn is correlated closely with the Holy Spirit (152–53, 164–67). As with Baur, the assumption once again is that this purely internal Christianity inevitably requires transient social and cultural "forms" for the purposes of "common life and public worship" (181; see further 180–88, 190–91, 197–98, 207–8, which also includes a likening of them to a protective "bark"). If the apostles were initially less explicit than Paul regarding the status of their Judaism as mere "husk" to Christianity's "kernel," the fact that they, "in the strength of Christ's spirit ... broke through these barriers" and "ultimately associated themselves with Paul's principles"—"That Peter did so we know for certain; of others we hear that they at least acknowledged their validity"—is considered by Harnack "the most remarkable fact of the apostolic age" (179–80). Cf. Reuss, *History of Christian Theology*, 1:348, who characterizes the "Judaeo-Christianity" of the New Testament—in contrast to the "Judaizing Opponents" of Paul (cf. 1:304–15)—as "religious ideas which arose in the Churches of Jewish origin, from the unconscious and spontaneous action of the various influences brought into contact within them, and before the progress of events, or the ascendancy of the privileged organs of God's truth, had succeeded from freeing the Gospel element from its accidental envelope."

61. See Hoennicke's conclusion in *Judenchristentum*, 367–77, esp. 368: "Die Gefahr des Judaismus, der Verjudung des Evangeliums, war, vor allem durch Paulus, glücklich bei Seite gedrängt worden. Die Kraft des Judaismus war gebrochen. Eine besondere Gefahr drohte von judaistischer Seite nicht mehr ... Daß der Judaismus keine Bedeutung für die Entstehung der katholischen Kirche gehabt hat, habe wir gesehen." Hort concludes that from the time of the supposed flight to Pella, the whole Judean Church was "probably not Judaistic except to a certain extent in practice as distinguished from principle," with the exception of the more marginal, sectarian Ebionites (180; cf. 175); the Diaspora Revolt in any event "made an impassable chasm between the Jews and the Christians of Palestine, and made intermediate forms of belief and practice almost impossible" (*Judaistic Christianity*, 178; further 164–202).

62. Harnack, *History of Dogma*, 290; cf. 291: "completely insignificant"; 293: "no significance at all"; 294: "Ebionism"—which for Harnack, as for Baur, is synonymous with "Jewish Christianity" (cf. 289 n. 1)—"was to all intents and purposes discarded early as the first century." Harnack's reconstruction would become the target of intensive criticism in a range of seminal studies in the twentieth and early twenty-first centuries; see Chapter 4 below on Jean Daniélou and Marcel Simon; also Lieu, "'Parting of the Ways'"; and King, *What Is Gnosticism?*, 55–70.

63. Harnack, *History of Dogma*, 43 and 46–47.

64. Harnack, *What Is Christianity?*, 199–200 (emphasis mine).

65. Harnack, *History of Dogma*, 17; cf. 21–22 for his defense of this point; and further, e.g., x and 11; cf. *What Is Christianity?*, 199–205, which treats this transformation with great ambivalence. Hort, rejecting "that imaginary reconstruction of the history of the Second Century" that assumed "what was not purely Pauline . . . was either purely Judaistic" or an amalgamation of the two, sides with Harnack: "In reality the great mass of Gentile Christianity, the ancestor of all subsequent Christianity, was none of these things . . . there was infinitely more Hellenizing than Judaizing" (*Judaistic Christianity*, 192–93).

66. Hort is quite explicit about his concern with "books of the New Testament which have been wrongly regarded as having a Judaistic character" (*Judaistic Christianity*, 9; cf. 147–63); cf. Hoennicke, *Judenchristentum*, 184–201, which extends the defense to include 1 Clement and Hermas as well; cf. Reuss, *History of Christian Theology*, esp. 1:307–11 on Revelation; and 1:308, 1:415–24, and 2:229–37 on James.

67. Hoennicke explains the origins of Ebionism as the result of syncretism among Jewish Christians after the fall of the temple (*Judenchristentum*, 228–40). Cf. the speculation of Hort (*Judaistic Christianity*, 200) that the Ebionites originated only after the edict of Hadrian. While people like Hegesippus and other "maintainers of St. James's tradition . . . might easily in a generation or two become merged in the great Church," "it was likely enough that others would be driven into antagonism to the Gentile Church . . . and become Judaistic in principle as well as practice," and thus increasingly isolated.

68. See Chapter 2 above.

69. Schliemann, *Clementinen*, 1–16, and on Baur in particular, 41–48. Schliemann anticipates all the key points of the counternarrative that would be developed in more seminal forms by Ritschl and Lightfoot.

70. Schliemann, *Clementinen*, 368, characterizing Baur's view: "Gleich das ursprüngliche Judenchristenthum, mithin die ursprüngliche Gestalt des Christenthums, ist ihm Ebionitismus"; cf. 43 (emphasis original): "*daß schon das älteste Judenchristenthum ein ebionitisches gewesen ist.*" Schliemann considers Baur's view to be a renewal of Toland's; see 364–65 and 368–70.

71. E.g., Schliemann, *Clementinen*, 371: "so ist . . . zu zeigen, daß die ursprüngliche Form des Christenthums, wie sie aus den Schriften der judenchristlichen Apostel erkannt wird, zwar eine durch den Einfluß des Judenthums bedingte, keineswegs aber eine ebionitische war . . . und sodann, daß die unmittelbar nachapostolische Zeit ebenfalls den ebionitischen Irrthümern fern gestanden."

72. See, e.g., Schliemann, *Clementinen*, 371–72: "Die äußeren Formen des Judenthums blieben, nur die Anerkennung Jesu von Nazareth als des Messias unterschied die Christen von den Juden." On the inadequacy of these Jewish "forms"

as a vehicle for Christian consciousness, see, e.g., 373–74: "Dem äußerlichen Festhalten an den Formen des Judenthums entsprach als der tiefere Grund der äusern Gebundheit eine ähnliche innere Gebundheit des christlichen Bewußtseins"; 378: "Gebundenheit des religiösen Bewußtseins durch die jüdische Denkweise"; also 376, where he cites the author of the Letter of James as an example: "die Eigenthümlichkeit des christlichen Bewußtseins bei ihm keinesweges einen völlig entsprechenden Ausdruck findet."

73. See Schliemann, *Clementinen*, 14, on the early "heretics," and 375–76 on the apostles: "Als Christus seine Jünger verließ, da hafteten diese noch zu sehr an seiner äußern sinnlichen Erscheinung . . . so konnte auch bei den Aposteln der neue Glaube nicht mit einem Mal die Beschränktheit des [Jewish] Standpunkts überwinden."

74. Schliemann, *Clementinen*, 375–76; cf. 391: "Zwar waren die übrigen Apostel ungeachtet der Verschiedenheit ihres Standpunkts mit Paulus durch die Einheit des christlichen Geistes verbunden und erkannten ihn als ihren Mitapostel an." Accordingly, as is typical of the counternarrative, the clash Paul reports between himself and Peter in Antioch (Gal 2:11–14) is interpreted in terms of Peter and Barnabas being momentarily "untrue to their principles" (389, *ihren Grundsätze untreu*).

75. Schliemann, *Clementinen*, 376–83. Like Ritschl and Lightfoot, Schliemann, citing Acts 10, notes that a special intervention of the Holy Spirit was still required for Peter to overcome his Jewish limitations where Cornelius was concerned (383–84).

76. Schliemann, *Clementinen*, 14: "das eben ein eigenthümlicher Vorzug der christlichen Wahrheit ist, sich in einer Mannigfaltigkeit der Form offenbaren zu können, daß grade diese Verschiedenheit der Betrachtungsweisen der christlichen Glaubenslehre jene ihr eigenthümliche Festigkeit und Vollständigkeit verleiht . . . Allein die Richtungen, welche in voller Reinheit in den neutestamentlichen Schriften vorliegen, traten in der Folge mehr und mehr einseitig auf, schlossen sich gegen die übrigen ab und bildeten sich zum Theil Häresien aus. So tritt die judenchristliche Anschauungsweise, welche sich ungetrübt und verklärt in einzelnen neutestamentlichen Schriften . . . findet, im Ebionitismus einseitig, getrübt und verunreinigt hervor."

77. See the distinction articulated in the extensive note in Schliemann, *Clementinen*, 371–72 (emphasis original): "Das Wort '*Judenchristen*' bezeichnet nie eine *Richtung*, sondern nur die *Abstammung*. Wo ich von einer *judenchristlichen Auffassung* rede, verstehe ich die Erfassung des Christenthums, welche durch den frühern jüdischen Standpunkt nothwendig bedingt ist, in der sich allerdings der frühere Standpunkt, aber keineswegs in einer das Christenthum wesentlich trübenden Weise—was die Ausdrücke *judaisirende, judaistische* Richtung besagen—zu erkennen gibt. Die *judenchristliche* Auffassung war in ihrem Recht, keineswegs aber die *judaisirende* . . . Der Ausdruck '*judaisirende, judaistische*

(judenzende) Schriften' bezeichnet nie die Abstammung, sondern die *Richtung*, welche *jüdische Elemente in ungehöriger Weise ins Christenthum überträgt.*"

78. See Ritschl, *Entstehung*, 104 ("das ursprüngliche jüdische Christenthum"). Criticizing Baur and Schwegler in particular, he argues that "die Darstellung der Geschichte des jüdischen Christenthums" suffers among other things from the fact that "die Terminologie ungewiß ist."

79. Ritschl, *Entstehung*, 105–6.

80. Ritschl, *Entstehung*, 106, 107, pointing out that the term does not necessarily imply ethnic descent, since even "born gentiles" would have been able to exhibit this *Richtung*.

81. Ritschl, *Entstehung*, 107–8: "Deshalb bleibt als die passendste Bezeichnung des Christentums, welches durch die Rücksicht auf die jüdische Nationalität und Sitte bedingt ist, so daß darunter auch die Species des Judenchristenthums befaßt wird, der Titel 'jüdisches Christenthum,' 'jüdische Christen' übrig." In Ritschl's book, then, the early apostles and the New Testament works associated with them are "Jewish Christian," but not "Jewish-Christian"; see, e.g., the treatment of 1 Peter, James, and Revelation in *Entstehung*, 108–24 (esp. 115, 119, 120). The broader category, unlike the narrower one, appears to be more closely correlated with ethnic derivation; thus the *Urapostel* are said to observe Jewish customs "als geborene Israeliten" (124).

82. Contrast his treatment of the Letter of James on one hand with the Apocalypse of John on the other: the former cannot be called *judaistische*, but only *alttestamentliche* (115), while the latter has "the most *judaistische* coloring" of any work in the New Testament (120). Neither in any event is to be considered *judenchristliche*: "Der Brief des Jakobus ist kein Dokument des Judenchristenthums" (115); and John too is "nicht judenchristlich" (120).

83. Lightfoot, *Galatians*, 294; cf. 318: "the primitive ages of Jewish Christianity." Cf. also "Jewish Christendom" (303) and "the Jewish Churches" (295, 311).

84. Variants of "Judaize" are repeatedly applied both to Paul's opponents in Galatia (e.g., 350, 371, 372, and passim) and to the "sects" of the postapostolic era (e.g., 218, 331). Paul's opponents are also sometimes characterized as "Judaic" (372; cf. 373: "half-Judaic, half-Christian brotherhood of the dispersion"), with Pharisaic and Essene Ebionites as forms of "Judaic Christianity" (323).

85. Lightfoot, *Galatians*, 331, differentiating the "Hebrew Christianity" of Hegesippus from the "Samaritan Christianity" of Justin as types of "Palestinian doctrine" opposed to the "Judaizing sects"; cf. the characterization of Hegesippus, whom Lightfoot identifies as Catholic rather than Ebionite, as "a thorough Hebrew in all his thoughts and feelings" (332). Interestingly, Lightfoot generally refrains from applying any of these qualifying terms directly to the apostles themselves, who are normally differentiated from Paul simply as "the Apostles of the Circumcision"; see, e.g., *Galatians*, 292, 293, 294, 351, 352, 371, 372; cf. "Church of the Circumcision" on 301–2 (in contrast to Church of the

Gentiles), 349, 365. That they are nonetheless "Hebrew Christians" in Lightfoot's sense is the clear implication of his argument.

86. Hort, *Judaistic Christianity*. The characterization of the broad aim of the lectures
quoted here is that of their editor, J. O. F. Murray (v). Murray observes Hort's
"genuine admiration for the genius of F. C. Baur, from whom the whole discussion started" despite the fact that "he was very far from accepting Baur's conclusions" (vi). He draws particular attention to Hort's acceptance of "the genuineness and the historical accuracy of all the leading Christian documents"
(esp. the New Testament) on one hand and "the parts played by the Apostolic
leaders during the period of transition before the Old Order had finally given
place to the New" on the other (vii).

87. See Hort, *Judaistic Christianity*, 1–6 (the quotation comes from p. 5). "Judaic" is
thus used in a general sense that applies to "nearly all Christianity" insofar as
"the faith of Christians is but the ripening and perfection of the faith of the
Old Covenant" (4–5). The term "Jewish Christianity" is used only in passing, as
in his reference to the "evidence respecting the Jewish Christianity of the latter
part of the Fourth Century and of the early part of the Fifth" (10), or to "the
dangers to faith which inevitably beset that form of Jewish Christianity which
we have seen to have been legitimate in Palestine, the adoption of the Gospel
without any disuse of the Law"—a "combination," he notes, " which "only for
a time . . . could be legitimate" (157).

88. Seeberg, *Lehrbuch der Dogmengeschichte*, 201: "Man kann aber auch unter 'Judenchristentum' eine Denkweise verstehen, die das ursprüngliche Christentum mit
spezifisch jüdischen Anschauungen und Tendenzen so versetzt, daß es dadurch
in seinem wesentlichen Gehalt modifiziert wird . . . Die entscheidende Diffe-
renz zu der heidenchristlichen Anschauung besteht also nicht in der materi-
ellen Aneignung jüdischer Ideen und Formen, sondern in der formalen Anerkennung ihrer Heilsnotwendigkeit."

89. Harnack, *History of Dogma*, 289.

90. See Harnack, *History of Dogma*, 287–89 (*Lehrbuch der Dogmengeschichte*, 271–73),
which gives an extended and very forceful rejection of the sort of broadening
of the category "Jewish Christianity" commonly deployed in response to Baur.
Harnack thus uses the term much as Baur had, which is to say more or less
synonymously with Ebionism (289 n. 1 [273 n. 1]). The central difference is simply his exemption of the apostles from that category. Interestingly, however, in
Harnack's hands the incarnational model of early Christianity allows him to
characterize "original Christianity"—while adamantly not "Jewish Christianity"—as having been at least "in appearance" a "Christian Judaism" insofar as it
"took possession of the whole of Judaism as religion, the creation of a universal
religion on Old Testament soil" (287 [271]: "Das ursprüngliche Christenthum
ist seiner Erscheinung nach christliches Judenthum gewesen, die Schöpfung
einer universalen Religion auf dem Boden der ATlichen"). Thus Papias's escha-

tology, e.g., was "not Jewish Christian, but Christian [*nicht judenchristlich . . . sondern christlich*]"; likewise, those with an adoptionist Christology "thought about the Redeemer not in a Jewish Christian, but in a Christian manner [*nicht judenchristlich, sondern christlich*]." Other such appropriations, he says, "may be described as Jewish, or as Christian; but the designation Jewish Christian must be rejected" as misleading (288 [272]). An analogous renarrowing of "Jewish Christianity" to the Ebionites was advocated in the mid-twentieth century by Hans Joachim Schoeps, though on less normative grounds; see Chapter 4 below.

91. Harnack, *History of Dogma*, 289 (*Lehrbuch der Dogmengeschichte*, 273). Despite his own insistence, Harnack himself periodically lapses into a more general use of such terms, as for example when describing the transition "from the first, Jewish Christian [*judenchristlichen*], generation of these believers to the Gentile Christians [*Heidenchristen*]" as one of the two "great transitions" in the "history of the Gospel" (71 [69]). The substantive "Jewish Christianity"—though not in the compound form *Judenchristenthum*—is used elsewhere with the same broad meaning: "The Gentile Christians [*die Christen aus den Heiden*] were little able to comprehend the controversies which stirred the Apostolic age within Jewish Christianity [*des jüdischen Christenthums*]" (*History of Christian Dogma*, 51 [50]).

92. Hoennicke, *Judenchristentum*, 18; the three subcategories are treated respectively in chap. 2, 3, and 4 of his book. On the widespread adoption of such a broader understanding of Jewish Christianity in subsequent scholarship, see further Chapter 4 below.

93. Schonfield, *History of Jewish Christianity*. Schonfield appears equally sympathetic to Paul and to his opponents, laying the blame for their separation on Gentile Christians who had run amok because of the "unexpected literalness" with which they interpreted Paul's theological statements about the law (30–31).

94. See, e.g., Schonfield, *History of Jewish Christianity*, 71, referring to Jews converted to Catholicism in the post-Constantinian era as "a new type of Jewish Christian" that includes even Epiphanius—who is in fact pictured on the cover of Schonfield's book with the legend "A Fourth Century Jewish Christian"! Cf. further p. 88: "The history of Jewish Christianity from the seventh century to the present day is principally a record of individual converts, who, such was the intolerance of the times, scarcely dare to acknowledge their Jewish extraction for fear of persecution."

95. The quotations are taken from Schonfield, *History of Jewish Christianity*, 11–13. Schonfield writes self-consciously against the backdrop of Nazi Germany, characterizing his present era as one in which "the 'Times of the Gentiles'" is "run[ning] out" (13). See also his pointed critique of Hort's characterization of Jewish Christianity as an anachronism that had gradually died a natural death: "If there was a death at all, which there is good cause to doubt . . . it

was matricide. Far from becoming a futile anachronism [Jewish Christianity's] spirit and human activity has persisted until the present day, and is even now undergoing a revival on a scale unknown since apostolic times. Jewish Christianity has always existed to supply that of which the Church has stood in need—the Messianic vision" (*History of Jewish Christianity*, 9).

96. See Schonfield, *History of Jewish Christianity*, 11, where, apparently alluding to liberal Protestant Christology, he notes with evident satisfaction that "we can mark in our own day, the beginnings of the return of the great Gentile Churches to the simpler faith in Christology of the early Jewish Christians." Note in this connection his positive appraisal of Toland's "vindication" (p. 7) of Jewish Christianity in *History of Jewish Christianity*, 150–52, esp. 150: "Our highest tribute must be reserved for a Gentile author . . . who . . . first perceived and set forth the fundamental difference in the constitution of Jewish and Gentile Christianity."

Chapter 4. The Legacy of Christian Apologetics in Post-Holocaust Scholarship

1. See already Schonfield, *History of Jewish Christianity* (1936), on which, see Chapter 3. Jewish scholarship on Jewish Christianity remains an understudied topic; see now, however, Reed, *Jewish-Christianity*, 361–88.

2. Simon, *Verus Israel*, 237–40. References to *Verus Israel* throughout this book refer to McKeating's English translation, with periodic cross-references to the underlying French in parentheses.

3. Daniélou, *Theology of Jewish Christianity*, 10 (emphasis original). The English version, "far from being merely a translation" of the original French (*Théologie du Judéo-christianisme* [1958]), represents a substantially revised edition (ix).

4. Schoeps's *Theologie und Geschichte des Judenchristentums* was published in 1949. A condensed and in minor ways reconsidered version was published as *Das Judenchristentum* in 1964 and translated into English as *Jewish Christianity* in 1969.

5. Cf. the treatment of the definitional issue in Schoeps, *Theologie*, 7–8 and 256–57, with Schoeps, *Jewish Christianity*, 9: "'Jewish Christians' in the broadest sense signifies all Christians of Jewish blood. As the designation of a group this name is ambiguous and open to misunderstanding . . . In this book, therefore, 'Jewish Christianity' is not used as a designation of origin but as the designation of the point of view of a party." The circumstances under which Schoeps composed his major study are noted in its Foreword (*Theologie*, iii).

6. Schoeps, *Theologie*, 7: "Mit dem Terminus 'judenchristlich' wird in dieser Arbeit nicht jede Äußerung eines Christen jüdischer Abstammung belegt, sondern nur Dokumentierungen eines vom großkirchlichen verschiedenen judenchristlichen Gruppenstandpunktes."

7. According to Schoeps, the characterization of the first generation of Jesus's followers as *judenchristlich* is accurate only if the term is used "in the genetic

sense" (*im genetischen Sinne*). Any other sense is "false and leads to serious confusion" (*Theologie*, 256). Cf. Schoeps, *Jewish Christianity*, 18: "as a group with a separate destiny and distinctive doctrinal views, Jewish Christianity first appeared at the moment of its organizational separation from the rest of primitive Christianity."

8. Schoeps, *Theologie*, 7–8: "Aus Justin (Dial. 47) wissen wir, daß noch um die Mitte des 2. Jahrhunderts zwei besondere Gruppen von Christen jüdischer Abstammung unterscheidbar waren, eine gemäßigte, die in der Kirche blieb ... und eine radikale, die das Zusammenleben mit den Heidenchristen ablehnte ... Uns interessiert hier ausschließlich die intransigente Partei ... Für sie allein werden wir in dieser Arbeit die Bezeichnung 'judenchristlich' und 'ebionitisch' ... synonym gebrauchen." Like Baur's critics, Schoeps correlates the Ebionites particularly with "extremists" who opposed Paul rather than with the apostolic community more generally; see Schoeps, *Jewish Christianity*, 18–20, and *Theologie*, 259: "die extreme, judenchristliche Gruppe in der Urgemeinde ... die wir als die eigentlichen Ahnen der späteren Ebioniten ansehen dürfen." Unlike Ritschl and Lightfoot, however, he considers "Nazoraean" simply to have been another name for that same group (*Theologie*, 10; cf. *Jewish Christianity*, 11).

9. Daniélou, *Theology of Jewish Christianity*, 10 n. 21.

10. In the revised English edition of *Opposition to Paul in Jewish Christianity* (1989), Luedemann's impression was that "at the moment Daniélou's understanding of the matter, despite some sharp criticisms, enjoys the greatest success" (29). The same assessment continued to be registered into the 1990s by Mimouni; see "Pour une définition nouvelle," 164, an edited version of which was published in 1998 in *Le judéo-christianisme ancien* (see p. 43) and subsequently translated into English in *Early Judaeo-Christianity* in 2012 (see p. 28). Cf. the recent observation in Carleton Paget, *Jews, Christians and Jewish Christians*, 25: "So many is the place in a book about early Christian theology where we will find the adjective 'Jewish Christian' used to describe something Jewish-sounding ... Such usage may not imply an endorsement of Daniélou's wider thesis ... but ... it comes close to something that Daniélou would recognize."

11. Daniélou, *Theology of Jewish Christianity*, 2.

12. Daniélou, *Theology of Jewish Christianity*, 1, 8, 10 (emphasis original). John Kloppenborg has pointed out to me that Daniélou represents a twentieth-century Roman Catholic approach to theology exemplified also by Yves Congar and Karl Rahner (e.g., Rahner, "Development of Dogma," "Considerations on the Development of Dogma," and "Basic Observations"). In response to Harnack's liberal Protestant notion of a core Christian doctrine corrupted and subsequently restored by Luther, this approach imagined dogma developing as part of an organic, dialectical relationship of revelation and history—a process that necessarily results in differing doctrinal formulations. I am indebted to Professor Kloppenborg for this illuminating observation and the accompanying references.

13. Daniélou, *Theology of Jewish Christianity*, 407 and 408, characterizing Christianity as an "unchanging faith" that nevertheless "has in every generation brought forth things new and old out of its treasures to meet human need." For Daniélou, then, the study of Jewish Christianity can serve to "remind us of truths and resources in the Christian faith which our own age has forgotten or underemphasized."

14. Daniélou, *Theology of Jewish Christianity*, 4 and 7. It is tempting to correlate such statements with Daniélou's otherwise inexplicable decision to leave the New Testament—which he considered "a distinctive and inspired creation" that "has for Christians the force of a Rule of Faith" (1)—largely to the side in his analysis of early Jewish Christian theology. Note also in this connection that *The Theology of Jewish Christianity* was the first installment of a three-volume account, *The Development of Christian Doctrine before the Council of Nicaea*, the second and third books of which treated "Hellenistic Christianity" (*Gospel Message and Hellenistic Culture*) and "Latin Christianity" (*The Origins of Latin Christianity*), respectively.

15. The preceding quotations are taken from Daniélou, *Theology of Jewish Christianity*, 4 and 55–56 (emphasis mine). Note the taxonomic ambiguity created by the idea that "heresies" only had elements "in common with Jewish Christianity." The Jerusalem community led by James, on the other hand, is characterized as "perfectly orthodox in its Christianity" despite remaining "attached to certain Jewish ways of life" (8).

16. Note in this connection that Daniélou cited with approval Simon's thesis—also formulated specifically against Harnack—that "Judaism remained a live and active force" of influence on Christianity "right down into the fourth century" (*Theology of Jewish Christianity*, 10). See further on Simon below.

17. Thus, e.g., Simon's criticism of Daniélou, on which see below. The extensive and insightful analysis in Kraft, "In Search of 'Jewish Christianity,'" comes closest, pointing out that "this 'Jewish Christian theology' would be related to actual early Christians as the Platonic world of ideas is thought to be related to the empirical world" (86). On the other hand, the supernatural foundation of the theory resurfaces explicitly in Longenecker's *Christology of Early Jewish Christianity*, which fills the gap left by Daniélou by focusing particularly on the New Testament; thus, e.g., p. 9: "it need be recognized that theological conviction on the part of early Jewish Christians was the product of both immediacy of revelation and providential development; that is, that both an initial consciousness and a process of gestation were involved in the formulation of early doctrine ... [A] distinctive appreciation of the 'Christ-event' (incarnation, ministry, passion, and resurrection)—as interpreted to an extent by Jesus himself and as illuminated by the Spirit—was common to all early Christians and basic to all genuinely Christian thought."

18. Klijn, "Study of Jewish Christianity," 426; cf. already Munck, "Jewish Christianity in Post-Apostolic Times," 113: "The danger in extending the conception of

'Jewish Christianity' [as Daniélou has done] . . . lies in the fact that it may easily end up making everything Jewish-Christian. There is nothing else left."

19. Taylor, "Phenomenon of Early Jewish-Christianity," 313.

20. The correlation of these divisions, together with the ostensibly sociological notion of a "mainstream" Christianity, finds particularly succinct expression in Quispel, "Discussion of Judaic Christianity," 84: "the main stream of Jewish Christianity did continue the apostolic tradition of Jerusalem and is therefore called 'orthodox Jewish Christianity.'" This continuity between ecclesiastical and modern critical historiography is noted by Strecker in the supplement "On the Problem of Jewish Christianity" appended to Walter Bauer's classic *Orthodoxy and Heresy in Earliest Christianity*: "The Jewish Christians . . . in a highly one-sided presentation . . . were deprecated as an insignificant minority by comparison with the 'great church' [in ecclesiastical heresiology]. Thus implicitly the idea of apostasy from the ecclesiastical doctrine also was applied to them. The more recent treatments have for the most part followed the older pattern of ecclesiastical historiography without contradiction" (241–42).

21. Munck, "Jewish Christianity in Post-Apostolic Times," 114 (emphasis original), adding that it is "unreasonable to name it after its Jewish inheritance, however justified Daniélou may be in stressing this in the face of the lack of understanding of this aspect" by scholars such as Harnack and Bultmann (cf. 108–9).

22. Munck, "Jewish Christianity in Post-Apostolic Times," 114 and 104; further Munck, "Primitive Jewish Christianity and Later Jewish Christianity."

23. Longenecker, *Christology*, 2–4.

24. Murray, "Defining Judaeo-Christianity," 308.

25. Klijn, "Study of Jewish Christianity," 426–27 (emphasis original).

26. Riegel, "Jewish Christianity," 415, suggesting that "'Judaeo-Christianity' . . . be used as a general term to refer collectively to the many Jewish-Christian ideas existing in the first few centuries after Christ."

27. Murray, "Defining Judaeo-Christianity," 303.

28. Murray, "Jews, Hebrews and Christians." The central basis for this proposed taxonomy is a distinction between those who "wished to identify themselves by relationship to Jerusalem, its temple, and its scribal establishment," whom Murray calls "Jewish," and "dissenting" groups that did not, whom he calls "Hebrews" (199). "Judaistic" and "Hebraistic" Christians, on the other hand, are used in connection with the "Sub-Apostolic Church," where one increasingly has to take into account "not merely 'Jews' and 'Hebrews' who have become Christians, but also converts from outside the Israelite world" (205). Neither this set of distinctions nor those proposed in his earlier article are advocated in Murray's subsequent entry on "Jewish Christianity" in the *Dictionary of Biblical Interpretation*.

29. Malina, "Jewish Christianity or Christian Judaism," 46 and 49–50. Malina's "hypothetical" account of Christian Judaism is oddly devoid of references to any actual ancient data that belong in the category.

30. For Simon's appreciative and yet critical appraisal of Daniélou, see the "Postscript" to the second edition of *Verus Israel* (411–15, here 414). Ongoing reflection on the definitional and terminological problems eventually led him to suggest renaming Daniélou's category *christianisme sémitique*; see Simon, "Réflexions," 66; cf. Simon, "Problèmes," 10.

31. Studies published since the 1990s that endorse some variation on Simon's law-based approach include Luedemann, *Opposition to Paul*, 28–32; Strecker, "Judenchristentum"; Taylor, "Phenomenon of Early Jewish Christianity"; Mimouni, "Pour une définition nouvelle"; Mimouni, *Le judéo-christianisme*, 39–72; Jones, *Ancient Jewish Christian Source*, 164 n. 21; Wilson, *Related Strangers*, 143–59; Kaestli, "Où en est le débat sur le judéo-christianisme?"; Carleton Paget, "Jewish Christianity"; Stemberger, "Judenchristen"; and Verheyden, "Jewish Christianity, a State of Affairs"; so also Gregory, "Hindrance or Help," citing a "significant convergence of opinion" on the matter (389). Reed's entry on "Jewish Christianity" in the *Dictionary of Early Judaism* seems to favor this definition at least for analytical purposes.

32. The Foreword to the French edition of Simon's *Verus Israel* is quite explicit in this regard (5). For whatever reason, that Foreword was not reproduced in the English edition. See further Baumgarten, "Marcel Simon's *Verus Israel*."

33. See already Parkes, *Conflict of the Church and the Synagogue*. Cf. Simon, *Verus Israel*, xiii, which characterizes early Jewish-Christian relations as a "situation in which brothers were ranged in enmity against each other in battle over an inheritance." See further on the general dynamic Boyarin, *Dying for God*, 1–21; also Becker and Reed, eds., Introduction to *Ways That Never Parted*, esp. 4–16.

34. Simon, *Verus Israel*, x.

35. Simon, *Verus Israel*, xiii and 385. "The Conflict of Orthodoxies" is the subject of Part II of the book (chaps. 5–8) and "Contact and Assimilation" the subject of Part III (chaps. 9–12). In this sense, Simon's work goes far beyond the schematic characterization of the "parting of the ways" model offered by Becker and Reed in *Ways That Never Parted*, 4–5.

36. Simon, *Verus Israel*, xviii. The section on "Contact and Assimilation" (see preceding note) opens with a chapter titled "The Fate of Jewish Christianity."

37. Simon is explicitly critical of such "préoccupations apologétiques" in Dix's *Jew and Greek* (a work Daniélou had cited at the outset of his own study); see Simon, "Réflexions," 61.

38. Simon, *Verus Israel*, 238 (278, "groupement intermédiaire entre l'Eglise et la Synagogue, il se distingue de l'une et de l'autre"). Simon is quite clear that his interests in "the ties of relationship and dependence that connect Catholic Christianity with Judaism" are not particularly concerned with "the Jewish contribution to the constitution of the Church" in beliefs, organization, rites, etc., but simply the nature of those social relationships themselves in the second through the early fifth centuries (xiii).

39. Simon, *Verus Israel*, xii and xv; see further Part I (chaps. 1–4) of Simon's study. Nonetheless, where universalism and particularism are concerned, this is perhaps only a matter of emphasis, as Simon can still trace the final split of Christianity and Judaism to "the moment when the Church became fully conscious of its own autonomy and universal mission" (xii).

40. The preceding quotations are from Simon, *Verus Israel*, 237–38.

41. Cf. Taylor's observation regarding the hyphen that is implied, even if not literally written, when the category is used in anything other than a purely ethnic sense: "It is bi-religious rather than ethnic-religious in application. Judaism and Christianity as two distinct *religions* are, in Jewish-Christianity, combined" ("Phenomenon of Early Jewish Christianity," 314–15). Taylor well recognizes that "the term is judgemental and anachronistic" (315): "The Jewish-Christians of the first century would not have considered themselves to be combining two religions." Indeed, "the division between what is somehow exclusively Christian and what is Jewish is an impossible one to make in the early Church" (317). She nonetheless continues to deploy the category along the lines of Simon's approach.

42. Munck, "Jewish Christianity in Post-Apostolic Times," 107 (with my own emphasis on the last clause). Munck argues that it is "the obscurity surrounding Jewish Christianity" that "has helped to support the theory that Christianity was a Jewish sect from the beginning," based particularly on Eusebius's account of the flight to Pella and the fact that "the Pseudo-Clementine writings and the so-called Jewish-Christian gospels bore witness that Jewish-Christian communities of this kind had survived."

43. For a convenient survey of such movements, see Horsley and Hanson, *Bandits, Prophets, and Messiahs*.

44. Longenecker, *Christology*, 6; cf. 9, which posits revelation, divine providence, and more specifically illumination provided by "the Spirit" as the grounds for "the uniqueness of Christian theology" and the basis of "all genuinely Christian thought." In a later treatment of the problem of definition, Simon, while broadly critical of Longenecker's approach, agrees that at least as far as the claim that Jewish Christianity can be distinguished from Judaism by "sa foi en Jésus" is concerned, "les choses sont en effet assez claires" ("Réflexions," 68).

45. Cf. in this respect Wellhausen's Jesus, who, if a Jew rather than a Christian, was nonetheless "more than Jewish"—indeed, so much so that "what is un-Jewish in him, what is human, is more characteristic than what is Jewish." See further on this Betz, "Wellhausen's Dictum," whose English rendering of Wellhausen's German I cite here (86–87). Cf. also, more recently, Theissen's sociological analysis of *Urchristentum* as "semiotic cathedral" in *A Theory of Primitive Christian Religion*.

46. Simon, *Verus Israel*, 238: "It was Christian as regards faith in Jesus, it was Jewish as regards the scrupulousness with which it observed the law." The specific content of this faith is framed variously over the course of Simon's publications.

Cf. *Verus Israel*, 66: "The Jewish Christians knew who the Son of Man was, and this is what distinguished them from the generality of Jews, for whom the Son of Man remained a great anonymous figure"; "Problèmes," 1: "le christianisme implique, au minimum, la conviction que Jésus est l'un des prophètes d'Israël"; "Réflexions," 55: "chrétiens parce qu'ils reconnaissent en Jésus le Messie."

47. Simon, "Réflexions," 57: "Même Etienne et les Hellénistes peuvent encore être étiquetés judéo-chrétiens ... Ce n'est en fait qu' à partir de Saint Paul que judéo-christianisme et christianisme cessent être coextensifs." Cf. the slightly different formulation of the matter in *Verus Israel*, 237: "until the preaching of St. Stephen and St. Paul, Jewish Christianity was the only kind of Christianity in existence."

48. Simon, *Verus Israel*, 237 (277), with McKeating's translation of the first clause modified to give a somewhat more literal rendering of the key phrase "dont la religion reste mêlée d'éléments judaïques." McKeating's use of an active construction ("those Christians who continued to mix their religion with elements drawn from Judaism") amounts to the same thing in any event.

49. Cf. Simon, "Problèmes," 7: "le judéo-christianisme représente une synthèse plus ou moins heureuse et logique, ou, si l'on préfère, une syncrèse de christianisme et de judaïsme."

50. The taxonomic logic is reminiscent of that which led Justin and Epiphanius to classify still earlier figures such as Socrates and Abraham as unwitting Christians.

51. See Chapters 2 and 3 above.

52. E.g., Simon, *Verus Israel*, xii (11), correlating the second-century separation of Christianity and Judaism into "distinct structures" with "the moment when the Church became fully conscious of its own autonomy and universal mission [depuis le moment où la première a pris une claire conscience de son autonomie et de sa mission universelle]." Cf. p. 65, where Judaism's ability to "adapt" to the destruction of the temple is contrasted with Christianity's experience of a "more positive bonus from the event," namely, a fuller consciousness of its own "originality." The echo is even clearer in Simon's original French: "Cette originalité ... c'est après la catastrophe surtout que l'Eglise elle-même en prend une pleine conscience" (87).

53. Simon, *Verus Israel*, 239, identifying "the syncretizing sects described by the Church's heresiologists" as "a third type of Jewish Christianity."

54. Simon, *Verus Israel*, 238–39, moving seamlessly from an early Catholic heresiological perspective to his own historical analysis—and pointing out that such a description accounts only for "what might be called" Jewish Christianity "in its classical form." The primary "correction" he emphasizes is a distinction between this "classical form" and "other manifestations of Christian life and thought that did not stem so directly from the original apostolic form of Christianity but that just as surely deserve the name of Jewish Christianity." See more on the latter below.

55. See the Postscript Simon added to the second edition of *Verus Israel* (esp. 409–17), as well as the subsequent treatments in "Problèmes" and "Réflexions."

56. Simon, "Problèmes," 1: "Il n'est pas trés facile ... de préciser le dosage des deux éléments requis pour qu'il y ait vraiment judéo-christianisme. Du côté chrétien, les choses sont relativement simples ... Il en va tout autrement lorsqu'il s'agit de définir la dose de judaïsme nécessaire pour qu'un chrétien puisse être étiqueté judéo-chretien."The idea that Christianity is more easily defined than Judaism, which is the underlying (but typically unspoken) assumption of the scholarly preoccupation with parsing the "Jewishness" of Jewish Christianity, finds similarly clear expression in Broadhead's *Jewish Ways of Following Jesus*, 46–50; see further on this Jackson-McCabe, "Orthodoxy, Heresy, and Jewish Christianity," 180–82.

57. Simon, "Réflexions," 66: "Encore serait-il peut-être préférable, puisque le judaïsme comportait lui aussi tout un secteur imprégné d'hellénisme et que Daniélou laisse en dehors, de son enquête de parler de christianisme sémitique plutôt que de judéo-christianisme. C'est néanmoins cette dernière appellation qui s'est imposée dans l'usage commun. Acceptons-la donc, avec les réserves nécessaires."Thus his subsequent distinction between "judéo-christianisme *lato sensu*" and "un judéo-christianisme au sens le plus précis" (73–74).

58. Simon, *Verus Israel*, 414; cf. "Problèmes," 2, 6–8; and "Réflexions," 54–59.

59. Note in this respect Simon's lamenting of the limitations in French for distinguishing between "des chrétiens d'origine juive" and "des chrétiens qui judaïsent" in "Problèmes," 2–3; cf. "Réflexions," 54–56.

60. See Cohen, *Beginnings of Jewishness*, 175–97, esp. 185–92. Cohen concludes that "Christian usage"—which is by far the dominant usage—"is largely shaped by Paul," who chastised Peter in Gal 2:14 for supposedly compelling Gentiles to "Judaize." "If *x* is a Christian, the tone of the word *ioudaïzein* is invariably polemical and abusive ... To call a Christian practice 'judaizing' is to label it, not to explain it" (194, 196); cf. Fonrobert, "Jewish Christians," 250–52; further Mason, "Jews, Judeans, Judaizing," esp. 144–58.

61. Simon, "Réflexions," 56–57: "Il fixe donc la position officielle de l'Eglise sur la question de l'observance juive. Nous sommes fondés par conséquent à voir là ligne de démarcation entre le chrétien de type normal et le judéo-chrétien." Cf. Simon, "Problèmes," 7–8, and more generally *Verus Israel* 237–38.

62. Simon, *Verus Israel*, 239–40.

63. Simon, "Réflexions," 74; cf. *Verus Israel* 310–21.

64. Simon's definition is adopted more or less as is, e.g., by Kaestli, "Où en est le débat?," 248–50; cf. Gregory, "Hindrance or Help," 389–92.

65. Luedemann, *Opposition to Paul in Jewish Christianity*, considers Simon's "methodological approach" to the problem of defining the category to be "in a class by itself" and deserving of "unqualified endorsement" (28). He nonetheless emphasizes that from the 50s on, such Torah observance, in "both the liberal and conservative wings of Jerusalem Jewish Christianity," was correlated with

anti-Paulinism (115; cf. 30–31; cf. Simon, "Réflexions," 71). In practice, then, criticism of Paul alone is seen as providing sufficient grounds for positing the existence of Jewish Christianity, as in Luedemann's analysis of Rom 3:8 (109–110). In the postapostolic era, in contrast, such anti-Paulinism may be indicative only of a "Jewish-Christian past" (197–98), as in his analysis of the Letter of James. This text "does not correspond to the definition of 'Jewish Christian'" insofar as it "never even hints that the so-called ceremonial law is still valid" (146). It is rather "an off shoot of an anti-Pauline Jewish Christianity, whose author . . . is no longer to be considered a Jewish Christian"; it casts, therefore, only "a refracted light on the theology and history of Jewish Christianity" (148–49). Such use of anti-Paulinism as a criterion for Jewish Christianity, on the other hand, was later explicitly rejected by Carleton Paget, "Jewish Christianity," 740.

66. See Carleton Paget, "Jewish Christianity," 735 and 739–41.

67. Strecker, "Judenchristentum," 311 ("jüdischen Struktur von Theologie und Lebenshaltung"). Contrast Taylor, "Phenomenon," 327: "There was no recognizable peculiar theology to link all the groups that have been called 'Jewish-Christian' together."

68. Horrell, "Early Jewish Christianity," 138, pointing out that such traditions were nonetheless ultimately separable from practice and thus could be "incorporated into the 'mainstream' of developing Christian orthodoxy" even as orthodoxy "abandon[ed] . . . Jewish praxis and . . . adopt[ed] an anti-Jewish posture." Cf. in this respect Luedemann's anti-Paulinism, on which see note 65 above.

69. Stemberger, "Judenchristen," 228–29; cf. Mimouni, "Pour une définition nouvelle," 184: "Le judéo-christianisme ancien est une formulation récente désignant des juifs qui ont reconnu la messianité de Jésus, qui ont reconnu qui n'ont pas reconnu la divinité du Christ, mais qui tous continuent à observer la Torah." Jones reports that Mimouni clarified to him orally that "by 'Jews' he understands . . . anyone who observes the Torah as defined there" (*Ancient Jewish Christian Source*, 164 n. 21). Note also, however, Mimouni's likening of "Judaizers" to "God-fearers" (*theosebeis*) in apparent contrast to "Jews," in *Le judéo-christianisme*, 17.

70. Simon, *Verus Israel*, 239. Simon remained steadfast in rejecting such a combined definition as too "narrow" (*Verus Israel*, 237; "Réflexions," 54) and "arbitrary" ("Problèmes," 2).

71. Jones, *Ancient Jewish Christian Source*, 164 n. 21 (emphasis original); cf. Jones, *Pseudoclementina*, 453.

72. Carleton Paget, "Jewish Christianity," 740–41.

73. Simon, *Verus Israel*, 237.

74. Jones, *Ancient Jewish Christian Source*, 164 n. 21.

75. Horrell, "Early Jewish Christianity," 136–37, identifying the "key question" to be addressed in the article as "What became of this essentially Jewish Christianity which characterized the whole Christian movement at its point of origin?";

Carleton Paget, "Jewish Christianity," 742; Stemberger, "Judenchristen," 228: "Der Herkunft nach ist die gesamte Kirche judenchristlich."

76. Reed, "'Jewish Christianity' after the 'Parting of the Ways,'" 200.

77. See Carleton Paget, "Jewish Christianity," 740–41.

78. Mimouni, *Le judéo-christianisme*, 39–40: "les judéo-chrétiens dont il est question ici ne sont pas exactement ceux du Ier siècle ... Pour la période qui va jusqu'en 135, en effet, il ne paraît pas nécessaire d' s'étendre sur la définition du judéo-christianisme car le christianisme n'est encore qu'un courant à l'intérieur du judaïsme." These remarks are apparently an attempt to clarify the point made (still more vaguely) in the original version of the article, namely that the Jewish Christians with whom he was concerned are not "ceux du Nouveau Testament" ("Pour une définition nouvelle," 162). For the historical reconstruction informing these remarks, see *Le judéo-christianisme*, 11–24.

79. Initially published in *Catholic Biblical Quarterly* in 1983 and subsequently developed in a different version as the Introduction in Brown and Maier, *Antioch and Rome*, 1–9.

80. Brown, "Not Jewish Christianity," 74–75 (emphasis mine). When Brown later says that the question of "which type of Jewish Christianity first came to Rome" is more helpful than the notion that "Jewish Christianity was replaced or outnumbered by Gentile Christianity" at Rome (78), he is apparently using "Jewish Christianity" in a purely ethnic sense; cf. p. 74, where such a replacement is said to be "intelligible" only insofar as "the ethnic origin of the respective Christians is the issue."

81. Brown and Maier, *Antioch and Rome*, 2; thus the title of the original essay.

82. Brown, "Not Jewish Christianity," 74–75.

83. See further on this point Taylor, "Phenomenon of Early Jewish Christianity." Taylor aims her critique primarily at "the generalized use" of the category as an "umbrella term" (313; cf. 327) while continuing to make use of it as defined along Simon's lines. Cf. more recently Gregory, "Hindrance or Help," which similarly objects not to the category per se (which he too defines in Simon's terms), but to the mischief it can create in interpretation of texts like the so-called Jewish Christian Gospels.

84. See Carleton Paget, "Definition," 51–52.

85. Boyarin, "Rethinking Jewish Christianity," on which see Chapter 5 below.

Chapter 5. Problems and Prospects

1. See esp. Lieu, "'Parting of the Ways'"; Boyarin, *Dying for God*, 1–21; further Becker and Reed, eds., *Ways That Never Parted*.

2. Simon, *Verus Israel*, 237.

3. See further on this in Chapter 6 below.

4. This is the common assumption, for example, that makes possible the testy exchange between Jerome and Augustine about how to interpret Paul's account

of a conflict between himself and Peter in Galatians 2. For more on this argument, see White, ed., *Correspondence*; further Myers, "Law, Lies and Letter Writing."

5. See, e.g., Goodman, "Modeling the 'Parting of the Ways.'"

6. Cf. King, "Which Early Christianity?," 71–74, calling it "one of the most promising new approaches" to making sense of early Christian diversity.

7. See among many others esp. Lieu, *Neither Jew Nor Greek?*; Lieu, *Christian Identity*; Boyarin, *Dying for God*; and Collins, *Invention of Judaism*.

8. Boyarin, *Border Lines*, 1 and 21.

9. Broadhead, *Jewish Ways of Following Jesus*, 389 (emphasis original); cf. Becker and Reed, eds., *Ways That Never Parted*.

10. Boyarin, *Dying for God*, 6; cf. Ruether, "Judaism and Christianity."

11. Lieu, *Neither Jew Nor Greek?*, 226–27.

12. Boyarin (*Dying for God*, 20) uses the term "Christian Judaism" as "an intentionally startling name" for all forms of Christianity before the fourth century. Cf. the more targeted uses in, e.g., Zetterholm, *Formation of Christianity*; Kampen, *Matthew within Sectarian Judaism*; Marshall, *Parables of War*; and Draper, "Holy Vine." Contrast the derogatory deployment of this taxonomic move by Epiphanius, who dismisses the Nazoraeans as "complete Jews and nothing else" (*Pan.* 29.7.1, *ta panta de eisin Ioudaioi kai ouden heteron*); similarly Morgan, *Moral Philosopher*, 374; and Hort, *Judaistic Christianity*, 5.

13. Eisenbaum, *Paul Was Not a Christian*. For sketches of the general outlines of this line of interpretation, see Gager, *Reinventing Paul*; and Zetterholm, *Approaches to Paul*, 127–63; further Nanos and Zetterholm, eds., *Paul within Judaism*.

14. See esp. Mason, "Jews, Judeans, Judaizing," and the essays produced in response to it in Law and Halton, eds., *Jew and Judean*; further Boyarin, "Rethinking Jewish Christianity"; and Collins, *Invention of Judaism*, esp. 1–19. On the question of "religion" in antiquity more generally, see Nongbri, *Before Religion*; also Barton and Boyarin, *Imagine No Religion*. For my own approach to the use of these terms, see the Introduction, above.

15. On this notion of redescription, see esp. Smith, "Sacred Persistence"; and Smith, "'End' of Comparison"; cf. his more recent statement in *Relating Religion*, 28–32.

16. King, "Which Early Christianity?," 74–80 (here 74 and 80).

17. Among Boyarin's many relevant publications, see esp. those listed in the bibliography.

18. Boyarin, *Dying for God*, 17, citing Simon, *Verus Israel*, 182.

19. Boyarin, *Dying for God*, 8 and 9–10, citing linguistic wave theory as his analogy.

20. Boyarin, *Border Lines*, 21.

21. Boyarin, *Dying for God*, 10–11. "Following this model, there could be and would have been social contact, sometimes various forms of common worship, all up and down the continuum of 'Jews' and 'Christians.' This social continuity pro-

vided for the possibility of cultural interaction and shared religious development" (10).

22. Boyarin, *Border Lines*, 19–20; cf. the discussion of "membership gradience" on pp. 25–26, where Judaism and Christianity are contrasted with a category like "bird," which has "definite borders": "One is either a bird or not . . .*Judaism* and *Christianity*, I want to claim, are categories more like *red* and *tall* than like *bird* . . . One cannot be both a *bird* and a *fish*, but one can be both a *tall* man and a *short* man . . . Just as certain entities can be more or less tall or red, I wish to suggest they can be more or less Christian (or Jewish) as well. And just as certain entities can be tall and short given different perspectives, so too can certain people or groups be Christian or Jewish from different perspectives, or both." Note at the same time, however, the concern he registers elsewhere regarding "the theologically founded anachronism of seeing Jews (and thus Jewish Jesus folk also) as more or less 'Jewish' insofar as they approach the religion . . . of the Rabbis" (*Jewish Gospels*, 24).

23. Boyarin, *Dying for God*, 11, and suggesting in a footnote that such problems are endemic to scholarly analysis of the relations between Christians and Jews in antiquity (141 n. 40).

24. Boyarin, *Border Lines*, 21, clarifying that by "fairly early on" he means "the mid-second century."

25. See Boyarin, *Dying for God*, 8–9; cf. 9–10: "This model allows us to see Judeo-Christianity (not in its modern sense of a homogenized common culture) as a circulatory system within which discursive elements could move from non-Christian Jews and back again, developing as they moved around the system." Thus the subtitle of his subsequent study, *Border Lines: The Partition of Judaeo-Christianity*. I follow his latter spelling, "Judaeo-Christianity," throughout unless quoting *Dying for God* directly.

26. For the temporal dimension of the category, see, e.g., Boyarin, *Border Lines*, 32–33: "at [the] very end of late antiquity, at the end of late ancient Judaeo-Christianity, rabbinic Judaism undergoes what is a virtual revolution in consciousness." Note at the same time his brief—but seemingly very significant—footnoted caveat to the idea that Judaism and Christianity "finally emerged from the womb as genuinely independent children of Rebecca" in the fourth century: "But perhaps even then, not completely" (*Dying for God* 6 and 135 n. 15). On Hort and Daniélou, see Chapters 3 and 4, respectively.

27. Boyarin, *Dying for God*, 6; cf. Boyarin, *Border Lines*, 7: "the suppressed versions of Judaeo-Christianity."

28. Boyarin, *Dying for God*, 20.

29. Cf. Boyarin, *Border Lines*, 20: "I am not denying that in the second, third, and fourth centuries, there were religious groups that were more Christian than others . . . I am also not, of course, claiming that there were no Jewish groups that were not Christian at all, but rather that the various Christian groups

formed a dialect cluster within the overall assortment of dialects that constituted Judaism (or perhaps better Judaeo-Christianity) at the time." Cf. Boyarin, *Jewish Gospels*, 22: "The model of family resemblance therefore seems apt for talking about a Judaism that incorporates early Christianity as well." The variability in Boyarin's taxonomic language can be understood in light of his notion of "membership gradience," in which "certain people or groups [can] be Christian or Jewish from different perspectives, or both" (*Border Lines*, 25).

30. Boyarin, "Rethinking Jewish Christianity," 8, with specific reference to the use of the term in 2 Maccabees; cf. Boyarin, *Jewish Gospels*, 2: "We are talking about the complex of rituals and other practices, beliefs and values, history and political loyalties that constituted allegiance to the People of Israel, not a religion called Judaism." Cf. Mason, "Jews, Judaeans, Judaizing."

31. Boyarin, "Rethinking Jewish Christianity," 12. Nongbri is unpersuaded by Boyarin's argument regarding the late antique invention of "religion"; see esp. *Before Religion*, 53–57.

32. See Boyarin, "Rethinking Jewish Christianity," 22–27 (here 23, 22, and 24, respectively). The "explosion of interest" in such groups Boyarin detects in the era of Epiphanius and Jerome basically comes down to these two men themselves, who were the first to identify a "Nazoraean" heresy (and who, perhaps not coincidentally, were also personally acquainted with one another). While the treatment of the Ebionites by Epiphanius in particular is far more extensive than earlier accounts, interest in the group is equally if not more apparent in the late second and early third centuries, when they are discussed by Irenaeus, Tertullian, Hippolytus, and Origen. For a survey of the testimony, see Klijn and Reinink, *Patristic Evidence*, 19–43.

33. Boyarin, "Rethinking Jewish Christianity," 24.

34. Boyarin, "Rethinking Jewish Christianity," 8.

35. See Chapter 1.

36. On "Ebionite" as a self-designation, see Chapter 6.

37. See the discussion of Toland in Chapter 1.

38. Boyarin, "Rethinking Jewish Christianity," 8.

39. "There is no Judaism" is the heading given to the first phase of the argument in Boyarin, "Rethinking Jewish Christianity," 8.

40. Boyarin, "Rethinking Jewish Christianity," 10 and 13; cf. 8. The notion of "disembedding" (e.g., p. 9) is taken from Schwartz, *Imperialism and Jewish Society*; see already Boyarin, *Border Lines*, 11–13.

41. Note at the same time, however, that despite its anachronism, Boyarin permits himself use of the term "Judaism" in *Jewish Gospels* "as a convenience to refer to that part of Jewish life that was concerned with obedience to God, worship, and belief" (3).

42. Boyarin, *Border Lines*, 29.

43. Cf. Boyarin, *Jewish Gospels*, 7: "The terms 'Christian Jews' and 'non-Christian Jews' that I distinguish throughout this book might be surprising to people

who think of Christians and Jews as opposites. But if we look closely at the first few centuries after Christ, we begin to see that this is precisely the way we ought to view the history of the religion of the Jews at that time." Cf. his inclusion of proselytes, God-fearers, and *gerim* among "different types of Jews" (23).

44. Reed, "'Jewish Christianity' after the 'Parting of the Ways,'" 190–91 nn. 5 and 8.

45. The first and last quotations come from Luomanen, *Recovering Jewish-Christian Sects*, 10. The second is from Luomanen, "Ebionites and Nazarenes," 83. With respect to Boyarin, Luomanen emphasizes that "it is also clear that the ways started to separate much earlier locally" (*Recovering Jewish-Christian Sects*, 10).

46. Broadhead, *Jewish Ways of Following Jesus*, 1–2.

47. Boyarin, *Dying for God*, 17. Of course Boyarin, as we have seen, had something quite different in mind.

48. Broadhead, *Jewish Ways of Following Jesus*, 1; see further 28–58, esp. 47–50 on the problem of "defining Jewishness."

49. Luomanen's approach was first articulated in a Finnish article jointly authored with Matti Myllykoski (cf. Luomanen, "Where Did Another Rich Man Come From?" 269 n. 60). It has remained basically consistent over his subsequent publications. For the fullest explanation, see Luomanen, *Recovering Jewish-Christian Sects*, 8–14; cf. "Where Did Another Rich Man Come From?" 265–69; also Luomanen, "Ebionites and Nazarenes," 83–85.

50. Luomanen, "Ebionites and Nazarenes," 84; cf. his concern with "eisegesis" in *Recovering Jewish-Christian Sects*, 13.

51. Luomanen, *Recovering Jewish-Christian Sects*, 9–10. For analogous polythetic approaches, see Murray, "Jewish Christianity"; Hill, "Jerusalem Church," 39–45; and Arnal, "Q Document." I advocated an analogous approach to differentiating Christianity and Judaism—though not, however, as the basis for any notion of a "Jewish Christianity"—in an earlier treatment of the problem (Jackson-McCabe, "What's in a Name?"). For my current understanding of the limitations of this approach, see below.

52. Luomanen, *Recovering Jewish-Christian Sects*, 8–9.

53. See esp. Luomanen, *Recovering Jewish-Christian Sects*, 10–12 (here 10 and 12). Cf. Luomanen, "Where Did Another Rich Man Come From?," 268–69, from which comes the quotation regarding "a Jewish Christianity on its own" (269); also Luomanen, "Ebionites and Nazarenes," 84.

54. Reed, *Jewish-Christianity*; see esp. the engagement with Boyarin's argument against the category on pp. xxi–xxvii. Perhaps not accidentally, revisions to the previously published essays collected in this volume include the introduction of a literal hyphen into the category "Jewish-Christianity" where formerly there was none. I am grateful to Professor Reed for sharing the page proofs with me before the book's publication, which made it possible for me to account for it here.

55. Reed, *Jewish-Christianity*, xxi–xxii (emphasis original).

56. See Reed, *Jewish-Christianity*, xxiii–xxvii. In particular, Reed finds the category useful for her twin aims of "expos[ing] the predominantly Christian frameworks" within which Jewish antiquity and Christian antiquity have been analyzed (xxvii) and integrating "Jewish-Christian" sources more fully into Jewish studies. These aims correspond to Parts One and Two of her book, respectively.

57. Reed, *Jewish-Christianity*, xxiii ("for now"; "at least for the present moment") and xxiv.

58. Reed, *Jewish-Christianity*, xx; cf. xxi, xxiv, xxvi, and 408.

59. Reed, *Jewish-Christianity*, xxv–xxvi. Reed is quite explicit that her use of the term signals "no claim for any direct one-to-one correspondence to any discrete social group or movement in the premodern eras here under analysis, nor even to any clear-cut discourse surrounding a self-claimed identity in the relevant premodern literature." Given its redescriptive nature, therefore, her definition is not "globally applicable or apt for every inquiry" but rather "provisionally useful at our present moment precisely due to its status as metalanguage" (xxvi).

60. Among the central aims of Reed's book is "to use the very rubric of 'Jewish-Christianity' as a lens through which to probe the power and limits of our own scholarly practices of sorting and studying 'religions'" (*Jewish-Christianity*, xvi). Accordingly, she is less interested in "telling any singular history of 'Jewish-Christianity'" than in "the potential of these sources to unsettle the narrowly presentist narratives commonly told of the Jewish and Christian past" (xxvi).

61. Reed, *Jewish-Christianity*, 394; cf. 395, characterizing this as "the question of the precise moment *after which* we can speak of two separate paths that can be traced to our present, as understood in our terms, peering back in retrospect for that determinative moment when 'Christianity' became a 'religion' distinct from 'Judaism.'" She cites in this connection Seth Schwartz's observation that this quest to identify "moments in which everything changed" is less "an explanatory strategy" than "an intellectual style" oriented around "being provocative" ("How Many Judaisms?," 231).

62. Reed, *Jewish-Christianity*, 398–99, citing Brubaker, "Ethnicity, Race, and Nationalism."

63. Reed, *Jewish-Christianity*, 390–91, relating this model specifically to Erickson's psychological theory of individuation. Cf. 390: "In both cases [i.e., Erickson's theory and "late twentieth century discourse about 'identity'"], the process is treated as the teleological emergence of a core self, constructed in consecutive stages that reach a climactic turning point, thereafter culminating in a distinct, bounded, and stable entity."

64. Reed, *Jewish-Christianity*, 396 and 398.

65. Reed, *Jewish-Christianity*, 396 and 428 (citing Brubaker, "Ethnicity without Groups," 169); cf. 399: "When one finds early Patristic passages with special resonance with our present-day contrasts of Judaism and Christianity ... it can be tempting to herald them as marking a point of 'origin' (or 'invention,'

'construction,' etc.) after which their predominance to this day is treated as if instant and/or inevitable ... however, it is unclear just how representative these particular modes of knowledge ordering were in their own time." The critique of "groupism" is drawn from Brubaker, "Ethnicity without Groups," on which see further *Jewish-Christianity*, 424–25.

66. Reed, *Jewish-Christianity*, 422; cf. 398: "Some Church Fathers—such as Ignatius, Tertullian, Epiphanius, and John Chrysostom—clearly contributed to the creation of conceptual taxonomies that define 'Christian' and 'Christianity' in contradistinction to 'Jew' and 'Judaism' in a manner that presages and perhaps even influences early modern articulations of the very notion of 'religion(s).' To treat these particular Patristic sources as uniquely representative of their own time, however, risks eliding what we find familiar from our present with what we posit as the dominant approaches to partitioning social and lived realities in the past—or, in other words: mistaking our modern ways of organizing knowledge about antiquity for our reconstruction of ancient ways of organizing knowledge"; also 411–12: "a scholarly conversation that purports to be about Jews and Christians is actually largely about a discussion of Christians, told from Christian sources, from within Christian classificatory schemes, and with an eye to the rest of Christian history and scholarship."

67. Cf. Reed, *Jewish-Christianity*, 400: "However influential in the *longue durée*, after all, Patristic polemical passages contrasting *Ioudaismos* and *Christianismos* were only part of the picture in Late Antiquity. When one ceases to read these passages as if descriptive reportage or ethnographical survey, it is possible to see them as products of creative acts of categorization that formed part of a continuum of experimentation with different modes of categorizing difference in Late Antiquity. Some examples ... can be found among those works that scholars now call 'Jewish-Christian.'"

68. It is to this end that Reed, following Brubaker and Cooper ("Beyond 'Identity'"), proposes shifting our concern with *identity* to questions of *identification*—which, it is suggested, foregrounds matters of agency with "more fine-grained attention to specific agents, settings, power relations, and social ramifications" (*Jewish-Christianity*, 436; further 401–21).

69. Reed, *Jewish-Christianity*, 422; cf. 424: "A focus on 'Jewish-Christianity' ... opens up some different lines of inquiry, oriented less toward the question of the prehistory and invention of our concept of 'religion' and more toward the question of what has been omitted as a result—and how such omissions, moreover, might skew our understanding of Late Antiquity more broadly."

70. Reed, *Jewish-Christianity*, 399.

71. Reed, *Jewish-Christianity*, 399. Cf. 408: "If the category 'Jewish-Christianity' is surely anachronistic ... it is perhaps in a manner that helps to expose what is also anachronistic about projecting our present sense of 'Judaism' and 'Christianity' back into the late antique past."

72. Reed, *Jewish-Christianity*, 420–21.

73. Reed, *Jewish-Christianity*, 399.
74. This was already my intention in putting together the volume *Jewish Christianity Reconsidered*. The conclusion of some readers that I was defending the category "Jewish Christianity"—which caught me quite off guard, to say the least—apparently resulted from my failure to make this distinction sufficiently clear.
75. Reed, *Jewish-Christianity*, 400.
76. See further on this problem Jackson-McCabe, "Orthodoxy, Heresy, and Jewish Christianity," esp. 179–83.
77. On Toland, Morgan and Baur, and Baur's critics, see respectively Chapters 1, 2, and 3 above.
78. "Contact and Assimilation" is the title of Part Three of Simon, *Verus Israel*. It opens with a lengthy chapter titled "The Fate of Jewish Christianity." See further Chapter 4 above.
79. Simon, *Verus Israel*, 238. On Schoeps, see Chapter 4 above.
80. Simon, *Verus Israel*, 238: "It was Christian as regards faith in Jesus." See further on this point in Chapter 4 above.
81. Cf. Boyarin and Luomanen, on whom see immediately above. This question of theorizing Christianity—far from an inconsequential matter about which one might merely "cavil" (cf. Boyarin, "Rethinking Jewish Christianity," 28)—seems to me a central desideratum in post-Christian, post-Parting-of-the-Ways-paradigm scholarship.
82. Note that "faith in Christ" has not been treated as a straightforward equivalent of Christianity even by Christians in practice, as is clear from the long history of conflict about who the "real" Christians are.
83. For a helpfully succinct analysis of the relationship of culture and identity, see Lincoln, *Holy Terrors*, 51–54. The "built-in ambiguity" he observes regarding the category "culture" applies equally well to Christianity as one particular species of it (51): "it can refer both to a group or community (as when 'my culture' = my people) and to some *x* that is a prime source of collective identity (as when 'our culture' = our habits, customs, and so forth)."
84. There is little reason to assume, e.g., that if some in Galilee did in fact flock to Jesus (as the Gospels tell it) in order to access his believed-in power over demons and illness, they did so on the understanding that they were "Christians," let alone practitioners of a "Christianity" distinct from Judean piety. The same goes for Jesus himself, who—as the charismatic leader of a dissident movement—might plausibly be identified as the inventor of the meme of an authoritatively powerful Jesus in the first place. Cf. also in this respect Betz's suggestion, based on the ritual invocation of Jesus in a number of ancient spells, that Jesus was sometimes integrated into a broadly Hellenistic magical culture whose practitioners seemed "keen to adopt and adapt every religious tradition that appeared useful to [them] . . . In the hands of magicians of this type, the gods from the various cults gradually merged . . . [T]here was no longer

any cultural difference between the Egyptian and the Greek gods, or between them and the Jewish god and the Jewish angels" (Betz, ed., *Greek Magical Papyri*, xlvi). Cf. Bohak's discussion of analogous appeals to the power of Jesus in what otherwise appear to be ancient and medieval Jewish spells (*Ancient Jewish Magic*, 277–78), with which one might compare already Mark 9:38–40 and Acts 9:13–14. Even the specific belief in Jesus as miracle-working "messiah" taken up to heaven until his return at a final judgment would eventually become as Islamic as Christian (e.g., Qur'an 3:45; 4:157, 171–72; 5:17, 72, 75; 9:30, 31) and belief that he was an incarnate deity sometimes adopted by devotees of the god Vishnu in India.

85. Townsend, "Who Were the First Christians?," 213–14.
86. Cf. Reed, *Jewish-Christianity*, 400.

Chapter 6. Beyond Jewish Christianity

1. How a group conceptualizes itself in relation to perceived others does, to be sure, have important sociological consequences. Cf. the analytical distinction drawn between "sects" and "cults" in Stark and Bainbridge, *Future of Religion*, 19–37. Translated into the language of identity, the distinction boils down largely to whether a group lays claim to an already existing identity (a "sect") or presents itself as an altogether new one (a "cult"). There is, however, no simple correlation between taxonomic separation and social separation. According to Stark and Bainbridge's analysis, "sects" and "cults" both exhibit social behaviors ranging from significant isolation to integration and interaction with those deemed "other." For a recent and illuminating application of the concept of "sect" to the early Jesus movement, see Kampen, *Matthew within Sectarian Judaism*.

2. Such questions continue to revolve largely around the interpretation of Paul's letters, both as our earliest evidence for the Jesus movement and as prime evidence for this movement's spread beyond Judeans. For recent discussion, see the essays collected in Nanos and Zetterholm, eds., *Paul within Judaism*.

3. Our historical knowledge of Ignatius, including both the dates of his letters and his status as bishop, is notoriously limited. See, e.g., Robinson, *Ignatius of Antioch*, 1–6 and 89–126, who dates him to the early second century. Barnes, "Date of Ignatius," argues for a date in the 140s.

4. For a recent treatment of the early history of the terms "Christian" and "Christianity," see Townsend, "Who Were the First Christians?"; on the importance of Antioch in this regard, see Zetterholm, *Formation of Christianity*.

5. All translations of Ignatius's letters are taken from Ehrman, *Apostolic Fathers*, unless otherwise noted, with two exceptions: I routinely render Ignatius's *Ioudaios* as "Judean" to emphasize its analogy with other ancient peoples rather than as a religious designation; similarly, I render *Christianismos* as "Christianism" in order to better historicize it in juxtaposition with analogous concepts such as *Ioudaïsmos* and *Hellēnismos*.

6. For helpful context in this respect, at least from the perspective of the Roman community to whom Ignatius wrote, see Lampe, *From Paul to Valentinus*, 397–402. Lampe correlates a "collegial presbyterial system of governance" (397) closely with a sense of community across an otherwise "fractionated" Roman community, and indeed across the empire more generally.

7. Cf. in this respect "the believing Judeans" (*hoi pisteusantes Ioudaioi*) in the *Martyrdom of Peter and Paul* cited by Skarsaune ("Jewish Believers," 6). Skarsaune also cites *tous pepisteukotas autō* [Jesus] *Ioudaious* in John 8:31; here, however, the phrase is used with a pointed ambivalence, as the unfolding dialogue in 8:31–59 makes clear; see note 19 below.

8. Ign. *Trall.* 8.2. Ehrman's translation of *tois ethnesin* as "the outsiders" is understandable, if perhaps overly generic; cf. Lake, *Apostolic Fathers*, "the heathen."

9. Skarsaune, "Jewish Believers," 5–7. Such phrases, in fact, make up the bulk of ancient "analogies" he cites for his category of "Jewish believers."

10. Cf. in this respect the portrayal of Jesus groups as resident aliens in their respective regions in the address of the Martyrdom of Polycarp, on which see further below.

11. See, e.g., Hall, *Ethnic Identity in Greek Antiquity*; and Hall, *Hellenicity*; cf. Mason's analysis of *-izo,-ismos* terms as indicating "the 'going over to, adopting of, or aligning with' a people or culture other than one's own" ("Jews, Judeans, Judaizing," 145).

12. E.g., Ign. *Eph.* 20.2: "Jesus Christ—who is from the race of David according to the flesh [*kata sarka ek genous Dauid*]"; cf. Rom 1:3. A relativizing of "fleshly" realities vis-à-vis spiritual ones is a recurring trope in Ignatius's letters; e.g., *Rom.* 9.3, 8.3; *Magn.* 6.2; *Phld.* 7.1; cf. the contrast between "unbelievers" as those who bear "the stamp of this world" and believers as those who bear "the stamp of God the Father" (*Magn.* 5.3). Cf. further the remarkable sentiment expressed (at least in some manuscripts) in his letter to the Romans that "nothing visible is good" (*Rom.* 3.3, *ouden phainomenon kalon*).

13. Mason argues strenuously that such *-ismos* constructions, here and elsewhere, connote specifically a "movement from one group to another" rather than a reification of the relevant cultural system ("Jews, Judeans, Judaizing," 151; see further 144–50). At least in this case, however, such an interpretation would render Ignatius's twin notions of "living according to Christianism" (*Magn.* 10.1, *kata Christianismon zēn*) and "living according to Judaism" (8.1, *kata Ioudaismon zōmen*) redundant at best.

14. Cf. Ehrman's translation: "It is outlandish to proclaim Jesus Christ and practice Judaism." Lake's "monstrous," in the first LCL edition of the *Apostolic Fathers*, nicely conveys a notion of the monstrous as that which violates order.

15. The Martyrdom of Polycarp is addressed both to the local "church of God" (*tē ekklēsia tou theou*) in Philomelium "and to all . . . everywhere, who belong to the holy and universal church" (*kai pasais tais kata panta topon tēs hagias kai katholikēs*

ekklēsias); cf. 8.1: "the entire universal church throughout the world" (*pasēs tēs kata tēn oikoumenēn katholikēs ekklēsias*); also 5.1, "the churches throughout the world" (*tōn kata tēn oikoumenēn ekklēsiōn*). The "elect" are contrasted with the "unbelievers" in 16.1. Translations of the Martyrdom of Polycarp are based on those of Ehrman in LCL, though I have altered them freely here and in what follows.

16. Mart. Pol. 3.2, "the pious race of Christians" (*theosebous genous tōn Christianōn*); cf. "the race of the righteous" in 14.1 and 17.1. See further Lieu, *Neither Jew Nor Greek?*, 52–60, and more extensively Buell, *Why This New Race*, who provides a thoughtful treatment of the issues involved in translating this ancient idea with the English "race" (5–21). This translation becomes especially useful for capturing the distinction drawn by some ancients between a generic human race—normally correlated with themselves!—and the "ethnic ones" who represent deviations from it; see below.

17. Mart. Pol. 13.1; cf. 17.1–18.1, where the Judeans in Smyrna, in apparent synergy with "the Evil One," indirectly pressure the government of Smyrna to allow Polycarp's corpse to be burned rather than given over to the Christians for ritual treatment. A similar theme of Judean hatred of Christians is registered in Justin, *Dial.* 39 and 93; cf. also John 8:31–59.

18. The miraculous circumstances surrounding Polycarp's death are said to underscore the difference between "the unbelievers"—apparently synonymous with "the entire multitude of both Gentiles and Jews who lived in Smyrna" who had "cried out with uncontrollable rage" to ensure his death—and "the elect" (Mart. Pol. 16.1; cf. 13.1–2). Cf. 19.1, where Polycarp's fame is such that "he is spoken of in every place, even by the nations [*kai hypo tōn ethnōn*]." Ehrman's rendering of *ethnōn* as "outsiders" here is very much to the point, even if obscuring, for my purposes, the taxonomic implications.

19. Quintus functions as the anti-type to Polycarp, ultimately engaging in precisely those practices the text considers incompatible with Christian identity. See Mart. Pol. 4: "But there was a person named Quintus, a Phrygian who had recently come from Phrygia, who was overcome with cowardice once he saw the wild beasts . . . [T]he insistent pleas of the proconsul convinced him to take the oath and offer a sacrifice"; contrast 9.3–10.1. Phrygians, notably, are stereotypically portrayed as cowards in ancient Greek literature; see Hall, *Hellenicity*, 180. Cf. in this respect the ambivalent status of "the Judeans who had believed in [Jesus]" and yet nevertheless sought to kill him in John 8:31–59.

20. See Irenaeus, *Haer.* 3.3.4. Irenaeus claims to have seen Polycarp in his "early youth" and recommends his letter to the Philippians (which in turn recommends Ignatius's letters; Pol. *Phil.* 13) as a place to find "the preaching of the truth." The Epilogue to the Martyrdom of Polycarp indicates that a copy was owned by Irenaeus (22.2). Later tradition, perhaps in the interest of bolstering claims of apostolic succession, seems to overstate the matter by framing

Irenaeus as a "disciple" of Polycarp and a witness to his execution in Rome; cf. Eusebius, *Hist. eccl.* 4.14 and 5.20; also Mart. Pol. 22.2, noting the alternative version given in the Moscow manuscript. For a general account of the social network to which Irenaeus belonged, see Behr, *Irenaeus of Lyons*, 13–71.

21. For analysis of Irenaeus's Roman community as "fractionated," see the very illuminating work of Lampe, *From Paul to Valentinus*. Irenaeus uses the term "Christian" in fragment 13 in *ANF* 1.570. A central concern with heresy is of course obvious in his major extant work, *Against Heresies*. It is also apparently the context in which the *Demonstration of the Apostolic Preaching* was written even if, as some have suggested, its concluding reference to *Against Heresies* is part of a later addition (cf. Behr, *Irenaeus of Lyons*, 68). See esp. the preface, which indicates that the work will allow its reader "to confound all those who hold false opinions" (1), particularly "all heretics . . . [who] <corrupt> those who receive the poison of their teaching" (3). The *Demonstration*, unfortunately, is extant only in an Armenian version; here and throughout I rely on the English translation in Behr, *St. Irenaeus of Lyons*. Translations from *Against Heresies* are from *ANF* unless otherwise noted.

22. See, e.g., Irenaeus, *Epid.* 1.8: "the God of all—both of the Jews and of the Gentiles and of the faithful . . . to the faithful He is as Father . . . while to the Jews He is as Lord and Lawgiver . . . and to the Gentiles He is as Creator and Almighty." As the passage continues, a catalogue of those who will not escape God's judgment places "a Jew" and "a Gentile" alongside "a sinful believer" (i.e., not "the faithful" per se) and "an [apostate] angel" (on which see immediately below).

23. Irenaeus, *Epid.* 5; cf. 11–16; and for the phrase "race of Adam," *Epid.* 33. Behr renders Irenaeus's apparent use of *logikos* in *Epid.* 5 as "verbal"; my rendering of it as "rational" highlights the importance of the term in relation to Irenaeus's understanding of natural law, on which see below.

24. Irenaeus, *Epid.* 16–18, 23; cf. Gen 6:1–7 and esp. 1 En. 6–11. Irenaeus thus characterizes the era before Christ as "the dominion of apostate angels" (83). See further 61, which imagines a future in which "men of different races and <dis>similar customs" who "had become bestial" will be "gathered in one place <in one> name" and "acquire, by the grace of God, righteous conduct, changing [their] wild and untamed nature."

25. Irenaeus, *Epid.* 23. The Egyptians, Arabs, Libyans, and "those who dwell in Phoenicia," e.g., are said to descend from the race of Ham (*Epid.* 20; cf. Gen 10).

26. A similar idea is found in the fragment from Methodius preserved in Epiphanius, *Pan.* 4.64.12–62; see further Jackson-McCabe, *Logos and Law*, 127–30.

27. On this Stoic theory and its various adaptations by Jewish and Christian authors, see Jackson-McCabe, *Logos and Law*, 30–133. On Irenaeus in particular, see immediately below.

28. See esp. Irenaeus's interpretation of the consequences of Babel in *Epid.* 23. The Judeans are identified as descendants of Abraham and, more specifically, of

Jacob and Judah; he thus can refer to them also as "sons of Israel" or simply "Israel"; see *Epid.* 24–25, 51, 57. Regarding their territory, see *Epid.* 24, "the land which is now called Judaea," and cf. 57, "the land of the Jews"; regarding language, note the references to Hebrew in 43, 51, 53.

29. See esp. Irenaeus, *Haer.* 4.15.1, with which cf. 4.13; see further the discussion in Jackson-McCabe, "Letter of James and Hellenistic Philosophy," 68–69.

30. Irenaeus, *Epid.* 95; cf. 89: God "does not want the redeemed to turn back to the Mosaic legislation, for the law was fulfilled by Christ." Apparently drawing on Gal 3:19–29, Irenaeus associates God's role as "Lord and Lawgiver" of the Judeans with an "intervening period" between humanity's general abandonment of God and the coming of Christ. Specifically, God brought the Judeans into "slavery by means of the law" so that they could "learn" in an era that had otherwise forgotten God; cf. *Epid.* 8 and 17–23.

31. Irenaeus, *Epid.* 95, citing in former times the adoption of Canaanite worship and prophecy by "the people," and in more recent times acknowledging "a temporal Caesar as their king" rather than the "Son of God" (apparently alluding to John 19:15).

32. Cf. Irenaeus, *Epid.* 21 and 42 with 89–95, which interprets the phrase "my chosen race, my people" from Isa 43:20 (Septuagint, *to genos mou to elekton, laon mou*) with reference to the calling of the Gentiles (89). Accordingly, only a select few of the race of Shem who died before Christ will be saved, namely the patriarchs, the prophets, and the righteous who "feared God and died in righteousness, and had the Spirit of God within them" (56). In *Epid.* 35 and 92 Irenaeus seems to include himself and his presumed readers among the Gentiles who had been made righteous. For the contrast of Church and Synagogue, see the interpretation of Isa 54:1 ("Rejoice, O barren one") in *Epid.* 94.

33. Irenaeus, *Epid.* 58, 59; cf. 64: "All these testimonies concerning [David's] Seed make known both the race and the place where he was going to be born."

34. This retrojection of Irenaeus's own values—of those things "which alone are true" (*Haer.* 4.3.4; cf. *Epid.* 1)—onto the apostles takes the concrete form of a claim of historical succession that ensures the essential continuity between the apostles and his own Church; see *Haer.* 3.1–4; cf. *Epid.* 3 and 98. The crucial link Irenaeus identifies between the apostles and himself is none other than Polycarp, who was not only "instructed by apostles" but also "appointed bishop of the Church in Smyrna" by them, and whom Irenaeus saw in his "early youth" (*Haer.* 3.3.4).

35. See Irenaeus, *Epid.* 41: John the Baptist was sent to prepare the Judeans for Christ; the apostles, in turn, having been sent by Christ "into the whole world, realized the call of the Gentiles, showing mankind the way of life ... cleansing their souls and bodies by the baptism of water and the Holy Spirit ... and in this way they established the churches"; cf. *Epid.* 86, where Irenaeus finds in biblical prophecy references to "the apostles who, sent by the Lord, preached to the whole world ... from Judaea and from Jerusalem, to relate the word of

God to us . . . they were going to preach to all the earth." Cf. Tertullian, *Praescr.* 8, which describes the apostles as having been "ordained to be teachers to the Gentiles" (*nationibus destinati doctores apostoli*). Matt 28:19 is likely in the background here.

36. On the relation of Marcion and Valentinus to the Roman community to which Irenaeus belonged, see Behr, *Irenaeus of Lyons*, 21–47, esp. 25–34; further Lampe, *From Paul to Valentinus*, esp. 241–56, 292–318, 381–96. Interestingly for our purposes, Marcion and Valentinus seem not only to have derived from the same social network to which Irenaeus belonged, but to have assumed the same basic taxonomic distinction between Jesus groups and their culture and Judeans and theirs assumed by other intellectual leaders within it. Indeed, in their cases the disavowal of Judean culture was even more thoroughgoing than Irenaeus's.

37. Irenaeus, *Haer.* 1.26.2, *perseverant in his consuetudinibus, quae sunt secundum legem, et iudaico charactere vitae.* See also 3.11.7, 3.21, 4.33.4, 5.1.3; further Klijn and Reinink, *Patristic Evidence*, 105–7, whose text and translation I cite here.

38. See his general remarks in the Preface (1–3) and Conclusion (98–100) of *Demonstration of the Apostolic Preaching*. For the phrase "dominion of the apostate angels," see *Epid.* 83, and cf., e.g., *Haer.* 4.41. A demonic origin of heresy is also postulated by Justin, on whom, see Brakke, *Gnostics*, 108–9. For further context, see Chapter 1 above.

39. One could also fruitfully examine Justin, who belonged to the same broad Roman community to which Irenaeus migrated, and with whose writing Irenaeus was familiar (*Haer.* 4.6.2). First Peter, which knows "Christian" as a term of identity (4:16), is also apparently written from Rome ("Babylon") to a similar network of communities beyond it in Asia Minor (1:1). More difficult to locate are works like 2 Peter, *Epistle to Diognetus*, and Athenagoras's *Legatio pro Christianis.* On the development of the "new race" theory in particular, see Buell, *Why This New Race.*

40. If we must be skeptical regarding the extent to which texts produced by the intelligentsia within a group reflect the thinking of its rank and file, we should also be skeptical regarding the ability of the intelligentsia to depart too radically from the general assumptions of that rank and file. Cf. in this respect Lampe's suggestion (albeit in a different context) that "the victory of orthodoxy was thus also a 'majority decision': the followers of the heretics were numerically outnumbered; orthodoxy, easily comprehended by the masses, constituted the 'Great Church' . . . Whoever has this 'Great Church' behind him succeeds. It is a simple law of gravity" (*From Paul to Valentinus*, 383–84).

41. Giorgio Jossa, e.g., can still argue that a "remarkable break with respect to the Judaism of the time" was at work already during Jesus's lifetime, and that the "paschal experiences" of the disciples were "not comparable" at any rate to other issues that diversified the Judaism of the time (*Jews or Christians?*, 59 and 67). See Jackson-McCabe, Review.

42. The long-standing scholarly treatment of Paul as the epitome of Christianity has been increasingly challenged in recent decades. See among others Gager, *Reinventing Paul*; Eisenbaum, *Paul Was Not a Christian*; and cf. the essays collected in Nanos and Zetterholm, eds., *Paul within Judaism*. For analysis of those with whom Paul was arguing in his letters, see Sumney, "Paul and Christ-believing Jews"; and more fully Sumney, *"Servants of Satan."*

43. See already Baur, "Christuspartei" (1831); Schliemann, *Die Clementinen* (1844); also Schoeps, *Theologie und Geschichte des Judenchristentums* (1949); Strecker, *Das Judenchristentum in den Pseudoklementinen* (1958); more recently, among others, Jones, *Pseudoclementina Elchasaiticaque inter Judaeochristiana* (2012); and Reed, *Jewish-Christianity and the History of Judaism* (2018).

44. See Jones, "Pseudo-Clementines"; also Jones, *Ancient Jewish Christian Source*, 1–38. Cf. the recent attempt to sort this out in Stanton, "Jewish Christian Elements."

45. Especially important with respect to the *Homilies*, which is my central concern here, are the studies in Reed, *Jewish-Christianity*; see also Duncan, *Novel Hermeneutics*; Carlson, *Jewish-Christian Interpretation*; and a number of the essays in Bremmer, ed., *Pseudo-Clementines*.

46. On the provenance of the *Homilies*, see Jones, *Pseudoclementina*, 38, and further 86–92. The work portrays Peter installing such leaders as extensions of his own special authority throughout his missionary journey: first in Caesarea Maritima before departing "for the Nations" (3.60–72) and subsequently in the Gentile cities themselves, including Tyre (7.5.3), Sidon (7.8.3), Beirut, (7.12.2), and Laodicea (20.23). Unfortunately (but interestingly), Peter's experience in Antioch is not narrated.

47. I rely on the critical edition of Rehm, Irmscher, and Paschke, *Pseudoklmentinen I, Homilien*. Further citations are to this edition and given parenthetically in the text. Translations of the *Homilies* are based largely on *ANF*, though I have altered them freely where it seemed helpful to do so.

48. *Hom.* 8.10.3–4; cf. 18.3.2: this law was not yet established "in writing" (*engraphōs*) "from the times of Adam until Moses." The link between reason, natural law, and such "freedom" is decidedly Stoic; see Jackson-McCabe, *Logos and Law*, 145–51.

49. These ideas surface throughout the *Homilies*, but see esp. 10.6: "you were at first made to be rulers and lords of all things. You who have his image in your bodies have in like manner the likeness of His judgment in your minds. Since, then, behaving like irrational animals [*alogois zōois*], you have destroyed the human soul [*tēn anthrōpou psychēn apōlesate*] … If, therefore, you receive the law of God, you become men [*anthrōpoi ginesthe*] … Therefore … return to your first nobility; for it is possible if you become conformed to God by good works … and by reason of your likeness to Him, you shall be reinstated as lords of all"; cf. 10.7, 11.4, and 19.21, and cf. the comparison of Gentiles with "irrational animals"

(*alogois zōois*) in 3.5.4. On the punishment of the soul after death, see e.g. 7.4, 9.9, 11.11. Cf. Irenaeus, *Epid.* 61.

50. *Hom.* 8.18–19. The diet in question is summarized as "shedding blood, or tasting dead flesh, or filling themselves with that which is torn of beasts, or that which is cut, or that which is strangled, or aught else that is unclean [*ē allou tinos akathartou*]" (8.19.1). In the *Homilies*, then, there is no question of reduced dietary restrictions for Gentiles comparable to the so-called Apostolic Decree of Luke-Acts (Acts 15:28–29) or the Noahide laws of the Talmud.

51. See *Hom.* 11.2, 11.11, and 9.15. Relevant passages once again are scattered throughout the *Homilies*, but cf. esp. 9.9: "For the demons, [having] power by means of the food given to them, are admitted into your bodies by your own hands; and lying hid there for a long time become blended with your own souls"; cf. 9.12.1, where people who are so afflicted "consent to the evil thoughts suggested by the demons, as if they were the reasoning [*logismō*] of their own souls"; also 10.10, where this demonic power (here and elsewhere depicted as "the serpent") seduces humans through the promise of a better *logismos*; further 10.11–14 and 10.20.3. Thus the claim that those who worship idols are "acting altogether without right reason" (10.23.4, *mēde orthō logismō poiountes*), and that, conversely, those who have (true) *logismos* worship neither animals nor the elements, but only God (10.9.5).

52. On the origin of human suffering, see esp. 8.11. The correlation of demonic food with disease, possession, and other forms of human suffering is developed at length in *Hom.* 9.8–23, esp. 9.12: "the demons who lurk in their souls induce them to think that it is not a demon that is distressing them, but a bodily disease, such as some acrid matter, or bile, or phlegm, or excess of blood, or inflammation of a membrane, or something else . . . For the universal and earthly soul, which enters on account of all kinds of food, being taken to excess by over-much food, is itself united to the spirit, as being cognate, which is the soul of man; and the material part of the food being united to the body, is left as a dreadful poison to it. Wherefore in all respects moderation is excellent."

53. See on this esp. *Hom.* 9.1–7. Egyptians, e.g., are especially associated with astrology (e.g., 10.16–18, 14.11) and magic (e.g., 5.3.4, 2.22.3), and Persians and Britons with inbreeding and public sex, respectively (19.19). The *Homilies* portrays this as a historical devolution from a primal monarchy into polyarchy (9.2.3); cf. in this respect its characterization of Jesus as preaching "the kingdom of the invisible God" enjoyable by anyone who "would reform his manner of living" (1.6.2).

54. See further 4.12–25; cf. Reed, *Jewish-Christianity*, 123: "Clement here argues that elite 'pagans' are the least pious of all precisely because of their education." The Homilist singles out Homer, Hesiod, and Orpheus as those widely extolled as "the wisest of the ancients" but who were in fact inspired by demons (cf. 6.3 and 6.17 and further 6.3–25); cf. also the treatment of the founders of various schools of Greek philosophy—and above all Socrates as paragon—in 5.18–19.

The contrast with Justin, who counts Socrates and Heraclitus as Christians (*1 Apol.* 46.3), could scarcely be starker. Note also that the *Homilies* interpret philosophical attempts to allegorize Greek myth—even if arising from some small vestige of "right reason" (*tou orthou logismou*) beneath the overlay of demonic reasoning (10.18.4)—as a fruitless and even positively harmful exercise (see further Carlson, *Jewish-Christian Interpretation*, 13–50). Insofar as the whole idea of living in accord with nature is a Greek philosophical value, the notion that Greek education is diametrically opposed to life in accord with nature is both an ironic and a fundamentally subversive claim.

55. The Alexandrian philosophers who mock Barnabas as a "Barbarian" are addressed by Clement as "your Greek multitude, being of one *psychē*" (1.11.8)—a characterization that is perhaps to be taken somewhat literally in light of the demonic psychology informing the *Homilies*; cf. the definition of the Jew and Greek in terms of praxis in *Hom.* 11.16.3, on which see further below. Regarding the transportability of Greek culture, note esp. the example of Simon Magus, the primary "enemy" of the *Homilies*: while of the Samaritan *ethnos*, his teaching is linked particularly to Greek myths (2.25.3, *Hellēnikois mythois*) and Greek *paideia* (2.22.2–3), albeit also blended with (equally transportable) Egyptian magic (2.22.3; cf. 2.26 and 32).

56. *Hom.* 4.19. Preconversion exposure, on the other hand, can be considered providential insofar as those who were "educated in the learning of the Greeks, especially in the atheistic doctrines . . . might be the better able to refute them" (15.4; cf. 13.7.3–4).

57. E.g., *Hom.* 14.5.2, where Peter says, "I and my tribe [*phylon*] have had handed down to us from our ancestors the worship of God [*ek progonōn theon sebein*]"; cf. 16.14.4, "being furnished by our fathers [*ek paterōn*] with the truths of the Scriptures, we know that there is only one who has made the heavens and the earth, the God of the Judeans [*theon Ioudaiōn*], and of all who choose to worship him"; cf. 10.26.3, "the accustomed faith of the Hebrews" (*tēn Hebraiōn synēthē pistin*). Abraham is identified as *archēgetēs* of the Jewish *ethnos* in 2.16.5, particularly in connection with Isaac and Jacob, the latter of whom is subsequently identified as "the father of the twelve tribes" (2.52.2, *hos dekaduo phylōn hyparxas patēr*).

58. The term *Ioudaioi* seems to be the most comprehensive term of identity in the *Homilies*, conjuring up simultaneously a people, its territory (e.g., 1.7.2, 7; 1.8.2–4), and its distinctive customs and especially piety (e.g., 4.7.2, *ta Ioudaiōn*; cf. 13.4.1, *tēs hēmeteras thrēskeias tēn politeian*). That being said, participation in these latter practices is deemed sufficient in itself for inclusion in the category (11.16.3–4, on which see further below). The terms "Hebrew" and "sons of Israel," in contrast, seem to be used more specifically as terms of ancestral descent. Thus, e.g., the contrast between "the Hebrews" and those "who are called from the Gentiles" in 8.5, which also states that "even the Hebrews who believe

Moses, and do not observe the things spoken by him, are not saved"; cf. the use of "sons of Israel" in 2.19. One who ceases to be a Gentile, then, becomes a *Ioudaios* or a *Ioudaia*—also called a proselyte to the *Ioudaioi* (13.7)—but not a Hebrew.

59. *Hom.* 8.5.4; cf. 18.3: God "did not lay down a law in writing from the times of Adam to Moses ... but he had a written law from Moses to the present times."

60. See esp. *Hom.* 2.38 on the Seventy and on "the Scribes and the Pharisees," esp. the interpretation of Matt 23:2–3 in 3.18–19: "'Listen to them' [the Scribes and the Pharisees], he [Jesus] said, as entrusted with the key of the kingdom, which is knowledge, which alone can open the gate of life, through which alone is the entrance to eternal life." In the present of the text, the "Scribes and Pharisees" can hardly be anyone other than the rabbis; see further Reed, *Jewish-Christianity*, 320–28.

61. The correlation of Jewish law with reason and natural law is a common trope in Jewish works familiar with Greek philosophy; cf. 4 Maccabees, Philo, the *Apostolic Constitutions*, and the Letter of James, and see further Jackson-McCabe, *Logos and Law*, esp. 87–133. To be sure, in the *Homilies* the formulaic phrase "books current among the Judeans" (3.38.1, 16.2, 16.15.3) is to be understood in light of its theory that the present form of the Torah also includes wrong-headed passages inserted sometime after the era of the Seventy; see esp. Carlson, *Jewish-Christian Interpretation*. The correlation of Jewish scriptural law with reason is in any event clear, most notably in the discussion of ritual behaviors surrounding menstrual and sexual impurity in *Hom.* 11.28–30, esp. 11.28.1–2: "purification, not approaching to a man's own wife when she is in separation [is necessary], for so the law of God commands ... If purity be not added to the worship of God [*tē tou theou thrēskeia*], you would roll pleasantly like the dung-flies. Wherefore as man, having something more than the irrational animals, namely rationality [*dio hōs anthrōpoi echontes ti pleion tōn alogōn zōōn (to logikoi einai)*], purify your hearts from evil by heavenly reasoning, and wash your bodies in the bath." The correlation of Jewish dietary restrictions to the natural order is a similarly clear implication of the work as a whole. Note, e.g., the portrayal of the Giants as having "turn[ed], contrary to nature [*para physin*], to the eating of animals ... [T]hey, on account of their bastard nature, not being pleased with the purity of food, longed after the taste of blood" (8.15); cf. more generally the link between eating such food and physical maladies (e.g., 7.1–3 and 7.6–11).

62. On the postulated difference in Judean psychology, see esp. *Hom.* 9.16.1. This is to be understood in light of a resistance to demonic worship in general and avoidance of demonic food in particular. Indeed, Judeans are immune only insofar as they observe the Torah; cf., e.g., 8.22.3: Not only are Gentile nations "polluted in body and soul" and "tyrannized over by sufferings and demons," but also "some of our nation [*tines tou hēmeterou ethnous*], who by evil deeds having

been brought under the power of the prince of wickedness" in the manner of the called who did not obey. See further 11.16, which distinguishes the demonic diseases that issue in eternal punishment from the merely transitory punishments given to pious but imperfect Judeans for the purpose of "settlement of accounts."

63. The phrase is found in *Hom.* 13.4.1; cf. 9.20.1: "For we are of the same nature as you, just not of the same piety [*tēs gar autēs hymin esmen physeōs, all' ou thrēskeias*]."

64. Cf. Reed, *Jewish-Christianity*, 138: "In *Hom.* 11.16.2–4, which is unparalleled in the *Recognitions*, 'Jew' and 'Greek' are redescribed in a manner unconnected to ethnicity or lineage." Translating *theosebēs* as "Godfearer" in the *Homilies* is misleading, however, insofar as this translation conjures up Gentiles who worshipped the Judean God without becoming proselytes (*pace* Reed, *Jewish-Christianity*, 202). As in the passage cited here, *theosebēs* applies equally well to born Judeans as to made ones—the latter of which are in any event styled precisely as "proselytes" (cf. 13.7.3, *tis Ioudaiois prosēlytos*). Thus, e.g., the Judeans to whom Jesus preached in the homeland are themselves styled precisely as "God-worshippers" in 17.6.3–4 (*pros theosebeis*; cf. 1.6.2, *Ioudaiois*); cf. also 7.4.3, *hoi theon sebontes . . . Ioudaioi*.

65. Cf. esp. *Hom.* 10.6: "Therefore approach with confidence to God, you who at first were made to be rulers and lords of all things: ye who have His image in your bodies, have in like manner the likeness of His judgment in your minds. Since, then, by acting like irrational animals, you have lost the soul of man from your soul [*epei oun alogois zōois eoikota praxantes (tēs psychēs) tēn anthrōpou psychēn apōlesate*], becoming like swine, you are the prey of demons. If, therefore, you receive the law of God, you become men [*ean oun tou theou nomon anadexēsthe, anthrōpoi ginesthe*] . . . Therefore do not refuse, when invited, to return to your first nobility; for it is possible, if ye be conformed to God by good works. And being accounted to be sons by reason of your likeness to Him, you shall be reinstated as lords of all."

66. *Hom.* 8.5.4: "There would have been no need for the coming of either Moses or Jesus if [the Hebrews and the Nations] were willing to discern from themselves that which is reasonable [*eiper aph' heautōn to eulogon noein eboulonto*]"; cf. 3.31.2 and 3.32.1. The implication of the work as a whole is that humans have an innate disposition toward piety by virtue of their rationality but require an authoritative prophetic voice to adjudicate in practice between conflicting human views about what right reasoning entails; cf. esp. 1.18–19 where the obscuring of the "will of God" by wicked human thoughts and behaviors is compared to smoke filling a house: "Wherefore it behooves the lovers of truth, crying out inwardly from their breasts, to call for aid, with truth-loving reason," so that someone can clear out the smoke. That person is the True Prophet, who "alone is able to enlighten the souls of men, so that with our own eyes we may be able

to see the way of eternal salvation." Cf. 2.5–8, 2.12.1, 3.11.1, 3.54.1; also 19.2.2, 19.7.1.

67. *Hom.* 8.6.2; cf. 8.5.3–4: "Since, therefore, both to the Hebrews and to those who are called from the Nations, believing in the teachers of truth is of God, while excellent actions are left to every one to do by his own judgment, the reward is righteously bestowed upon those who do well ... Neither is there salvation in believing in teachers and calling them lords."

68. Cf. Reed, *Jewish-Christianity*, 195: "by the logic of *Hom.* 8.5–7, no Jewish mission is needed; Jews will be saved through the teachings of Moses." On the corruptions in the Torah and Jesus's role in discerning them, see esp. *Hom.* 3.47–57; further Carlson, *Jewish-Christian Interpretation*, esp. 77–109. Note also, however, the caveat in *Hom.* 8.7.1: "Neither, therefore, are the Hebrews condemned on account of their ignorance of Jesus, by reason of Him who has concealed him, if doing the things commanded by Moses, they do not hate Him whom they do not know."

69. See *Hom.* 8.7.5: "if any one has been thought worthy to recognize both [Moses and Jesus] as preaching one doctrine, that man has been counted rich in God." Note also the reticence expressed about publicly acknowledging the group's theory of false scriptural passages: "For we do not wish to say in public that these chapters are added to the Bible, since we should thereby perplex the unlearned multitudes, and so accomplish the purpose of this wicked Simon. For they not having yet the power of discerning, would flee from us as impious; or, as if not only the blasphemous chapters were false, they would even withdraw from the word. Wherefore we are under a necessity of assenting to the false chapters ... and to give in private an explanation of the chapters that are spoken against God to the well-disposed after a trial of their faith" (2.39). Cf. the dynamic assumed in the concluding command to Ezra in 4 Ezra 14:24–26: "But prepare for yourself many writing tablets ... and I will light in your heart the lamp of understanding, which shall not be put out until what you are about to write is finished. And when you have finished, some things you shall make public, and some you shall deliver in secret to the wise." The relationship of Jesus and his disciples to Judeans portrayed in the *Homilies* is in this sense interestingly analogous to that of Valentinus and his disciples to Christians, on which see Lampe, *From Paul to Valentinus*, 387–91.

70. The *Homilies* interact at various points with Matt 23. Note esp. 11.28–29, which is careful to point out that Jesus's criticisms were aimed only at "certain of the Scribes and Pharisees among us"—namely the hypocritical ones—"not with respect to all." While the issue there, as in Matthew, is a disjuncture between internal and external purity, the central criticism in *Hom.* 3.18–19 is this: They have been "entrusted with the key of the kingdom, which is knowledge, which alone can open the gate of life, through which alone is the entrance to eternal life ... [T]hey possess the key, but those wishing to enter they do not suffer to

do so"; cf. in this connection 3.5: "the wicked one, not loving God less than the good one, is exceeded by the good in this one thing only, that he, not pardoning those who are impious on account of ignorance ... desires the destruction of the impious; but the good one desires to present them with a remedy." Cf. Reed, *Jewish-Christianity*, 191–94. This endorsement of the Pharisees' claim to be the keepers not only of divine law but of authorized interpretations of the Torah dating back to Moses is remarkable—not least in light of the starkly different appraisal in the fragments from the so-called Nazoraean commentary on Isaiah preserved by Jerome, on which see below.

71. *Hom.* 8.6.5. In 8.22 the image is one of inviting the Nations to a banquet to which the Judean *ethnos* has already been invited; cf. the allusion to Matt 8:11 in *Hom.* 8.4; also 3.49.1, which identifies Jesus as "the expectation of the Nations" à la Gen 49:10. It is in this sense that Jesus can be said to have come "for the salvation of all the world [*pantos tou kosmou*]" (12.7.5); even here, however, cf. the depiction of Moses in 2.52.2 as one "who prophesied the law of God for the whole age [*panti tō aiōni*]." Cf. Reed, *Jewish-Christianity*, 195: "the appointed task of Jesus and his apostles [in the *Homilies*] is solely to save 'pagans.'"

72. Jesus's location in Judea is noted repeatedly in *Hom.* 1.7.1, 7; 1.8.3; 15.2. Cf. 17.6.3–6, where Peter explains that Jesus spoke in short declarations rather than extended arguments because he was addressing his words "to the pious [*pros theosebeis*] who had knowledge enough to enable them to believe the things uttered by him ... for his statements were not strange to what was customary for them [*tēs autōn synētheias*] ... as to a people [*laō*] who were able to understand him, to whom we also belong." The disciples were given more elaborate private explanations only when things were not fully understood—which in any case, it is said, "rarely happened." Presumably this included above all the matter of textual corruptions in the Judean scriptures.

73. On Peter's special authority, see esp. *Hom.* 4.5.2 and 17.19. Although he is in Caesarea Maritima when the story opens (1.15), the bulk of the narrative is framed around his pursuit of Simon into "Gentile" territory—specifically, his travels north up the coast from city to city until he reaches Antioch. The fact that the "heretic" Simon goes out among the Nations (2.17.3, *eis ta ethnē*) before Peter is interpreted in terms of a more general doctrine of syzygies ("pairs"), in which inferior things precede superior ones (2.15–18; cf. 2.33, 7.2–4). As Reed observes (*Jewish-Christianity*, 198–99), the *Homilies*' emphasis on Peter's relationship to Gentiles stands in marked contrast to his portrayal by Eusebius, not to mention Gal 2:7–10. On the other hand, it is again reminiscent of Irenaeus (and Tertullian) in this respect; see note 35 above.

74. See, e.g., Peter's summary exhortation in *Hom.* 7.4 to the Gentiles of Sidon who had become "dead in your souls to God and were smitten in your bodies": "And the things which are well-pleasing to God are these: to pray to Him, to ask from Him, recognizing that He is the giver of all things, and gives with

discriminating law; to abstain from the table of devils, not to taste dead flesh, not to touch blood; to be washed from pollution; and the rest in one word—*as the God-fearing Judeans have heard, do you also hear* [*ta de loipa heni logō hōs hoi theon sebontes ēkousan Ioudaioi, kai hymeis akousate hapantes*], recovering one mind in many bodies ... And so understanding from yourselves what is reasonable, and doing it, you will become dear to God, and will obtain healing."

75. For language of regeneration, see esp. *Hom.* 19.23.6: "we can show you how, being born again and changing your origin [*anagennētheis kai tēn genesin hypallaxas*] and living lawfully, you will obtain eternal salvation"; cf. 1.7.5, and cf. 10.6: "Since, then, behaving like irrational animals [*alogois zōois*], you have destroyed the human soul [*tēn anthrōpou psychēn apōlesate*] ... If, therefore, you receive the law of God, you become men [*anthrōpoi ginesthe*] ... Therefore ... return to your first nobility; for it is possible if you become conformed to God by good works ... and by reason of your likeness to Him, you shall be reinstated as lords of all." On the assumed initiation ritual, see esp. the account of Clement's baptism (11.35), which, not coincidentally, comes on the heels of an extensive treatment of baptism and the more general matter of purity in 11.24–33; cf. the account of the baptism of Clement's mother in 13.9–12 and more generally the account of a mass baptism in Tyre in 7.5: "all sat down together in the marketplaces in sackcloth and ashes, grieving ... and repenting their former sins."

76. *Hom.* 2.19.3. The text is difficult at this point, but the basic sense of the passage is clear: by exchanging the *politeia* of her own people for the "lawful" *politeia* of the Judeans (cf. 2.20.1), she ceases to be "ethnic" and can thus access divine healing. Note at the same time that after this change she can still be identified as "the Canaanite" with respect to her ancestry (4.1; cf. 3.73).

77. Nicetas and Aquila are introduced in 2.1–2 and become key characters in the story, not least since—in a dramatic twist—they turn out to be Clement's own long-lost brothers Faustinus and Faustinianus; for their backstory, see esp. *Hom.* 2.20–21 and 13.1–8.

78. *Hom.* 4.7.2, *pasēs Hellēnikēs paideias*; see further the accounts of his and his family's earlier lives in 12.8–11, 12.15–18, and 14.6–10, and note also the contrast between Clement's "refined habits" and the spare living of Peter in 12.6.

79. Cf. *Hom.* 5.28.2: "although I have examined many doctrines of philosophers, I have inclined to none of them, excepting only that of the Judeans." It is all the more remarkable that Clement is here recalling words he had spoken to Appion even before, apparently, hearing about Jesus. Indeed, already at that juncture Clement is portrayed as having recognized that it is from Judeans—not Greeks or Egyptians—that one can learn "both to understand and to do the things that are pleasing to God" (5.26.3); see further 5.2–24, which, however, stands in some tension with the opening portrayal of Clement in *Hom.* 1.1–5.

80. Cf. Reed, *Jewish-Christianity*, 201: "To learn the truth ... Clement must travel to its source in Judaea (1.7)." For the Homilist, then, while Judean piety (like

Hellenism) is transportable beyond its originating territory and *ethnos*, it is not "disembedded" from them, let alone from Judean culture more generally as a "religion" in Boyarin's sense of the term ("Rethinking Jewish Christianity," 13, 15–16; following Schwartz, *Imperialism and Jewish Society*, 179).

81. *Hom.* 11.35.1–2. Notably, it is only at this point that Clement can begin to eat with Peter (cf. 1.22, 3.39). Cf. *Hom.* 13.4.3–4, where Peter subsequently explains to Clement's mother that she should not be insulted when Clement, in turn, will not eat with her: "we do not live with all indiscriminately; nor do we take our food from the same table as Gentiles, inasmuch as we cannot eat along with them, because they live impurely . . . But when we have persuaded them to have true thoughts, and to follow a right course of action, and have baptized them with a thrice-blessed invocation, then we dwell with them. For not even if it were our father, or mother, or wife, or child, or brother, or any other one having a claim by nature on our affection, can we venture to take our meals with them; for our *thrēskeia* compels us to make a distinction"; cf. further 13.9 and 14.1.

82. The earlier tension between Appion and Clement is narrated in a lengthy flashback in *Hom.* 5; see esp. 5.2–3 and 26–29; cf. Josephus, *Against Apion*, and see further Bremmer, "Apion and Anoubion in the *Homilies*," 79–90. I follow the *Homilies'* rendering of his name when describing its story.

83. *Hom.* 4.7.2–3. Cf. Clement's earlier derisive embrace of the characterization of Jesus and his disciples, and Judeans more generally, as barbarians in order to shame the Greek philosophers of Alexandria: "to your own injury you laugh at the truth, which, to your condemnation, consorts with the barbarians, and which you will not entertain when it visits you" (1.11.5; cf. 1.11.1).

84. Though the *Homilies* does not use the term *Ioudaïsmos*, this debate between Clement and Appion is precisely the sort of thing Mason has in mind in his analysis of the meaning of it and other such *-ismos* terms in the ancient literature; see "Jews, Judeans, Judaizing," 144–50.

85. Cf. Reed's observations in "From Judaism and Hellenism to Christianity and Paganism," 428–29: "The religion of Peter and Clement is described wholly in terms of Judaism . . . [Clement] affirms the description of his conversion as apostasy from Hellenism and affiliation with Judaism"; cf. the revised version of these lines in Reed, *Jewish-Christianity*, 121–22.

86. Another, and quite ironic, similarity between Irenaeus and the *Homilies* is that both are thoroughly indebted to precisely that culture they otherwise so adamantly disavow: Judean culture in the case of Irenaeus, and Greek philosophy in the case of the *Homilies*.

87. Cf. Peter's words to the Gentile multitudes in *Hom.* 8.22.4: "the Father . . . has ordered us, through the Prophet of the Truth, to come into the partings of the ways, that is, to you, and to invest you with the clean wedding-garment, which is baptism, which is for the remission of the sins done by you, and to bring the

good to the supper of God by repentance, although at the first they were left out of the banquet."

88. It is scarcely accidental that the famed anti-Jewish writer Appion is second only to Simon Magus as the central opponent in this text. Their purported alliance, in fact, is explained with reference to their common hatred of Judeans (*Hom.* 5.2).

89. There is no more warrant for introducing a third term like "Christianity" here than in connection with Philo's distinction between "proselytes," who "left their country, their kinsfolk and their friends for the sake of virtue and piety," and the "native born," who required no such movement (*Spec. Leg.* 1.51–53). Note in this connection the asymmetrical use of the preposition "from," e.g., in *Hom.* 8.5.3: "both to the Hebrews and to those who are called from the Nations [*Hebraiois te kai tois apo ethnōn keklēmenois*], believing in the teachers of truth is of God"; cf. 8.7.1–2: "Neither are the *Hebraioi* condemned on account of their ignorance of Jesus, by reason of Him who has concealed him, if, doing the things commanded by Moses they do not hate him whom they do not know. Neither are those from among the Nations [*hoi apo ethnōn*] condemned, who know not Moses on account of Him who has concealed him, provided that these also, doing the things spoken by Jesus, do not hate Him whom they do not know." While "Hebrew" is thus apparently a function of ancestry in the *Homilies, Ioudaios* is defined first and foremost with reference to participation in salient aspects of Judean culture; see 11.16.3–4, on which see above. Cf. in this respect Rev 2:9, which takes the same approach to "Judean," albeit with a more sectarian, exclusivistic edge: *tēn blasphēmian tōn legontōn Ioudaious einai heautous kai ouk eisin alla synagōgē tou satana.*

90. The Homilist, as far as I have noted, does not use the term *Ioudaïsmos,* but rather *ta Ioudaiōn,* "the things of the Judeans" (e.g., 4.7.2). While the types of practices we might today separate out as "religion" are integral to these "Judean things," the expression is better understood broadly with reference to a culture on the analogy of "Hellenism" (cf. 4.8.2, *ta patria ethē . . . ta Hellēnōn*) than to a "religion" on the analogy of modern notions of Christianity and Judaism.

91. The distinction between descriptive and redescriptive projects is seemingly blurred, e.g., in the importation of "Christianity" into Reed's otherwise indispensable, pioneering efforts to engage "the specific issue of identity and polemics in the Pseudo-Clementines" ("From Judaism and Hellenism to Christianity and Paganism," 427); see, e.g., pp. 434–35 (with which cf. Reed, *Jewish-Christianity,* 139 and 141): "The *Homilies* . . . embrace a complementary connection between Judaism and true Christianity . . . Similarly, the 'debate with Appion' is pivotal to the *Homilies'* efforts to present Christians and Jews as a united front in the fight against . . . 'pagan' culture . . . The *Homilies* depict Judaism's perennial conflict with Hellenism as continued by all authentic Christians—even Gentile Christians." Cf. Jones, *Pseudoclementina,* 37: "The

author tends … to equate Christianity and Judaism." Such imposition of a notion of Christianity quite extraneous to the text's self-understanding is precisely the work done by the category "Jewish Christianity." Descriptively speaking, the *Homilies* do not seem to me to be evidence for the negotiation of a Christian identity at all, but rather a Judean one precisely analogous to that attributed to its presumed "Hellenistic Jewish source" (Reed, *Jewish-Christianity*, 131). Indeed, one might well reckon not only with the possibility that the Homilist was effectively dismissing "a great many of its fellow Christians as merely 'Greeks'" (*Jewish-Christianity*, 141), but that he may well have chafed at the suggestion that he was himself a fellow "Christian" at all given the widespread "not-Judean" connotations of that name.

92. See esp. Irenaeus, *Haer.* 1.26.2; also 3.11.7, 3.21, 4.33.4, and 5.1.3.

93. See Chapter 1.

94. See Chapter 3.

95. The question of *essential* continuities or similarities, if central to Christian, Ebionite, and Judean (in the *Homilies*) self-definition, is so methodologically problematic as to be all but meaningless within a critical history of culture; cf. Smith, "Fences and Neighbors."

96. For a fuller treatment of the evidence, particularly with an eye to this question of self-understanding, see Jackson-McCabe, "Ebionites and Nazoraeans." I draw freely on that essay in what follows.

97. Discussion most frequently revolves around the Pseudo-Clementine literature and the so-called Jewish Christian gospels. On the former, see above. For a recent treatment of the problems surrounding the latter, see Luomanen, *Recovering Jewish-Christian Sects and Gospels*.

98. See Jackson-McCabe, "Ebionites and Nazoreans," 189–92.

99. Note the special interest in naming these sects both in the letter from Acacius and Paul requesting Epiphanius's account of them (1.9) and in Epiphanius's own opening remarks (e.g., Proem I, 1.2, 5.2; cf. the incipit of *Anacephalaeosis I*, "the mothers and original names of all the sects"). See further Chapter 1 above.

100. Jesus and the apostles themselves, of course, are exempt from this heresiological sourcing game. The assumption is that their teachings are sui generis, having been revealed from a superhuman, superhistorical realm.

101. Cf. here Ignatius's use of *atopos* with respect to those who mix Christianism and Judaism (*Magn.* 10.3), as well as Jerome's strategy for dealing with the Nazoraeans: "since they want to be both Jews and Christians, they are neither Jews nor Christians" (*Ep.* 112.13). Elsewhere Jerome takes a different tack, calling Ebion *semi-Christianus et semi-Judaeus*—but all "heretic"! See *Comm. Gal.* 3.13–14 (Klijn and Reinink, *Patristic Evidence*, 204–5); cf. in this respect Ign. *Trall.* 6.1–2; Tertullian, *Praescr.* 7.9–13.

102. Carleton Paget, *Jews, Christians and Jewish Christians*, 344. Cf. Origen, *Princ.* 4.3.8, *Hom. Gen.* 3.5, *Comm. Matt.* 16.12. Epiphanius combines the polemical

accounts of the name found among the group's critics with the theory of a historical figure called Ebion by suggesting that "the poor wretch was named prophetically by his father and mother" (*Pan.* 30.17.1–3).

103. Cf. Bauckham, "Origin of the Ebionites," 177–78; Skarsaune, "Ebionites," 452; and Carleton Paget, *Jews, Christians and Jewish Christians*, 347.

104. The Jewish character of the group is of course the central recurring theme in the heresiological reports; for details, see Jackson-McCabe, "Ebionites and Nazoraeans," 196–97.

105. Skarsaune, "Ebionites," 425; further Carleton Paget, *Jews, Christians and Jewish Christians*, 344–49. Bauckham ("Origin of the Ebionites," 177–80) points out the particular connection between this idea and eschatological inheritance of the covenantal land.

106. See 4QpPs^a 2.9–12 (on Ps 37:11): "And the poor shall inherit the land ... Its interpretation concerns the congregation of the poor who will tolerate the period of distress and will be rescued from all the snares of Belial. Afterwards, all who shall inherit the land will enjoy and grow fat with everything"; cf. 3:10 (on Ps 37:21–22): ... "Its interpretation concerns the congregation of the poor [for of them is] the inheritance of the whole world" (translations from García Martinez, *Dead Sea Scrolls Translated*). See further Bauckham, "Origin of the Ebionites," 179.

107. For a recent analysis of this long-standing issue, see Carleton Paget, *Jews, Christians and Jewish Christians*, 345–46. Cf., e.g., Matt 5:3 and esp. Jas 2:5: "Has God not chosen the poor of the world [*tous ptōchous tō kosmō*] to be rich in faith and inheritors of the kingdom that he promised to those who love him?" Note also the cogent conclusion in Jones, *Pseudoclementina*, 513: "It is hard to imagine any use of the word 'poor' among the early believers without some religious overtones."

108. Cf. Origen, *Comm. ser. Matt.* 79; Ps.-Tertullian, *Haer.* 3; and Epiphanius, *Pan.* 30.26.2 and 30.33.4–30.34.5; further Skarsaune, "Ebionites," 438–39; Broadhead, *Jewish Ways*, 211–12.

109. For the Ebionite rejection of Paul, see Irenaeus, *Adv. Haer.* 1.26.2; Origen, *Hom. Jer.* 19.12; Origen, *Cels.* 5.66; and Epiphanius, *Pan.* 30.16.8–9 and 30.25.1–14. Tertullian, conversely, interprets Paul as arguing against both the practice (*Praescr.* 32.2–5) and the Christology (*Praescr.* 32.11; cf. *Virg.* 6.1) of Ebion.

110. Cf. Eusebius's similarly global comment regarding the diabolical force inspiring "sorcerers" and others "to slip in under the appellation of the Christians" (*goiētōn tēn Christianōn prosēgorian hypoduomenōn*), with the same evil demon said to be at work in the Ebionites (*Hist. eccl.* 3.26.4–3.27.1).

111. Note in this connection the common suggestion that the appellation "Christian" only ever became a self-designation at all when members of the Jesus movement began appropriating a name first applied to them from the outside; see, e.g., *TDNT* 9:536–37 (*chriō*, etc.). See more recently Townsend's intriguing proposal that *Christianoi* was coined specifically as a designation for Gentile

groups ("Who Were the First Christians?"). Zetterholm, on the other hand, suggests it may have begun as an "intra-Jewish designation for a Jewish messianic synagogue in Antioch" (*Formation of Christianity*, 94–96, here 96). Thus even if we are to take seriously Origen's portrayal of Ebionites as positively "boasting to be Christians" (*Christianoi einai auchountes*), it is unclear in what contexts and with what intentions this may have been done (*Cels.* 5.61; text from Klijn and Reinink, *Patristic Evidence*, 134).

112. Thus, e.g., Epiphanius on the Nazoraeans: "People like these are refutable at once and easy to detect . . . and are Jews and nothing else [*kai Ioudaioi mallon kai ouden heteron*]" (29.9.1); cf. 29.7.1. It is to be noted in this connection that Epiphanius presents this characterization in opposition to their own supposed self-understanding: they did not themselves, he says, "keep the name 'Judeans' . . . but [took] 'Nazoraeans'" instead.

113. Ps.-Tertullian, *Haer.* 2; text and translation in Klijn and Reinink, *Patristic Evidence*, 124–25. Cf. Jerome, *Expl. Dan.*, Prol. (Klijn and Reinink, *Patristic Evidence*, 218–19), which clarifies "Ebionite" as referring to "another kind of Jew" (*Ebionitam, qui altero genere Iudaeus est*).

114. Origen, *Cels.* 2.1 (Klijn and Reinink, *Patristic Evidence*, 134–35), *Ebiōnaioi chrēmatizousin hoi apo Ioudaiōn ton Iēsoun hōs christon paradexamenoi*; cf. in the same passage "those from the Jews who believe in Jesus" (*hoi apo Ioudaiōn eis ton Iēsoun pisteountes*), with which cf. also *Comm. Matt.* 16.12. Cf. Eusebius, *Onom.* p. 301, 32–34 (Klijn and Reinink, *Patristic Evidence*, 150–51), *Hebraiōn hoi eis Christon pisteusantes, Ebiōnaioi kaloumenoi*.

115. Epiphanius, *Pan.* 30.1.5: *Ioudaion de heauton homologōn Ioudaiois antikeitai*, framing the issue of their right to the name in purely cultural terms of belief and practice and conceding that Ebion "does agree with them [i.e., Judeans] in part [*kaitoi symphōnōn autois en merei*]." Cf. Eusebius's portrayal of the Ebionites as "a heresy of so-called Jews [*hairesis . . . kaloumenōn tinōn Ioudaiōn*] who claim to believe in Christ" (*Dem. ev.* 7.1 [Klijn and Reinink, *Patristic Evidence*, 138–39]). Interestingly, Epiphanius takes precisely the opposite tack with the Nazoraeans, arguing that they are nothing other than Judeans despite their supposed rejection of that name in favor of "Nazoraeans" (*Pan.* 29.7.1, 29.9.1).

116. Origen, *Princ.* 4.3.8, alluding to Rom 9:8; cf. Matt 15:24 and 10:5–6. The Ebionites' special reverence for the Gospel of Matthew is a common feature of reports of them beginning with Irenaeus, *Haer.* 1.26.2.

117. Epiphanius (*Pan.* 30.16.8–9) relates that Paul was said to be a son of Greek parents who became circumcised only after falling in love with the daughter of the high priest, and who then became hostile to the law as a result of unrequited love; cf. his extensive refutation of the charge in *Pan.* 30.25.1–14. Cf. Origen's (unfortunately vague) reference to the fact that "up to the present day the Ebionites strike [Paul] the Apostle of Jesus Christ with shameful words incited by the unlawful word of the high priest" (*Hom. Jer.* 19.12, alluding to Acts 23:3 [Klijn and Reinink, *Patristic Evidence*, 126–29]).

118. Jerome, *Ep.* 112.13: "What shall I say of the Ebionites who claim to be Christians? Until now a heresy is to be found in all parts of the East where Jews have their synagogues; it is called 'of the Minaeans' and cursed by the Pharisees to now. Usually they are named Nazoreans." Tertullian, while aware of the heresy of "Ebion" (e.g., *Praescr.* 10.7, 33.5), describes "Nazoraean" simply as "the name Jews call *us*" (*Marc.* 4.8 [Klijn and Reinink, *Patristic Evidence*, 108–9], *et ipso nomine nos Iudaei Nazarenos appellant*). See further Schaeder, "*Nazarenos, Nazoraios,*" *TDNT* 4:874–79. I have drawn freely in what follows on an earlier treatment of the issues surrounding the supposed Nazoraean group in Jackson-McCabe, "Ebionites and Nazoraeans," 198–204.

119. Justin, *Dial.* 47.1–3 (following the translation in Falls, *Dialogue with Trypho*). In Justin's view, interestingly, while Judeans who try to compel Christians to observe Jewish law will not be saved, the Gentiles they successfully persuade nonetheless probably will be.

120. Origen, *Cels.* 5.61 (Klijn and Reinink, *Patristic* Evidence, 134–35). Ebionites are typically associated more straightforwardly with the identification of Jesus as a human being rather than God; cf. Jackson-McCabe, "Ebionites and Nazoraeans," 197. Cf. Justin, *Dial.* 48.

121. See Chapter 4 above; thus, e.g., Pritz, *Nazarene Jewish Christianity*.

122. See further Jackson-McCabe, "Ebionites and Nazoraeans," 198–200; cf. Jones, *Pseudoclementina*, 514.

123. Cf. in this respect Epiphanius's strategy regarding Ebion: "But since he is midway between all the sects, as one might say, he amounts to nothing" (*Pan.* 30.1.4); also Ignatius's use of *atopos* in *Magn.* 10.3, on which see above.

124. Cf. Epiphanius, *Pan.* 29.6.7 and 29.7.1. The notice about the group's secession from the apostolic community in *Pan.* 29.5.4 is based on Eusebius's account of Philo's Therapeutae, whom Epiphanius (like Eusebius) takes to be early followers of Jesus; cf. *Hist. eccl.* 2.16–17, which, however, makes no mention of Nazoraeans in this connection.

125. The five fragments generally accepted as belonging to this work are found in Jerome, *Comm. Isa.* 8.11–15, 8.19–22, 9.1, 29.17–21, 31.6–9. For discussion, see Schmidtke, *Neue Fragmente*, 108–23; Klijn, "Jerome's Quotations"; Pritz, *Nazarene Jewish Christianity*, 57–70; Kinzig, "Nazoraeans," 474–77; and Luomanen, *Recovering Jewish-Christian Sects*, 71–75. Broadhead (*Jewish Ways*, 166–71) entertains the possibility that at least some of the content from Jerome, *Comm. Isa.* 11.1–3 might also have come from this work. The rationale for doing this is rather thin, however, and the passage is not included in the following analysis. I use the text and (with minor modifications) translation in Klijn and Reinink, *Patristic Evidence*, 220–25, unless otherwise noted.

126. The earliest possible date is established by its reference to R. Meir, who was active in the mid-second century. Pritz (*Nazarene Jewish Christianity*, 68) reasonably suggests a date "in the mid-third century, and at least after 200, when the

Mishnah was compiled"; so too Luomanen, *Recovering Jewish-Christian Sects*, 75. Whether Jerome had access to the original Hebrew or Aramaic of this work or only some already translated fragments of it is a matter of dispute.

127. Cf. Cohen, *From the Maccabees to the Mishnah*, 226: "the rabbis see themselves not as 'Pharisees' but as 'the sages of Israel.' Neither the Mishnah nor any other rabbinic work betrays a Pharisaic self-consciousness"; see further Reed, *Jewish-Christianity*, 295–329. The "Scribes and Pharisees" are explicitly referenced in four of the five extant fragments (*Comm. Isa.* 8.11–15, 8.19–22, 9.1, and 29.17–21) and are clearly in view in the fifth (on Isa 31:6–9); cf. the analogously recurring critique in the fragments of the so-called *Gospel of the Nazoraeans*, on which see Luomanen, *Recovering Jewish-Christian Sects*, 110–19.

128. For discussion of the puns underlying Jerome's (or his source's) Latin, see Schmidtke, *Neue Fragmente*, 113–14; Klijn, "Jerome's Quotations," 250; Pritz, *Nazarene Jewish Christianity*, 61–62; and Kinzig, "Nazarenes," 475 nn. 66 and 67.

129. *Mishnayot* likely underlies the use of *deuterōseis* here; see Strack and Stemberger, *Introduction to the Talmud and Midrash*, 65; and Pritz, *Nazarene Jewish Christianity*, 66–68. On the historical problems in the text's rabbinic genealogy, see Pritz, *Nazarene Jewish Christianity*, 59–62; and Strack and Stemberger, *Introduction to the Talmud and Midrash*, 65–78.

130. The fragment on Isa 8:11–15 points out that Shammai and Hillel "were born not long before the Lord." On the interpretation of Zebulon and Naphtali as the land of Israel more generally, see Klijn, "Jerome's Quotations," 251, who rightly notes the contrast with Matt 4:12–17.

131. Regarding Gentiles, note also the reference to "the philosophers and every perverse dogma" in Jerome, *Comm. Isa.* 31.6–9; cf. Luomanen, *Recovering Jewish-Christian Sects*, 75.

132. Cf. Klijn, "Jerome's Quotations," 254: "the Jewish leaders do not seem to be representatives of the Jewish people as a whole. Although the Jewish leaders reject the Christian message, the people is called upon to repent."

133. Note in this connection that the rabbis' domination of Jewish society during this era was not nearly so complete as has often been imagined; see Schwartz, *Imperialism and Jewish Society*.

134. See Jerome, *Comm. Isa.* 9.1, quoted above. Unfortunately, how exactly the group understood the significance of Paul—in comparison, say, to Jerome and Epiphanius as opposed to the so-called new perspective on Paul advanced in the recent reconstructions of Gager, Eisenbaum, and others—is unknown.

135. Cf. in this respect, e.g., Psalms of Solomon 17; also the Gospel of Matthew, on which see further Kampen, *Matthew within Sectarian Judaism*, 184–202.

136. It is perhaps noteworthy in this connection that Jerome links these same "Nazoraeans" to a gospel closely related to the one we now call Matthew; for a recent treatment of the matter, see Luomanen, *Recovering Jewish-Christian Sects*, 83–119. With reference to the interpretation of Isa 9:1–4 in particular,

cf. esp. Matt 23:4: "They tie up heavy burdens, hard to bear, and lay them on the shoulders of others," which comes in the context of a wider criticism that "Pharisees and scribes" "break the commandment of God for the sake of [their] tradition" (15:3).

137. Jerome's statement on his approach to translation in his Epistle 57, written in response to an accusation that he had produced a misleading translation of a letter of Epiphanius to John of Jerusalem, is worth bearing in mind. "I have always aimed," he writes, "at rendering sense, not words [*non verba, sed sententias transtulisse*]"; cf. 57.5.2, on translating from Greek: with the lone exception of "the holy scriptures where even the order of the words is a mystery, I render sense for sense and not word for word [*non verbum e verbo sed sensum exprimere de sensu*]." Jerome cites a variety of prior authorities for this approach, who (among other things) convey "the sense" but do "not invariably keep the words of the original" (57.6); whose "omissions, additions, and alterations" result from "substituting the idioms of his own for those of another tongue" (57.5); and who, in short, "like a conqueror [lead] away captive into his own tongue the meaning of the originals" (57.6). I follow the Latin text in PL 22, and the translation in *Nicene and Post-Nicene Fathers*, Series 2, vol. 6.

138. Matt 28:15: "And this story is still told among Judeans [*para Ioudaiois*] to this day." For a recent treatment of this line in Matthew, see Kampen, *Matthew within Sectarian Judaism*, 180.

139. It is perhaps not accidental that the one similarly puzzling reference to "Judeans" in Matt 28:15 also occurs at the same time an active mission among the Nations first comes into view (cf. Matt 27:16–20; contrast 10:5, 15:24).

140. For a survey of the term's earliest usage, see Cohen, *Beginnings of Jewishness*, 69–106, esp. 75, on its usage already before the Common Era: "*Hoi Ioudaioi* is the most common way by which 'the Judaeans' of specific places identify themselves ... The ethnic reference of 'Judaean' was so strong that both the Judaeans themselves and the Greeks and Romans had a sense that all Judaeans everywhere somehow belonged to a single group."

141. On Eusebius, see Johnson, "Identity, Descent, and Polemic," 54–55; on Epiphanius, see Chapter 1 above.

142. Cf. in this respect, e.g., the broadly analogous (albeit more militaristic) scenario imagined in Psalms of Solomon 17, which also alludes to Isaiah at several points (Collins, *Scepter and the Star*, 49–56). Here too the Messiah will purge "Israel" both of sinful leaders that arose within it and of the Gentile practices imported from outside it in a process that will eventually encompass "the whole earth" (17:30). While "the Nations" will acknowledge Israel's God and serve "under the yoke" of his Messiah, there is no hint that they will adopt Israel's law, let alone that they will themselves become Israelites. Indeed, once Israel's tribes are redistributed upon the land, "the alien and the foreigner will no longer live near them" (17:28). There seems to have been an ongoing difference of opinion

among Judeans who believed these prophecies were being fulfilled through Jesus about how to negotiate the practical implications of actual such Gentiles; cf. Gal 2; Acts 15; Justin, *Dial.* 47.

143. Epiphanius, *Pan.* 29.7.7–8; cf. 30.2.7–9 and 30.34.6. It has long been acknowledged that there is some relationship between at least some of the writings attributed to the Ebionites by Epiphanius and what we now call the Pseudo-Clementine literature; see further Jones, *Pseudoclementina*, 50–113.

144. Wellhausen, *Einleitung*, 114. See the very perceptive observations in Betz, "Wellhausen's Dictum," 86–87, whose English rendering of Wellhausen's German is cited here.

Bibliography

Arnal, William. "The Q Document." In *Jewish Christianity Reconsidered: Rethinking Ancient Groups and Texts*, edited by Matt Jackson-McCabe, 119–54. Minneapolis: Fortress, 2007.

Baird, William. *History of New Testament Research*. 3 vols. Minneapolis: Fortress, 1992–2013.

Barnes, Timothy D. "The Date of Ignatius." *Expository Times* 120 (2008): 119–30.

Barton, Carlin A., and Daniel Boyarin. *Imagine No Religion: How Modern Abstractions Hide Ancient Realities*. New York: Fordham University Press, 2016.

Bauckham, Richard. "The Origin of the Ebionites." In *The Image of the Judaeo-Christians in Ancient Jewish and Christian Literature*, edited by Peter J. Tomson and Doris Lambers-Petry, 162–81. WUNT 158. Tübingen: Mohr Siebeck, 2003.

Bauer, Walter. *Orthodoxy and Heresy in Earliest Christianity*. 2nd ed. with appendices by Georg Strecker. Translated by a team from the Philadelphia Seminar on Christian Origins and edited by Robert A. Kraft and Gerhard Krodel. Philadelphia: Fortress, 1971. Repr., Mifflintown, PA: Sigler, 1996.

Baumgarten, Albert I. "Marcel Simon's *Verus Israel* as a Contribution to Jewish History." *Harvard Theological Review* 92 (1999): 465–78.

Baur, Ferdinand Christian. "Die Christuspartei in der korinthischen Gemeinde, der Gegensatz des petrinischen und paulinischen Christenthums in der ältesten Kirche, der Apostel Petrus in Rom." 1831. Reprinted in *Ausgewählte Werke in Einzelausgaben*, 1:1–145. Edited by Klaus Scholder. 5 vols. Stuttgart-Bad Cannstaatt: F. Frommann, 1963–1975.

Baur, Ferdinand Christian. *The Church History of the First Three Centuries*. 3rd ed. Translated by Allan Menzies. 2 vols. London: Williams and Norgate, 1878. Translation of *Kirchengeschichte der drei ersten Jahrhunderte*. Tübingen: Fues, 1863.

Baur, Ferdinand Christian. *History of Christian Dogma*. Edited by Peter C. Hodgson. Translated by Robert F. Brown and Peter C. Hodgson. Oxford: Oxford University Press, 2014. Translation of *Lehrbuch der christlichen*

Dogmengeschichte. 3rd ed. Leipzig: Fues, 1867. 1st ed., Stuttgart: Becher's Verlag, 1847.

Baur, Ferdinand Christian. *Paul the Apostle of Jesus Christ: His Life and Works, His Epistles and Teachings.* Translated by A. P. 2 vols. London: Williams and Norgate, 1873–1875. Reprinted as two volumes in one, Peabody, MA: Hendrickson, 2003. Translation of *Paulus, Der Apostel Jesu Christi. Sein Leben und Wirken, seine Briefe, und seine Lehre. Ein Beitrag zu einer kritischen Geschichte des Urchirstenthums.* Edited by Eduard Zeller. 2 vols. Leipzig: Fues, 1866–1867.

Becker, Adam H., and Annette Yoshiko Reed, eds. *The Ways That Never Parted: Jews and Christians in Late Antiquity and the Early Middle Ages.* Minneapolis: Fortress, 2007.

Behr, John. *Irenaeus of Lyons: Identifying Christianity.* Oxford: Oxford University Press, 2013.

Behr, John, trans. *St. Irenaeus of Lyons: On the Apostolic Preaching.* Popular Patristics Series 17. Crestwood, NY: St. Vladimir's Seminary Press, 1997.

Betz, Hans Dieter, ed. *The Greek Magical Papyri in Translation Including the Demotic Spells. Volume One: Texts.* 2nd ed., with an updated bibliography. Chicago: University of Chicago Press, 1992.

Betz, Hans Dieter. "Wellhausen's Dictum 'Jesus Was Not a Christian but a Jew' in Light of Present Scholarship." *Studia Theologica* 45 (1991): 83–110.

Bohak, Gideon. *Ancient Jewish Magic: A History.* Cambridge: Cambridge University Press, 2008.

Boyarin, Daniel. *Border Lines: The Partition of Judaeo-Christianity.* Divinations: Rereading Late Ancient Religion. Philadelphia: University of Pennsylvania Press, 2004.

Boyarin, Daniel. *Dying for God: Martyrdom and the Making of Christianity and Judaism.* Figurae: Reading Medieval Culture. Stanford, CA: Stanford University Press, 1999.

Boyarin, Daniel. *The Jewish Gospels: The Story of the Jewish Christ.* New York: New Press, 2012.

Boyarin, Daniel. "Rethinking Jewish Christianity: An Argument for Dismantling a Dubious Category (to Which Is Appended a Correction of My *Border Lines*)." *Jewish Quarterly Review* 99 (2009): 7–36.

Brakke, David. *The Gnostics: Myth, Ritual, and Diversity in Early Christianity.* Cambridge, MA: Harvard University Press, 2010.

Bremmer, Jan N. "Apion and Anoubion in the *Homilies.*" In *The Pseudo-Clementines*, edited by Jan N. Bremmer, 73–92. Studies on Early Christian Apocrypha 10. Leuven: Peeters, 2010.

Bremmer, Jan N., ed. *The Pseudo-Clementines.* Studies on Early Christian Apocrypha 10. Leuven: Peeters, 2010.

Broadhead, Edwin. *Jewish Ways of Following Jesus: Redrawing the Religious Map of Antiquity.* WUNT 266. Tübingen: Mohr Siebeck, 2010.

Brown, Raymond E. "Not Jewish Christianity and Gentile Christianity but Types of Jewish/Gentile Christianity." *Catholic Biblical Quarterly* 45 (1983): 74–79.

Brown, Raymond E., and John P. Maier. *Antioch and Rome: New Testament Cradles of Catholic Christianity*. New York: Paulist, 1983.

Brubaker, Rogers. "Ethnicity, Race, and Nationalism." *Annual Review of Sociology* 35 (2009): 21–42.

Brubaker, Rogers. "Ethnicity without Groups." *European Journal of Sociology* 43 (2002): 163–89.

Brubaker, Rogers, and Frederick Cooper. "Beyond 'Identity.'" *Theory and Society* 29 (2000): 1–47.

Buell, Denise Kimber. *Why This New Race: Ethnic Reasoning in Early Christianity*. New York: Columbia University Press, 2005.

Byrne, Peter. *Natural Religion and the Nature of Religion: The Legacy of Deism*. Routledge Religious Studies. London: Routledge, 1989.

Cain, Andrew, ed. *St. Jerome: Commentary on Galatians*. Fathers of the Church. Washington, DC: Catholic University of America Press, 2010.

Cameron, Averil. "Jews and Heretics—A Category Error?" In *The Ways That Never Parted: Jews and Christians in Late Antiquity and the Early Middle Ages*, edited by Adam H. Becker and Annette Yoshiko Reed, 345–60. Minneapolis: Fortress, 2007.

Carlson, Donald H. *Jewish-Christian Interpretation of the Pentateuch in the Pseudo-Clementine Homilies*. Minneapolis: Fortress, 2013.

Carleton Paget, James. "The Definition of the Terms *Jewish Christian* and *Jewish Christianity* in the History of Research." In *Jewish Believers in Jesus: The Early Centuries*, edited by Oskar Skarsaune and Reidar Hvalvik, 22–52. Peabody, MA: Hendrickson, 2007.

Carleton Paget, James. "Jewish Christianity." In *The Cambridge History of Judaism, Volume Three: The Early Roman Period*, edited by William Horbury, W. D. Davies, and John Sturdy, 731–75. Cambridge: Cambridge University Press, 1999.

Carleton Paget, James. *Jews, Christians and Jewish Christians in Antiquity*. WUNT 251. Tübingen: Mohr Siebeck, 2010.

Carleton Paget, James. "The Reception of Baur in Britain." In *Ferdinand Christian Baur und die Geschichte des frühen Christentums*, edited by Martin Bauspiess, Christof Landmesser, and David Lincicum, 335–86. WUNT 333. Tübingen: Mohr Siebeck, 2014.

Champion, Justin. *John Toland: Nazarenus*. British Deism and Free Thought 1. Oxford: Voltaire Foundation, 1999.

Champion, Justin. "John Toland: The Politics of Pantheism." *Revue de synthese* 2–3 (1995): 259–80.

Champion, Justin. *The Pillars of Priestcraft Shaken: The Church of England and Its Enemies, 1660–1730*. Cambridge Studies in Early Modern British History. Cambridge: Cambridge University Press, 1992.

Champion, Justin. *Republican Learning: John Toland and the Crisis of Christian Culture, 1696–1722.* New York: Manchester University Press, 2003.

Cohen, Shaye J. D. *The Beginnings of Jewishness: Boundaries, Varieties, Uncertainties.* Berkeley: University of California Press, 1999.

Cohen, Shaye J. D. *From the Maccabees to the Mishnah.* Library of Early Christianity. Philadelphia: Westminster, 1989.

Collins, John J. *The Invention of Judaism: Torah and Jewish Identity from Deuteronomy to Paul.* Taubman Lectures in Jewish Studies 7. Oakland: University of California Press, 2017.

Collins, John J. *The Scepter and the Star: The Messiahs of the Dead Sea Scrolls and Other Ancient Literature.* AYBRL. New York: Doubleday, 1995.

Colpe, Carsten. *Das Siegel der Propheten. Historischen Beziehungen zwischen Judentum, Judenchristentum, Heidentum, und frühem Islam.* ANTZ 3. Berlin: Institut Kirche und Judentum, 1990.

Daniel, Stephen H. *John Toland: His Methods, Manners, and Mind.* Kingston: McGill-Queen's University Press, 1984.

Daniélou, Jean. *The Theology of Jewish Christianity.* Vol. 1 of *The Development of Christian Doctrine before the Council of Nicaea.* Translated by John A. Baker. London: Darton, Longman & Todd, 1964. Translation and revision of *Théologie du judéo-christianisme.* Tournai: Desclée, 1958.

Dix, Gregory. *Jew and Greek: A Study in the Primitive Church.* Westminster: Dacre, 1953.

Draper, Jonathan. "The Holy Vine of David Made Known to the Gentiles through God's Servant Jesus: 'Christian Judaism' in the Didache." In *Jewish Christianity Reconsidered: Rethinking Ancient Groups and Texts,* edited by Matt Jackson-McCabe, 257–83. Minneapolis: Fortress, 2007.

Droge, Arthur J. *Homer or Moses? Early Christian Interpretations of the History of Culture.* Hermeneutische Untersuchungen zur Theologie 26. Tübingen: Mohr Siebeck, 1989.

Duddy, Thomas. *A History of Irish Thought.* New York: Routledge, 2002.

Duncan, Patricia A. *Novel Hermeneutics in the Greek Pseudo-Clementine Romance.* WUNT 395. Tübingen: Mohr Siebeck, 2017.

Ehrman, Bart D., trans. *The Apostolic Fathers.* 2 vols. LCL. Cambridge, MA: Harvard University Press, 2003.

Eisenbaum, Pamela. *Paul Was Not a Christian: The Original Message of a Misunderstood Apostle.* New York: HarperOne, 2009.

Falls, Thomas B., trans. *St. Justin Martyr. Dialogue with Trypho.* Revised with a New Introduction by Thomas P. Halton. Selections from the Fathers of the Church 3. Washington, DC: Catholic University Press of America, 2003.

Flower, Richard. "Genealogies of Unbelief: Epiphanius of Salamis and Heresiological Authority." In *Unclassical Traditions.* Vol. 2 of *Perspectives from East and West in Late Antiquity,* edited by Christopher Kelly, Richard Flower, and Michael Stuart Williams, 70–87. Cambridge: Cambridge University Press, 2011.

Fonrobert, Charlotte. "Jewish Christians, Judaizers, and Christian Anti-Judaism." In *Late Ancient Christianity*, edited by Virginia Burrus, 234–54. Vol. 2 of *A People's History of Christianity*, edited by Denis R. Janz. Minneapolis: Fortress, 2005.

Fouke, Daniel C. *Philosophy and Theology in a Burlesque Mode: John Toland and 'The Way of Paradox.'* Amherst, NY: Humanity Books, 2007.

Fruchtenbaum, Arnold G. *Hebrew Christianity: Its Theology, History, and Philosophy.* Washington, DC: Canton, 1974.

Gager, John G. *Reinventing Paul.* Oxford: Oxford University Press, 2000.

García Martinez, Florentino. *The Dead Sea Scrolls Translated: The Qumran Texts in English.* Leiden: Brill, 1994.

Gawlick, Günter, ed. *Thomas Morgan: The Moral Philosopher.* Facsimile reprint in one volume. Stuttgart-Bad Cannstatt: Frommann (Holzboog), 1969.

Goodman, Martin. "Modeling the 'Parting of the Ways.'" In *The Ways That Never Parted: Jews and Christians in Late Antiquity and the Early Middle Ages*, edited by Adam H. Becker and Annette Yoshiko Reed, 119–29. Minneapolis: Fortress, 2007.

Gregory, Andrew. "Hindrance or Help: Does the Modern Category of 'Jewish Christian Gospel' Distort Our Understanding of the Texts to Which It Refers?" *Journal for the Study of the New Testament* 28 (2006): 387–413.

Hall, Jonathan M. *Ethnic Identity in Greek Antiquity.* Cambridge: Cambridge University Press, 2000.

Hall, Jonathan M. *Hellenicity: Between Ethnicity and Culture.* Chicago: University of Chicago Press, 2002.

Harnack, Adolf von. *History of Dogma. Volume 1.* Translated from the 3rd ed. by Neil Buchanan. New York: Dover, 1961. Translation of *Lehrbuch der Dogmengeschichte.* Vol. 1 of *Die Entstehung des kirchlichen Dogmas.* 3rd ed. Freiburg: Mohr (Siebeck), 1894.

Harnack, Adolf von. *What Is Christianity?* Fortress Texts in Modern Theology. Translated by Thomas Bailey Saunders with an introduction by Rudolf Bultmann. Philadelphia: Fortress, 1986. Translation of *Das Wesen des Christentums: Sechzehn Vorlesungen vor Studierenden aller Fakultäten im Wintersemester 1899/1900 an der Universität Berlin gehalten.* Leipzig: J. C. Hinrichs, 1901.

Harris, Horton. *David Friedrich Strauss and His Theology.* Cambridge: Cambridge University Press, 1973.

Harris, Horton. *The Tübingen School: A Historical and Theological Investigation of the School of F. C. Baur.* With a new preface by the author and a foreword by E. Earle Ellis. Grand Rapids: Baker, 1990.

Hilgenfeld, Adolf. *Judenthum und Judenchristenthum: Eine Nachlese zu der 'Ketzergeschichte des Urchristenthums.'* Leipzig: Fues (Reisland), 1886. Repr., *Judentum und Judenchristentum: Eine Nachlese zu der Ketzergeschichte des Urchristenthums.* Hildesheim: Georg Olms, 1966.

Hill, Craig C. "The Jerusalem Church." In *Jewish Christianity Reconsidered: Rethinking Ancient Groups and Texts*, edited by Matt Jackson-McCabe, 39–56. Minneapolis: Fortress, 2007.

Hodgson, Peter C. *Ferdinand Christian Baur on the Writing of Church History*. Library of Protestant Thought. New York: Oxford University Press, 1968.

Hodgson, Peter C. *The Formation of Historical Theology: A Study of Ferdinand Christian Baur*. New York: Harper & Row, 1966.

Hodgson, Peter C. "Hegel's Christology: Shifting Nuances in the Berlin Lectures." *Journal of the American Academy of Religion* 53 (1985): 23–40.

Hoennicke, Gustav. *Das Judenchristentum im ersten und zweiten Jahrhundert*. Berlin: Trowitzsch, 1908.

Holl, Karl, ed. *Epiphanius. Ancoratus und Panarion*. Leipzig: Hinrichs, 1915.

Horrell, David G. "Early Jewish Christianity." In *The Early Christian World*, edited by Philip F. Esler, 1:136–67. 2 vols. London: Routledge, 2000.

Horsley, Richard A., with John S. Hanson. *Bandits, Prophets, and Messiahs: Popular Movements in the Time of Jesus*. Harrisburg, PA: Trinity Press International, 1999.

Hort, Fenton John Anthony. *Judaistic Christianity: A Course of Lectures*. Edited with a preface by J. O. F. Murray. Cambridge: MacMillan, 1901.

Irinischi, Eduard, and Holger M. Zellentin. "Making Selves and Marking Others: Identity and Late Antique Heresiologies." In *Heresy and Identity in Late Antiquity*, 1–27. TSAJ 119. Tübingen: Mohr Siebeck, 2008.

Jackson-McCabe, Matt. "Ebionites and Nazoraeans: Christians or Jews?" In *Partings: How Judaism and Christianity Became Two*, edited by Hershel Shanks, 187–205. Washington, DC: Biblical Archaeology Society, 2013.

Jackson-McCabe, Matt. "'Jewish Christianity' and 'Christian Deism' in Thomas Morgan's *The Moral Philosopher*." In *The Rediscovery of Jewish Christianity*, edited by F. Stanley Jones, 105–22. HBS 5. Atlanta: Society of Biblical Literature, 2012.

Jackson-McCabe, Matt, ed. *Jewish Christianity Reconsidered: Rethinking Ancient Groups and Texts*. Minneapolis: Fortress, 2007.

Jackson-McCabe, Matt. "The Letter of James and Hellenistic Philosophy." In *Reading the Epistle of James: A Resource for Students*, edited by Eric Mason and Darian Lockett, 45–71. Resources for Biblical Study. Atlanta: SBL Press, 2019.

Jackson-McCabe, Matt. *Logos and Law in the Letter of James: The Law of Nature, the Law of Moses, and the Law of Freedom*. NovTSup 100. Leiden: Brill, 2001. Repr., Atlanta: Society of Biblical Literature, 2010.

Jackson-McCabe, Matt. "Orthodoxy, Heresy, and Jewish Christianity: Reflections on Categories in Edwin Broadhead's *Jewish Ways of Following Jesus*." In *The History of Religions School Today*, edited by Thomas R. Blanton IV, Robert Matthew Calhoun, and Clare K. Rothschild, 169–83. WUNT 340. Tübingen: Mohr Siebeck, 2014.

Jackson-McCabe, Matt. "The Politics of Pseudepigraphy and the Letter of James." In *Pseudepigraphie und Verfasserfiktion in frühchristlichen Briefen*, edited by Jörg Frey, Jens Herzer, Martina Janssen, and Clare K. Rothschild, 599–623. WUNT 246. Tübingen: Mohr Siebeck, 2009.

Jackson-McCabe, Matt. Review of *Jews or Christians?* by Giorgio Jossa. *BTB* 39 (2009): 230–31.

Jackson-McCabe, Matt. Review of *The Ways That Never Parted,* edited by Adam H. Becker and Annette Yoshiko Reed. *BTB* 38 (2008): 189–90.

Jackson-McCabe, Matt. "What's in a Name? The Problem of 'Jewish Christianity.'" In *Jewish Christianity Reconsidered: Rethinking Ancient Groups and Texts,* edited by Matt Jackson-McCabe, 7–38. Minneapolis: Fortress, 2007.

Johnson, Aaron P. "Identity, Descent, and Polemic: Ethnic Argumentation in Eusebius' *Praeparatio Evangelica.*" *Journal of Early Christian Studies* 12 (2004): 23–56.

Jones, F. Stanley. *An Ancient Jewish Christian Source on the History of Christianity: Pseudo-Clementine* Recognitions *1.27–71.* Texts and Translations 37, Christian Apocrypha Series 2. Atlanta: Scholars Press, 1995.

Jones, F. Stanley. "From Toland to Baur: Tracks of the History of Research into Jewish Christianity." In *The Rediscovery of Jewish Christianity: From Toland to Baur,* edited by F. Stanley Jones, 123–36. HBS 5. Atlanta: Society of Biblical Literature, 2012.

Jones, F. Stanley. *Pseudoclementina Elchasaiticaque inter Judaeochristiana: Collected Studies.* Orientalia Lovaniensia Analecta 203. Leuven: Peeters, 2012.

Jones, F. Stanley. "The Pseudo-Clementines: A History of Research." In *Pseudoclementina Elchasaiticaque inter Judaeochristiana: Collected Studies,* 50–113. Orientalia Lovaniensia Analecta 203. Leuven: Peeters, 2012.

Jones, F. Stanley, ed. *The Rediscovery of Jewish Christianity: From Toland to Baur.* HBS 5. Atlanta: Society of Biblical Literature, 2012.

Jossa, Giorgio. *Jews or Christians? The Followers of Jesus in Search of Their Own Identity.* Translated by Molly Rogers. WUNT 202. Tübingen: Mohr Siebeck, 2006.

Kaestli, Jean-Daniel. "Où en est le débat sur le judéo-christianisme?" In *Le déchirement. Juifs et chrétiens au premier siècle,* edited by D. Marguerat, 243–72. *Monde de la Bible* 32. Geneva: Labor at Fides, 1996.

Kampen, John I. *Matthew within Sectarian Judaism: An Examination.* AYBRL. New Haven: Yale University Press, 2019.

Kim, Young Richard. *Epiphanius of Cyprus: Imagining an Orthodox World.* Ann Arbor: University of Michigan Press, 2015.

King, Karen L. *What Is Gnosticism?* Cambridge, MA: Harvard University Press, 2003.

King, Karen L. "Which Early Christianity?" In *The Oxford Handbook of Early Christian Studies,* edited by Susan Ashbrook Harvey and David Hunter, 66–84. Oxford: Oxford University Press, 2008.

Kinzig, Wolfram. "The Nazoraeans." In *Jewish Believers in Jesus: The Early Centuries,* edited by Oskar Skarsaune and Reidar Hvalvik, 463–87. Peabody, MA: Hendrickson, 2007.

Kittel, Gerhard, and Gerhard Friedrich, eds. *Theological Dictionary of the New Testament.* Translated by Geoffrey W. Bromiley. 10 vols. Grand Rapids: Eerdmans, 1964–1976.

Klijn, A. F. J. "Jerome's Quotations from a Nazoraean Interpretation of Isaiah."
RSR 60 (1972): 241–55.

Klijn, A. F. J. "The Study of Jewish Christianity." *NTS* 20 (1973–74): 419–31.

Klijn, A. F. J., and G. J. Reinink. *Patristic Evidence for Jewish-Christian Sects.*
NovTSup 36. Leiden: Brill, 1973.

Kraft, Robert A. "In Search of 'Jewish Christianity' and Its 'Theology': Problems
of Definition and Methodology." In *Judéo-christianisme: Recherches historiques et
théologiques offertes en homage au Cardinal Jean Daniélou. RSR* 60 (1972): 81–92.

Lake, Kirsopp, trans. *The Apostolic Fathers.* 2 vols. LCL. Cambridge, MA: Harvard
University Press, 1985–1992.

Lampe, Peter. *From Paul to Valentinus: Christians at Rome in the First Two Centuries.*
Translated by Michael Steinhauser and edited by Marshall D. Johnson. Minneapolis: Fortress, 2003.

Law, Timothy Michael, and Charles Halton, eds. *Jew and Judean: A MARGINA-
LIA Forum on Politics and Historiography in the Translation of Ancient Texts.* Mar-
ginalia: Los Angeles Review of Books; published as an e-book on August 26,
2014. Available at http://marginalia.lareviewofbooks.org/jew-judean-forum/.

Le Boulluec, Alain. *La notion d'hérésie dans la littérature grecque IIe–IIIe siècles.*
2 vols. Paris: Études Augustiniennes, 1985.

Leland, John. *A View of the Principal Deistical Writers that have Appeared in England
in the last and present Century.* 3rd ed. London: Benj. Dod., 1757. Reprint edited
by René Wellek. 3 vols. British Philosophers and Theologians of the 17th and 18th
Centuries. New York: Garland, 1978.

Lemke, Hella. *Judenchristentum zwischen Ausgrenzung und Integration: Zur Geschichte eines exegetisches Begriffes.* Hamburger Theologische Studien 25. Munster:
LIT, 2001.

Lieu, Judith M. *Christian Identity in the Jewish and Graeco-Roman World.* Oxford:
Oxford University Press, 2004.

Lieu, Judith M. *Neither Jew Nor Greek? Constructing Early Christianity.* London:
T & T Clark, 2005.

Lieu, Judith M. "'The Parting of the Ways': Theological Construct or Historical
Reality?" In *Neither Jew Nor Greek? Constructing Early Christianity,* 11–29. London: T & T Clark, 2005.

Lightfoot, J. B. *The Epistle of St. Paul to the Galatians: With Introductions, Notes, and
Dissertations.* London: Macmillan, 1865. Repr., Grand Rapids: Zondervan, 1972.

Lincicum, David. "F. C. Baur's Place in the Study of Jewish Christianity." In *The
Rediscovery of Jewish Christianity: From Toland to Baur,* edited by F. Stanley Jones,
137–66. HBS 5. Atlanta: Society of Biblical Literature, 2012.

Lincoln, Bruce. *Holy Terrors: Thinking about Religion after September 11.* Chicago:
University of Chicago Press, 2003.

Longenecker, Richard N. *The Christology of Early Jewish Christianity.* London:
SCM, 1970. Repr., Vancouver: Regent College Publishing, 2001.

Luedemann, Gerd. *Opposition to Paul in Jewish Christianity.* Translated by M. Eugene Boring. Minneapolis: Fortress, 1989.

Luomanen, Petri. "Ebionites and Nazarenes." In *Jewish Christianity Reconsidered: Rethinking Ancient Groups and Texts,* edited by Matt Jackson-McCabe, 81–118. Minneapolis: Fortress, 2007.

Luomanen, Petri. *Recovering Jewish-Christian Sects and Gospels.* Supplements to *Vigiliae Christianae.* Texts and Studies of Early Christian Life and Language 110. Leiden: Brill, 2012.

Luomanen, Petri. "Where Did Another Rich Man Come From? The Jewish-Christian Profile of the Story about a Rich Man in the '*Gospel of the Hebrews*' (Origen, *Comm. in Matth.* 15.14)." *VC* 57 (2003): 243–75.

Malina, Bruce J. "Jewish Christianity: A Select Bibliography." *Australian Journal of Biblical Archaeology* 6 (1973): 60–65.

Malina, Bruce J. "Jewish Christianity or Christian Judaism: Toward a Hypothetical Definition." *JSJ* 7 (1976): 46–56.

Manns, Frederic. *Bibliographie du Judeo-christianisme.* Preface by P. B. Bagatti. Studium Biblicum Franciscanum Analecta 13. Jerusalem: Franciscan Printing Press, 1979.

Marcus, Joel. "Jewish Christianity." In *The Cambridge History of Christianity, Volume 1: Origins to Constantine,* edited by Margaret M. Mitchell and Frances M. Young, 87–102. Cambridge: Cambridge University Press, 2006.

Marshall, John W. *Parables of War: Reading John's Jewish Apocalypse.* Waterloo, Ontario: Wilfrid Laurier University Press, 2001.

Mason, Steve. "Jews, Judaeans, Judaizing, Judaism: Problems of Categorization in Ancient History." *JSJ* 38 (2007): 457–512.

McGiffert, Arthur Cushman. *A History of Christianity in the Apostolic Age.* New York: Scribner's Sons, 1897.

Mimouni, Simon Claude. *Le judéo-christianisme ancien. Essais historiques.* Paris: Cerf, 1998. Translated by Robyn Fréchet as *Early Judaeo-Christianity: Historical Essays.* Leuven: Peeters, 2012.

Mimouni, Simon Claude. "Pour une définition nouvelle du judéo-christianisme ancien." *NTS* 38 (1992): 161–86.

Morgan, Thomas. *The Moral Philosopher. In a Dialogue between Philalethes a Christian Deist, and Theophanes a Christian Jew.* Facsimile of the second edition with a new introduction by John Vladimir Price. History of British Deism. London: Routledge/Thoemmes, 1995.

Munck, Johannes. "Jewish Christianity in Post-Apostolic Times." *NTS* 6 (1959–1960): 103–16.

Munck, Johannes. "Primitive Jewish Christianity and Later Jewish Christianity: Continuation or Rupture?" In *Aspects du judéo-christianisme. Colloque de Strasbourg 23–25 avril 1964,* 77–93. Paris: Presses Universitaires de France, 1965.

Murray, Robert. "Defining Judaeo-Christianity." *Heythrop Journal* 15 (1974): 303–10.

Murray, Robert. "Jewish Christianity." In *A Dictionary of Biblical Interpretation*, edited by R. J. Coggins and J. L. Houlden, 341–46. London: SCM; Philadelphia: Trinity Press International, 1990.

Murray, Robert. "Jews, Hebrews and Christians: Some Needed Distinctions." *Novum Testamentum* 24 (1982): 194–208.

Myers, Jason A. "Law, Lies and Letter Writing: An Analysis of Jerome and Augustine on the Antioch Incident (Galatians 2:11–14)." *Scottish Journal of Theology* 66 (2013): 127–39.

Myllykoski, Matti. "'Christian Jews' and 'Jewish Christians': The Jewish Origins of Christianity in English Literature from Elizabeth I to Toland." In *The Rediscovery of Jewish Christianity: From Toland to Baur*, edited by F. Stanley Jones, 3–41. HBS 5. Atlanta: Society of Biblical Literature, 2012.

Nanos, Mark D., and Magnus Zetterholm, eds. *Paul within Judaism: Restoring the First-Century Context to the Apostle*. Minneapolis: Fortress, 2015.

Nicholl, H. F. "John Toland: Religion without Mystery." *Hermathena* 100 (1965): 54–65.

Nongbri, Brent. *Before Religion: A History of a Modern Concept*. New Haven: Yale University Press, 2013.

O'Neill, J. C. "The Study of the New Testament." In *Nineteenth Century Religious Thought in the West*, edited by Ninian Smart, John Clayton, Patrick Sherry, and Steven T. Katz, 3:143–78. 3 vols. Cambridge: Cambridge University Press, 1985.

Palmer, Gesine. *Ein Freispruch für Paulus: John Tolands Theorie des Judenchristentums mit einer neuasgabe von Tolands 'Nazarenus' von Claus-Michael Palmer*. ANTZ 7. Berlin: Institut Kirche und Judentum, 1996.

Parkes, James. *The Conflict of the Church and the Synagogue: A Study in the Origins of Antisemitism*. New York: Hermon, 1974.

Patrick, David. "Two English Forerunners of the Tübingen School: Thomas Morgan and John Toland." *Theological Review* 14 (1877): 562–603.

Pritz, Ray A. *Nazarene Jewish Christianity: From the End of the New Testament Period until Its Disappearance in the Fourth Century*. Jerusalem: Hebrew University Magnes Press, 2010.

Quispel, G. "The Discussion of Judaic Christianity." *VC* 22 (1968): 81–93.

Rahner, Karl. "Basic Observations on the Subject of Changeable and Unchangeable Factors in the Church." In *Theological Investigations. Volume 14: Ecclesiology, Questions in the Church, the Church in the World*, 3–23. Translated by David Bourke. New York: Seabury, 1976.

Rahner, Karl. "Considerations on the Development of Dogma." In *Theological Investigations. Volume 4: More Recent Writings*, 3–35. Translated by Kevin Smyth. Baltimore: Helicon, 1966.

Rahner, Karl. "The Development of Dogma." In *Theological Investigations. Volume 1: God, Christ, Mary and Grace*, 39–77. Translated by Cornelius Ernst. Baltimore: Helicon, 1961.

Rauschen, Gerhard, and Josef Martin. *Quinti Septimii Florentii Tertulliani Librum de Praescriptione Haereticorum addito S. Irenaei Adversus Haereses libro III, 3–4.* Florilegium Patristicum IV. Bonn: Hanstein, 1930.

Reed, Annette Yoshiko. "From Judaism and Hellenism to Christianity and Paganism: Cultural Identities and Religious Polemics in the Pseudo-Clementine *Homilies.*" In *Nouvelles intrigues Pseudo-clémentines/Plots in the Pseudo-Clementine Romance,* edited by Frédéric Amsler et al., 351–61. Publications de l'Institut romand des sciences bibliques 6. Lausanne: Zèbre, 2008.

Reed, Annette Yoshiko. "Jewish Christianity." In *Dictionary of Early Judaism,* edited by John J. Collins and Daniel Harlow, 810–12. Grand Rapids: Eerdmans, 2010.

Reed, Annette Yoshiko. "'Jewish Christianity' after the 'Parting of the Ways.'" In *The Ways That Never Parted: Jews and Christians in Late Antiquity and the Early Middle Ages,* edited by Adam H. Becker and Annette Yoshiko Reed, 189–231. Minneapolis: Fortress, 2007.

Reed, Annette Yoshiko. *Jewish-Christianity and the History of Judaism: Collected Essays.* TSAJ 171. Tübingen: Mohr Siebeck, 2018.

Reed, Annette Yoshiko, and Lily Vuong. "Christianity in Antioch: Partings in Roman Syria." In *Partings: How Judaism and Christianity Became Two,* edited by Hershel Shanks, 105–32. Washington, DC: Biblical Archaeology Society, 2013.

Rehm, Bernhard, Johannes Irmscher, and Franz Paschke. *Die Pseudoklmentinen I, Homilien.* Berlin: Akademie Verlag, 1969.

Reuss, Édouard. *History of Christian Theology in the Apostolic Age.* Translated by Annie Harwood. 2 vols. London: Hodder and Stoughton, 1872–1874. Translation of *Histoire de la théologie chrétienne au siècle apostolique.* 2 vols. 3rd ed. Strasbourg: Treuttel et Wurtz, 1864.

Reventlow, Henning Graf. "Judaism and Jewish Christianity in the Works of John Toland." *Proceedings of the Sixth World Congress of Jewish Studies* 3 (1977): 111–16.

Riegel, Stanley K. "Jewish Christianity: Definitions and Terminology." *NTS* 24 (1978): 410–15.

Ritschl, Albrecht. *Die Entstehung der altkatholischen Kirche. Eine kirchen- und dogmengeschichtliche Monographie.* 2nd ed. Bonn: Adolph Marcus, 1857.

Robinson, Thomas A. *Ignatius of Antioch and the Parting of the Ways: Early Jewish-Christian Relations.* Peabody, MA: Hendrickson, 2009.

Ruether, Rosemary Radford. "Judaism and Christianity: Two Fourth-Century Religions." *Studies in Religion* 2 (1972): 1–10.

Runesson, Anders. "The Question of Terminology: The Architecture of Contemporary Discussions on Paul." In *Paul within Judaism: Restoring the First-Century Context to the Apostle,* edited by Mark D. Nanos and Magnus Zetterholm, 53–77. Minneapolis: Fortress, 2015.

Saldarini, Anthony J. *Matthew's Christian-Jewish Community.* CSHJ. Chicago: University of Chicago Press, 1994.

Schliemann, Adolph. *Die Clementinen nebst den verwandten Schriften und der Ebio-nitismus, ein Beitrag zur Kirchen- und Dogmengeschichte der ersten Jahrhunderte.* Hamburg: Perthes, 1844.

Schmidtke, Alfred. *Neue Fragmente und Untersuchungen zu den judenchristlichen Evangelien. Ein Beitrag zur Literatur und Geschichte der Judenchristen.* Texte und Untersuchungen zur Geschichte der altchristlichen Literatur 37/2. Leipzig: Hinrichs, 1911.

Schoeps, Hans Joachim. *Jewish Christianity: Factional Disputes in the Early Church.* Philadelphia: Fortress, 1969.

Schoeps, Hans Joachim. *Theologie und Geschichte des Judenchristentums.* Tübingen: Mohr (Siebeck), 1949.

Schonfield, Hugh J. *The History of Jewish Christianity: From the First to the Twentieth Century.* London: Duckworth, 1936. Repr., 2009.

Schott, Jeremy. "Heresiology as Universal History in Epiphanius's *Panarion.*" *Zeitschrift für Antikes Christentum/Journal of Ancient Christianity* 10 (2006): 546–63.

Schwartz, Seth. "How Many Judaisms Were There? A Critique of Neusner and Smith on Definition and Mason and Boyarin on Categorization." *Journal of Ancient Judaism* 2 (2011): 208–38.

Schwartz, Seth. *Imperialism and Jewish Society, 200 B.C.E. to 640 C.E.* Jews, Christians, and Muslims from the Ancient to the Modern World. Princeton, NJ: Princeton University Press, 2001.

Schwegler, Friedrich Carl Albert. *Das Nachapostolische Zeitalter in den Hauptmomenten seiner Entwicklung.* 2 vols. Tübingen: Fues, 1846.

Schweitzer, Albert. *The Quest of the Historical Jesus: A Critical Study of Its Progress from Reimarus to Wrede.* Translated by William Montgomery. New York: MacMillan, 1968.

Seeberg, Reinhold. *Lehrbuch der Dogmengeschichte. Erster Band: Die Anfänge des Dogmas im nachapostolischen und altkatholischen Zeitalter.* Sammlung Theologischer Lehrbücher. 2nd ed. Leipzig: Deichert, 1908.

Simon, Marcel. "Problèmes du judéo-christianisme." In *Aspects du judéo-christianisme. Colloque de Strasbourg 23–25 avril 1964,* 1–17. Paris: Presses Universitaires de France, 1965.

Simon, Marcel. "Réflexions sur le judéo-christianisme." In *Christianity, Judaism and Other Greco-Roman Cults: Studies for Morton Smith at Sixty. Part Two: Early Christianity,* edited by Jacob Neusner, 53–76. Studies in Judaism in Late Antiquity 12. Leiden: Brill, 1975.

Simon, Marcel. *Verus Israel: A Study of the Relations between Christians and Jews in the Roman Empire AD 135–425.* Translated by H. McKeating. London: Littman Library of Jewish Civilization, 1996. Translation of *Verus Israel: Étude sur les relations entre chrétiens et juifs dans l'empire Romain (135–425).* 2nd ed. Paris: de Boccard, 1964.

Skarsaune, Oskar. "The Ebionites." In *Jewish Believers in Jesus: The Early Centuries*, edited by Oskar Skarsaune and Reidar Hvalvik, 419–62. Peabody, MA: Hendrickson, 2007.

Skarsaune, Oskar. "Jewish Believers in Jesus in Antiquity—Problems of Definition, Method, and Sources." In *Jewish Believers in Jesus: The Early Centuries*, edited by Oskar Skarsaune and Reidar Hvalvik, 3–21. Peabody, MA: Hendrickson, 2007.

Slater, W. F. "Hort's Lectures on 'Judaistic Christianity.'" *Expositor* 2 (7th ser.) (1895): 128–50.

Smith, Jonathan Z. *Drudgery Divine: On the Comparison of Early Christianities and the Religions of Late Antiquity*. CSHJ. Chicago: University of Chicago Press, 1990.

Smith, Jonathan Z. "The 'End' of Comparison: Redescription and Rectification." In *A Magic Still Dwells: Comparative Religion in the Postmodern Age*, edited by K. C. Patton and B. C. Ray, 237–41. Berkeley: University of California Press, 2000.

Smith, Jonathan Z. "Fences and Neighbors: Some Contours of Early Judaism." In *Imagining Religion*, 1–18. CSHJ. Chicago: University of Chicago Press, 1982.

Smith, Jonathan Z. *Relating Religion: Essays in the Study of Religion*. Chicago: University of Chicago Press, 2004.

Smith, Jonathan Z. "Sacred Persistence: Toward a Redescription of Canon." In *Imagining Religion*, 36–52. CSHJ. Chicago: University of Chicago Press, 1982.

Sobel, B. Zvi. *Hebrew Christianity: The Thirteenth Tribe*. New York: Wiley, 1974.

Stanton, Graham. "Jewish Christian Elements in the Pseudo-Clementine Writings." In *Jewish Believers in Jesus: The Early Centuries*, edited by Oskar Skarsaune and Reidar Hvalvik, 305–24. Peabody, MA: Hendrickson, 2007.

Stark, Rodney, and William Sims Bainbridge. *The Future of Religion: Secularization, Revival, and Cult Formation*. Berkeley: University of California Press, 1985.

Stemberger, Günter. "Judenchristen." *RAC* 19:228–45.

Stephen, Leslie. *History of English Thought in the Eighteenth Century*. 3rd ed. Reprinted in 2 vols. New York: Harbinger, 1962.

Strack, H. L., and Günter Stemberger. *Introduction to the Talmud and Midrash*. Translated and edited by Markus Bockmuehl. Minneapolis: Fortress, 1996.

Strauss, David Friedrich. *The Christ of Faith and the Jesus of History: A Critique of Schleiermacher's The Life of Jesus*. Translated with an introduction by Leander E. Keck. Lives of Jesus. Philadelphia: Fortress, 1977.

Strauss, David Friedrich. *The Life of Jesus Critically Examined*. Edited by Peter C. Hodgson. Translated from the 4th ed. by George Eliot (Mary Anne Evans). Lives of Jesus. Philadelphia: Fortress, 1972.

Strecker, Georg. "Judenchristentum." *TRE* 17:310–25.

Strecker, Georg. *Das Judenchristentum in den Pseudoklementinen*. 2nd ed. Texte und Untersuchungen 70. Berlin: Akademie-Verlag, 1981.

Stroumsa, Guy G. *A New Science: The Discovery of Religion in the Age of Reason*. Cambridge, MA: Harvard University Press, 2010.

Sumney, Jerry. "Paul and Christ-believing Jews Whom He Opposes." In *Jewish Christianity Reconsidered: Rethinking Ancient Groups and Texts*, edited by Matt Jackson-McCabe, 57–80. Minneapolis: Fortress, 2007.

Sumney, Jerry. *"Servants of Satan," "False Brothers," and Other Opponents of Paul.* Journal for the Study of the New Testament Supplement Series 40. Sheffield: Sheffield Academic Press, 1999.

Taylor, Joan E. "The Phenomenon of Early Jewish-Christianity: Reality or Scholarly Invention?" *VC* 44 (1990): 313–34.

Theissen, Gerd. *A Theory of Primitive Christian Religion*. Translated by John Bowden. London: SCM, 1999.

Toland, John. *Nazarenus: Or, Jewish, Gentile, and Mahometan Christianity*. 2nd ed. London: Brotherton, Roberts & Dodd, 1718. http://gallica.bnf.fr/ark:/12148/bpt6k67828g

Toland, John. *The Theological and Philological Works of the Late Mr. John Toland*. London: W. Mears, 1732. Repr., Elibron Classics facsimile edition; Adamant Media: 2005.

Townsend, Philippa. "Who Were the First Christians? Jews, Gentiles and the *Christianoi.*" In *Heresy and Identity in Late Antiquity*, edited by Eduard Iricinschi and Holger M. Zellentin, 212–30. TSAJ 119. Tübingen: Mohr Siebeck, 2008.

Verheyden, Joseph. "Jewish Christianity, a State of Affairs: Affinities and Differences with Respect to Matthew, James, and the Didache." In *Matthew, James and Didache: Three Related Documents in Their Jewish and Christian Settings*, edited by Huub van de Sandt and Jürgen K. Zangenberg, 123–35. Symposium Series 45. Atlanta: Society of Biblical Literature, 2008.

Wellhausen, Julius. *Einleitung in die drei ersten Evangelien*. Berlin: Georg Reimer, 1905.

White, Carolinne, ed. *The Correspondence (394–419) between Jerome and Augustine of Hippo*. Studies in the Bible and Early Christianity 23. Lewiston, NY: Mellen, 1990.

White, L. Michael. *From Jesus to Christianity: How Four Generations of Visionaries and Storytellers Created the New Testament and Christian Faith*. New York: HarperOne, 2005.

Williams, Frank. *The* Panarion *of Epiphanius of Salamis*. Nag Hammadi and Manichaean Studies 63. 2 vols. 2nd ed. Leiden: Brill, 2009–2013. Repr., Atlanta: SBL Press.

Wilson, Stephen G. *Related Strangers: Jews and Christians 70–170 C.E.* Minneapolis: Fortress, 1995.

Young, Frances. "Did Epiphanius Know What He Meant by Heresy?" *Studia Patristica* 17 (1982): 199–205.

Zachhuber, Johannes. *Theology as Science in Nineteenth-Century Germany: From F. C. Baur to Ernst Troeltsch*. Changing Paradigms in Historical and Systematic Theology. Oxford: Oxford University Press, 2013.

Zetterholm, Magnus. *Approaches to Paul: A Student's Guide to Recent Scholarship.* Minneapolis: Fortress, 2009.

Zetterholm, Magnus. *The Formation of Christianity in Antioch: A Social-Scientific Approach to the Separation between Judaism and Christianity.* London: Routledge, 2003.

Index

Abel, 19

Abraham, 45, 148, 194n33; as *archēgetēs*,
257n57; Epiphanius on, 19–20, 178,
238n50; Irenaeus on, 152, 252n28;
Justin on, 194n31, 238n50

Acts of the Apostles, 168, 172–73, 192n15,
228n75, 249n84, 256n50, 267n117,
271n142; Baur on, 63, 67, 71, 73–75,
219n139; Lightfoot on, 79–80, 84,
87; Morgan on, 48; place in canon,
26, 67; Ritschl on, 82, 221n14; Simon
on, 117; Toland on, 26, 198n60,
200nn67–68

Adam, 64, 213n87; Epiphanius on, 17–20,
202n84; Irenaeus on, 151, 252n23;
Pseudo-Clementine *Homilies* on,
255n48, 258n59

Aelia Capitolina, 86–87

Alexandria, 58, 163, 257n55, 263n83

anachronism: avoiding, 125; Christianity as, 247n71; Jewish Christianity as 119, 132, 134, 231–32n95,
237n41, 247n71; Judaism as, 243n22,
244n41, 247n71; Torah observance
as, 225n59

angels, 249n84; apostate or fallen, 151,
154, 157, 252n22, 252n24, 254n38. *See
also* demons

animals, 157, 255n49, 256n51, 258n61,
259n65, 262n75; sacrifices of, 86,
199n64, 251n19

anti-Judaism, 67, 109

Antioch: community in, 145, 156, 181,
249n4, 267n111; conflict in, 14, 26,
73, 82, 84, 190n6, 200n69, 218n127,
223n40, 225n59, 228n74; liberal Hellenistic Christianity in, 72; Pseudo-
Clementine *Homilies* on, 156, 181,
223n40, 255n46, 261n73

anti-Paulinism, 68, 73–75, 78, 79, 85, 89,
91, 94, 103, 117, 240n65; as criterion
for Jewish Christianity, 240n65; of
Ebionites, 85

anti-Semitism, 1, 109. *See also* anti-Judaism; Jews: hatred of or by; Judeans:
hatred of or by

Apocalypse of John. *See* Revelation
(Apocalypse of John)

apocalypticism, 94

apologetics, Christian: hidden, 100, 110,
114, 140; historiography without,
111, 119, 122, 132; impact on scholarship of, 8, 47, 57, 100, 103, 111, 114,
122; "Jewish Christianity" and, 38,
40, 97, 122, 183; liberal Christian,
204n2; true or original Christianity
and, 51–52, 57. *See also* historiography: apologetic

apostates or apostasy, 191n13, 235n20,
263n85. *See also* angels: apostate or
fallen

apostles: apologetic claims refer to,
115; authority of (*see under* authority); Christianism or Christianity
of, 29–31, 34, 42, 78–79, 90, 92, 97,
115, 122, 123, 139, 145, 149, 180, 181,
205n12, 221n8; circumcision and
(*see* circumcision: Apostles or